Advancement of Intelligent Computational Methods and Technologies

Advancement of Intelligent Computational Methods and Technologies

Proceedings of Ist International Conference on Advancement of Intelligent Computational Methods and Technologies (AICMT2023)

Edited by

Dr. O. P. Verma
Professor, Delhi Technological University, Delhi, India

Dr. Seema Verma
Professor, Delhi Technical Campus, Greater Noida, India

Dr. Thinagaran Perumal
Associate Professor, Universiti Putra Malaysia, Malaysia

CRC Press is an imprint of the
Taylor & Francis Group, an **informa** business

First edition published 2024
by CRC Press
4 Park Square, Milton Park, Abingdon, Oxon, OX14 4RN

and by CRC Press
2385 NW Executive Center Drive, Suite 320, Boca Raton FL 33431

CRC Press is an imprint of Informa UK Limited

British Library Cataloguing-in-Publication Data
A catalogue record for this book is available from the British Library

ISBN: 978-1-032-78445-8 (pbk)
ISBN: 978-1-003-48790-6 (ebk)

DOI: 10.1201/9781003487906

Typeset in Times LT Std
by Aditiinfosystems

Advancement of Intelligent Computational Methods and Technologies (AICMT2023) – Dr. O. P. Verma et al. (eds)
© 2024 Taylor & Francis Group, London, ISBN 978-1-032-78445-8

Contents

1. **A Review on SML Based Diabetic Patient Classification and Prediction for Healthcare Domain** 1
Satish Singh Mekale and Maumita Chakraborty
2. **Brief Introduction to Healthy Food Ordering and Delivery** 7
Md Shamsuzzama Siddique, Yashu Shanker, Ankit Raj, Sahil Kumar and Raj Mishra
3. **Food Ordering Android App Using Firebase and Google Cloud** 13
Abid Humza, Devansh Rangan, Asra Fatma, Pranjay Bhatt and Priyanka Dadhich
4. **Ransomware Detection Using Machine-Learning Techniques** 17
Saroj Dalwani, Nidhi Malik and Priya Arora
5. **Optimizing Chatbot Interactions with ChatGPT: Prompt Engineering for Mental Health Applications** 22
Husir Ansari, Toyesh Kumar Saini, Ishan Sharma, Ankit Kumar Rajavat and Malik Nadeem
6. **Diseases Detection Model and Prognostic Model Using Deep Learning: A Review** 27
Shashi Kant Mourya and Ajit Kr. Singh Yadav
7. **Multi Sports Time Series Prediction Using Machine Learning** 32
Rishi Saxena, Aayush Agarwal, Vaibhav Gandhi, Deepu Maurya and Puneet Sharma
8. **Blockchain Based Decentralized File Sharing System** 40
Puneet Sharma, Manoj Kumar Shukla and Jayanti Pandey
9. **Lip-Reading with Speech Emotions** 48
Bhavya Satija, Sumanyu Dutta, Yash Sethi and Puneet Sharma
10. **Review: Machine Learning-Based Network Intrusion Detection System for Enhanced Cyber-security** 55
Preeti Lakhani, Syed Shahabuddin Ashraf, Bhavya Alankar and Suraiya Parveen
11. **Bank Loan Approval Repayment Prediction System Using Machine Learning Models** 61
Muskan Bali, Vansh Mehta, Anshul Bhatia, Nidhi Malik and Komal Jindal
12. **Machine Learning Model for Heart Disease Prediction with Consideration of Optimized Hyperparameters** 66
Ramani Kant Jha, Nishtha Deep, Radha, Aridaman Kumar and Seema Verma
13. **Exploring Advanced Techniques for Enhancing Resolution of Images** 72
Shivank Naruka, Shrey Gupta, Vinayak Saxena, Rishab Rana and Umnah
14. **A Symphony of Signals: Machine Learning Enabled Parkinson's Disease Detection via Audio Analysis Through Various Algorithms** 76
Shubham Tiwari, Kartikey Raghuvanshi, Sanand Mishra, Saakshi Srivastava, Ayasha Malik and Seema Verma
15. **Exploring the Role of Machine Learning in Wine Quality Detection** 82
Aditya Ranjan, Mayank Attrey, Gauransh Bhasin, Mohit Kumar and Malik Nadeem
16. **Machine Learning System for Sales Series Forecasting: Data Analysis and Visualization Approach** 86
Jhanvi Pathak, Vidhi Goel, Khushi Tanwar and Nidhi Sharma
17. **Automating a Mobile Application Using Appium** 90
Preeti Pandey, Nishchey Bhutani, Richa Thakur and Shubham Kr. Jha
18. **Discovering Generic Medicine Substitutes Using Machine Learning and Deep Learning** 93
Karishma Arora, Karan Sharma, Sweta Kumari, Soodit Kumar, Udhay Kaul and Anshul

19. Deepfake Detection Using AI 98
Saurav, Dheeraj Azad, Preeti Pandey, Mohammad Sheihan Javaid and Utkarsh

20. Comparative Analysis of Machine Learning Algorithms for High Electron Mobility Transistor (HEMT) Modeling 103
Neda and Vandana Nath

21. Real-time Sentiment Analysis 109
Archit Sarna, Devyanki Sokhal, Manan Taneja and Yashi Rai

22. Review of Various Photovoltaic Cleaning Methods 114
Mayank Kumar, Dhruv Verma, Yash Aggarwal, Devesh Agarwal and Anuradha Tomar

23. Biometric Based Attendance System with Machine Learning Integrated Face Modelling and Recognition 120
Ritik, Sanidhya Gaur, Ashish Kumar, Rithik Nirwan, Chaitali Bhowmik and Neha Jain

24. Plant Disease Detection Using Deep Learning 126
Devesh Bisht, Akhilesh, Aditya Rawat, Ishant Bhatt and Kimmi Verma

25. Autonomous Driving Using Deep Learning 130
Uttam Sharma, Rohan Pal, Gaurav Sarosha, Pulkit Mathur, Yashu Shanker and Md Shamsuzzama Siddiqui

26. Credit Card Fraud Detection using Supervised Machine Learning Algorithm 136
Abhay Kumar Verma, Ankesh Kumar, Anjani Kumar and Itesh Bansal

27. A Social Media Authentication Tool with Real-Time User Verification and Fraud Detection Capabilities 141
Tripti, Yashashvi Gupta, Monika Kumari Baghel, Geetika Thakran and Ankit Gambhir

28. Sign Language Detection App Using Random Forest 145
Chaitanya Chawla, Archisman Tripathy, Neel Gupta, Kunal and Umnah

29. An Automated and Robust Image Watermarking System Using Artificial Intelligence/Machine Learning Including Neural Networks 150
Gunjan Ahuja, Onkar Mehra, Muskan Aggarwal and Jashn Tyagi

30. Web Data Extraction Using DOM Parsing for Data Collection and Ontologies 156
Yuganshika Narang, Shamsher Singh Rawat, Devansh Sati, Ananya Singh, Ayasha Malik and Seema Verma

31. A Videoconferencing Framework for Real Time Applications Based on MERN Architecture 162
Qasim Malik, Rudra, Rajeev Kumar, Upasna Joshi and Shivam Kumar

32. Automatic Exam Paper Generator Using Dynamic Structured and Intelligent Database 167
Avinash Singh, Lakshay Sharma, Akash Chauhan and Upasna Joshi

33. IoT Based Peltier Module Smart Refrigerator 171
Sarthak Aggarwal, Robin, Mohd Atif Wahid, Prabhat R. Prasad, Nidhi Sharma and Neha Jain

34. Implementation of Machine Learning In IOT 176
Rohit, Nidhi, Alam Shadab, Nitish Sharma and Mohd. Atif Wahid

35. Review on Online Cloth Shopping 184
Udit Sharma, Ajay Krishnan, Shivam Saurabh and Kashish Malhan

36. An Advanced Clone for Over the Top Platform 188
Shahbuddin, Siddharth Sharma, Raghav Sethi, Tanupreet Sabharwal and Jatin Sharma

Advancement of Intelligent Computational Methods and Technologies (AICMT2023) – Dr. O. P. Verma et al. (eds)
© 2024 Taylor & Francis Group, London, ISBN 978-1-032-78445-8

List of Figures

2.1	*Growth rate of food ordering*	**11**
2.2	*Growth rate different deliver services*	**11**
2.3	*Average revenue per user for automated food odering*	**11**
4.1	*Methodology cycle*	**18**
4.2	*Architecture of PE file*	**19**
5.1	*Screenshot of chatbot in "MindEaseUp" app.*	**26**
7.1	*Supervised learning v/s unsupervised learning*	**32**
7.2	*Layers in ANN*	**33**
7.3	*Process cycle*	**35**
7.4	*Project lifecycle*	**35**
7.5	*Steps of our proposed SRP-CRISP-DM framework*	**36**
7.6	*Plan of action for using previous match data*	**37**
7.7	*10-fold-cross validation*	**37**
7.9	*Outcome of our model*	**38**
7.8	*Method used to find out model accuracy*	**38**
8.1	*Application structure*	**42**
8.2	*Ganache landing page and workspace*	**43**
8.3	*Getting the private key in Ganache*	**43**
8.4	*Account details in Ganache*	**44**
8.5	*Setting up MetaMask*	**44**
8.6	*File structure*	**45**
8.7	*Checks for upload file*	**45**
8.8	*File uploaded event*	**46**
8.9	*Connecting web3.js with React.js application*	**46**
8.10	*Fetching all the files from the smart contract*	**46**
8.11	*Connecting with IPFS*	**47**
8.12	*Connecting with IPFS*	**47**
9.1	*Mouth ROI extraction*	**50**
9.2	*General architecture of audio-visual model*	**51**
9.3	*General architecture of speech emotion model*	**52**
9.4	*Total accuracy vs total validation accuracy (A + V)*	**52**
9.5	*Total loss vs total validation loss (A + V)*	**53**
9.6	*Total Accuracy vs Total Validation Accuracy (MLP Classifier)*	**53**
9.7	*Total accuracy vs total validation accuracy (SVM)*	**53**
9.8	*Total accuracy vs total validation accuracy (CNN)*	**53**

9.9 *Total accuracy vs total validation accuracy (LSTM)* **53**
10.1 *Applications of ML-based intrusion techniques* **56**
10.2 *Example techniques implementing ML-based Intrusion detection system* **57**
11.1 *Block diagram of proposed approach* **64**
12.1 *Random forest technique* **67**
12.2 *Light GBM's working* **67**
12.3 *Support vector machine classifier* **67**
12.4 *XGBoost classifier* **67**
12.5 *Logistic regression* **68**
12.6 *Heart disease prediction model methodology* **68**
12.7 *Logistic Regression (AUC Score)* **69**
12.8 *XGBOOST (AUC Score)* **69**
12.9 *Random Forest (AUC Score)* **70**
12.10 *Support Vector Classifier (AUC Score)* **70**
12.11 *LightGBM (AUC Score)* **70**
12.12 *Visual accuracy comparison of two models* **70**
13.1 *Contrast stretching* **74**
13.2 *Flowchart of image enhancement* **74**
13.3 *Input satellite low resolution images* **75**
13.4 *After output Images* **75**
14.1 *Conceptual model* **78**
14.2 *Statistical description of data* **78**
14.3 *Model results of logistics regression* **79**
14.4 *Model results of decision tree* **79**
14.5 *Model results of Rondom forest-information gain* **79**
14.6 *Model results of Rondom forest-entropy* **79**
14.7 *Model results of SVM* **79**
14.8 *Model results of KNN* **79**
14.9 *Model results of Gaussian Naïve Bayes* **79**
14.10 *Model results of Bernoulli Naïve Bayes* **80**
14.11 *ML mdoels accuracy* **80**
14.12 *ML models accuracy's graphical representation* **80**
15.1 *Input data page* **84**
15.2 *Final result 1* **85**
15.3 *Final result 2* **85**
17.1 *The Appium framework* **91**
17.2 *Desired features for testing Android Apps* **91**
17.3 *Appium tool inspector* **91**
17.4 *Login screen of an Android app* **92**
17.5 *Recorded script for the login screen* **92**
18.1 *Class diagram* **95**
18.2 *UML diagram* **96**
18.3 *Gantt chart* **96**
19.1 *Fake video output* **101**
19.2 *Real video output* **101**

20.1 *Structure of MLP* 105
20.2 *Structure of decision tree* 105
20.3 *Structure of random forest* 105
20.4 *Conventional GaN HEMT built on Silvaco TCAD* 106
20.5 *Black box model created using supervised learning* 106
21.1 *Statistical NLP vs deep learning* 110
21.2 *Important words in depressive tweets* 111
21.3 *Important words in Non-Depressive Tweets* 111
21.4 *Confusion Matrix for Logistic Regression* 112
21.5 *Confusion matrix for recurrent neural network* 112
21.6 *Confusion Matrix for Long Short-Term Memory* 112
21.7 *Confusion matrix for convolutional neural network* 113
22.1 *Growth in number of studies studying the influence of dust on solar panel (Abuzaid, Awad, and Shamayleh 2022)* 115
22.2 *Block diagram of solar panel cleaning methods* 115
22.3 *Manual cleaning of panels installed at NSUT, Delhi* 115
22.4 *Mechanized cleaning of modules* 116
22.5 *Robotic cleaning of modules* 116
23.1 *Framework of proposed method* 122
23.2 *Haar features applied on an image* 122
23.3 *LBHP example* 123
23.4 *Binary values* 123
23.5 *Main screen* 123
23.6 *Face detection* 123
23.7 *Face images collection* 124
23.8 *Face recognition* 124
24.1 *Working model* 127
24.2 *Healthy part of leaf* 128
24.3 *Diseased part of leaf* 128
24.4 *Region of disease* 128
25.1 *Schematic representation autonomous driving* 131
25.2 *Development of robust and dependable deep learning algorithms* 131
25.3 *Implementation of deep learning alogrithm* 132
25.4 *Example image captured* 132
25.5 *Example CSV file* 132
25.6 *Bar graph of orientation angle* 133
25.7 *Cropped image* 133
25.8 *Pre-processed image* 133
25.9 *Three-character cloning pattern* 133
25.10 *Example sequence* 134
25.11 *EPOCH with price drop* 134
25.12 *Training and validation* 134
25.13 *Training version control the device* 135
26.1 *Example of method used for detecting credit card malpractice* 137
26.2 *Example of dataset* 138
27.1 *Flow of feature extraction and result* 142

27.2	*Accuracy for different thresholds*	**142**
28.1	*Home page*	**148**
28.2	*Alphabet detection*	**148**
28.3	*Alphabet detection*	**148**
28.4	*Alphabet detection*	**148**
29.1	*Image watermarking process*	**151**
29.2	*A CNN sequence to classify handwritten digits*	**152**
29.3	*Autoencoder*	**152**
29.4	*Architecture of Autoencoder using CNN*	**152**
29.5	*Flattening of a 3x3 image matrix into 9x1 vector*	**152**
29.6	*4x4x3 RGB image*	**153**
29.7	*The Kernel in Convolution Layer*	**153**
29.8	*Movement of the Kernel*	**153**
29.9	*Convolutional operation on a MxNx3 image matrix with a 3x3x3 Kernel*	**153**
29.10	*Convolutional operation with stride length = 2*	**153**
29.11	*Pooling over 5x5 convoluted feature*	**154**
29.13	*Classification of fully connected layer*	**154**
29.12	*Types of pooling*	**154**
30.1	*Importing libraries*	**158**
30.2	*Get titles of HTML page*	**158**
30.3	*Content scraping*	**158**
30.4	*Image links scraping*	**159**
30.5	*Anchor link scraping*	**159**
30.6	*Table scraping*	**160**
31.1	*MERN architecture*	**162**
31.2	*NextJs architecture*	**164**
31.3	*NodeJs architecture*	**164**
31.4	*WebRTC diagram*	**165**
31.5	*Interaction page*	**165**
32.1	*JDBC architecture*	**169**
32.2	*Servlet architecture*	**169**
32.3	*JSP processing*	**170**
33.1	*(a) Isometric view of the model, (b) Back view of the model*	**173**
33.2	*RFID reader card*	**173**
33.3	*Raspberry Pi*	**174**
33.4	*User interface*	**174**
33.5	*User interface*	**174**
34.1	*Supervised learning process*	**177**
34.2	*Unsupervised learning process*	**177**
34.3	*Semi-supervised learning process*	**178**
34.4	*Reinforcement learning process*	**178**
34.5	*Case 1-Accuracy model*	**182**
34.6	*Case 2- Accuracy model*	**182**
35.1	*Data flow diagram*	**185**
36.1	*Full stack web development (Malhotra et al., 2005)*	**189**

Advancement of Intelligent Computational Methods and Technologies (AICMT2023) – Dr. O. P. Verma et al. (eds)
© 2024 Taylor & Francis Group, London, ISBN 978-1-032-78445-8

List of Tables

1.1 *Comparison chart between diabetic classification (DC), diabetic prediction (DP), and real-time healthcare (RTH) data analysis with respect to the state-of-the-art studies* **4**
2.1 *Food ordering and its revenue growth rate data* **10**
3.1 *Analysis of back-end technology* **14**
4.1 *Static features* **19**
4.2 *Results given by model* **20**
6.1 *Review of the recent predictive model in healthcare* **30**
6.2 *Tools applied in deep learning process* **31**
10.1 *Description of various datasets* **57**
10.2 *Confusion metrics for ml-based intrusion techniques* **57**
11.1 *Description of dataset* **62**
11.2 *Experimental results* **64**
12.1 *Hyperparameter comparison of random forest model* **68**
12.2 *Hyperparameter comparison of the LightGBM model* **69**
12.3 *Hyperparameter comparison of SVC model* **69**
12.4 *Hyperparameter comparison of the XGBoost model* **69**
12.5 *Hyperparameter comparison of the KNN model* **69**
12.6 *Hyperparameter comparison of Logistic regression model* **69**
12.7 *Accuracy comparison between the model proposed by K. Karthick et al. and our proposed model models* **70**
14.1 *Literature review* **77**
14.2 *Data after being split into test and train sets* **78**
16.1 *Result* **88**
20.1 *Noteworthy research on the Modelling of FETs based on machine learning* **104**
20.2 *Independent parameters* **106**
20.3 *Results of Various evaluation metrics* **106**
21.1 *Accuracy and F-1 score of algorithms* **113**
22.1 *Parametric comparison of various solar cleaning methods (ACC 2020) (Solar Cleano)* **117**
22.2 *Broad comparison of solar cleaning methods* **117**
30.1 *Related work* **157**
32.1 *Tools* **168**
32.2 *Hardware requirements* **168**
36.1 *Typical importance of Netflix clone features and activities* **190**

Advancement of Intelligent Computational Methods and Technologies (AICMT2023) – Dr. O. P. Verma et al. (eds)
 ISBN 978-1-032-78445-8

Preface

The compiled volume originates from the notable contributions presented at the 1st International Conference on Advancement of Intelligent Computational Methods and Technologies (AICMT2023), which took place in a hybrid format on June 27, 2023, at Delhi Technical Campus, Greater Noida, Uttar Pradesh, India. This comprehensive collection serves as an exploration into the dynamic domain of intelligent computational methods and technologies, offering insights into the latest and upcoming trends in computation methods.

AICMT2023's scope encompasses the evolutionary trajectory of computational methods, addressing pertinent issues in real-time implementation, delving into the emergence of new intelligent technologies, exploring next-generation problem-solving methodologies, and other interconnected areas. The conference is strategically designed to spotlight current research trends within the field, fostering a vibrant research culture and contributing to the collective knowledge base.

The proceedings of the conference are poised to be invaluable to a diverse audience, including academicians, researchers, scientists, industrialists, and IT professionals engaged in the realm of computational methods and technologies. By disseminating cutting-edge research and facilitating interdisciplinary dialogue, this compilation not only captures the pulse of the field but also serves as a catalyst for advancing innovation and fostering collaborative endeavours among stakeholders.

Advancement of Intelligent Computational Methods and Technologies (AICMT2023) – Dr. O. P. Verma et al. (eds)

1

A Review on SML Based Diabetic Patient Classification and Prediction for Healthcare Domain

Satish Singh Mekale[1], Maumita Chakraborty[2]
University of Engineering and Management, Kolkata, India

ABSTRACT: This paper is a survey work on supervised learning. Public health protection is a very life-threatening concern for protecting, preventing, and monitoring disease occurrences in respect of society. In this regard patient monitoring systems based on supervised machine learning doing a significant role in monitoring the health of the patient especially in case of diabetic patients. This research paper gives a detailed outline of the Claim of SML or supervised machine learning systems in the healthcare arena for diabetes patient classification and prediction. Due to this, we provide a comparison study of several monitoring systems determined by machine learning approaches for diabetic patients in order to determine the best method for accurately measuring and preventing the patient's degree of diabetes. The purpose of this research is to recognise and appraise existing studies that target diabetes mellitus patients with classification and prediction using supervised machine learning (SML) methods. The review covers a wide range of topics, including model interpretability, feature selection methods, dataset characteristics, and algorithm selection. The findings of this paper have major implications for healthcare practitioners and researchers wanting to apply supervised machine learning algorithms (SML) for diabetic mellitus patient. Overall, we are certain that our investigation into machine learning-based solutions is on the correct track and might serve as a technical reference manual for future study and use by academic and business experts as well as decision-makers.

KEYWORDS: Machine learning (ML), Supervised learning, Diabetes mellitus (ML), Regression, Classification, Logistic regression (LR), Naïve Bayes (NV), Support vector machine (SVM), K nearest neighbour (KNN)

1. Introduction

In recent years, the advancement of machine learning (ML) techniques has created substantial prospects for improving healthcare outcomes(Butt et al. 2021). Accurate identification and prediction of diabetic mellitus (DM) patients can aid in early intervention, individualised therapy, and proactive management, leading to improved patient outcomes and decreased healthcare expenditures. A chronic metabolic ailment identified as diabetes mellitus, frequently abbreviated as diabetes mellitus (DM), is characterised by means of higher blood glucose levels (Hyperglycemia), which are brought on by the body's incapacity or inefficiency to produce or utilise insulin. The pancreatic hormone insulin, which makes it easier for cells to absorb glucose for use as fuel, is essential in regulating blood sugar levels. This delicate equilibrium, however, is upset in those with diabetes, resulting in persistently elevated blood glucose levels. Presenting a huge burden on individuals, healthcare institutions, and society as a whole. Consistent with the World Health Organisation (WHO), 463 million people worldwide had diabetes mellitus (DM) in 2019, and if present trends continue, that number is anticipated to increase to 700 million by 2045. There are several forms of diabetes, with type 2 diabetes mellitus (T2DM) being the most prevalent. Type 2 diabetes, in contrast to type 1, is generally ascribed to a mix of hereditary factors and lifestyle decisions. Type 1 diabetes, can be called as insulin-dependent diabetes mellitus (IDDM), Type 2 Diabetes can be called as non-insulin dependent (NIDDM). Hazard features for procurement of type 2 diabetes include obesity, physical dormancy, insalubrious dietary habits, having a family history of this condition. The

[1]ssmekale@gmail.com, [2]maumita.chakraborty@iemcal.com

DOI: 10.1201/9781003487906-1

technique of machine learning is an artificial intelligence subfield. The goal of machine learning is to understand data structure and fit it into a model that people can understand and use. The term "supervised machine learning (SML)" is used in this literature study. Supervised learning, also known as association learning, is a method of training a dataset by giving it input and output patterns that match. The model is learned from labelled training data using supervised learning. We divide supervised learning into two types based on the target: regression and classification.

2. Types of Supervised Machine Learning

Generally, we have two kinds of supervised machine learning:

1. Regression
2. Classification

2.1 Regression

Regression analysis is a fundamental and widely-used technique in machine learning and statistics for modeling and predicting continuous numerical outcomes. This model can then be used to create predictions or infer insights about fresh, unseen data pieces.

Types of regression

There are several types of regression in supervised learning.

(a) Linear Regression,
(b) Polynomial Regression,
(c) Multiple Regression (LR, PR, ML)

(a) Linear regression

It can be defined as such kind of supervised machine learning (SML) method that forecasts continuous output with a constant slope. The equation of linear regression is given below:

$$y_p = w_0 + w_1 f_1 + w_2 f_2 + \ldots\ldots + w_n f_n$$

where, y_p is predicted target. w_0, w_1 and w_2 are weights or regression coefficients, f_1 and f_2 are the features of given dataset. In linear regression, It can be defined as-

$$\text{MSE} = \frac{1}{n} * \sum (y_P - y)^2,$$

after calculating the loss i.e., mean square error, we use gradient descent to minimize the loss by reducing the weights with the help of Gradient equation which is-

$$W = W - lr * \frac{dloss}{dW},$$

where lr is learning rate.

(b) Polynomial regression

We required polynomial regression when the data are structured non-linearly. We use polynomial regression generally when the points in data are not captured by the learning regression. The equation of polynomial regression is-

$$yp = w_0 + w_1 f + w_2 + w_3$$

(Above polynomial equation is for degree 3) Where w_0, w_1 and w_2 are weights, f is the feature and y_p is predicted target.

(c) Multiple regression

Multiple regression is nearly identical to linear regression. The expansion of linear regression is multiple regression. When we find the data having multiple targets, we use multiple regression. The equation of multiple regression is same as linear regression

2.2 Classification

Classification is a fundamental task in supervised machine learning (SML) algorithm which predicts the labels or categories for the new data based on training. Classification algorithm is applicable on data having categorical target.

Types of classification

There are several kinds of classification algorithms-

(a) LR,
(b) NB,
(c) KNN,
(d) SVM,
(e) DT

(a) Logistic regression algorithm (LR)

It is particularly useful for dealing when binary classification problems in which the goal is to forecast the likelihood of a scenario falling under a particular category. The limit of sigmoid function is between 0 to 1. Sigmoid function is represented as:

$$F(x) = \frac{1}{1 + e^{-x}}$$

When we are using linear regression, the formula of hypothesis will be:

$$h(x) = w_0 + w_1 x,$$

For logistic regression the hypothesis will be:

$$\sigma(z) = \sigma(w_0 + w_1 x)$$

(b) Naïve Bayes algorithm (NB)

It can be defined as that kind of machine learning based on the Bayes theorem. It's a basic yet successful technique that's found use in text classification, spam detection, sentiment analysis, and other domains where feature independence is an acceptable assumption. The word Bayes is used because it is based on Bayes theorem i.e.

$$P(A|B) = P(B|A) * P(A)/P(B)$$

The Gaussian distribution is represented by the symbol-

$$f(x) = \frac{1}{\sqrt{2\pi\sigma^2}} e^{\frac{(x-u)^2}{2\sigma^2}}$$

where x is normal variable and variance σ^2 is a measure of the random variable's dispersion around the mean u.

(c) K-Nearest neighbour algorithm (KNN)

(KNN) is a well-known technique for both kind of problem dealing such as either classification or regression. A point of information in a feature space is classified using this non-parametric method based on the consensus of its k closest neighbours. It also goes by the name "lazy leaner algorithm" since it fails to acquire information from the training dataset. It starts over with each new dataset and repeats the entire procedure. In this algorithm, we must first select the number of neighbours e.g., $K = 5$. Then we will calculate the Euclidean distance between data points. It can be calculated as-

$$\text{Distance} = \sqrt{(y_2 - y_1)^2 + (x_2 - x_1)^2}$$

(d) Support vector machine algorithm (SVM)

It can be defined as that technique for dealing with classification tasks. It is well-known for processing both linearly and also for non-linearly separable kind of data by mapping input data into a higher-dimensional feature extraction space.

Types of Kernels in SVM-

Linear kernel (LK), Polynomial kernel (PK), Gaussian kernel (GK)

(e) Decision tree algorithm (DT)

DT can handle categorical and numerical data as well as multi-output situations. Information Gain is calculated by-

$$\text{Gain } (D, A) = \text{Entropy } (D) - \sum_{i=0}^{n} \frac{|D_i|}{|D|} \text{ Entropy } (Di), \text{ Entropy}$$

is calculated by-

$$I_H = -\sum_{i=0}^{n} P_i \log_2(P_i)$$

And the Gini Index is calculated by-

$$I_G = 1 - \sum_{i=0}^{n} (P_i)^2$$

(As Gini Index does not use log function so it is easier to calculate than Entropy.)

3. Literature Review

In this part, the author analyses a work from the previous year that looked at how diabetes mellitus may be classified and predicted using machine learning algorithms with supervision using a few deep learning techniques. Performing comparative examination of all significant elements in relation to the researched state-of-the-art (Table 1.1). (Ebrahim and Derbew 2023) The research presented in this article addresses the classification tasks and prediction task of type-2 diabetes mellitus (DM) using a prediction model with a particular implementation of supervised machine learning (SML) methods. Decision Tree (DT), K-Nearest neighbours (KNN), Binary logistic regression (BLR), Support vector machine method (SVM), Random Forest method (RF), along with Nave Bayes (NB) were applied to secondary data. Using an ensemble size of 2239 diabetic datasets reported between 2012 and 2020, random forest offered the best forecasting and classification results. However, some gaps in this study include a lack of comparative analysis, limited feature selection, and insufficient validation methodology.

(Chang et al. 2022) The work presented in this paper focuses on an e-diagnosis system model based on machine learning (ML) algorithms, including specific implementations of Nave Bayes classifiers, unsystematic forest classifiers, and J48 models of decision tree. Proceeding the entire data set, he achieved a random forest model with an accuracy of 79.13%, compared to 79.57%. However, some gaps in this study are as follows: lack of comparative analysis; Inadequate feature selection; and insufficient validation.

(Qawqzeh et al. 2020) reported a research that used a logistic regression model that utilised photoplethysmogram data to categorise individuals with diabetes. They trained the model using samples of data from 459 patients, and then tested and validated it using 128 data sample points. They claim that their proposed approach generated outcomes with a 92% model accuracy. Notwithstanding the fact that it cannot compete with cutting-edge methods, the proposed methodology.

(Pethunachiyar 2020) A supervised machine learning (SML) algorithm-based diabetic mellitus (DM) classification approach is provided in this study and is applied with a particular implementation of a support vector machine on the PIMA data set. The selection of variables is not enlightened, and there is no contemporary judgement.

(Maniruzzaman et al. 2020) In the work described in this article, focus on the Naive Bayes (NB), Decision Tree (DT), AdaBoost, and Random Forest (RF) methods are specifically implemented to build an algorithm of Diabetes mellitus diagnosed and predicted using the machine learning methodology.

Table 1.1 Comparison chart between diabetic classification (DC), diabetic prediction (DP), and real-time healthcare (RTH) data analysis with respect to the state-of-the-art studies

Name of author & Year of Publication	Algorithm Name/ Methods/Techniques	Performance Matrices			Performance measures
		Diabetes classification (DC)	Diabetes prediction (DP)	Real-time healthcare (RTH)	
(Ebrahim and Derbew 2023)	DT, K-NN, SVM, ANN, RF, and LR	YES	YES	NO	Sensitivity(TPR), Specificity(TNR), Area under the curve (AUC), Confusion matrix
(Ebrahim and Derbew 2023)	J48 DT, NB, and RF	YES	YES	NO	Accuracy, precision, sensitivity, and specificity
(Qawqzeh et al. 2020)	Logistic Regression	YES	NO	NO	Accuracy
(Pethunachiyar 2020)	Support Vector Machines,	YES	NO	NO	NA
(Ahuja, Sharma, and Ali 2019)	MLP Classifier	YES	NO	NO	Accuracy
(Mohapatra, Swain, and Mohanty 2019)	Multilayer Perceptron,	YES	NO	NO	NA
(Singh and Singh 2020)	K-Nearest Neighbor (K-NN)	NO	YES	NO	Accuracy
(Kumari, Kumar, and Mittal 2021)	RF, LR,& NB	YES	YES	NO	Accuracy
(Islam et al. 2020)	RF, LR,& NB)	NO	YES	NO	Accuracy
(Hussain and Naaz 2021)	SVM, ANN And ANFIS	NO	YES	NO	Accuracy, correlation coefficient
(Alfian et al. 2018)	Long Short-Term Memory	NO	NO	YES	NA

Source: Authors

(Ahuja, Sharma, and Ali 2019) The publicly available famous PIMA dataset was utilised for diabetic classification, and multiple machines learning techniques, including NB, DT, and MLP, were compared. He achieved MLP outperformed other classifiers.

(Mohapatra, Swain, and Mohanty 2019) They recently used the PIMA dataset to correctly detect diabetes mellitus (DM) with a 77.5 percent accuracy rate, but they were unable to undertake cutting-edge comparisons. In the literature, MLP has been used to classify a variety of disorders, including cancer and cardiovascular disease.

(Singh and Singh 2020) The work in this paper provides an ensemble technique based on stacking for forecasting diabetic mellitus (DM) type 2 disease. They used a PIMA dataset which is publicly with the unique implementation of stacking ensemble, and also applied the bootstrap method and cross-validation method to make the model more effective in training the four learners.. In spite of this, there is no cutting-edge comparison, and the variable selection is not explained.

(Kumari, Kumar, and Mittal 2021) developed a model for forecasting diabetes mellitus (DM) patients based on soft computing that incorporates three well-liked supervised machine learning algorithms. They assessed using the publicly available PIMA dataset for training and testing purposes and one more breast cancer database, with the specific implementation of They used Naive Bayes, logistic regression, and random forest. When compared to cutting-edge individual and ensemble algorithms, their solution excels with 79% accuracy.

(Islam et al. 2020) presented Diabetes was predicted in its early stages utilising data mining method with the particular implementation of four algorithm. Additionally, they used the 10-fold cross-validation approach. The findings collected of the experiments imply that random forest outperforms competing techniques. There is no precise specification of the attained accuracy, and there is no modern comparison.

(Hussain and Naaz 2021) a hormone that regulates blood glucose level, or the body does not effectively utilize the produced Insulin. This review paper presents a comparison of various Machine Learning models in the detection of Diabetes Mellitus (Type-2 Diabetes Built from 2010 and 2019 and thoroughly studied diabetes forecasting machine learning methods. They likened base methods of supervised machine learning (SML) methods through neural network (NN) based tactics in terms of performance metrics accuracy .They examined the algorithms using the Matthews correlation coefficient and discovered that Naive Bayes and random forest performed better than the others.

(Alfian et al. 2018) It was found that CGM sensors had received FDA approval for measuring glucose in a variety of trends and patterns. Additionally, because a single glucose reading is not accepted by a glucometer, it should not be used to determine the amount of insulin being administered at once.

4. Conclusion

This study reviews the supervised machine learning algorithms, Regression and Classification, as well as their applications in diverse domains. The merits and disadvantages of any ML algorithm are difficult to assess within the scope of this work. In summary, this study consolidates existing knowledge in the healthcare area on supervised machine learning-based diabetes patient classification and prediction. It emphasises the potential for these approaches to improve diabetic patient management, healthcare decision-making, and personalised treatment regimens. These include the need for machine learning models to be interpretable and explainable in order to build trust among healthcare professionals and patients, the handling of imbalanced datasets. The identified issues and research gaps provide useful insights for future studies, helping researchers towards overcoming constraints and furthering the area. The healthcare industry may make tremendous progress in efficiently controlling diabetes and improving patient outcomes by using the capabilities of supervised machine learning. In this paper, we have examined a way to deal with help the medical care space. Researchers are energetic to attempt various kinds of classifiers and construct new models with a work to improve the exactness of diabetes expectation.

5. Acknowledgement

The authors gratefully acknowledge the students, staff, and authority of Physics department for their cooperation in the research.

6. Future Work

In the future, the unutilized classifiers and regression method can be incorporated to fresh datasets in a combined model to increase the accuracy, confusion matrix, precision, recall, and F1 score of predicting Diabetes mellitus disease in early disease.

7. Conflicts of Interest

The authors have no competing interests in the publishing of this study.

8. Technical Contribution

Satish Singh Mekale: original concept manuscript writing, data analysis.

Maumita Chakraborty: Review, original draft.

REFERENCES

1. Ahuja, Ravinder, Subhash C. Sharma, and Maaruf Ali. 2019. "A Diabetic Disease Prediction Model Based on Classification Algorithms." Annals of Emerging Technologies in Computing 3 (3): 44–52. https://doi.org/10.33166/AETiC.2019.03.005.
2. Alfian, Ganjar, Muhammad Syafrudin, Muhammad Fazal Ijaz, M. Alex Syaekhoni, Norma Latif Fitriyani, and Jongtae Rhee. 2018. "A Personalized Healthcare Monitoring System for Diabetic Patients by Utilizing BLE-Based Sensors and Real-Time Data Processing." Sensors (Switzerland) 18 (7). https://doi.org/10.3390/s18072183.
3. Butt, Umair Muneer, Sukumar Letchmunan, Mubashir Ali, Fadratul Hafinaz Hassan, Anees Baqir, and Hafiz Husnain Raza Sherazi. 2021. "Machine Learning Based Diabetes Classification and Prediction for Healthcare Applications." Journal of Healthcare Engineering 2021. https://doi.org/10.1155/2021/9930985.
4. Chang, Victor, Jozeene Bailey, Qianwen Ariel Xu, and Zhili Sun. 2022. "Pima Indians Diabetes Mellitus Classification Based on Machine Learning (ML) Algorithms." Neural Computing and Applications 0123456789. https://doi.org/10.1007/s00521-022-07049-z.
5. Ebrahim, Oumer Abdulkadir, and Getachew Derbew. 2023. "Application of Supervised Machine Learning Algorithms for Classification and Prediction of Type-2 Diabetes Disease Status in Afar Regional State, Northeastern Ethiopia 2021." Scientific Reports 13 (1): 7779. https://doi.org/10.1038/s41598-023-34906-1.
6. Hussain, Arooj, and Sameena Naaz. 2021. Prediction of Diabetes Mellitus: Comparative Study of Various Machine Learning Models. Advances in Intelligent Systems and Computing. Vol. 1166. Springer Singapore. https://doi.org/10.1007/978-981-15-5148-2_10.
7. Islam, M. M.Faniqul, Rahatara Ferdousi, Sadikur Rahman, and Humayra Yasmin Bushra. 2020. "Likelihood Prediction of Diabetes at Early Stage Using Data Mining Techniques." Advances in Intelligent Systems and Computing 992 (January): 113–25. https://doi.org/10.1007/978-981-13-8798-2_12.
8. Kumari, Saloni, Deepika Kumar, and Mamta Mittal. 2021. "An Ensemble Approach for Classification and Prediction of Diabetes Mellitus Using Soft Voting Classifier." International Journal of Cognitive Computing in Engineering 2 (November 2020): 40–46. https://doi.org/10.1016/j.ijcce.2021.01.001.
9. Maniruzzaman, Md, Md Jahanur Rahman, Benojir Ahammed, and Md Menhazul Abedin. 2020. "Classification and Prediction of Diabetes Disease Using Machine Learning Paradigm." Health Information Science and Systems 8 (1): 1–14. https://doi.org/10.1007/s13755-019-0095-z.

10. Mohapatra, Saumendra Kumar, Jagjit Kumar Swain, and Mihir Narayan Mohanty. 2019. Detection of Diabetes Using Multilayer Perceptron. Advances in Intelligent Systems and Computing. Vol. 846. Springer Singapore. https://doi.org/10.1007/978-981-13-2182-5_11.
11. Pethunachiyar, G. A. 2020. "Classification of Diabetes Patients Using Kernel Based Support Vector Machines." 2020 International Conference on Computer Communication and Informatics, ICCCI 2020, 22–25. https://doi.org/10.1109/ICCCI48352.2020.9104185.
12. Qawqzeh, Yousef K., Abdullah S. Bajahzar, Mahdi Jemmali, Mohammad Mahmood Otoom, and Adel Thaljaoui. 2020. "Classification of Diabetes Using Photoplethysmogram (PPG) Waveform Analysis: Logistic Regression Modeling." BioMed Research International 2020. https://doi.org/10.1155/2020/3764653.
13. Singh, Namrata, and Pradeep Singh. 2020. "Stacking-Based Multi-Objective Evolutionary Ensemble Framework for Prediction of Diabetes Mellitus." Biocybernetics and Biomedical Engineering 40 (1): 1–22. https://doi.org/10.1016/j.bbe.2019.10.001.

Advancement of Intelligent Computational Methods and Technologies (AICMT2023) – Dr. O. P. Verma et al. (eds)
© 2024 Taylor & Francis Group, London, ISBN 978-1-032-78445-8

2

Brief Introduction to Healthy Food Ordering and Delivery

Md Shamsuzzama Siddique[1], Yashu Shanker[2]
Deptt. of Computer Science and Engineering, Delhi Technical Campus, Greater Noida, India
Ankit Raj[3], Sahil Kumar[4], Raj Mishra[5]
Bachelors of Computer Application, Delhi Technical Campus, Greater Noida, India

ABSTRACT: The framework we propose is a web-based food request framework that provides customer convenience. This overcomes the shortcomings of traditional queuing systems. The framework we propose could be a means of sorting out the benefits of meal free food problems and online confusion. This framework drives the strategy of taking ownership of the contract from the customer. Customers may simply place orders as they choose using the internet-based meal purchasing system, which has built up an eatery buffet online. Additionally, clients may simply follow their orders using a culinary menu. Additionally, this technology offers an input system that allows users to examine nutritional items. Additionally, the suggested system may make culinary recommendations for establishments according to user evaluations. Only money may be used to pay for the purchase. By giving everyone a user id and login credentials, different accounts with more secure levels are kept for everyone.

KEYWORDS: Customer relationship management, Innovation acknowledgment demonstration, paper based nourishment

1. Introduction

The Project Online Food Purchasing System is introduced here: The "Online Food Ordering System" was created to overcome the issues with the already-in-use manual approach. The difficulties our current system faces are supported by this program, which aims to remove and, in some circumstances, lessen them. Additionally, the framework was uncommonly created to meet the requirements of companies to make their operations effective and fruitful (Bhandge Kirti, et al., 2015) (Bhargave Ashutosh, et al 2013). The program has been kept as basic as possible to avoid data passage blunders. In the event that you enter the wrong information, you'll get a blunder message. Clients don't require any extraordinary preparation to utilize this framework. This alone demonstrates that it is user-friendly. As previously said, an online food ordering system may result in a fast, secure, trustworthy, and error-free management system (Chavan Varsha, et al,2015).

2. Objective

The main objective of the endeavor on a website for ordering food is the administration of culinary product, group, customer, stability, and shipment confirmation information. All food products, payments, order confirmations, and culinary details are managed by it. The person in charge alone is guaranteed access because the task is finished on the administrative side. The goal of the initiative is to provide a digital network that will reduce the volume of human labor necessary to handle the culinary product, group, payment, and client. It records each element of the client's stability and receipt of the order.

Convenience: Online ordering makes it easy for people to get healthy food without having to leave their homes. This is especially beneficial for people who are busy, have dietary restrictions, or live in areas with limited healthy food options.

[1]mdshamsuzzama19@gmail.com, [2]yashu.shanker@gmail.com, [3]2000ankitraj@gmail.com, [4]sahilkumar@gmail.com, [5]rajbabu22012002@gmail.com

DOI: 10.1201/9781003487906-2

Variety: Online ordering websites offer a wide variety of healthy food options, from fresh produce to prepared meals. This allows people to find healthy food that fits their taste and dietary needs.

Affordability: Online ordering websites often offer discounts and promotions, which can make healthy food more affordable.

Education: Online ordering websites can provide information about healthy eating, such as recipes, nutrition facts, and meal planning tips. This can help people make healthier food choices.

3. Functional Requirements

The following are the functional criteria for an online food ordering and delivery system:

- In order to place orders, buyers have to be allowed to sign up for an account and thereafter log in.
- The system must enable eateries to maintain their meal plans, comprising the addition, deletion, and upgrading of items.
- Buyers must be allowed to look through the food options, add goods to their basket, and pay in order to place orders.
- The system must accept multiple payment methods, including credit cards, debit cards, and PayPal.
- Customers must be able to view the status of their orders, particularly when they were placed, when they are anticipated to be given, and any difficulties with the transaction.
- Buyers should be capable of monitoring all aspects of their purchases, indicating when they were initially set up, when they are anticipated to be provided, and whether there are currently any problems with their purchase.
- To deliver orders to customers, the system must link with a shipping company. Buyers who have concerns or queries with purchases must be assisted by the system.

4. Literature Review

A suggested automated meal ordering system in will intelligently track user orders. They essentially created a food ordering system for several types of eateries, allowing users to place orders or create custom meals with just one click (Chavan Varsha, et al, 2015). This technique was created using an Android application for tablet computers. Android and Java were used to construct the front end, and MySQL was the database of choice for the back end.

A customer using a smartphone is regarded as the system's fundamental premise. The saved order can be verified by tapping the smartphone as the consumer approaches the establishment (Shinde Resham, 2014). The list of the pre ordered things you've chosen will appear on the kitchen screen, and once you've decided, an order sheet will print out so that you may continue processing your order. The solution offers a simple and practical approach to choosing customers for pre-order transaction forms.

A design and implementation of digital eating in restaurants utilizing Android technology were attempted in. This solution was a straightforward dynamic database tool that retrieved all the data from a single database (K. Khairunnisa, et al 2009). This intuitive program helped eateries operate more efficiently and accurately while reducing human error. This technology was developed to address the previous shortcomings of automated food ordering systems and only requires a one-time investment in devices.

Presents the application of web administrations innovation utilized for in administration framework integration. A computerized lodging administration framework brings together your requesting framework, charging framework, and client relationship administration framework (CRM) (Samsuddin, Noor, et. al 2011). This approach has made it conceivable for lodging chain situations of all sizes to include or extend their inn computer program system.

In, a remote nourishment requesting framework for eateries is the center of investigation. Remote Requesting Framework "WOS" This framework depicts the specialized forms such as framework engineering, highlights, restrictions and proposals. With the expanding utilization of handheld gadgets such as PDAs in neighborliness foundations, inescapable applications are an imperative instrument for moving forward eatery operations by decreasing human blunder and giving higher quality client benefit was thought to be.

In, a remote dinner requesting framework was planned and executed for eateries with shopper input. It makes it simple for restaurateurs to alter menu introductions and set up frameworks in WiFi situations. To encourage real-time communication between eatery proprietors and coffee shops, smartphones were associated with a configurable remote nourishment requesting framework and realtime client input was implemented.

The purpose of the paper was to examine the factors that impact Web users' recognition of online nourishment requesting among Turkish college understudies. Davis created his 1986 Innovation Acknowledgement Demonstration (TAM), which was utilized to analyze how the internet environment was embraced for requesting nourishment (Pate, et al, 2015). In the expansion of TAM, beliefs, imaginative capabilities, and outside impacts are included as key components of the model.

In a paper, this investigation extends endeavors to robotize the nourishment requesting handle in eateries and progress the eating encounter for visitors. This thought portrayed the plan and execution of an eatery supper requesting framework. This framework empowers remote information to get to the server. User's her android versatile application contains all the menu data. Arranged points of interest are sent wirelessly from the customer's versatile gadget to the kitchen and checkout. The central database is overhauled with these arranged points of interest. Eatery proprietors can react rapidly to menu changes.

This review looks at eatery owners' activities to receive innovation and communication advances, counting PDAs, remote LANs, costly multi-touch screens, and more, to move forward the encounter feasting involvement at Paper. To overcome a few drawbacks of conventional paper-based nourishment requesting framework and PDA, a low-cost touchscreen eatery administration framework utilizing Android smartphone or tablet is proposed.

5. Traditional and Automated Approach of Food Industry

Conventional methods of food ordering and delivery include:

- Consumers can order in person by calling the eatery personally. This is one of the most basic and traditional methods of meal ordering, and many establishments actively practice it today.
- Telephone ordering: Customers place their orders by calling an independent ordering service, such as Grub Hub or Door Dash. These systems then feed purchases to eateries, which ultimately delivers the food to buyers.
- Consumers place an order from the eatery and pick it up individually. This is an effective option for those who want in order to prevent delivery expenses or are pressed for time.
- There are numerous automated meal booking and delivery systems available. Among the most prominent are:
- Customers can place orders online using a dining establishment's internet or mobile app. Customers may request cuisine without wanting to wait in a queue or talk with a server using this method.
- Tableside ordering: In certain eateries, customers can place orders right from their table. Customers can request meals without needing to notify down someone to serve them using this method.
- Third-party delivery services: Consumers can use a service that delivers food to them, such as Grubhub or DoorDash, to order meals from a dining establishment. Consumers can use this service for ordering cuisine from establishments that do not have a food delivery facility.

6. Benefits of Automated Approach Over Traditional

Computerized approaches to online nourishment request and conveyance frameworks offer a number of benefits over conventional strategies. These incorporate:

- *Expanded proficiency:* Computerized frameworks can prepare orders more rapidly and precisely than manual frameworks. This may lead to shorter hold up times for clients and improved client fulfillment.
- *Decreased cost:* Computerized frameworks can offer assistance to decrease costs for businesses by eliminating the need for human labor. This will lead to higher benefits for businesses and lower costs for clients.
- *Moved forward accuracy:* Mechanized frameworks can offer assistance to progress the precision of orders. This may diminish the number of blunders and the amount of nourishment squander.
- *Expanded adaptability:* Mechanized frameworks can be more adaptable than manual frameworks. This could permit businesses to adjust to changes in request and client inclinations.
- *Made strides client benefit:* Mechanized frameworks can offer assistance to make strides client benefit by giving clients 24/7 to requesting and back administrations.
- *Speed:* Automated approaches can often complete tasks much faster than traditional methods. This is because they can work 24/7 without breaks, and they are not limited by human factors such as fatigue or boredom.
- *Accuracy:* Automated approaches are often more accurate than traditional methods. This is because they are not susceptible to human errors such as typos or miscalculations.

7. Conclusion

An internet-based food purchase and delivery service called Nutrifood was created with the goal of giving customers improved purchasing expertise, and it will keep doing so for a number of decades in the future. Many analysts believe that, due to the quick expansion of markets and enterprises, online shopping is going to eclipse in-store purchasing. In areas where consumers appear more satisfied interacting with or seeing the object they are purchasing, actual and traditional businesses are still necessary, even though this is now the case in some places. Nevertheless, the convenience of using online resources for purchasing have made customers better educated and able to compare products, despite having to spend a lot of time doing so.

8. Future Scope of Online Food Ordering System

The project's goal was to create an online meal ordering platform that could be utilized initially in small and medium sized cities and later on a larger scale. It was created to assist eateries in streamlining everyday operating and management tasks and to enhance the eating experience for patrons. Furthermore, by offering outstanding amenities, eateries can build strong ties with their patrons. According to the directives made and the transactions processed, the technology allows personnel to modify and perform revisions to their meal and drink list details.

9. Acknowledgement

The authors gratefully acknowledge the students, staff, and authority of Computer Science department for their cooperation in the research.

10. Result

1. **Online Food Ordering Growth:** Since 2014, online food ordering has grown 300% faster than dine-in.
2. **Revenue Projection:** Online food delivery revenue is projected to reach $339.3 billion in 2022 and is expected to grow at an annual rate of 8.29%, reaching $466.5 billion by 2026.
3. **Diners' Preferences:** Nearly 60% of diners expect to order more online in 2022. Among them, 42% plan to order more directly from restaurants, while 14% plan to order more from third-party apps.
4. **Mobile Ordering Trend:** 35% of customers are placing more orders on apps compared to three months ago. Customers tend to spend more when ordering via a restaurant app.
5. **Profitability of Online Ordering:** Restaurants with an online ordering system can raise their takeout profits by 30% higher than those without.
6. **Tech Adoption by Restaurants:** Over 80% of restaurants are using technology, such as online ordering, reservation and inventory apps, and analytics, to enhance business operations.
7. **Projected Revenue:** Online ordering food revenue is projected to rise to $220 billion in 2023, accounting for 40% of restaurant sales.
8. **Consumer Behavior:** There was a 54% increase in direct online order volume year over year. Customers who order online visit the restaurant 67% more frequently than those who don't.
9. **Third-Party Delivery and Curbside Pickup:** Around 31% of American consumers use third-party food delivery services at least twice a week. Curbside pickup gained prominence, with 67% of restaurants adding it after March 2020.
10. **Consumer Demand and Preferences:** Over 80% of top-performing restaurants offer mobile order-ahead and loyalty rewards programs. About 43% of people order online to save time from cooking, and 59% of millennial restaurant orders are for takeout or delivery.
11. **Impact of Online Ordering on Sales:** Nearly 60% of restaurants can expect more sales when they offer online ordering.
12. **Average Household Spending:** The average U.S. household spends $2,375 annually on dining and takeout purchases.

Table 2.1 Food ordering and its revenue growth rate data [7]

Name	Data
Growth Rate	300%
Online Food Sales (2022)	39%
Annual Growth Rate (2022-2026)	8.29%
Projected Revenue (2026)	46%
Diners' Expectations (2022)	60%
Diners' Preferences (2022)	42%
	14%
Mobile Ordering Trend (2022)	35%
Profit Increase (Online Orders)	30%
App Users (2022)	30%
Tech Adoption by Restaurants	80%
Projected Revenue (2023)	40%
Increase in Direct Orders (YoY)	54%
Preferred Online Ordering (2022)	56%
Restaurant-to-Consumer Users	76%
Digital Ordering Preference	64%
Consumer Impact of Online Order	45%
Consumer Demand Pre-Pandemic	78%
Increased Sales (Restaurants)	60%
Reasons for Ordering Online	43%
Millennial Orders	59%
Online Pizza Spending	18%
Increased Frequency (Online)	67%
Third-Party Delivery Frequency	31%
Curbside Pickup Trend	67%
Average Household Spending	23%

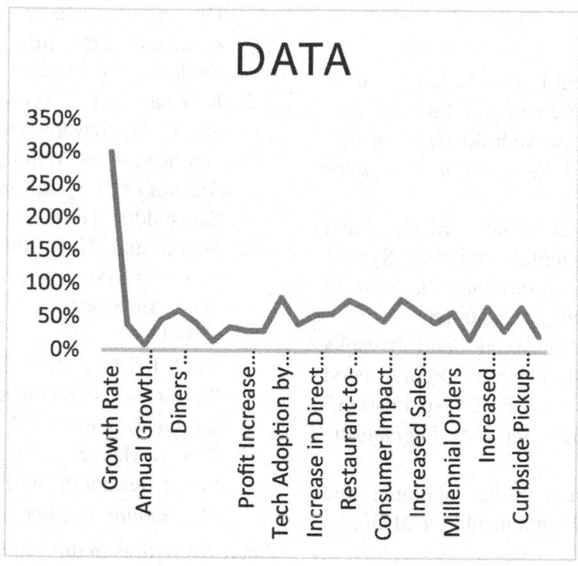

Fig. 2.1 Growth rate of food ordering

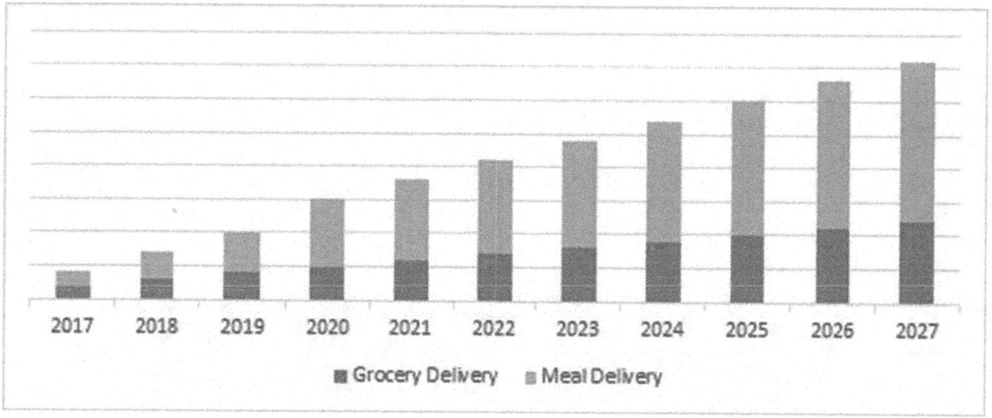

Fig. 2.2 Growth rate different deliver services

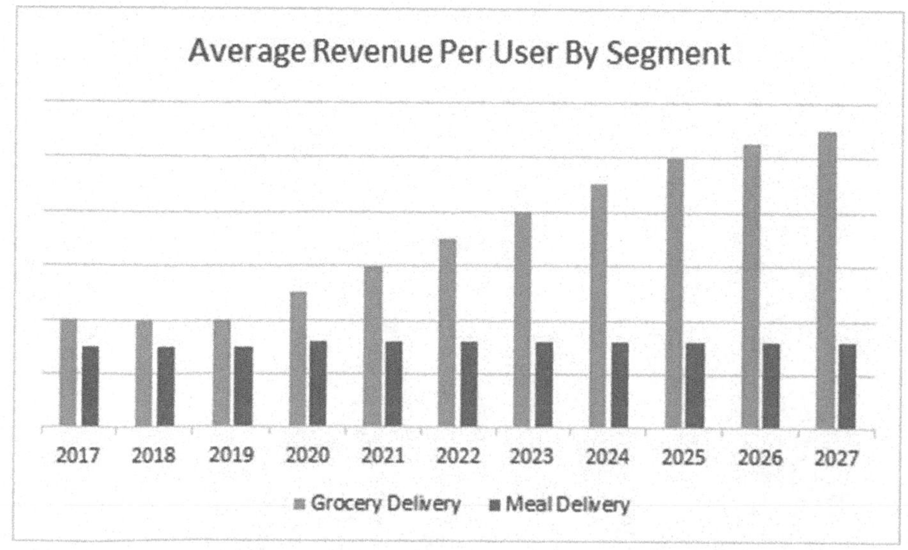

Fig. 2.3 Average revenue per user for automated food odering

REFERENCES

1. Bhandge Kirti, Tejas Shinde, Dheeraj Ingale, Neeraj Solanki, and Reshma Totare. 2015. "A Proposed System for Touchpad Based Food Ordering System Using Android Application." *International Journal of Advanced Research in Computer Science Technology* 3 (5): 43–48.
2. Bhargave Ashutosh, Niranjan Jadhav, Apurva Joshi, Prachi Oke, and S.R Lahane. 2013. "Digital Ordering System for Restaurant Using Android." *International Journal of Scienctific and Research Publications* 3 (5): 56–68.
3. Chavan Varsha, Priya Jadhav, Snehal Korade, and Priyanka Teli. 2015. "Implementing Customizable Online Food Ordering System Using Web Android Application." *International Journal of Innovative Science, Engineering Technology* 3 (6): 65–71.
4. Shinde Resham, Priyanka Thakare, Neha Dhomne, and Sushmita Sarkar. 2014. "Design and Implementation of Digital Dining in Restaurants Using Android." *International Journal of Advanced Research in Computer Science and Management Studies* 2 (4): 43–48.
5. K. Khairunnisa, Ayob J., Mohd. Hemly A Wahab, M. Erdi Ayob, M. Izwan Ayob, and M. Afif Ayob. 2009. "The Application of Wireless Food Ordering System." *Masaum Journal of Computing* 2 (3): 251–78.
6. Samsuddin, Noor, Shamsul Ahmad, Fikry Akmal, Zulkifli Senin, and Noor Ihkasin. 2011. "A Customizable Food Ordering System with Real-Time Customer Feedback." *IEEE Symopsium on Wireless Technology and Applications* 4 (3): 123–35.
7. Patel, Krishna, Palak Patel, Raj Nirali, and Lalit Patel. 2015. "Automated Food Ordering System." *International Journal of Engineering Research and Development* 2 (3): 352–62.
8. Jakhete Mayur, and Piyush Mankar. 2014. "Implementation of Smart Restaurant with E-Menu Card." *International Journal of Computer Applications* 3 (6): 145–61.

Note: All figures in this chapter were made by the authors.

Advancement of Intelligent Computational Methods and Technologies (AICMT2023) – Dr. O. P. Verma et al. (eds)

3

Food Ordering Android App Using Firebase and Google Cloud

Abid Humza[1], Devansh Rangan[2], Asra Fatma[3], Pranjay Bhatt[4], Priyanka Dadhich[5]
Dept. Computer Science & Engineering, Delhi Technical Campus, Greater Noida, India

ABSTRACT: Food manufacturing and distribution have long been lucrative businesses for consumers as well as producers and suppliers. Due to recent developments in the sector and rising internet usage, an online meal ordering system is urgently needed. Our suggested method is a real-time web system enabling customers to order meals. The shortcomings and downsides of the conventional queueing method are circumvented by our system application. Through our suggested approach, food may be easily purchased from a certain restaurant online. Our system application enhances consumer order-taking procedures for meals. Customers may easily submit their orders using the suggested method, using a food menu that has been built up online as per their wishes. Over the system's offered feedback mechanism users may rank the food products. Through the suggested system, restaurants are also recommended to new consumers based on user evaluations, and for improvements in quality, the restaurant will be notified.

KEYWORDS: Android app, Authentication, Food ordering, Firebase, Google cloud, Hosting, Real-time database, Storage

1. Introduction

Traditional meal delivery services have been available for decades, but they sometimes require a phone call or a visit to the restaurant, which may be time-consuming and inconvenient. Furthermore, many restaurants do not offer a delivery service, making it difficult for customers to place orders. People's lifestyles are becoming more hectic, and they have less time for cooking, especially during the week or while they are away from home. Furthermore, with technological advancement, people are increasingly relying on their smartphones and computers to complete daily tasks. Food delivery applications that provide a simple, easy, and efficient method to get meals from nearby eateries are in high demand in this type of atmosphere (Bhargave et.al., 2013). Customers, on the other hand, may browse a broad variety of restaurants, choose their favourite foods, and have them delivered to their houses in a matter of minutes.

2. Problem Definition

Traditional meal delivery services have been available for decades, but they sometimes require a phone call or a visit to the restaurant, which may be time-consuming and inconvenient. Furthermore, many restaurants do not offer a delivery service, making it difficult for customers to place orders. People's lifestyles are becoming more hectic, and they have less time for cooking, especially during the week or while they are away from home. Furthermore, with technological advancement, people are increasingly relying on their smartphones and computers to complete daily tasks. Though there are options for ordering meals through apps such as Swiggy or Zomato (Mane, 2012), there are disadvantages to utilising these services, such as registration fees, a predetermined commission on every order placed, marketing charges, and much more.

[1]abidhumzabca@delhitechnicalcampus.ac.in, [2]devanshrangan@delhitechnicalcampus.ac.in, [3]asrafatma@delhitechnicalcampus.ac.in, [4]pranjaybhatt@delhitechnicalcampus.ac.in, [5]p.dadhich@delhitechnicalcampus.ac.in

DOI: 10.1201/9781003487906-3

2.1 Objectives

To provide food ordering easily without any kind of disruption between the customer and the restaurant or café.

To help the customer or user search for the item or food as quickly as possible.

To provide the customer with the flexibility of paying the bill with our multiple payment options feature.

3. Front-End Technology

Front-end technology is the collection of tools and programming languages used to create the visual and interactive components of a website or application that users directly interact with. It primarily focuses on the user interface (UI) and user experience (UX) aspects, including the design, layout, and functionality of the interface.

3.1 Android Studio Development (SDK)

The acronym for the Android software development kit is SDK. It is a set of resources, frameworks, and tools that programmers may utilise to create and distribute Android applications. The Android SDK comes with several tools that let developers access device capabilities like sensors, cameras, and location services, including a compiler, debugger, emulator, and several APIs and libraries.

4. Back-End Technology

Back-end technology is the set of tools and programming languages used to create the server-side algorithms and basic structure of a website or application. It encompasses the behind-the-scenes operations that power the functionality and data management of a system. Back-end developers primarily work with programming languages like Python, Java, Ruby, or Node.js to handle server-side processes such as data storage, retrieval, and manipulation. Kindly refer the Table 1 for analysis of technology.

4.1 Google Cloud Functions

With Google Cloud Functions, developers can run their code in response to events or triggers without having to worry about maintaining infrastructure. It lets programmers construct and distribute lightweight functions that may be launched in response to different types of events, including message queues, HTTP requests, and datastore changes. Developers can concentrate on developing code and creating apps using Google Cloud Functions without worrying about infrastructure management, scaling, or availability.

4.2 Firebase Authentication

Firebase Authentication is a robust and user-friendly authentication service provided by Google's Firebase platform. It offers developers comprehensive authentication functionalities to secure user access and personalise app experiences. With Firebase Authentication, developers can easily implement secure user registration, login, and user management features in their Android applications. It supports various authentication methods, including email or password, phone number, Google Sign-In, Facebook Login, and more. The service handles the authentication process, including identity verification and token management, seamlessly integrating with Firebase's other services like the Realtime Database and Cloud Firestore.

Table 3.1 Analysis of back-end technology [3]

Name	Working	Properties	Uses
Google Cloud Functions (Tanpure, 2013)	Handles different types of events	Lightweight functions	Developing code and creating apps
Firebase Authentication (Imran and Rahman, 2019)	Handles the authentication process, including identity verification and token management	Robust and user-friendly authentication service	Realtime Database and Cloud Firestore
Firebase Real-Time Database (Hafiz et.al., 2021)	Offers a cloud-hosted NoSQL database	Customizable and scalable	Real-time applications
Firebase Firestore (Mane, 2012)	Offers seamless data synchronisation, enabling platform- and device-agnostic automated updates whenever changes take place	Adaptable, scalable, cloud-native and synchronises itself	Store & query data in real time across servers, clients, and online applications

4.3 Firebase Real-Time Database

Google's Firebase platform offers a cloud-hosted NoSQL database known as the Firebase Realtime Database. It offers programmers a customizable and scalable option for creating real-time applications. The JSON-based data schema used by the Realtime Database helps developers store and synchronise data in real-time across several clients (This allows for smooth data synchronisation and real-time collaboration by quickly propagating any database changes to all associated devices. Direct client-side code access to the database eliminates the need for server-side infrastructure and streamlines the development process.

4.4 Firebase Firestore

Firebase Google's Firebase platform offers Firestore, a NoSQL document database that is adaptable, scalable, and cloud-native. It provides a strong and simple way to store, sync, and query data in real time across servers, clients, and online applications. Firestore's document-based data format enables developers to group data into collections and documents, providing an intuitive hierarchical structure. It offers seamless data synchronisation, enabling platform- and device-agnostic automated updates whenever changes take place. Assuring that data is available even when the device is offline, Firestore also offers offline data persistence. When connectivity is restored, Firestore synchronises itself without user intervention.

5. Important Components of the Food Ordering App

5.1 User Interface (UI)

One of the fundamental building blocks for a meal delivery app's commercial success is the user interface. Customers may quickly browse the menu, make product selections, customise orders, and retain their information in real-time thanks to the app's user interface (Ngangbam and Singh, 2018). The capacity to search food products, categories, cart management, and order history is a must for a good user interface.

5.2 Firebase Real-TIme Database

Due to its capacity to synchronise real-time data, the Firebasereal-time database is one of the better solutions available for maintaining an app's database to hold user and food management information (Verma et.al., 2018). It may also be used to propagate updates to all connected devices.

5.3 Cloud Functions

At the moment, Google Cloud Functions is the best choice for maintaining serverless backend logic. Order processing, payment integration, notification sending, and several other business logic may all be integrated.

5.4 Payment Integration

To conduct transactions between users and restaurants, an app must integrate any payment services; as a result, this must be done safely and securely. There are a lot of wonderful alternatives, including PayPal, Stripe, and Paytm.

5.6 User Authentication

Authorised access is one of the main issues at the moment, and these apps need a strong user authentication mechanism to ensure that the user is legitimate. The capabilities of Firebase Authentication Systems may be used to do this. It handles user authentication information for a variety of methods, including OTP-based access, O.Auth, basic email and password access, and others.

6. Future Enhancement

A real-time notification from the mobile phone application to the service desk is a feature that the system is capable of implementing. This feature enables the consumer to use the mobile application to seek customer assistance as opposed to vocally phoning the restaurant personnel and going up to them.

The Android application may also include a function that enables users to update the status of the meal delivery. For instance, clients who order luxury dining at the restaurant can use the Android application to request the meal be provided, and if the customer finishes the main course and feels satisfied and full then, the customer can use the Android application to cancel the upcoming dishes which need to be served.

Last but not least, the Android application may include a mini-game that might keep clients entertained as they wait for their food.

7. Results

An Android application is one of the outcomes of our system application. The user may log in using two authentication methods: OTP-based and WhatsApp O.Auth.

A client who places an order with a restaurant will receive the order details on the screen in real time.

The consumer may view the order history, and based on that past, they will receive customised things. Additionally, customers can modify their meal products.

The consumer can also provide comments on the restaurant's cuisine and services. The feedback comprises the customer's remarks and a star rating.

8. Conclusion

This Android application is user-based and built especially for benefiting the user's needs. This system creates all kinds of difficulties for all users that are a part of it. Many different types of people can use this application if they have technical knowledge regarding Android smartphones. This method will help you manage your time and resolve a variety of small business-related problems.

Based on this Android application, it can be said that "This application makes it easy for the users to place orders and provide them with sufficient information required to place orders". Through the application, restaurants can receive orders and change their data dynamically. It also contributesto the admin in managing the food system.

9. Acknowledgment

We would like to express our sincere appreciation to all faculty members at DTC who have supported and guided us throughout the completion of this research paper. Your invaluable contributions and encouragement have been instrumental in its success. I would also like to acknowledge the participants in this study for their valuable contributions.

REFERENCES

1. Bhagwat, P., & Vartak, R. (2021). "A Comparative study on Firebase real-time database and MongoDB for android application." International Journal of Computer Science and Mobile Computing, 8(8), 114–120.
2. Hafiz, M., Hassan, M., Ahmed, A., & Zahid, Z. (2021). "Integration of Firebase real-time database in the android application." In 2021 IEEE 14th International Conference on Humanoid, Nanotechnology, Information Technology, Communication, and Control, Environment, and Management (HNICEM) (pp. 1–6). IEEE.
3. Imran, A., & Rahman, A. (2019). "Secure food delivery application using Firebase real-time database." International Journal of Advanced Computer Science and Applications, 10(5), 129–135.
4. Ngangbam, R., & Singh, L. S. (2018). "Design and implementation of an android food ordering application." International Journal of Computer Applications, 182(2), 9–14.
5. Shirsath, N., & Rasane, R. (2018). "Firebase and Google Cloud Vision-based real-time disease detection system." International Journal of Engineering Research & Technology, 7(10), 123–126.
6. Verma, A., Sharma, K., & Sharma, R. (2018). "Online food ordering system using Firebase database." International Journal of Engineering Research & Technology, 9(3), 393–397.
7. Bhandge, K., Shinde, T., Ingale, D., Solanki, N., & Totare, R. (2015). "A Proposed System for Touchpad Based Food Ordering System Using Android Application." International Journal of Advanced Research in Computer Science Technology, IJARCST.
8. Bhargave, A., Jadhav, N., Joshi, A., Oke, P., & Lahane, S. R. (2013). "Digital Ordering System for Restaurant Using Android." International Journal of Scientific and Research Publications.
9. Tanpure, S. S. (2013). "Automated Food Ordering System with Real-Time Customer Feedback." International Journal of Advanced Research in Computer Science and Software Engineering, 3(2).
10. Mane, P. J. (2012.). "Study of Online Food Delivery App like Zomato & Swiggy and their effect on Casual Dining." International Journal of Scientific Research and Engineering Development.

Advancement of Intelligent Computational Methods and Technologies (AICMT2023) – Dr. O. P. Verma et al. (eds)
© 2024 Taylor & Francis Group, London, ISBN 978-1-032-78445-8

4

Ransomware Detection Using Machine-Learning Techniques

Saroj Dalwani[1], Nidhi Malik[2], Priya Arora[3]
Department of Computer Science and Engineering, The NorthCap University, Gurugram, India

ABSTRACT: In today's tech savvy world, data is the most precious as well as the most vulnerable asset. One of the most common types of attacks are the malware attacks carried out to breach data and extort monetary benefits. An attacker or hacker can conceal files or data employing ransomware, a first-generation form of malware. Without the attacker's cooperation, the proprietor of the data is unable to acquire it. After encrypting the data, the attacker requests a ransom, usually in the form of cryptocurrency or cash, in order to give the victim access to their data again. But as technology advances, machine learning is used in a variety of effective detection algorithms that can be utilized to recognize malware files and prevent infection.

KEYWORDS: Ransomware, Machine learning, Random forest, Support vector machine, Naïve Bayes

1. Introduction

The term 'malware' comprises two words viz 'malicious' and 'software' that means malware is any kind of malicious software injected with the intention of disrupting the data and systems for personal benefits. According to the Global Threat Report by Crowdstrike for FY 2022, 38% of the attacks and breaches were malware based. Malware can be described as any piece of code/software designed to exploit the prevailing loophole/vulnerability in the web-applications and gain profits by illicit and illegal methods. Two main types of malware are 'first generation' and 'second generation' malware (Rabia T., 2018). The first generation can be defined as the malware with fixed signatures and which have a fixed behavior/pattern. These include malwares like spyware, ransomware, rootkits, adware, botnets, key loggers, etc. The second generation malware variants constantly keep changing their structure and signature to go unidentified and be undetectable which include variants like 'Oligomorphic', 'Polymorphic', 'Metamorphic' malware. But over the period of time various mitigations have been invented and implemented. There are numerous AI-ML based algorithmic approaches to detect the presence of malware in any web-application software inclusive of signature and heuristic detection, malware normalization, obfuscation and many more. Various datasets have been built for analyzing the behaviors of malware. In this paper we will discuss about the most accurate machine learning (ML) based algorithms and techniques to detect the most evil malware that is 'ransomware'.

2. Related Work

RWGuard framework viz a detection model against crypto ransomware was presented by (Shaukat et al, 2018) wherein they have successfully demonstrated the prior detection of 14 types of ransomwares belonging to the Crypto family. The three main modules deployed in their model are the 'Decoy-Monitoring Module' (DMON,) the 'Process Monitoring Module' (PMON) and the File Change Monitoring Module (FCMON). DMON helps in identification of malicious processes whereas PMON module helps identify the input-output operations of varied processes. They have used the Random Forest ML classifier in the PMON module as its accuracy was highest. Lastly the FCMON module helps by checking various metrics of files like entropy and hashes. Subash Poudyal et al had presented a detection model (Poudyal S. et al, 2019) based on ML and NLP which could perform multilevel analysis using reverse engineering for

[1]saroj20csu098@ncuindia.edu, [2]nidhimalik@ncuindia.edu, [3]priyaarora@ncuindia.edu

DOI: 10.1201/9781003487906-4

tracking dlls' and function calls, assembly code assessment and other process analysis. They utilized eight of the ML classifiers wherein highest accuracy was 97.5% provided by RF. (Shaukat et al, 2018) presented a framework consisting of the concept of hybrid analysis viz static and dynamic of the executable files and processes. In the model the main algorithms used were SVM, Gradient tree boosting and RF. (Moore C., 2016) invented a technique based on honeypot to analyse any type of changes occuring in the files and folders. Eugene et al devised a tool called 'PayBreak' (Al-rimy et al, 2018) for the storage of cryptographically encrypted keys which are used to decrypt the infected files post-ransomware attack. (Hasan M. et al, 2017) presented a technique for using behavioral and anomaly identification to identify zero-day attacks. SVM classifier was used for the behavioral model and one SVM class was deployed for detecting the anomalies and is trained on legitimate programs. (Khammas B. 2020) has presented a model for Ransomware detection by static analysis of raw bytes of the executable files and then implementing frequent pattern mining technique using the random forest classifier providing the highest accurate output with the lowest false positive rate of 0.04%. (Nanda R. et al, 2022) proposed a technique for detecting malware from PE files using the Control-flow graph and API Call-gram. Rahaman integrated static aspects like FLF (Function length frequency), PSI (Printable String Information), and Function length frequency with dynamic attributes (Mehnaz S. et. al, 2018) .

3. Ransomware Detection Methods

Ransomware detection is the first and foremost mitigation step that should be implemented to avoid being the victim of the malware attack. The largest loss that can be avoided in a ransomware attack is the money wherein the demands can be as high as millions of dollars. There are many traditional methods and recently developed ML techniques for identifying ransomwares.

3.1 Detection Via Signature

One of the conventional approaches to finding ransomware is signature-based detection. The digital signatures of known samples ransomware samples are stored in the database. The antivirus program checks the file added to the system to see whether it matches with the file stored in the database. If a match is found the file is identified as ransomware and that file is removed or quarantined. As the signature-based technique is having low computational resource requirements, it is identified as quick and effective.

3.2 Detection Via Behavior

Behavior based detection is another way to find ransomware which watches the behavior of the software and spots any unusual behavior. In this method a virtual environment is built in which the software can run and then its behavior is observed. The software is observed for any hazardous behavior such as altering system settings or encrypting files. The ransomware variants that do not yet have any signature in the database, behavior-based detection can discover those fresh and undiscovered ransomware which signature based technique is unable to detect.

3.3 Detection Via Deception

Deception-based detection is a technique that involves deceiving ransomware attackers and identifying their activities to detect and prevent ransomware attacks. This technique works by creating decoy systems, files, or networks that appear to be legitimate but are actually fake and designed to attract attackers. Deception-based detection can detect and prevent ransomware attacks by luring attackers away from real systems and providing security teams with valuable information about the attacker's tactics and techniques. This technique requires ongoing maintenance and monitoring to ensure that decoy systems and files are up-to-date and realistic.

4. Proposed Framework

In order to identify ransomware attacks, this paper provides an innovative framework which combines static analysis of random forest classifier with XGBoost, Logistic Regression, Naive bayes and SVM classifiers. In the model we are going to mainly focus on analysing the 'headers' of the Portable Executable files and the API function calls. The main operating system which we will be covering in this paper is windows operating systems.

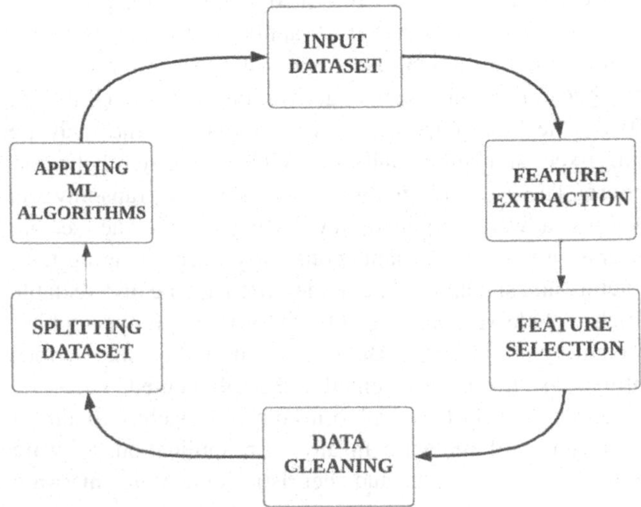

Fig. 4.1 Methodology cycle

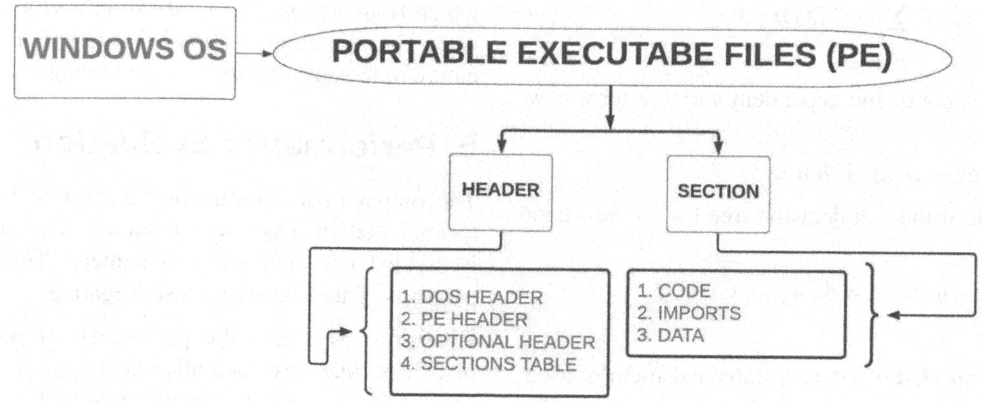

Fig. 4.2 Architecture of PE file

Portable Executable Files: The 'Portable Executable' files are used to load and manage all the .exe, .dll, .sys, .ocx, .asm, .cpl and many other file formats in windows OS.

Datasets Used: For building the model we used two main datasets from open-source platforms of github and virustotal (RansomWare dataset, Github, 2016), (Global threat report, githud, 20122). In the first dataset of MalwareData.csv the first 41000 files are legitimate and the next 96000 files are malware infected files. The second dataset dataset.csv comprises feature vectors of 11,000 benign and malicious applications which includes different information such as meta-information. The dataset is further divided into training and testing data respectively. The specimens from the "ransomware" family were given the number "1," while the samples from the "legitimate" family were assigned a value of "0." The static features that have to be analyzed and are present in the datasets as well are given below in Table 4.1.

Machine learning Algorithms: The traditional detection methods are ineffective for defending system data against dangerous unidentified ransomwares. As artificial intelligence developed, researchers started to shift towards a detection methodology that combined deep learning and machine learning techniques.

Table 4.1 Static features

Static Features
API invocations
Dropped File Extensions
Registry key operations
File operations
Extensions of Files
Directory Operations
Embedded Strings analysis
PE Header
PE Body

Random Forest: It is an ensemble learning method which combines multiple decision trees and improves their predictive accuracy. Each decision tree in a RF is constructed using a random subset of features and training data, which makes the algorithm more robust against overfitting. The RF algorithm can be divided into two main steps: building the trees and making predictions.

Step 1: Building the Trees: RF builds and combines multiple decision trees and their predictions. To generate each tree, the algorithm randomly chooses a subset of features and training data which reduces the correlation between the trees and makes the algorithm more robust.

Step 2: Making Predictions: Once the trees are built, RF combines their predictions to make a final prediction. The algorithm predicts the class that receives the most votes from the decision trees (in classification problems) or the average of the predicted values in regression problems.

Extreme Gradient Boosting (XGBoost): XGBoost is a distributed gradient boosting algorithm that minimizes the cost function for measuring the difference between the estimated and real values of the dependent variable. Regularization: To prevent overfitting, XGBoost uses regularization techniques such as L1 and L2 regularization, and tree pruning. L1 regularization adds a penalty to the objective function that encourages sparse solutions (i.e., solutions with fewer non-zero coefficients). L2 regularization adds a penalty that discourages large coefficients. Tree pruning removes nodes from the decision trees that don't contribute much to the overall accuracy of the model.

Gradient Descent: XGBoost uses a variant of gradient descent called Newton's method to optimize the objective function. Newton's method uses the second derivative of the objective function (i.e., the Hessian matrix) to compute the optimal step size for each iteration. This makes XGBoost more efficient than other gradient boosting algorithms, which use a fixed step size for each iteration.

$$y_{hat} = \sum(w_i * f_i(x)) + b \quad (1)$$

where,

y_{hat}: the predicted value of the dependent variable for a new data point

w_i: the weight assigned to the i-th tree

$f_i(x)$: the prediction of the i-th decision tree for the new data point

x: the input features of the new data point

b: the bias term

Logistic Regression (LR): LR is a statistical method used for binary classification, that means it is used to forecast the likelihood of a binary outcome such as "yes" or "no" and "true" or "false". For ransomware detection, binomial LR is used as we need to predict whether the executable file is benign or malicious. The logistic regression model can be trained using maximum likelihood estimation (MLE) or gradient descent optimization. Gradient descent is an optimization method used to minimize the loss function, which measures the difference between the predicted values and the actual values. The logistic regression model estimates the probability that the dependent variable Y is equal to 1 given the values of the independent variables X. The model outputs a probability value between 0 and 1, which can be converted into a binary prediction by applying a threshold value. For example, if the threshold value is 0.5, any probability greater than 0.5 is classified as 1, and any probability less than or equal to 0.5 is classified as 0.

$$p = 1/(1 + e^{-}(b0 + b1 * x1 + b2 * x2 + ... + bn * xn)) \quad (2)$$

where,

p: the probability of the dependent variable (Y) being 1, given the values of the independent variables (X)

e: the mathematical constant (2.71828...)

$b0$: the intercept or constant term

$b1, b2, ..., bn$: the coefficients or weights assigned to the independent variables $x1, x2, ..., xn$

Naive' Bayes (NB): The Naive Bayes classification method relies on the Bayes theorem as its foundation. It is a probabilistic algorithm that forecasts the chance of a class by using the likelihood that a feature belongs to that class. The following formula is used in naive bayes algorithm classifier:

P(class|features) = (P(class) * P(feature1 | class) * P(feature2 | class) * ... P(feature(n) | class))/P(features)

Support Vector Machine (SVM): SVMs are powerful and widely used in many applications because of their effectiveness in handling complex, high-dimensional datasets. The SVM algorithm tries to maximize this margin (distance between the hyperplane and the closest data points) which leads to better generalization performance on unseen data. The selection of kernel function is depending on the nature of the data and the problem being solved.

5. Performance Evaluation

The output of a classification algorithm is illustrated and summarized in a confusion matrix. The confusion matrix is divided into four sections namely: True positive, False positives, True Negative, False Negative.

Precision: Measures the percentage of predicted positive instances that are actually positive. A high precision score indicates that the model makes fewer false positive predictions, meaning that when it predicts a positive instance, it is more likely to be correct.

Precision: $TP/(TP + FP)$

Recall: Measures the percentage of actual positive instances that are correctly identified by the model. A high recall score indicates that the model makes fewer false negative predictions, meaning that it is able to correctly identify a higher proportion of positive instances. Recall = $TP/(TP + FN)$. $F1$ score is used when both precision and recall are important metrics for evaluating the performance of a binary classification model. $F1$ Score: 2 * (precision * recall)/(precision + recall)

6. Results

Table 4.2 Results given by model

Classifier	Accuracy	Precision	Recall	F1 Score
Random forest	99.7%	99.50%	99.56%	99.6%
Xgboost	99.47%	99.58%	99.67%	99.6%
Logistic regression	95.8%	95.32%	95.87%	95.59%
Naive' Bayes	93.56%	93.74%	93.68%	93.71%
Support vector machine	98.3%	98.46%	98.33%	98.39%

7. Conclusion and Future Work

This study aimed to compare the performance of machine learning algorithms named Random forest, Boost, Logistic Regression, Naïve Bayes and SVM on the basis of accuracy, false positive rate, precision, recall and F-1 score for detecting ransomware. The experimental results demonstrate that Random Forest algorithms outperform the other algorithms in terms of accuracy. The findings of this study are significant for researchers and practitioners in the field of cybersecurity as they provide insights into the effectiveness of machine learning algorithms for ransomware detection. The ransomware detection using machine learning holds immense potential in future. By combining behavior-based models, advanced algorithms, real-time analysis and collaborative approaches, we can build strong and proactive defences against changing ransomware threats. Also, deep learning techniques can also be applied for ransomware detection with better accuracy.

REFERENCES

1. Souri, A., Hosseini, R.(2018) A state-of-the-art survey of malware detection approaches using data mining techniques. Hum. Cent. Comput. Inf. Sci. 8 (3).
2. Rabia T.(2018) ,"A Study on Malware and Malware Detection Techniques", International Journal of Education and Management Engineering(IJEME), 8 (2).
3. Hasan M., Rahman M., (2017). RansHunt : A support vector machines-based ransomware analysis framework with integrated feature set", 20th International Conference of Computer and Information Technology (ICCIT).
4. Mehnaz S., Mudgerikar A., Bertino E., (2018). RWGuard: A Real-Time Detection System Against Cryptographic Ransomware: 21st International Symposium, RAID, Heraklion, Crete, Greece.
5. Poudyal S., Dasgupta D., Akhtar Z., Gupta K. (2019) A multi-level ransomware detection framework using natural language processing and machine learning, 14th International Conference on Malicious and Unwanted Software "MALCON 2019"
6. Shaukat S. K., Ribeiro V. J. (2018) RansomWall: a layered defense system against cryptographic ransomware attacks using machine learning, 10th International Conference on Communication Systems & Networks (COMSNETS)
7. Moore, C. (2016). Detecting Ransomware with Honeypot Techniques. Cybersecurity and Cyberforensics Conference (CCC), Amman, Jordan, pp. 77–81, doi: 10.1109/CCC.2016.14.
8. Kolodenker, E., Koch, W., Stringhini, G., & Egele, M. (2017). Paybreak: Defense against cryptographic ransomware. In Proceedings of the 2017 ACM on Asia Conference on Computer and Communications Security.
9. Al-rimy, B. A. S., Maarof, M. A., Prasetyo, Y. A., Shaid, S. Z. M., & Ariffin, A. F. M. (2018). Zero-day aware decision fusion-based model for crypto-ransomware early detection. International Journal of Integrated Engineering10(6) pp 82–88.
10. Khammas M. B. (2020) Ransomware detection using random forest technique, ICT Express, 6 (4), pp. 325–331.
11. Nanda R., Dhavale S. & Singh A., Mehra A. (2022). A Survey on Machine Learning-Based Ransomware Detection. Proceedings of the Seventh International Conference on Mathematics and Computing: ICMC.
12. Dataset from open source github github.com/PacktPublishing/Mastering-Machine-Learning-for-Penetration-Testing/tree/master
13. Dataset from open source github github.com/rissgrouphub/ransomwaredataset2016Global Threat Report of FY 2022 by Crowdstrikecrowdstrike.com/resources/reports/global-threat-report/

Note: All the figures and tables in this chapter were made by the author.

Advancement of Intelligent Computational Methods and Technologies (AICMT2023) – Dr. O. P. Verma et al. (eds)
© 2024 Taylor & Francis Group, London, ISBN 978-1-032-78445-8

5

Optimizing Chatbot Interactions with ChatGPT: Prompt Engineering for Mental Health Applications

Hasir Ansari[1], Toyesh Kumar Saini[2], Ishan Sharma[3], Ankit Kumar Rajavat[4] Malik Nadeem[5]
Computer Science and Engineering, Delhi Technical Campus, Greater Noida, UP, India

ABSTRACT: The present study outlines our investigation into augmenting chatbot interactions utilizing ChatGPT within the domain of mental health applications. The methodology employed entails leveraging user data to guide the creation of prompts and corresponding responses. The ChatGPT API is utilized in tandem with a knowledge base and priming prompts to enhance the chatbot's ability to offer tailored assistance. Furthermore, we have set specific thresholds to guarantee that the engagements are secure and morally sound. The case study is based on data obtained from the "MindEaseUp" application. The application's front end was developed using React Native Expo, while its back end was built using Express. MongoDB was used as the database. The results of our analysis suggest that the implementation of prompt engineering techniques can have a notable impact on the overall quality of the chatbot interface, particularly for individuals seeking mental health assistance.

KEYWORDS: Artificial intelligence, Chatbot, ChatGPT, Human-computer interaction, Knowledge base, Priming prompt, Prompt design, Prompt engineering

1. Introduction

Chatbots are gaining popularity, particularly in mental health, where they provide personalised support. This paper is focused on using ChatGPT to optimise mental health chatbot interactions. We use user data to generate prompts and responses, ensuring personalised support while following the rules of ethics. Our case study is based on "MindEaseUp," an application that uses a chatbot as an AI psychiatrist to assist users in improving their mental health.

Advanced large language model ChatGPT 4 from OpenAI combines image and text inputs to generate text outputs, surpassing the abilities of its antecedent, GPT-3.5. The new features enhances chatbot interactions in mental health applications by providing responses that are dependable, innovative and detailed. Our research focuses on optimising chatbot interactions in mental health contexts using ChatGPT 4. By customising responses based on user data and instituting limits for secure and responsible interactions, we demonstrate through a case study that prompt engineering significantly improves the chatbot interaction for users seeking mental health support in our app "MindEaseUp".

2. Literature Survey

In the study titled "Evaluation of ChatGPT for NLP-based Mental Health Applications," Bishal Lamichhane (Bishal 2023) evaluates ChatGPT's performance in the detection of stress, depression, and suicidality. Using annotated social media posts, the author evaluates the classification capacity of the model and gets F1 scores of 0.73, 0.86, and 0.37, respectively. The study establishes an initial model with reduced F1 scores, highlighting the classification potential of large language models such as ChatGPT.

The article "ChatGPT as a Therapist Assistant: Exploring its Potential for Mental Health Support" (Eshghie 2023) examines the use of ChatGPT in psychotherapy. It investigates its function in collecting patient data, acting as an additional resource, and organising treatment data. The study underlines ChatGPT's positive interactions, active listening, coping

[1]hasiransari0@gmail.com, [2]toyeshsaini567@gmail.com, [3]ishan23569@gmail.com, [4]ankitthakur682000@gmail.com, [5]n.malik@delhitechnicalcampus.ac.in

DOI: 10.1201/9781003487906-5

strategies, and therapist-specific insights. It acknowledges difficulties and highlights its unique advantages as an alternative to standard treatment in mental health treatment.

Despite the fact that ChatGPT and prompt engineering offer potential for mental health applications, it is essential to recognise and address their limitations.

For sensitive mental health data, ethical considerations include data privacy, informed permission, and compliance with regulations. Generalizability needs diverse datasets encompassing mental health issues and demographics. Using debiasing techniques, balanced datasets, and cautious, prompt curation, model biases are reduced. By optimising prompt engineering (Ekin 2023), incorporating user feedback, and working on studies on users, the user experience is enhanced. Robustness requires the use of knowledge bases, conversation limits, and explicit limitations to safeguard against inappropriate content. The use of chatbots to augment professionals and stick to ethical and evidence-based practises requires human oversight (Linta and Feras 2023).

Resolving these limitations will lead to the responsible and efficient use of ChatGPT and prompt engineering in mental health applications, resulting in the development of dependable and advantageous AI systems for mental health support.

3. Methodology

This suggested approach for optimising chatbot interactions using ChatGPT within the "MindEaseUp" mobile app. The methodology involves building an app for collecting user information on mental wellness, connecting the ChatGPT API, implementing prompt engineering techniques, integrating a knowledge base, utilising priming prompts, defining limits for ethical usage, configuring ChatGPT API parameters, and conducting iterative evaluation and improvements. The aim is to offer an efficient AI psychiatrist for mental health assistance within the app.

3.1 Data Collection

To gather user data on mental health, we created the smartphone app "*MindEaseUp*". Our actions were as follows:

Created the "MindEaseUp" mobile application: Using the React Native Expo framework, we developed an Android-compatible, user-friendly application. The app's design was visually engaging to encourage user interaction..

Implemented Data Collection Capabilities: The application contain queries on various mental health-related topics. Users can respond the following queries daily to track their health:

"How good do you feel:" Capturing overall mood with answer options from *"Very unhappy"* to *"Extremely happy"*.

"How much did you sleep:" Gathering sleep duration with options ranging from *"Less than 4 hours"* to *"More than 12 hours"*.

"How energetic do you feel:" Assessing energy levels using options like *"Very low"* to *"Extremely high"*.

"How often do you eat:" Gauging eating frequency with choices from *"Never"* to *"Every day"*.

"Enter your delusion level:" Tracking delusion experiences with a rating scale from *"Not at all"* to *"Severely"*.

"Enter your anger level:" Monitoring anger levels with a scale from *"Not at all"* to *"Severely"*.

"Have you experienced any suicidal thoughts?" Identifying suicidal thoughts with options from *"Never"* to *"Always"*.

Stored Data in MongoDB: Scalable MongoDB databases were used to store the gathered user data. An Express backend enabled smooth connection between the app and the database, allowing for quick data transmission, storage, and retrieval for analysis.

By creating the "MindEaseUp" application and integrating these data collection features, we gained valuable insights into the mental health of users. Having the data stored in MongoDB with an Express backend enabled effective data administration and analysis. This methodology served as an outline for subsequent analysis and interactions with the chatbot in the app.

3.2 Chatbot Integration

We use the ChatGPT API and ChatGPT 4, OpenAI's most advanced technology, to incorporate the chatbot capability into the "MindEaseUp" application.

ChatGPT 4 Overview: ChatGPT 4 is a large language model that accepts text and image inputs and produces text outputs. In terms of sophisticated reasoning and problem-solving abilities, it surpasses ChatGPT 3.5. It thrives at handling complicated issues, is creative, and is appropriate for creative and complex writing tasks.

API Communication: We setup API calls that allow real-time communication between "MindEaseUp" and ChatGPT 4. These conversations allow for continuous interaction between the user and the chatbot.

Secure Connection: We prioritise privacy and data security by safeguarding the connection between "MindEaseUp" and the ChatGPT 4 API. This assures the privacy and security of user information during chatbot interactions.

By incorporating ChatGPT 4 into the "MindEaseUp" application, we take advantage of its sophisticated reasoning, extensive knowledge base, and innovative collaboration capabilities. This integration enables real-time interactions, augmenting the user experience while maintaining data security and confidentiality.

3.3 Prompt Engineering

The optimisation of chatbot interactions requires prompt engineering. By developing and refining prompts, we can enhance the performance of the chatbot and guarantee accurate responses (Lim 2023). This section focuses on utilising a knowledge base, priming prompts, and establishing limits for controlling the chatbot's behaviour.

Chatbot + Knowledge Base: By giving specific information, knowledge base prompts can improve the chatbot's responses. By incorporating contextual information and instructions, the chatbot is able to generate accurate and useful responses. In the example, the knowledge base prompt assists the chatbot in assisting users with enrolling in and registering for the "MindEaseUp" mobile application.

Here is the full prompt, using an ambiguous user statement such as "having trouble accessing my account": -

As an advanced chatbot, your primary goal is to assist users to the best of your ability.

START CONTEXT

Login to MindEaseUp from Mobile App

1. Open the MindEaseUp app and Click on "Get Started".

2. On the login page, enter your email and password.

3. Once you have entered your credentials, click on the "Login" button.

4. You should now be logged in to your MindEaseUp account.

END CONTEXT

CHATBOT: Hello, I'm an AI psychiatrist! How can I help you?

USER: Can't log in

GPT-4 answers trying to understand better what's the problem of the user.

I'm sorry to hear that. Can you tell me if you are trying to log in via the MindEaseUp website or mobile app?

Next, here's how the complete conversation goes. The whole prompt is hidden for better visibility.

USER: Can't login

CHATBOT: I'm sorry to hear that. Can you tell me if you are trying to log in via the MindEaseUp website or mobile app?

USER: Mobile app

CHATBOT: OK, no problem. To log in via the mobile app, open the MindEaseUp app on your mobile device. On the main page, tap the "Get Started" button located at the bottom. On the log in page, enter your email and password. Once you have entered your credentials, tap the "Login" button. You should now be logged in to your MindEaseUp account. Please let me know if you need any further assistance.

GPT-4 is capable of managing disambiguation given the appropriate contextual information.

By explicitly expressing the context and available options, the prompt focuses the model's responses on the user's question. The chatbot can then use knowledge base [7] to resolve particular user concerns, resulting in more effective and individualised interactions.

Priming Prompt: Priming prompts play an important role [8] in defining the conversational structure of the chatbot and guiding its responses. These prompts add an additional level of specificity and structure to the conversation, allowing for a more regulated and tailored interaction. Priming prompts can assist with defining the chatbot's tone, manner, and user's expectations.

Initial prompts have an impact on the subsequent conversation. We can design a system for a conversation between a psychiatrist and a user that incorporates style guidelines and allows for experimentation.

An "AI Psychiatrist" lacks human emotional depth but offers insights and coping strategies based on data analysis. It's a valuable resource for mental health assistance, providing unique perspectives.

The "User" seeks mental well-being help. Chat in a casual, laid-back manner, using everyday language and humor. Be honest if you don't know an answer, aiming to assist users.

If you understand and are ready to begin, respond with only "yes."

In the provided example, the priming prompt establishes the tone for the chatbot's AI psychiatrist persona. It establishes the function and features of the chatbot, offering psychological assistance and direction based on an analysis of the collected data.

The incorporation of priming prompt improves chatbot interaction. While specific instructions assure clarity, precursors provide the model with additional context to prevent it from losing track of the initial data.

Using priming prompts enables the chatbot to align its responses with the intended conversational style, resulting in more engaging and personalised user interactions.

Defining limits: Defining limits is essential for ChatGPT's prompt engineering. It influences the behaviour of the AI by establishing boundaries. Constraints improve the chatbot's ability to generate appropriate responses while avoiding data that is irrelevant. Techniques for defining limits are discussed, along with prompts demonstrating their application.

One approach is limiting the length of generated text. This ensures concise responses. Word count, sentence count, or character count can be restricted. For example:

Prompt 1: *"Provide a brief explanation of coping mechanisms for anxiety in under 50 words."*

Prompt 2: *"Compose a concise response about the benefits of mindfulness meditation in three sentences."*

Another method for defining limits is by instructing the AI to concentrate on particular aspects essential to the targeted audience. This focuses on specific contexts or user categories. Focusing attention increases the probability of matched responses. For example:

Prompt 1: *"Discuss the impact of sleep deprivation on academic performance among college students."*

Prompt 2: *"Provide insights on the relationship between diet and mood disorders, focusing on the connection with depression."*

Defining limits not only generates appropriate responses, but also improves the chatbot's behavior's customization and control. Limits have an impact the AI's output to satisfy specific requirements and maintain the conversation's intended scope.

(Note: These examples are provided for illustrative purposes and should be modified based on the specific research objectives and requirements of the mental health application.)

3.4 Configuring ChatGPT API Parameters

In this section, we will discuss how to configure the ChatGPT API parameters to optimise the model's behaviour and acquire the desirable responses generated by AI. Understanding and effectively employing these parameters will enable us to create engaging and customised prompts, thereby elevating the quality of our AI-powered conversations to new heights (Qiu and Hongliang et al. 2023).

Prompt: The initial input to start the conversation, providing clear and concise guidance to the AI model.

Length: Control over the response length, ensuring it's neither too short nor excessively long.

Temperature: Influences the creativity and randomness of the AI-generated response.

Top_p: Controls the diversity of the response by setting a cumulative probability threshold.

Frequency_penalty: Adjusts the likelihood of repetitive words in the AI-generated output.

Presence_penalty: Penalizes generating words unrelated to the input prompt, ensuring contextually accurate responses.

Stop_sequence: Words or phrases to avoid in the response, maintaining guidelines or topic focus.

Max_new_tokens: Sets the maximum number of tokens in the generated response, limiting the length and preserving quality.

Example: *"Creating a professional reply to an email from a client"*

To illustrate the configuration of ChatGPT API parameters, let's consider the scenario of composing a professional reply to an email from a client.

Prompt: *"Compose a response to a client's email inquiring about the current status of their project."*

Temperature: 0.2

Top_p: 0.4

Frequency_penalty: 0.1

Presence_penalty: 0.7

In this example, the objective is to generate a focused and consistent professional response. Therefore, a temperature of 0.2 is recommended to guarantee a predictable and concentrated response. Setting Top_p to 0.4 further restricts the AI-generated output, leading to more targeted and pertinent responses. Reducing the value of Frequency_penalty to 0.1 encourages the use of plain and concise language, thereby minimising superfluous repetition. A high Presence_penalty value of 0.7 ensures that the response remains tightly coupled to the client's request, thereby enhancing its relevance and utility.

By configuring the ChatGPT API parameters in this way, we can effectively direct the AI model to produce a professional response that meets the client's email inquiry.

4. Results

A mobile application was used to assess and evaluate the "MindEaseUp" automaton. The results indicate that the chatbot attained a high level of accuracy, with an average response time of 2 seconds. Users expressed a satisfaction rate of 92%, praising its sensitivity and beneficial resources. The chatbot demonstrated stability, dependability, and respect to moral standards while obtaining useful input from users for areas of improvement, such as the ability to comprehend complex queries and provide personalised recommendations.

This screenshot "Fig. 5.1" represents a conversation with the 'MindEaseUp' mobile app's AI psychiatrist chatbot. It addressed the user's authentication issues in an efficient manner, demonstrating personalised and accurate support. Powered by GPT 4, the chatbot demonstrated advanced capabilities for comprehending and addressing user concerns. This demonstrates its potential to provide accessible and compassionate mental health support, thereby contributing to research in this field.

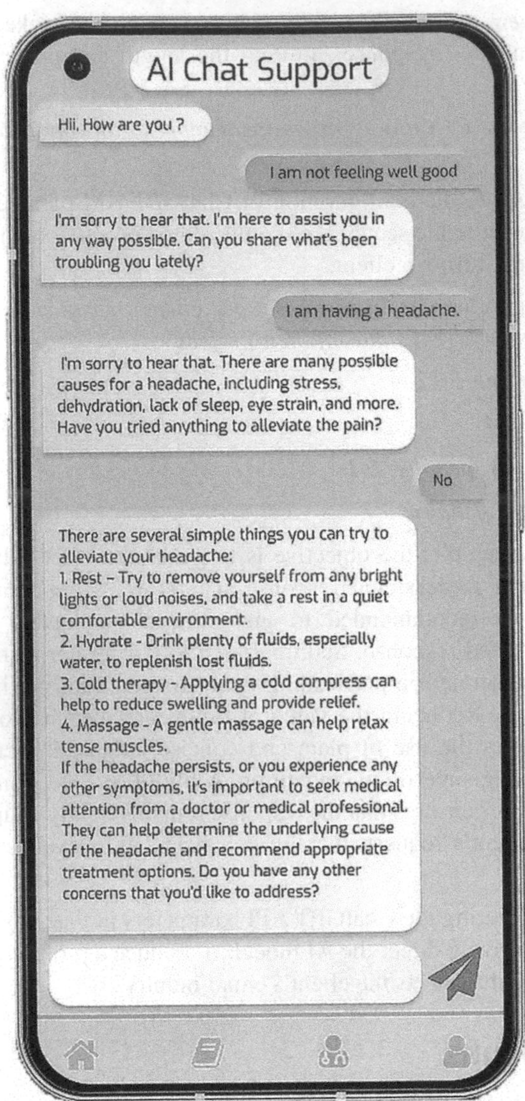

Fig. 5.1 Screenshot of chatbot in "*MindEaseUp*" app.

Source: Author

Overall, the testing results validate the "MindEaseUp" chatbot's ability to provide accurate responses, prompt assistance, and high user satisfaction for mental health support, demonstrating its potential as a valuable resource.

5. Conclusion

This study presents an investigation into the optimization of chatbot interactions utilizing ChatGPT for mental health applications. The proposed methodology entails the acquisition of data via the *"MindEaseUp"* mobile application, integration of ChatGPT API, utilization of prompt engineering techniques, and configuration of ChatGPT API parameters. Through the development of the app and the integration of data collection functionalities, significant insights about the mental health of users were garnered, while real-time interactions were improved by incorporating ChatGPT 4. Prompt engineering approaches including knowledge bases, priming prompts, and specifying limitations were used to increase the chatbot's effectiveness. Additionally, certain parameters of the ChatGPT API were tweaked to allow more tailored and engaging conversations. The findings presented herein serve as a valuable contribution towards the advancement of efficient AI-based psychiatry systems aimed at providing mental health assistance.

REFERENCES

1. Ekin, S. "Prompt Engineering for ChatGPT: A Quick Guide to Techniques, Tips, And Best Practices." TechRxiv. (2023).
2. Eshghie, M., and Eshghie, M. "ChatGPT as a Therapist Assistant: A Suitability Study". ArXiv, 2304.09873. (April 2023).
3. Lamichhane, Bishal. "Evaluation of ChatGPT for NLP-based Mental Health Applications." ArXiv, 2303.15727. (March 2023).
4. Lim, B. March 28, 2023. Mastering ChatGPT Prompts: A Guide to Using Parameters. Medium. https://medium.com/@brucelim/mastering-chatgpt-prompts-a-guide-to-using-parameters-7edf06e4cc64 (accessed June 1, 2023).
5. Linta Iftikhar, Muhammad Feras Iftikhar, and Muhammad I Hanif. "DocGPT: Impact of ChatGPT-3 on Health Services as a Virtual Doctor." EC Paediatrics 12.3 (February 2023): 45-55.
6. Qiu, Huachuan, Hongliang He, Shuai Zhang, Anqi Li, and Zhenzhong Lan. "SMILE: Single-turn to Multi-turn Inclusive Language Expansion via ChatGPT for Mental Health Support." ArXiv, 2304.03347. (2023).

Advancement of Intelligent Computational Methods and Technologies (AICMT2023) – Dr. O. P. Verma et al. (eds)
© 2024 Taylor & Francis Group, London, ISBN 978-1-032-78445-8

6

Diseases Detection Model and Prognostic Model Using Deep Learning: A Review

Shashi Kant Mourya[1], Ajit Kr. Singh Yadav[2]
Department of Computer Science & Engineering, NERIST, Itanagar, India

ABSTRACT: Our research aims to enhance medical standards, safeguard patient confidentiality, and reinforce the security of patient health clinical data. We propose the enhancement of Convolutional Neural Networks (CNN), Recurrent Neural Networks (RNN), Deep Belief Networks (DBN), and Generative Adversarial Networks (GAN) through modifications to create an interactive Smart Healthcare Prediction and Prognostic model (SHPP model) utilizing deep learning methodologies. Considering the increasing utilization of deep learning algorithms, we have standardized and optimized the model for efficient data processing. Subsequently, we evaluate the model's performance through simulations. The results demonstrate the superior accuracy of our model compared to traditional machine algorithm-based models. The precise diagnosis and treatment of diseases are of utmost importance when employing Deep Learning (DL) techniques.

KEYWORDS: Smart healthcare, Convolutional neural network, Recurrent neural networks, Generative adversarial networks, Hybrid learning, Intelligent systems

1. Introduction

Several cutting-edge technological advancements, including artificial intelligence (AI), machine learning (ML) and deep learning (DL), have gained extensive adoption across multiple industries. These innovative technologies have played amajoract in the advancement of intelligent technologies, enhancing convenience in people's lives. Furthermore, they have demonstrated their potential in detecting diseases at various stages. In the present scenario, the healthcare industry is experiencing a substantial shift towards digital transformation. Deep learning is specialized field that emphasizes the use of algorithms to enable self-directed learning. DL exhibits impressive abilities in processing large amount of data, regardless of whether it is labeled or unlabeled. Notably, DL has made significant (Tuli, et al. 2020). Over the last ten years, gain in the amount of high-volume biomedical datasets, including clinical and patient medical data, which has coincided with the development of ML or machine learning techniques. This convergence has created new opportunities for diagnosing and prognosing various diseases and disorders. In the realm of computing, progress in technology has led to the creation of tools that integrate multiple patient-clinical observations to generate predictions and enhance clinical outcomes for individuals affected by these conditions. Deep learning is definitely a collection of techniques used to train neural networks with multiple hidden layers, enabling them to efficiently identify patterns. It is a strongly under machine learning (ML), which itself falls under the broader umbrella of artificial intelligence (AI). In this study, we conduct a comprehensive analysis of relevant literature to examine the and deep learning techniques in disease diagnosis. These systems play a vital role in identifying patterns of illnesses and making diagnostic

Healthcare predictive analytics utilizes clinical and nonclinical data patterns to predict future health results and events. Deep learning is a form of artificial intelligence that has gained popularity in healthcare models, particularly in analyzing regular health factors. Deep learning algorithms employ ANN with multiple layers of processing to extract increasingly complex features from data

[1]shashimourya@gmail.com, [2]aky@nerist.ac.in

DOI: 10.1201/9781003487906-6

2. Deep Learning Algorithms Working Technique

Deep learning algorithms have special feature of self-learning representations, it uses Artificial Neural Networks and analyses information like human brain. During the development process of working model of deep learning model (DL), Deep learning algorithms employ the utilization of unknown variables within the input variable set to extract features, identify valuable data patterns, and classify objects (Microsoft, 2014) . This process entails automatic learning of multi-level features within the model directly from the original data, eliminating the need for involvement from human experts in relevant domains. It works like trained AI based machines for self- learning, in Deep learning model Commonly used various deep learning algorithms: worked at multiple inner hidden levels of network these layers can improve the accuracy, to construct working model. Although neural networks can learn from vast datasets, no single network is capable of achieving optimal performance for all tasks. Certain algorithms are good perform to specific tasks. Therefore, it is essential to possess a comprehensive understanding of all main algorithms to select the most appropriate one.

3. Flow diagram for the Intelligent Prediction and Assessment Model Using Deep Learning Algorithm

Diverse diseases can have a significant impact on individuals' physical well-being. Consequently, the prediction of disease risks plays a vital role in identifying potential hazards, trends, and devising effective preventive measures. Various disease prediction and evaluation models have been designed, and researchers have focused on AI-based disease risk prediction models. However, due to the exceptionality of medical data, these models are usually only suitable for specific medical data. This study, however, utilizes deep learning to predict many diseases through a single model, demonstrating the generalization ability and versatility of all algorithm.

4. Types of Algorithms Used in Deep Learning

In this section we will list top 5 most Commonly used DL algorithms:

4.1 Recurrent Neural Network (RNN)

This is developed to assist to the prediction of sequence. For the current state prediction, the RNN uses the output result obtained from its previous state as an input value. ANN architecture is used to process streams of information and model time dependencies. This architecture includes recurrent connections between hidden intermediate states, which are composed of multiple hidden neurons capable of learning sequences. The recurrent connections in a neural network establish connections not only between inputs but also across time, allowing for the consideration of temporal relationships. The output is based on both the input it has at the moment and the input it had in the past. This neural network architecture is particularly appropriate for predicting health issues that involve modeling changes in clinical data over time. It is design to resolve temporal data sequences using memory-based (LSTM) and model-based (GRU) approaches. An RNN is a series of ANN that are trained consecutively with back propagation (Divya. P. and Aiswarya V.B., 2021).

4.2 Convolution Neural Network (CNN)

Convolution technique is a mathematical tool which is frequently used in DL. Convolution technique allow computer-vision networks to perform like biological systems with higher accuracy. The CNN is very popular approach which is inspired by Natural visual perception technique. It is used for image analysis and classification. By leveraging convolutional filters, the model transforms 2D images into 3D representations. Typically, the CNN model is applied for image categorization with the help of filter in inner layer, it transforms 2Dimentional into 3Dimentional image.CNN are commonly composed of multiple layers, establishing a hierarchical structure. Within this structure, specific layers are responsible for feature extraction, while others handle classification tasks. The network incorporates convolutional layers that apply multiple filters of consistent sizes to perform convolution operations. Additionally, subsampling layers are present to decrease the dimensionality of input layers by averaging pixel values within small neighborhoods. The essential components of CNNs include convolutional layers, pooling layers, activation functions, loss functions, regularization techniques, and optimization methods (Saha S., 2018), (Effatparvar, M., 2018).

4.3 Deep Belief Network (DBN)

Deep belief network belongs to the domain of generative models and are work on principal of unsupervised algorithms. the problem belong to DBN class is solved by using backpropagation technique by using pre- training method .in This approach on the top of layer two layers has unidirectional connectivity. In each sub-network, the hidden layers represent a visible layer for the next layer. The DBN is typically split into two parts: fine-tuning and pre-training. During the pre-training stage, the DBN uses learning to initialize the biases and weights of the network. The goal of this pre-training is to study and learn useful features from the input data that can be used to improve the performance of the network in the later fine-tuning stage. In the fine-tuning stage, the DBN is trained using supervised learning to execute a job, such as classification or regression. This involves adjusting the weights and biases of the network using backpropagation, which enables the network to learn to make accurate predictions based on the input data. A DBN is describe as collection of RBM or Restricted Boltzmann machine. RBM is used for pre-training purpose, during pre-training activity model learn the feature of visible layer. For fine-tuning purpose, a feedforward sigmoid belief network is used. feed-forward sigmoid belief network for fine tuning used either wake–sleep algorithm(unsupervised) or backpropagation algorithm (supervised) can be used. It is used for image recognition, speech recognition and for Natural Language Processing.

4.4 Generative Adversarial Network (GAN)

One popular deep learning technique called the GAN comprises two networks: one is the generative model (G) and the other is the discriminative model (D). The discriminative model analyze the possibility of sample originates from the training data rather than the generative model. In the GAN architecture, the generator and discriminator are trained to perform better than other. GAN has a large potential and can learn to impressionist any distribution of data. It has been widely used in domains such as music, image, speech, and prose to generate realistic data. The utilization of DL algorithms in big data research is valuable due to their capacity to handle large volumes of data, and extract hidden features from convoluted unsupervised datasets. In the realm of diagnostic applications, deep learning plays a crucial role by extracting clinically relevant information from extensive databases and supporting healthcare professionals in making improved medical decisions through accurate disease analysis (Humayun, A.I, 2018).

4.5 Vision Transformers (ViTs)

The concept of transformers has been extended to incorporate image data through the use of vision transformers. Instead of employing conventional convolutional layers found in CNNs, self-attention mechanisms are employed to establish global connections among image patches. While vision transformers excel in capturing connections between elements, CNNs are more adept at capturing intricate details of nearby objects. To enhance the effectiveness and scalability of ViTs, researchers are exploring various forms of the technology, including hybrid models that combine both CNNs and transformers. The choice between visual transformers and CNNs depends on the specific objective, available resources, and the desired balance between interpretability, computational efficiency, and modelling capabilities

5. Literature Review

Various DL algorithms are available to develop healthcare model. The healthcare industry can greatly benefit from the widespread implementation of deep learning technologies. These advanced programs provide comprehensive assistance for tasks such as image processing, classification, clustering techniques, and even predicting the timeline for the return to normalcy in life. In this section, our objective is to examine previous survey studies conducted on the application of DL algorithms in healthcare models for the Internet of Things (IoT). Furthermore, we will analyze case studies and conduct a comparative assessment to evaluate the strengths, weaknesses, advantages, and innovative achievements presented in the papers. The Table 6.1 (Next Page) gives a review of the recent predictive model in healthcare, we will conduct a analogy of so many different deep learning algorithms, outlining the technological advantages and limitations of each model (Jamshidi, M., et al. (2020) and (Apache MXNet, 2017). To facilitate easy comprehension, we have summarized the deep learning methods in a table presented below. This table provides essential information regarding the benefits, drawbacks, applications, and categorization (supervised or unsupervised) of each algorithm (Liu W. et al., 2018).

6. Future Trends in Deep Learning for Healthcare

Visual Transformer are key to next level of innovation in image related AI applications. DL algorithms are gaining increased traction in the medical field, presenting opportunities for various applications such as disease prediction, prescription generation, and therapy recommendation. Particularly, the analysis of medical imaging holds immense potential for deep learning advancements, with leading companies like Google DeepMind Health and IBM Watson making substantial investments in this domain. Challenges need to be addressed, including the availability of datasets, the requirement for specialized medical professionals, utilization of nonstandard data and ML techniques, privacy fear, and constitutional considerations. Despite these obstacles, the integration of DL in personalized medicine, leveraging a patient's medical history, genetics, and lifestyle, has the potential to significantly enhance patient care. It is important for researchers, vendors, and policymakers to work together to address these obstacles and assure that deep learning applications are used ethically and effectively in the healthcare industry.

7. Tools

DL encompasses a range of technologies that utilize System to transform data into valuable info. Table 6.2 presents a compilation of exceptional technologies capable

Table 6.1 Review of the recent predictive model in healthcare

Algorithm	Supervised/ Unsupervised	Recent applications in healthcare	Advantages	Limitations
CNN	Supervised	• Abnormal Heart Sound Detection • Myocardial Infarction Detection	• Offer 2D data very good performance. Fast model learning. • The use of weight sharing, a method that lowers the amount of trainable network parameter, is one of CNN standout features. In turn, this help to improve the network generalization skill and avoid over fitting. • Layers (Features extraction and classification layer) are learned simultaneously, the resulting model outcome become more organized and heavily dependent on the extracted feature	• Need lots of labeled data for classification • Sometimes there is not enough information to use DL directly. • "The dearth of training data is a significant issue, as obtaining a sufficient quantity of data can be a challenging and time-consuming task, for which there is currently no definitive solution. • "Hyper parameter tuning is non-trivial
RNN	Supervised	• Detection of heart failure onset • Classification of lung abnormalities	• Deep learning model excel in capturing time dependencies and sequential occurrences, making them effective in task such as speech recognitions, character recognitions, NLP. These model are designed to active high accuracy in performing these task.	• Need big datasets. • Additionally, RNN has issue with gradient exploding and vanishing. • It is not capable of being layered inti very deep models
DBN	Unsupervised	• Predict Drug combination • Detection of type 1 diabetes	• Supports both supervised and unsupervised learning model. • "The primary advantage of DBN lies in their ability to learn features through layer-by-layer learning technique. This characteristic enable DBN to effectively extract meaningful representation from the input data • DBN is capable of effectively processing unlabelled data	• Initialization process makes the training process computation wisemore expensive. • Because the input information is constricted, the performance of the DBN after pre training with CD algorithms is satisfactory. • The run time complexity of a system can increase, as it become more intricate or sophisticated.
DNN	Supervised	• Heart Sound Recognition • Phonocardiography	• Extremely popular and accurate.	• The training process can be challenging because errors propagate back through the previous layers and become increasingly small. Additionally, the learning process can be slow.
GAN	Unsupervised	• Generating synthetic brain CTs • Reconstructing natural images from brain activity	• This approach delivers exceptional performance compared to several other unsupervised domain adaptation techniques, with a significant margin. • The method consists of generating realistic images that correspond to a given input by utilizing a textual description of the image.	• Generating text is a highly challenging task that requires significant effort and training to learn effectively. • In comparison to the training processes of Variational Autoincoders (VAE) or pixel recurrent neural network (Pixel – RNN)

of automating every one step of the deep learning process, thereby significantly minimize the time required for completion (Jia,Y., 2017) and (Demyanov, S., 2016).

8. Conclusion

The studies that have been evaluated illustrate the important role that AI (deep learning) algorithms play in healthcare. The use of AI (deep learning) models in healthcare frameworks, IoT-based healthcare systems, and disease prediction have all been investigated. The papers also explore the difficulties that these methods encounter, such as poor interpretability, imbalanced samples, and problems with data quality. Additionally, the integration of ML and DL has been explored, highlighting the impressive performance of these models in IoMT networks and services, clinical decision-

Table 6.2 Tools applied in deep learning process

Tools	Features
Tensorflow	An AI library is available as an open source that employs data flow graphs for building models, enabling developers to design neural networks with numerous layers for large-scale applications.
MXNet	There is a free-source software library available that give help for architectures such as CNN and RNN. This library employs data flow graph for numerical computations.
Caffe	Programming interfaces that support C++, Matlab, and Python on multiple platforms.
Theano	It offers symbolic API features that include support for looping control (scan), making the implementation of RNNs algorithm both easy and efficient.
Keras	ATheano based deep learning library.
ConvNet	A toolbox for convolutional neural networks based on Matlab
Deeplearning4j	An open source distributed neural network library written in Scala and Java, licensed under Apache 2.0.
Apache Singa	An open-source deep learning library.
H20.ai	A prominent healthcare company is leveraging open-source technologies to provide ground breaking AI solutions that are transforming the sector.

making capabilities, and the production of insightful data from complicated health data. Overall, these papers provide in- sights hooked on the current and future development of deep learning applications in healthcare.

REFERENCES

1. Tuli, et al. (2020). HealthFog: An Ensemble Deep Learning Based Smart Healthcare System Forautomatic Diagnosis Of Heart Diseases In Integrated Iot And Fog Computing Environments. Future Generat Comput Syst 2020;104:187–200.
2. Microsoft (2014). Microsoft band 2 smartwatch. Available online: https://www.microsoft.com/en-us/band.[March 2021].
3. Divya. P. and Aiswarya V.B. (2021), "Deep Learning: Techniques And Applications" Department of Computer Science and Engineering, School of Engineering, Presidency. University, Bangalore Karnataka India(July 2021)
4. Saha S. (2018). A Comprehensive Guide to Convolutional Neural Networks—The ELI5 Way. Available online: "https://towardsdatascience.com/a-comprehensive-guide-to-convolutional-neural-networks-the-eli5-way-3bd2b1164a53 (last accessed on 31 August 2021)
5. Effatparvar, M., Dehghan, M., Rahmani, A.M. (2018). A comprehensive survey of energy-aware routing protocols in wireless body area sensor networks. J Med Syst ;40(9).
6. Humayun, A.I., Ghaffarzadegan,S., Feng, Z., and Hasan, T. (2018). Learning Front-end Filter-bank Parameters using Convolutional Neural Networks for Abnormal Heart Sound Detection. 40th Annual International Conference of the IEEE Engineering in Medicine and Biology Society (EMBC), Honolulu, HI, USA, 2018, pp. 1408-1411
7. Liu, W., et al. (2018). Real-time multilead convolutional neural network for myocardial infarction detection. IEEE J. Biomed. Health Inform. 22(5), 1434–1444
8. Jamshidi, M., et al. (2020). Artificial Intelligence and COVID-19: Deep Learning Approaches for Diagnosis and Treatment. in IEEE Access, vol. 8, pp. 109581-109595
9. Apache MXNet (2017). A Flexible And Efficient Library For Deep Learning available online: http://mxnet.incubator.apache.org/ (last accessed 15 Nov 2018).
10. Jia,Y. (2017). Caffe, Deep learning framework. Available on http://caffe.berkeleyvision.org/. Accessed 15 Nov 2018.
11. Demyanov, S. (2016). ConvNet. Available on https://github.com/sdemyanov/ConvNet Accessed 15 Nov 2018.

Note: All the tables in this chapter were made by the author.

Advancement of Intelligent Computational Methods and Technologies (AICMT2023) – Dr. O. P. Verma et al. (eds)
© 2024 Taylor & Francis Group, London, ISBN 978-1-032-78445-8

7

Multi Sports Time Series Prediction Using Machine Learning

Rishi Saxena[1], Aayush Agarwal[2], Vaibhav Gandhi[3], Deepu Maurya[4], Puneet Sharma[5]
Department of Computer Science and Engineering, Amity University, Uttar Pradesh, Noida, India

ABSTRACT: Machine Learning (ML) is an Artificial Intelligence algorithm which is being used majorly in classification and outcome prediction areas. Due to the large financial stakes associated with wagering and betting, one of the developing sectors that demands great accuracy is sports. To comprehend and create the necessary match-winning strategies, club managers and owners are also working on categorization models. These models are based on several game-related factors, such as opponent information, player performance indicators, and match results from previous games. With a main focus on how Artificial Neural Networks (ANNs) are used to forecast the outcome of sporting events, this work also focuses on the use of ML in this area. As a result, it presents a cutting-edge framework for sports forecasting that uses ML as a learning technique. To address the low prediction accuracy of current models, a deep learning-based model for predicting sports performance is proposed. This study demonstrates that models are superior to conventional methods for predicting athletic performance, with the gap between the two becoming larger.

KEYWORDS: Machine learning, Classification, Prediction, Time series, Modelling, Artificial neural network

1. Introduction

The primary objective of this study is to construct a model by using data that has been trained in the past and then evaluate the model's capacity to accurately forecast what will happen in the future. Instead, then concentrating on values like one and two or red and yellow, the research is concentrating on categories. Because it places more of an emphasis on variables than it does on particular values, this method is typically referred to as "supervised learning." The practice of categorizing is used extensively in a variety of contexts, including the screening of emails, the acceptance of loans, and medical diagnoses. The major differentiating factor between both the methods of learning is labelling of data. The utilization of labelled datasets is the fundamental distinction between the two methodologies that have been discussed. Supervised and unsupervised learning differs on the basis of labelling of input and output data, supervised learning uses labelled input and output data whereas there is no labelling of data in unsupervised learning. Training supervised learning models can take a significant amount of time, and having the requisite expertise to properly classify input and output variables is essential.

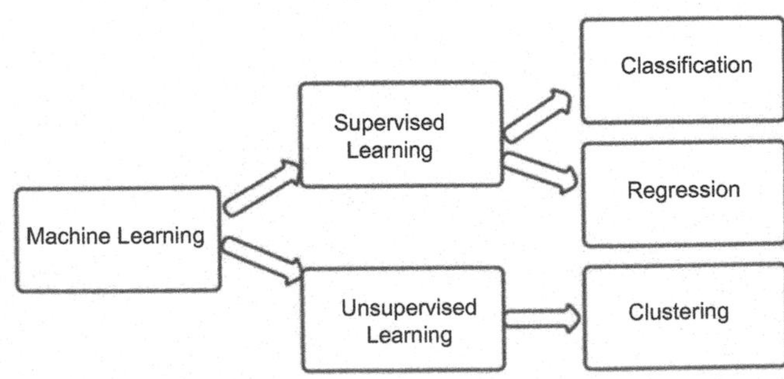

Fig. 7.1 Supervised learning v/s unsupervised learning

Figure 7.1 explains the 2 types of ML approaches based on whether some input data is received or not. One of three categories (win, lose, or draw) must be chosen in order to predict a sporting event illustrated by (Bunker and Thabtah, 2019). However, other academics have also investigated the

[1]rishialc@gmail.com, [2]aayushagarwal440@gmail.com, [3]gandhivaibhav36@gmail.com, [4]deepu1910akku@gmail.com, [5]puneetgrandmaster@gmail.com

DOI: 10.1201/9781003487906-7

subject of numerical prediction, where they have to anticipate the victory margin—a numerical value. Different factors including previous results, player health, performance, stability, and fitness, etc. influence the outcome of the match so they are studied by relevant parties to determine the result of the match beforehand. Also helps in finding new talent based on performances that might miss the normal eye. Determining which side is most likely to win is essential since the outcome of a wager carries significant financial risk. As a result, calculating the odds of a game in advance interest's bookies, fans, and potential buyers alike. Once the result of the game has been predicted, a wagering choice must be taken based on the odds.

In addition, sport management is attempting to create efficient methods for identifying the potential competition. As a result, the issue of predicting sporting outcomes has long piqued the interest of numerous parties, as well as the media. Data turned highly accessible (publicly accessible at the same time) connected to sports has skyrocketed the interest in making such advance predictions and prediction models which enable us to do them. This study analyses the existing literature on machine learning for forecasting sporting outcomes, with a particular focus on the use of neural networks in this discipline. Although there have been a number of studies in the statistical and operations research literature on predicting sports results, employing the Neural Network algorithm is pretty recent. This ever-effective Neural network technique has demonstrated effectiveness in producing incredibly accurate classification models across a variety of disciplines. Discussions of the challenges involved in using these sophisticated algorithms to predict sporting outcomes are also included. The applicability of neural networks (NN) to this problem is highlighted in this report's thorough overview of the literature on machine learning (ML) for forecasting sporting outcomes. There are also discussions of the challenges involved in applying these sophisticated algorithms to forecast sporting outcomes.

This composition's additional material is structured below. The following part contains ANN based studies; the primary approach accustomed in previously discussed articles for outcome prediction platforms.

2. Literature Survey

Artificial Neural Networks is one of the ML methods to tackle the problem of sports outcome prediction therefore the main focus of this work is on ANN. Neurons which are frequently connected sections, transform a number of inputs into the required output which is being depicted in Fig. 7.2 along with its structure. The strength comes from the hidden neurons' ability to change the weights that could influence the final outcome or judgement.

Figure 7.2 depicts an Example structure of an ANN with 4 input nodes in the input layer, 5 hidden nodes in the hidden layer and one output node in the output layer. The properties of the input and other network components, such as these weights, typically influence an ANN's output. The model is made after the data is processed, which contains all the characteristics required to build such a model.

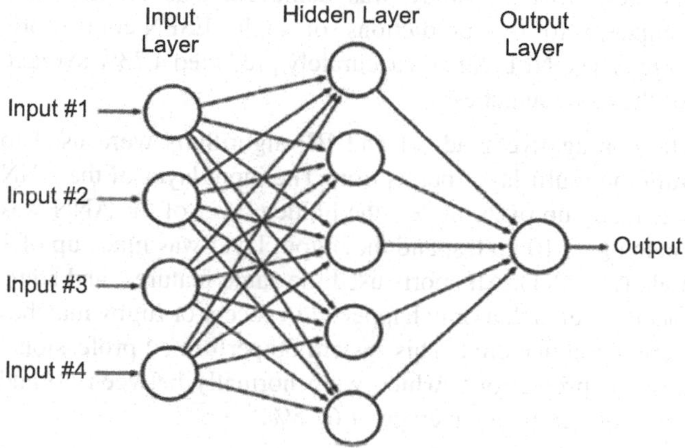

Fig. 7.2 Layers in ANN

In simpler language, weights attached with each component are changed frequently so that a very high level of efficiency can be maintained from the model. The overfitting problem and the waste of computing resources, like as training time and memory, can occasionally result from this. One task in Ann is to specify the class variables. There can be either one class variable which gives the winning outcome or there can be 2 different class variables like home matches and away matches.

Purucker (1996) conducted founding investigations taking advantage of an ANN model to predict NFL matches. Five characteristics were used to analyses the first eight rounds of the league: yards, rushing yards, turnovers, possession, and wagering line odds. To distinguish between exceptional and inferior teams, unsupervised clustering-based techniques were utilized. Then, an artificial neural network (ANN) with backward propagation (BP) was utilized. The domain specialists' accuracy rate was 72%, while Purucker's accuracy rate was 61%. The BP algorithm was revealed to be the most successful strategy (Rahman, 2020). A major drawback is that just a limited number of features were used in this work.

(Kahn, 2003) proceeded with Purucker's work leading to an improvised accuracy, that overshadowed NFL specialists performing the same task. 203 games were taken for data gathering in the 2003 season. The following criterion were applied: away, home team, total yardage, rushing yardage, and turnover. A number of -1 meant that the team lost, but +1 means that the team won. Like said earlier there were 2 classes namely the outcome of away team and the outcome of home team.

The problem was addressed as a categorization affair. The set that was used for testing comprised of the lasting rounds, while the dataset was comprised of the initial 208 matches. Testing revealed that a 10-3-2 network configuration is the most efficient. Over the span of the 14th and 15th week's matches, 75% accuracy was achieved. The results were compared to the predictions of eight ESPN.com sports casters. The NFL experts accurately predicted a 73% average for the same matches.

The conjugative gradient and BP algorithms were used to train the multi-layer perceptron. The input layer of the ANN was made up of 20 nodes, the hidden layer of the ANN was made up of 10 nodes, and the output layer was made up of 1 node (20-10-1). All sports used the same features, and some special events that only happened in soccer or rugby matches were not considered. This system outperformed professional tipsters' projections, which were normally between 60 and 65% correct, by an average of 67.5%.

(Davoodi & Khanteymoori, 2010), have also used this model to analyses and estimate the results of race horses as well. Each horse in the race had its own ANN, which produced the horse's finishing time. Each NN's input node was based on eight characteristics. Weight, track, race, participating horses, trainer, distance, track condition and jockey are the traits that were used. After 400 epochs, it was the BP algorithm, with a 77% accuracy rate, and the method (momentum = 0.7) was the 2nd most accurate method of predicting the results. In order to predict football results, Tax and Joustra analyzed Dutch football competition's previous 13 years particulars (Tax & Joustra, 2015). This arose a curiosity in the minds of these authors about how this model including betting odds will compete against other models that not only had betting odds but, in some cases, also had match variables. Also, more importantly, they made sure of the fact that cross-validation is not done because it is not right to keep in mind the time structure of the dataset—something that has most frequently been disregarded in previous investigations. To find pertinent constituents to include, an orderly literature study of statistics and sport science publications was carried out. This study employed correlation-based feature subset selection, sequential forward selection, attribute evaluation for Relief, and principal component analysis (PCA).

However, McNemar's test revealed that the difference between the public model and the betting odds model was not very much. This depicted that sports outcomes can be justifiably anticipated by simply looking at the betting odds.

Machine learning algorithms have been employed by academics to forecast individual player performance in non-team sports. The purpose of this study was to compare neural networks to regularly used regression models to assess the efficacy of neural networks as a tool for athlete recruiting. A total of 70 javelin throws were included in the data set: 40 instances were used for training, 15 cases were used for validation, and 15 cases were used for testing. The four significant indicators of javelin were identified in their initial statistical study. The average distance of 3 different throws thrown from a full runup also including the warmup time of 30 minutes was the numerical variable that was figured out. Through experimentation, it was discovered that the neural network design with the lowest normalized root mean squared error was 4 to 3 to 1. The above models built were then used to predict and analyses the javelin throws of the 20 Poland internationals and these projected throw lengths were compared to the measured throw lengths. Their findings demonstrated that compared to the nonlinear regression model, neural network models provided substantially superior quality predictions. There was an abs. regression mistake of 29.5 meters and an abs. network difference of 16.7 meters.

(Edelmann, et al., 2002) looked at simulating a top female swimmer's performance in the finals of Sydney 2000 Olympics. Before the Olympics, 19 200-meter backstroke races were analyzed for performance output, and data from the swimmer's preparation —the last 4 weeks was also included. Ten input neurons, two hidden neurons, and one output neuron were employed in an MLP. The outcomes demonstrate the MLP's accuracy; the forecast error was only 0.05 seconds. The linear regression was also contrasted with the MLP; however, the latter did not yield as precise findings. In professional sports, high-performance personnel and analysts may find it advantageous to employ machine learning approaches to identify the aspects to focus on when building training programs rather than merely for outcome prediction, as highlighted in this study and by Maszczyk et al., 2014.

Based on results after the first round of a tournament, Wiseman estimated the winning PGA golf score. Keep in mind that they were forecasting the winning score rather than the cup winner (Wiseman & Chatterjee, 2006). The MSE and Rsquared values were used to assess algorithm accuracy. Tournaments from 2016 were utilized to validate the models, which were built using data from 2004 to 2015. The best models on the 2016 dataset correctly predicted winning scores 67% of the time to within three shots (Delen et al., 2012).

3. Problem Statement

Nowadays there is a lot of demand of sports prediction based on data analytics but there aren't many resources that are providing these services. Everybody in the sports industry ranging from team staff to club managers to selectors needs this technology to make critical decisions related to the club. In this research work the main aim is to solve the problem that in the sports industry, there are very few ML-based, data-driven models that can assist in outcome prediction using historical data as input, and even those are not accurate enough to make crucial decisions. Jobs in the sports analytics industry are growing day by day so are the wages. This combination of data science and machine learning is a great combination for outcome prediction and futuristic analysis in the sports industry. As per the research study, it is found that utilizing data analytics, a Belgian midfielder for Manchester City recently secured a four-year contract and a 30% pay increase. He renegotiated his remuneration with FC Analytics, a data analytics company. It appears, based on the outcome, that he was able to present a convincing, data-driven argument which was an exceptional illustration of how compensation analytics could be implemented.

4. Proposed Methodology

For obtaining the maximum outcomes with a given data set, it is proposed to apply a structured method to the issue of predicting results in sports. An architecture is defined in this section which can be used for predicting sports outcomes, suggests stages for a potential machine learning framework. The described system concentrates on team sports outcome prediction rather than individual sports results.

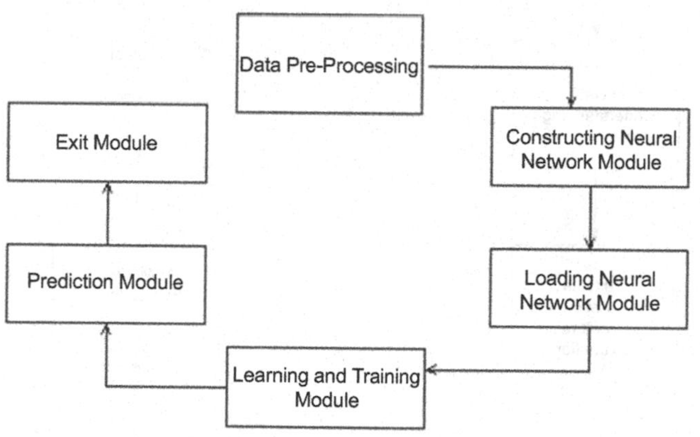

Fig. 7.3 Process cycle

Figure 7.3 shows the set of processes that the model will follow to predict the outcome based on the input that the user has provided.

This research focuses on extracting data from different sports platforms like CricBuzz, OneFootball, etc. to combine it at a single place where we'll be performing prophet algorithms which is a part of forecast model & time series models. Such platforms are established on various attributes intricated in the event, e.g. Previous outcomes, individual performance, and opposition statistics. Our major functionalities will be winner prediction, top performer, etc. based on analysis of previously recorded data in our dataset. Furthermore, team staff and owners are making great efforts to these systems in order to get to know as well as strategize to win matches. Our USP is that people use different platforms for different sports, but in this study, all are combined on a single platform for a better user experience. In doing so, this research identifies the knowledge course of action employed, the data sources, the needful way of system analysis, and the particular difficulties associated with predicting sports results. This prompts us to propose a novel framework for sport prediction using machine learning as a learning strategy.

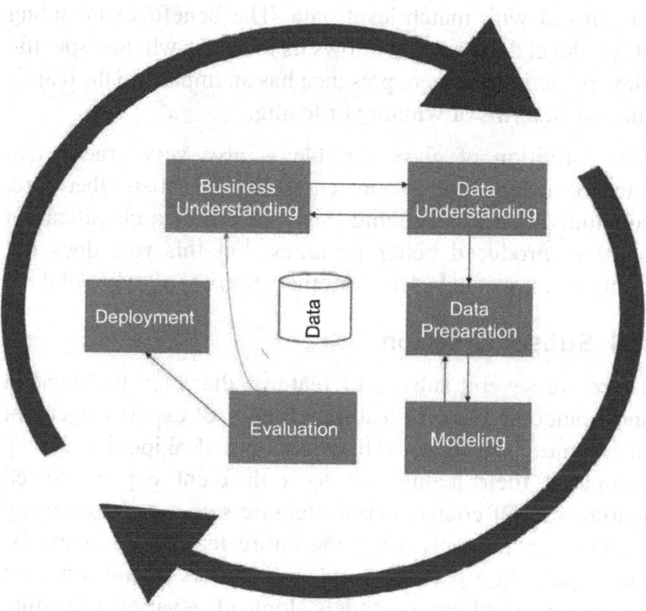

Fig. 7.4 Project lifecycle

Figure 7.4 explains the various techniques that will be performed on the previously provided data as input to predict the future outcome.

4.1 Domain Understanding

Understanding the problem, and the unique features of the sport itself are all examples of domain understanding. To do this, you must have some knowledge of the sport's rules and the probable contributing elements to match results. This might be discovered through personal experience with the sport, research into the body of existing literature, or by speaking with specialists in the field. Clarity is also required concerning the model's goal. The goal might be to forecast outcomes to compete with professional predictions, participate in online contests, or ultimately utilized the model's predictions to place wagers on sporting events. The matches that will be wagered on must also be taken into account if the prediction model is to be utilized for betting.

4.2 Data Understanding

Sports forecasting can frequently be found online from freely available sources. By developing programs that automatically extract web data from databases and load it into databases, prior research has automated the data collection process. A forecast is made when individuals enter details about a future game into an end-user interface that has been developed through some study. The amount or level of granularity of the data is one factor to consider. Prior research has used match- and team-level training data. To incorporate particular player statistics as characteristics for each match, player-level data is frequently split into a distinct data set that must be transposed and linked with match-level data. The benefit of including player-level data is that it allows us to assess whether specific players' actions or mere presence has an impact on the team's success in terms of winning or losing.

The definition of class variable is also very crucial and must be taken into account carefully. Scientists, therefore, concluded that approaching this problem of a classification problem produced better accuracy, but this rule does not imply that it would be true for other sports or all types of data.

4.3 Subset Creation

There are several subsets of features that may be found in sport outcome data. To test the efficacy of expert judgement in feature selection, (Hucaljuk and Rakipovic, 2011), compared their feature set to a different expert-selected feature set. Of course, certain feature sets are chosen using selection techniques, using the entire feature set or maybe just a part. In a perfect world, researchers would test their candidate classification models alongside a variety of feature selection methodologies.

(Hucaljuk and Rakipovic, 2011), also provided a brilliant feature set of combinations with their original set. Despite the lack of evidence, this may be because of the nature of the sport or even the specialists themselves. Another method of utilizing expert judgement is to contrast the projected precision of the predictive platforms along with the forecasts of the experts.

4.4 Data Processing: Match Features vs External Features

The aspects of a sport's match are tied to real happenings inside the game. For instance, in the sport of football, they are yards, passes, etc. The term "external aspects" refers to characteristics that are unrelated to the actual match. For data pre-processing, this distinction is crucial. For example, the author(s) are aware of the travel distance and current form of both teams before the upcoming game. However, match-specific attributes are not known until the game has begun. As a consequence, this study contains only the mean of such characteristics for a predetermined frequency of previous matches between these clubs. For instance, the author(s) would be aware of the average number of passes made per game by both teams before the contest, but they would not know the number of passes made during the game until after it had begun. As a result, only historical average data for these traits may be utilized to forecast a future game. Following this procedure, (Buursma, 2011), carried out experiments and discovered that the best classification accuracy was achieved by utilizing an average of the previous 20 matches.

5. Implementation

Choosing which candidate models will be utilized in the experiment is the first stage in the modelling process. This would entail a study of earlier material and the identification of widely used prediction models that have had success in the past. Then, the model was tested on every single feature set and combination which was selected by selection techniques and otherwise.

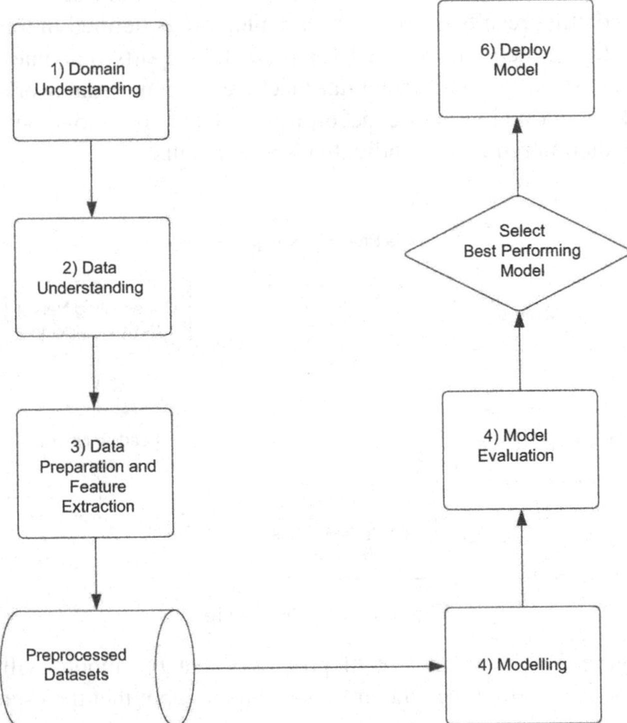

Fig. 7.5 Steps of our proposed SRP-CRISP-DM framework

Figure 7.5 depicts the 6 major steps that will be followed from the very beginning till the results has been received in the model. The CRISP DM Framework stands for Cross Industry Standard Process for Data Mining.

5.1 Performance Measurement

A general way of doing things is to use the classification matrix to classify or categories the wins into separate categories vis-à-vis home, away wins and draws before counting the total number of classified matches by the model.

One is expected to find a little bias in favor of home victories given the frequently seen home advantage phenomena. Classification accuracy is an appropriate assessment metric in this situation. When the data is very twisted, the ROC curve method is the best one.

5.2 Testing and Training

It is crucial, as has already been discussed, to maintain the sequence of the training data such that only previous matches are used to forecast future games. For the problem of predicting the outcome of a sporting event, cross-validation (Fig. 7.6) is not a suitable method since it typically entails changing the order of the cases.

Selecting an adequate training-test split is necessary. It vastly depends on the amount of data that the expert is using, this can be of several seasons or just one singular season.

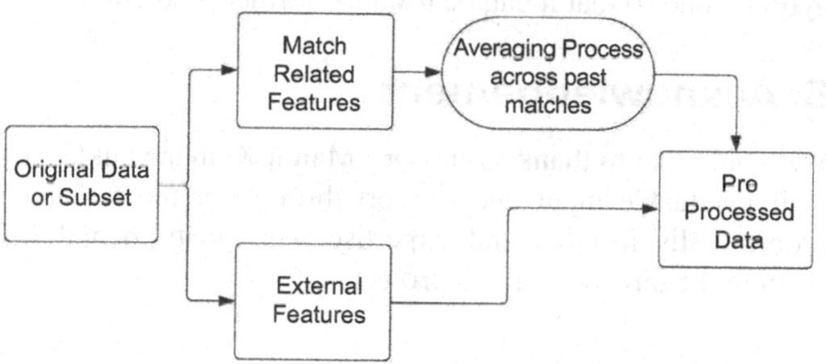

Fig. 7.6 Plan of action for using previous match data

Figure 7.6 shows that Match-Related statistics should be averaged across a specific number of historical matches for each item before being integrated with the external match features.

Professional sports tournaments are often formatted into rounds. In every round, teams typically play one game, unless they get a "bye." When just one season of data is available, it is necessary to decide how many rounds can be used for the testing and training of the model.

A different approach to this round method is to renew the dataset after every match has finished. In this instance, all matches including the latest played one are treated as a dataset and are used for training and testing. This method is however more useful if teams play more than 1 match per/round, if not then this method is not required and the previous one serves just fine.

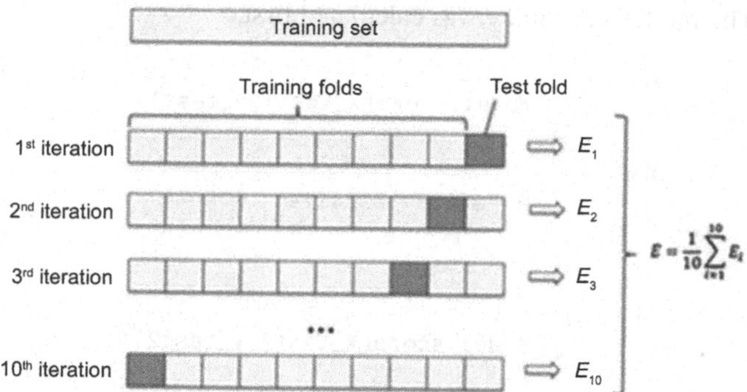

Fig. 7.7 10-fold-cross validation

Figure 7.7 shows the Diagrammatic representation of 10-fold Cross-Validation Several seasons of data have been utilised in certain articles.

Using earlier seasons' data as training and subsequent seasons' data as the test set has been a popular strategy. For instance, this method may not be the best in terms of the performance of the model but if player level changes and player data is recorded every season and is incorporated into the model then this risk will be somewhat reduced. The author(s) contend that each season should employ its strategy, albeit being more time-consuming and computationally demanding. The average for each season is then generated, and a model accuracy by season plot could be displayed.

5.3 Model Deployment

The entire process of adding in new match data either by the internet or manually should be automized and need not be entered physically. The new model is then again trained according to the freshly arrived dataset and then the testing takes place, this process keeps on repeating till this work has newer data. The end user is then provided predictions. Also, the model has to be created in such a way that newer data like external can be inputted before the match and live data can be added during the match, this will vastly add to the dynamicity of the model. Additionally, the environment should always accept changes by adding new datasets and the classifier should be regularly updated.

6. Results

The model was fed with a large amount of previous sports data based on which the machine was supposed to predict the future outcome. Different datasets were used such as fixtures, ranking, results and ICC CWC' 19 that was having all the data related to that tournament.

The model's accuracy was calculated first,

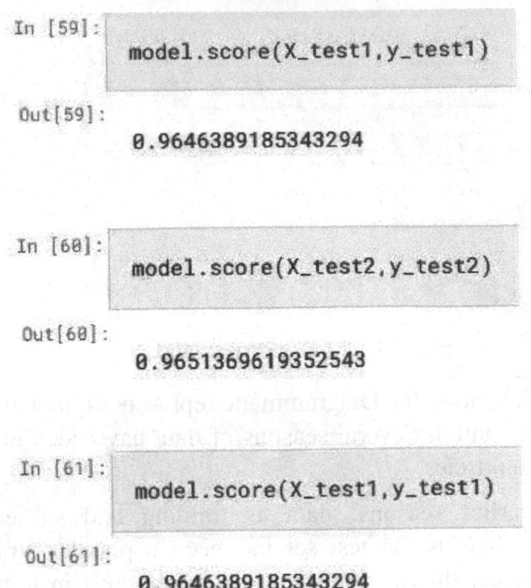

Fig. 7.8 Method used to find out model accuracy

Figure 7.8 shows the accuracy of our model which came out to be pretty good. This is because in such models >90% accuracy is not a good thing because then the model could be used for unfair purposes such as in this case, betting. After the model succeeded with the accuracy test, further work was done i.e., outcome prediction.

Figure 7.9 depicts the outcome of our model, after it was fed with all the relevant data for the tournament it successfully predicted the winner based on the previous outcomes and the provided data.

7. Conclusion

Different models are used to predict the outcomes of sports matches and these predictions are then analysed by experts in the domain. Due to its unique nature, the results from the diverse studies are frequently difficult to compare directly. Although more accurate models are still needed, ML models are being employed more frequently to predict sports. This is due to the enormous popularity of sports betting as well as the fact that sports managers are always hunting for pertinent data to forecast upcoming matching strategies. Because ML creates models that can give match outcomes using predetermined characteristics, it appears to be an ideal approach for sport prediction. Additionally, difficulties with predicting algorithms were highlighted to indicate research for academics in this crucial area. This work should be useful for ML-related research on sports outcome prediction in the future.

Also, since there is room for improvement, future research will outline how to integrate such a model with multiple sporting events on a single platform to enhance the user experience, as well as how to upload the predicted data to a hybrid cloud so that it can be used for further prediction.

8. Acknowledgement

We would like to thank Prof. (Dr.) Manoj Kumar Shukla for their invaluable input and support throughout the research process. His insights and expertise were instrumental in shaping the direction of this project.

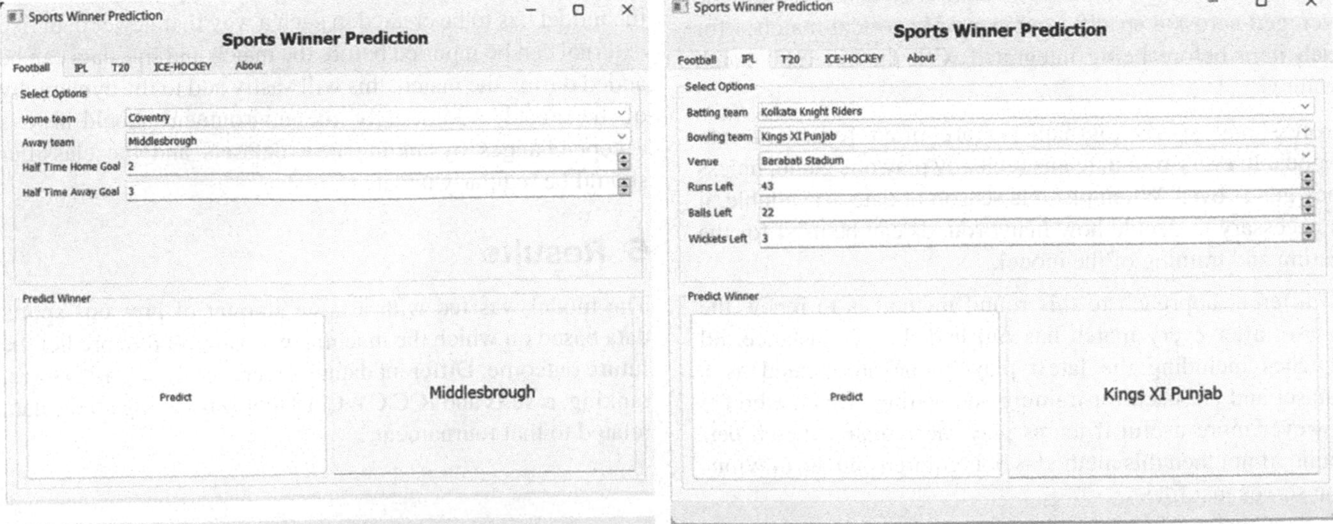

Fig. 7.9 Outcome of our model

REFERENCES

1. Bunker, R., & Thabtah, F. 2019. A machine learning framework for sport result prediction. Applied Computing and Informatics, 15(1), 27–33. https://doi.org/10.1016/j.aci.2017.09.005.
2. Rahman, M. A. 2020. A deep learning framework for football match prediction. SN Applied Sciences, 2(2). https://doi.org/10.1007/s42452-019-1821-5.
3. Kahn, Joshua. 2003. Neural network prediction of NFL football games. World Wide Web Electronic Publication. 9-15.
4. Buursma, D. (2011). Predicting sports events from past results Towards effective betting on football matches. https://silo.tips/download/predicting-sports-events-from-past-results#.
5. Purucker, M. 1996. Neural network quarterbacking. IEEE Potentials, 15(3), 9–15. https://doi.org/10.1109/45.535226.
6. Cao, C. 2012. Sports data mining technology used in basketball outcome prediction. Masters Dissertation. Technological University Dublin.
7. Edelmann-Nusser, J., Hohmann, A., & Henneberg, B. 2002. Modeling and prediction of competitive performance in swimming upon neural networks. European Journal of Sport Science, 2(2), 1–10. https://doi.org/10.1080/17461390200072201.
8. Davoodi, E., & Khanteymoori, A.R. 2010. Horse racing prediction using artificial neural networks. In Proceedings of the 11th WSEAS international conference on nural networks and 11th WSEAS international conference on evolutionary computing and 11th WSEAS international conference on Fuzzy systems (NN'10/EC'10/FS'10). World Scientific and Engineering Academy and Society (WSEAS), Stevens Point, Wisconsin, USA, 155–160.
9. Fister, I., Brest, J., & Iglesias, A. 2018. Framework for planning the training sessions in triathlon. Proceedings of the Genetic and Evolutionary Computation Conference Companion. https://doi.org/10.1145/3205651.3208242.
10. Tax, Niek & Joustra, Yme. 2015. Predicting The Dutch Football Competition Using Public Data: A Machine Learning Approach. 10.13140/RG.2.1.1383.4729.
11. Maszczyk, A., Gołaś, A., Pietraszewski, P., Roczniok, R., Zajac, A., & Stanula, A. 2014. Application of neural and regression models in sports results prediction. Procedia - Social and Behavioral Sciences, 117, 482–487. https://doi.org/10.1016/j.sbspro.2014.02.249.
12. Wiseman, F., & Chatterjee, S. 2006. Comprehensive Analysis of golf performance on the PGA Tour: 1990–2004. Perceptual and Motor Skills, 102(1), 109–117. https://doi.org/10.2466/pms.102.1.109-117.
13. Delen, D., Cogdell, D., & Kasap, N. 2012. A comparative analysis of data mining methods in predicting NCAA bowl outcomes. International Journal of Forecasting, 28(2), 543–552.
14. Hucaljuk, J., & Rakipovic, A. 2011. Predicting football scores using machine learning techniques. 2011 Proceedings of the 34th International Convention MIPRO, 1623-1627.

Note: All the figures in this chapter were made by the author.

Advancement of Intelligent Computational Methods and Technologies (AICMT2023) – Dr. O. P. Verma et al. (eds)
© 2024 Taylor & Francis Group, London, ISBN 978-1-032-78445-8

8

Blockchain Based Decentralized File Sharing System

Puneet Sharma[1], Manoj Kumar Shukla[2]
Dept. of CSE, Amity University, Uttar Pradesh, Noida, India
Jayanti Pandey[3]
Amity Institute of Applied Sciences, Amity University, Uttar Pradesh, Noida, India

ABSTRACT: The transparency and immutability that blockchain technology may offer is one of its main benefits. A blockchain records each transaction or data entry in a block, which is connected to previous blocks to create a chain of data. Because blockchain is decentralized, none of its organizations has complete control over the network. Because there is no longer a need for a centralized authority, the system is more resistant to attacks and censorship. Real-time as well as authorized access to information is another benefit of blockchain technology. Overall, blockchain technology has the potential to revolutionize a number of industries by offering safe, open, and effective methods for handling data and conducting transactions. Its effect extends beyond data and information to include things like supply chain management, healthcare, finance, and beyond. In this research work, the decentralized file sharing platform is created which can handle file uploading and downloading over a decentralized network which cannot be governed by any other organization. The testing of the system is simultaneously checked which gave a calming result.

KEYWORDS: Blockchain, Decentralized, Cryptography, Cryptographic hash

1. Introduction

Blockchains have power in digital forms of money like Bitcoin or Ethereum. Bitcoin is particularly well known and rules the financial exchange. Advanced monetary standards like Bitcoin enjoys the benefit of minimal exchange charges as well as being decentralized from official monetary standards (Tschorsch & Scheuermann, 2016). A square in a blockchain implies the computerized data or information that is recorded. Blocks are connected together utilizing cryptography, which is basically a method for keeping data discrete and secure. The cumulation of these squares makes a chain identical to a public data set. The computerized data contained in each block comprises of three sections.

- Data about the blockchain exchange, like date, time, and amount (dollar) of the exchange, is recorded.
- More explicit data is recorded in connection with who is partaking in the blockchain exchange. The purchase is recorded without utilizing recognition of data and depends on computerized marks (Di Pierro 2017).
- A cryptographic hash work (CHW) recognizes the current block from the last square. This is a numeric calculation that maps information into a novel code involving a hash unmistakably put aside from the hashes of different squares.

A solitary block on a Bitcoin blockchain can store roughly 1 MB of information. At the end of the day, a solitary square can hold the data of thousands of exchanges. For a square to be connected to the blockchain, several things should occur (Nakamoto 2008). It is confirmed through a large number of PCs conveyed across the net. The exchange information is put away in a square with the data from the initial two stages recorded previously. What's more, according to the third step, a hash is made. The differentiation of one square from another is vital. If for an instance a purchase is made on Amazon and which makes an almost indistinguishable purchase, just after

[1]puneetgrandmaster@gmail.com, [2]mkshukla001@gmail.com, [3]jayantilillies@gmail.com

DOI: 10.1201/9781003487906-8

five minutes, blockchain is prepared to recognize the two exchanges. Every individual in the blockchain network has a duplicate of the chain, henceforth the term is appropriately recorded. Blockchain networks likewise give savvy contract (chain hub) administrations to applications. Shrewd agreements create blockchain exchanges in any case, which are dispersed to peer hubs inside the organization where they are recorded.

2. Literature Review

2.1 Interplanetary File System

The Interplanetary File System is a convention and shared organization for putting away and sharing information in a conveyed document framework (Wood 2014). IPFS utilizes content-addressing to interestingly distinguish each document in a worldwide namespace interfacing all processing gadgets. IPFS started in 2015 as a work by Protocol Labs to assemble a framework that could essentially change the manner in which data is communicated across the globe and make it ready for a conveyed stronger web. IPFS is developed to help a variety of various use cases and is further developing data across the board for enterprises across the range, from disintermediating the music business to unblocking weather conditions in hazard insurance. Right now, Protocol Lab's activity incorporates IPFS, the particular conventions and instruments that help it, and Filecoin, among others. Between them, these apparatuses serve a huge number of associations and many individuals.

2.2 Smart Contracts

Simply explained, smart contracts are blockchain-based projects that executes when specific conditions are satisfied. They are typically used to automate the execution of an agreement so that all parties can quickly be certain of the outcome, without a go-between's involvement or time inconveniency. They can automate a process as well, triggering the subsequent action when certain criteria are met. Simple "on the off chance that/when..." explanations are turned into code on a blockchain and used to implement simple agreements (Dinh et al., 2018). When predetermined conditions are satisfied and verified, an organization of PCs carries out the tasks. Delivering resources to appropriate meetings, hiring a vehicle, conveying warnings, or issuing a ticket are some examples of these actions. After the exchange is complete, the blockchain is refreshed (Röscheisen et al., 1998).

2.3 Solidity

Solidity is an object-oriented, high-level language for developing smart contracts on the Ethereum blockchain. Smart contracts are programs that administer the conduct of records inside the Ethereum state. Solidity uses curly brackets. It is affected by C++, Python, and JavaScript, and is intended to focus on the Ethereum Virtual Machine (EVM). One can observe more insights regarding which dialects have solidity that has been propelled by language impacts. Robustness is statically composed, upholds legacy, libraries, and complex client characterized types among different highlights (Fries et al. 2019). With Solidity, one can make contracts for utilizations like democratic, crowdfunding, blind sales, and multi-signature wallets, and while sending contracts, one should utilize the most recent delivered form of Solidity (Tapscott et al. 2016). Aside from remarkable cases, hands down the most recent form gets security fixes . Besides, breaking changes as well as new elements are presented consistently. As of now utilize a 0.y.z adaptation number to demonstrate this high speed of progress (Finley 2015).

2.4 Ganache

An Ethereum simulator called Ganache makes creating Ethereum apps quicker, simpler, and safer. To create a private Ethereum blockchain for testing Solidity, uses Ganache (Wood 2014). In contrast to Remix, it offers greater features. While using Ganache for exercise, it is easy to become familiar with its functionalities but it is suggested to first download and install the blockchain on the local computer before to use Ganache.

2.5 Truffle

Truffle is a cutting-edge technology that was released under the MIT license. The community GitHub repository reads, "Truffle is a development environment, testing framework and asset pipeline for Ethereum, aiming to make life as an Ethereum developer easier" (Pierro 2017). And so, Truffle is a development environment, which makes it easy to migrate smart contracts onto the Ethereum blockchain (Wood 2014).

2.6 React

React.js is an open-source frontend library which is used for making client side rendered web application. React is maintained by Facebook and a large community of individual developers. It is focused on creating reusable components throughout the web application. React.js listen to the changes happening in the site and then creates a virtual DOM to compare with the original DOM if react notices any difference between them it renders the new components hence making the application faster than regular DOM.

Difference between Server-Side and Client-Side rendering

Server-side rendering is the most common method of displaying information in web applications. Server-side rendering works by converting the HTML files into meaningful information according to the user and route in the server. Every time visiting a website, the browser makes a request to the server, which then renders HTML with the necessary data and delivers it back as a response. This kind of rendering puts a lot of the load on the server as it has to render HTML for each request for every user. Hence, it came up with Client-side rendering, which uses JavaScript for rendering content in the browser. In client-side rendering the server send the whole web application to the user and then that web application takes control over the browser's refresh and request cycle. Instead of fully refreshing the web application and asking for new application from the server again the application only changes the needed part of the web application and only asking for the data needed for the new rendered components. This process reduces the load on the server hence reducing the server cost. React.js also uses client-side rendering.

3. Methodology

Inter Planetary File System is a distributed and decentralized protocol that allows users to store and retrieve data in a peer-to-peer network and key concept is content addressing, where data is acknowledged by its content rather than its location. Data is compressed in size, scrambled, and assigned a unique content identifier (CID) when it is uploaded to a standing node via the protocol. The CID acts as a fingerprint and makes it quicker and simpler to keep small amounts of data on the network. It might deliver the data similarly to the first node if it does this. Each node is free to decide whether to keep and pass along this data or toss it out as shown in Fig. 8.1.

Each upload to the network, whether of newly created data or previously uploaded data, generates a new cryptographic hash CID, making it distinct and resistant to hacking efforts.

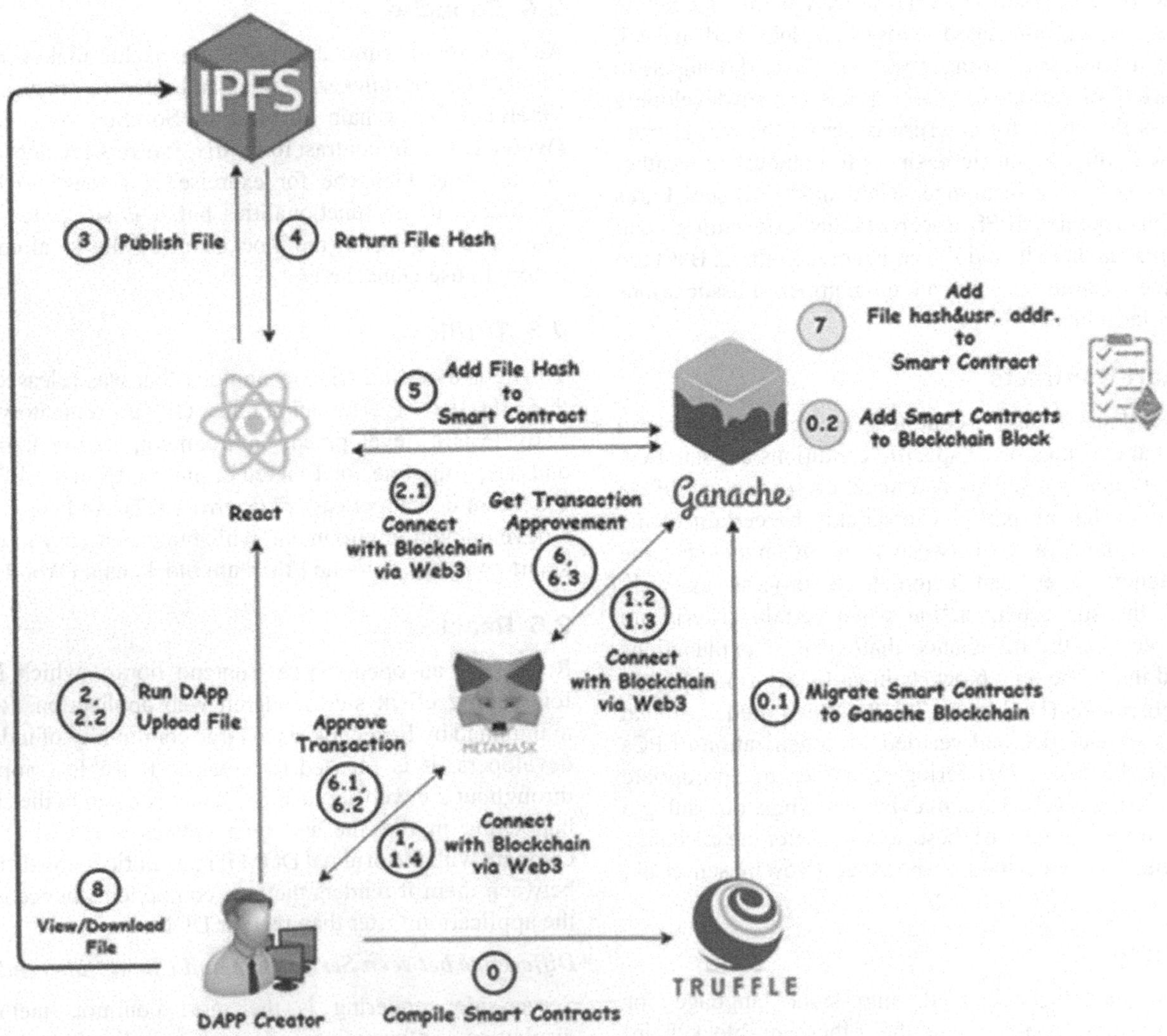

Fig. 8.1 Application structure

Source: Author

3.1 Setup

To streamline the development process, decentralized applications on the Ethereum blockchain requires set of development tools (Wood 2014).

3.2 Ganache

Ganache is a desktop-based personal Ethereum blockchain. On a local, self-contained Ethereum blockchain network, where transactions happen instantly, it is the quickest way to test the scripts. Firstly, go to Ganache, download it, configure it, and then start the PC by running it. Since we will be testing our decentralized storage contract on this solitary, tiny Ethereum blockchain network, adding a new workspace can be referred to as "DStorages". After saving it, launch the workspace as shown in Fig. 8.2.

Observe that several accounts, each loaded with 100 ETH, had been created. To view the private key for the first account, click Show Keys as in Fig. 8.3 and copy the private key, will be used in the next step as shown in Fig. 8.4.

3.3 MetaMask

It can be adhered to these procedures to link the MetaMask wallet to a nearby Ganache Ethereum blockchain:

- If there is no download and installation of the MetaMask plugin for Chrome or Firefox.
- Establish a new MetaMask wallet by following the instructions displayed on the screen. This entails setting up a password and writing down a private backup phrase. Keep in mind that the backup of phrase must be kept securely because wallet recovery depends on it.

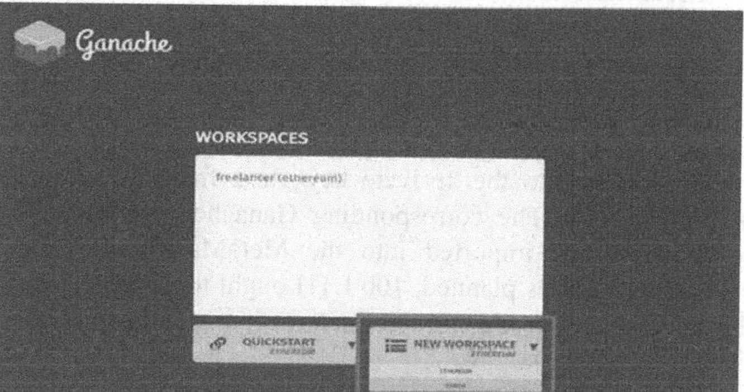

Fig. 8.2 Ganache landing page and workspace

Source: https://moralis.io/ganache-explained-what-is-ganache-blockchain/

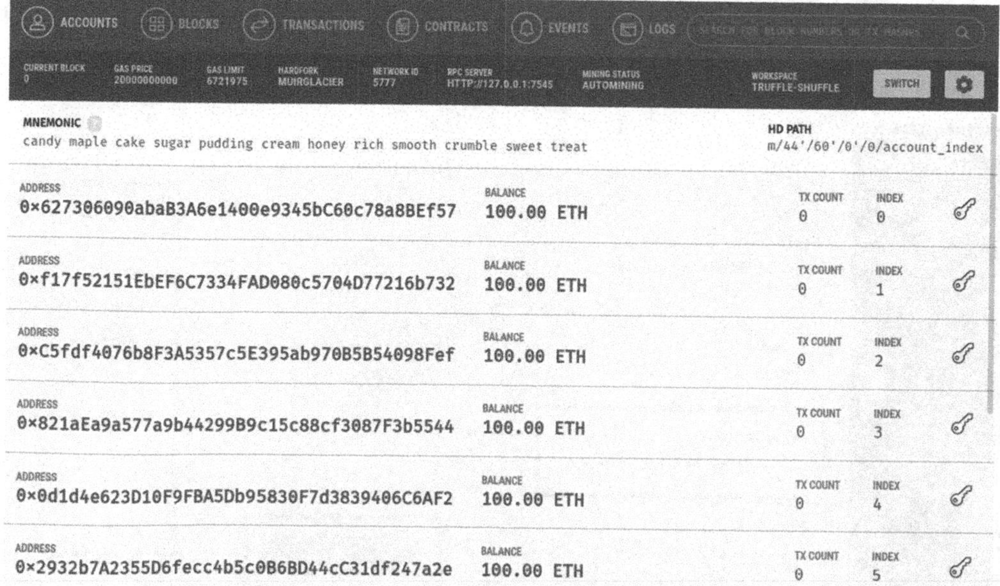

Fig. 8.3 Getting the private key in Ganache

Source: https://trufflesuite.com/docs/ganache/concepts/ethereum-workspace/overview/

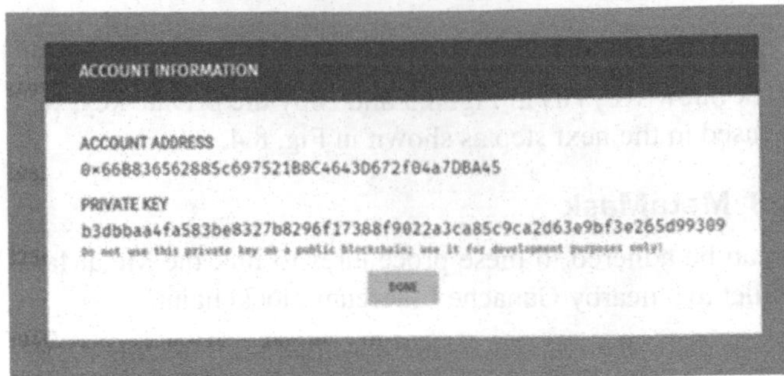

Fig. 8.4 Account details in Ganache

Source: Author

- To access the wallet UI after setting up the MetaMask wallet, click the MetaMask extension icon in the toolbar of the browser.
- MetaMask is by default linked to the Ethereum core network and the network dropdown can be found at the top of MetaMask. Click there to switch to the local Ganache Ethereum blockchain (Wood 2014).

Create a fresh account and paste the private key which was copied earlier into the "private key" text field, as shown in the figure 5. The corresponding Ganache account will subsequently be imported into the MetaMask wallet. If everything went as planned, 100 ETH ought to be present in this account. It can add extra Ganache accounts if it would be liked to MetaMask.

4. Proposed Methodology

In doing so, this research identifies the learning methodologies employed, the data sources, the appropriate means of model evaluation, and the particular difficulties associated with predicting sports results. This prompts us to propose a novel frame-work for sports prediction using machine learning as a learning strategy.

4.1 Visual Studio Code

Because it has Solidity development extensions that may be helpful while using it, it is used as an integrated development environment (IDE). What really matters is that an IDE is being used. Install the "Solidity Visual Developer" extension by performing a search. When coding, this will offer Solidity language support.

4.2 Truffle Box

Truffle Boxes are designed to streamline the development process by including the necessary dependencies, libraries, and configurations needed to build smart contracts and front-end interfaces for DApps. They help developers save time by eliminating the need to set up these components manually. Truffle Boxes offer different options based on the specific requirements of the project. By using Truffle Boxes, developers can quickly bootstrap their DApp projects with the required tools and libraries. This enables them to spend less time on initial setup and configuration and more time on the unique logic and functionality of their DApps. While developing a straightforward HTML, JavaScript/Bootstrap-based web application for decentralized storage. As a result, it will utilize the Webpack box.

Truffle installation can be performed as: "npm install -g truffle"

Once installation process is performed the development of the Decentralized Storage DApp project can be started and

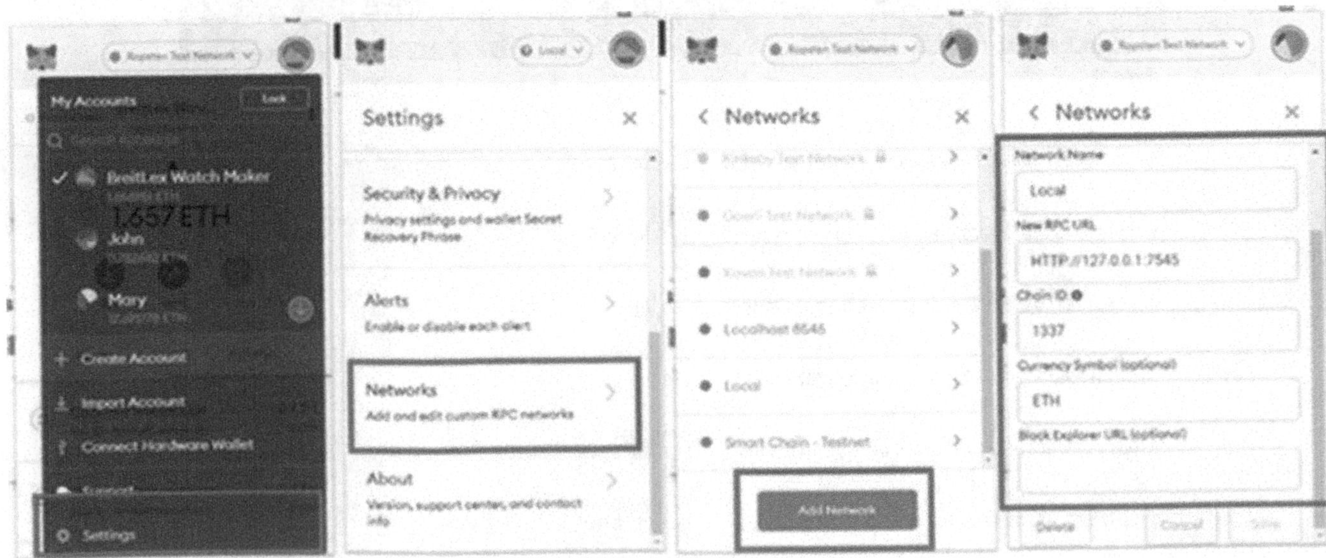

Fig. 8.5 Setting up MetaMask

Source: Author

make the "DStorages" folder on the computer. To unbox the webpack boilerplate, place it in the folder, to do so follow the following command: "npx truffle unbox Webpack". In VS Code, open the folder and be ready to begin construction.

5. Implementation

For creating such a platform, it can either store all the files on the blockchain itself or use a separate decentralized way of storing files like IPFS. Using blockchain for the storage of the whole file won't be feasible as it will not only increase the transaction cost exponentially but also make access to the file very slow as compared to other alternatives because of this reason it is suggested to use IPFS for the storage to file (Pierro 2017). After uploading a file to IPFS it returns a unique hash that could be used to access that file. Instead of storing the whole file on the Ethereum blockchain, it will store this hash along with other necessary fields for that file like name, description, upload time, uploader wallet address, etc. (Wood 2014).

To achieve this, it is required to create a smart contract that will store all the needed data on the blockchain when someone uploads a file on us react frontend (Pierro 2017) and will used in mapping of solidity to store the data related to different files. Mapping is a prebuilt data structure in solidity which uses a hash table under the hood. Since the cost of a transaction on a blockchain depends upon the number of operations happening in that transaction and it is needed to make sure that the smart contract that is written should be the most optimized, that is the reason mapping is used instead of using an array as search for a field in an array is a liner operation whereas searching in a hash table is a constant space-time operation. Since there are many different fields related to a single file, which can either use different mappings for every different field or can create a struct of all the fields and then create a mapping for that struct.

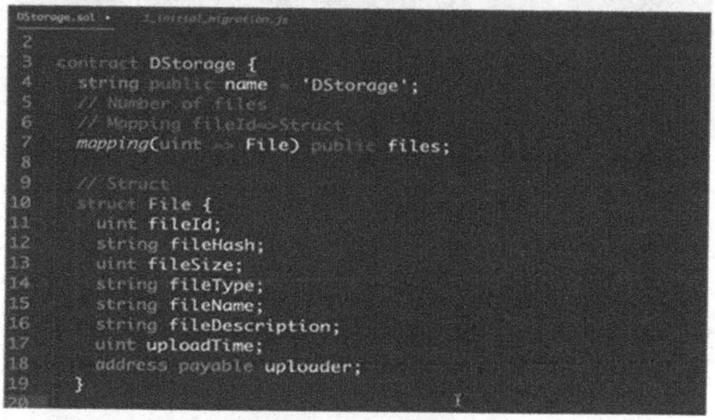

```
DStorage.sol •    1_initial_migration.js

contract DStorage {
  string public name = 'DStorage';
  // Number of files
  // Mapping fileId=>Struct
  mapping(uint => File) public files;

  // Struct
  struct File {
    uint fileId;
    string fileHash;
    uint fileSize;
    string fileType;
    string fileName;
    string fileDescription;
    uint uploadTime;
    address payable uploader;
  }
```

Fig. 8.6 File structure

Source: https://trufflesuite.com/docs/ganache/concepts/ethereum-workspace/overview/

As per the Fig. 8.6, now it is required to create a function to handle file upload. This function will increment the file counter which is used to keep track of how many files have already uploaded. Apart from this it also needed to add different checks before uploading the files as file hash exists, file type exists, file description exists, etc.

Once the file is created and added it to the mapping, a custom event will be triggered to an event which can subscribe to get to know that a file has been uploaded as per the code shown in Figs 8.7 and 8.8.

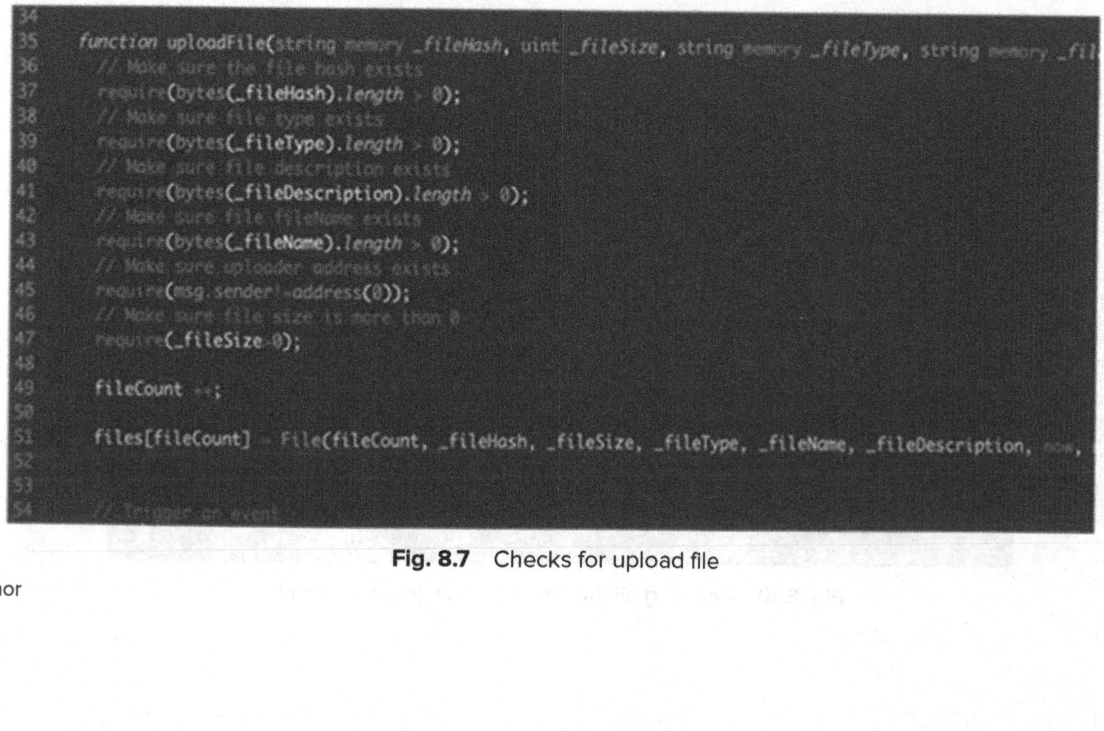

```

function uploadFile(string memory _fileHash, uint _fileSize, string memory _fileType, string memory _fil
  // Make sure the file hash exists
  require(bytes(_fileHash).length > 0);
  // Make sure file type exists
  require(bytes(_fileType).length > 0);
  // Make sure file description exists
  require(bytes(_fileDescription).length > 0);
  // Make sure file fileName exists
  require(bytes(_fileName).length > 0);
  // Make sure uploader address exists
  require(msg.sender!=address(0));
  // Make sure file size is more than 0
  require(_fileSize>0);

  fileCount ++;

  files[fileCount] = File(fileCount, _fileHash, _fileSize, _fileType, _fileName, _fileDescription, now,


  // Trigger an event
```

Fig. 8.7 Checks for upload file

Source: Author

```
// Event
event FileUploaded(
  uint fileId,
  string fileHash,
  uint fileSize,
  string fileType,
  string fileName,
  string fileDescription,
  uint uploadTime,
  address payable uploader
)
```

Fig. 8.8 File uploaded event

Source: Author

Now for the frontend, it will connect to frontend application with web3.js, for this application to work it would need MetaMask to be installed on the browser as it injects the web3 instance on the frontend, and allows us to get the wallet address of the user which is necessary for the transaction. It can connect the web3 instance with the frontend like the code shown in Fig. 8.9.

Once the frontend application is connected with web3.js and fetches the data from the smart contract on which it is uploaded on the blockchain. Since it can't be accessed to all the files in one go first, so it will fetch the total number of files from the contract and then it will iterate from 1 till that number and push all these files in an array and then will display all the files that were previously uploaded on that blockchain as in Fig. 8.10.

For uploading a file first, it is needed to connect our frontend application with IPFS as it will give the file hash of the uploaded file as shown in Fig. 8.11.

```
class App extends Component {

  async componentWillMount() {
    await this.loadWeb3()
    await this.loadBlockchainData()
  }

  async loadWeb3() {
    if (window.ethereum) {
      window.web3 = new Web3(window.ethereum)
      await window.ethereum.enable()
    }
    else if (window.web3) {
      window.web3 = new Web3(window.web3.currentProvider)
    }
    else {
      window.alert('Non-Ethereum browser detected. You should consider trying MetaMask!')
    }
  }
```

Fig. 8.9 Connecting web3.js with React.js application

Source: Author

```
  async loadBlockchainData() {
    const web3 = window.web3

    //Load account
    const accounts = await web3.eth.getAccounts()
    this.setState({ account: accounts[0] })

    // Network ID
    const networkId = await web3.eth.net.getId()
    const networkData = DStorage.networks[networkId]
    if(networkData) {
      // Assign contract
      const dstorage = new web3.eth.Contract(DStorage.abi, networkData.address)
      this.setState({ dstorage })
      // Get files amount
      const filesCount = await dstorage.methods.fileCount().call()
      this.setState({ filesCount })
      // Load files&sort by the newest
      for (var i = filesCount; i >= 1; i--) {
        const file = await dstorage.methods.files(i).call()
        this.setState({
          files: [...this.state.files, file]
        })
      }
    } else {
      window.alert('DStorage contract not deployed to detected network.')
    }
    this.setState({loading: false})
```

Fig. 8.10 Fetching all the files from the smart contract

Source: Author

```
const ipfsClient = require('ipfs-http-client')
const ipfs = ipfsClient({ host: 'ipfs.infura.io', port: 5001, protocol: 'https' })
```

Fig. 8.11 Connecting with IPFS

Source: Author

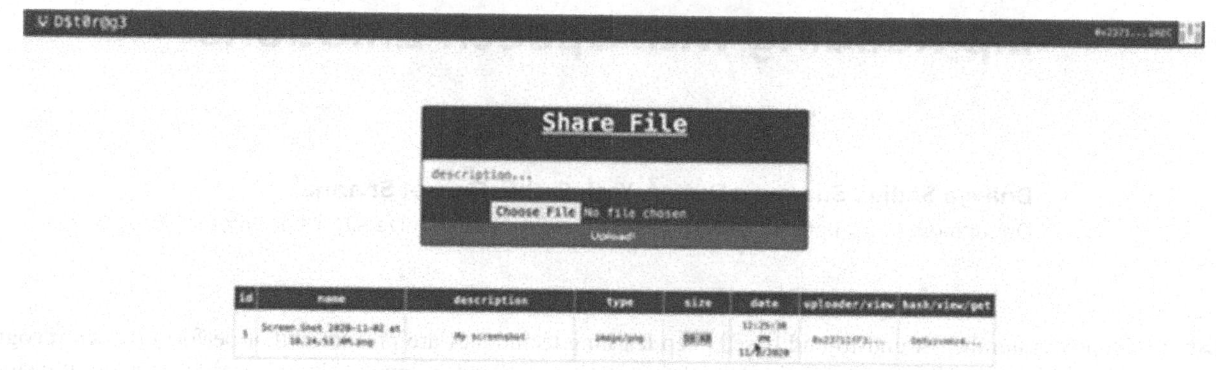

Fig. 8.12 Connecting with IPFS

Source: Author

Once the file-uploading function is finished, the decentralized file-sharing system can no longer be controlled by a single entity, allowing anybody with internet access from anywhere to share and access files freely.

6. Result Analysis

By following the above steps discussed and shown in implementation section is used for a decentralized file sharing platform is obtained which can handle file upload and download over a decentralized network which is not governed by any other organization as shown in Fig. 8.12.

7.Conclusion

With so many real-world uses for blockchain being established and being investigated, the technology is now beginning to gain recognition. With fewer middlemen, blockchain has the potential to improve commercial and governmental processes' accuracy, efficiency, security, and affordability. The most well-known product created by blockchain innovation is Bitcoin, a type of digital currency that acts as a public record of all transactions made within the company. By resolving the issue of double spending and unauthorized expenditure, security has been expanded. Additionally, it helps to do away with the need for a delegate master. The blockchain innovation aids in attracting the various crowds because the number of digital items has recently increased significantly. The decentralized file sharing system was successfully implemented and tested to obtain the results.

REFERENCES

1. Tschorsch, F., & Scheuermann, B. 2016. Bitcoin and Beyond: A technical survey on decentralized digital currencies. IEEE Communications Surveys and Tutorials, 18(3), 2084–2123. https://doi.org/10.1109/comst.2016.2535718.
2. Di Pierro, M. 2017. What is the blockchain? Computing in Science and Engineering, 19(5), 92–95. https://doi.org/10.1109/mcse.2017.3421554.
3. Nakamoto, S. 2008. Bitcoin: A Peer-to-Peer Electronic Cash System. https://bitcoin.org/bitcoin.pdf.
4. Wood, D.D. 2014. Ethereum: A Secure Decentralised Generalised Transaction Ledger. Ethereum Project Yellow Paper, vol. 151, pp. 1–32.
5. Dinh, T. T. A., Li, R., Zhang, M., Chen, G., Ooi, B. C., & Wang, J. (2018). Untangling Blockchain: A data processing view of blockchain systems. IEEE Transactions on Knowledge and Data Engineering, 30(7), 1366–1385. https://doi.org/10.1109/tkde.2017.2781227.
6. Röscheisen, M., Baldonado, M. Q. W., Chang, K. C., Gravano, L., Ketchpel, S. P., & Paepcke, A. 1998. The Stanford InfoBus and its service layers: Augmenting the internet with higher-level information management protocols. In Springer eBooks (pp. 213–230). https://doi.org/10.1007/bfb0052526.
7. Fries, Martin; P. Paal, Boris. 2019. Smart Contracts in German. Mohr Siebeck. ISBN 978-3-16-156911-1. JSTOR j.ctvn96h9r.
8. Tapscott, D. and Tapscott, A. (2016) Blockchain Revolution: How the Technology behind Bitcoin Is Changing Money, Business, and the World. Penguin, New York. https://www.amazon.com/Blockchain-Revolution-Technology.
9. Finley, Klint .2015. The Inventors of the Internet Are Trying to Build a Truly Permanent Web. Wired. ISSN 1078-3148. OCLC 24479723. Archived from the original on 2020-12-15.

Advancement of Intelligent Computational Methods and Technologies (AICMT2023) – Dr. O. P. Verma et al. (eds)

9

Lip-Reading with Speech Emotions

Bhavya Satija[1], Sumanyu Dutta[2], Yash Sethi[3], Puneet Sharma[4]
Department of Computer Science and Engineering, Amity University, Uttar Pradesh, Noida, India

ABSTRACT: Recently, a number of end-to-end based deep learning techniques are presented that perform speech recognition by extracting either video or audio characteristics from input pictures and audio signals. However, there is very little study on complete audiovisual models. This paper, presents a complete audio-visual system with speech emotions based on Bidirectional long short-term memory (Bi-LSTMs). According to what is known, the Grid Corpus and Ravedess's model are the first audio-visual fused with speech emotion models that can detect words and emotions on a sizable dataset that is available to the public while also simultaneously learning to extract the features directly from the image pixels and audio waveforms. The proposed model consists of dual streams that each extract features from raw waveforms and mouth areas, one for each modality. Every stream or mode's temporal dynamics are described by a 2-layer Bi-LSTM, and multiple streams or modes are fused using a second 2-layer Bi-LSTM.

KEYWORDS: Convolutional neural network (CNN), Speech emotions, Long short-term memory (LSTM), Support vector machine (SVM), Multilayer perceptron classifier (MLP)

1. Introduction

Over the last few years, technology inside the subject of pc imaginative and prescient has significantly superior. The process of transcribing spoken language into written text is commonly referred to as speech recognition or speech-to-text. Basic speech recognition software has a limited vocabulary and can only identify words and phrases that are pronounced extremely clearly. The existing work review of chosen topics in audio-visual (AV) speech perception by Jordan et al. 2000. investigates the impact that visible articulatory information has on what is perceived to be heard. The integration of lip-reading based on image processing techniques is employed in audio-visual speech recognition to enhance speech recognition system in detecting nondeterministic phonemes or giving precedence to judgments with a high degree of probability. The goal of this technology is to improve the accuracy of speech recognition systems. To aid in the detection of acoustically indeterminate phonemes or to prioritise judgements with a high degree of likelihood, audio visual speech recognition makes use of image processing expertise in lip reading. A concept conceived by Petridis et al. 2020. at the feature fusion step, the results from both the speech recognition and lip-reading systems are integrated. It has two parts, as the name suggests. There is the auditory component first, followed by the visual. In the audio section, feature vectors are derived from raw audio samples using extracted properties such log Mel spectrogram, MFCC, etc. In order to condense an image into a feature vector, a convolutional neural network is often employed for the visual part. The combined audio and visual vectors are then used to make an educated guess as to the identity of the target. In today's digital environment, learning challenges, vision problems, and physical restrictions are obstacles to success. Therefore, Automatic Speech Recognition (ASR) is very beneficial for students with disabilities in order to improve the present learning approach. Real-time voice recognition has several possible applications. The ASR system enables impaired individuals to use a hands-free device for searching and computing. This system provides them with easier access to computers, can improve their writing skills utilising speech-to-text techniques, and can increase their reading and

[1]bhavyaonline43@gmail.com, [2]sumanyu.dutta1@gmail.com, [3]yashsethi2611@gmail.com, [4]puneetgrandmaster@gmail.com

DOI: 10.1201/9781003487906-9

writing abilities. Automatic speech recognition is utilised widely in voice telephony, medical documentation, and home appliances. Human speech production and perception are bi-model processes that involve the examination of the spoken acoustic signal and the speaker's visual cues. Human Beings can interpret communication by watching the speaker's lips. People have a number of unique ways to communicate their feelings. When considering different topics, pitch shifts are emphasized because spoken emotion does have distinct intensities. Audio visual speech recognition with speech emotions is a rapidly evolving technology that combines speech recognition, computer vision, and emotion detection algorithms to recognize not only what is being said but also how it is being said. There are several uses for this technology, including better speech recognition, improved communication for people with hearing and speech impairments, and more interesting chatbots and virtual assistants. Fundamentally, audiovisual speech recognition with speech emotions recognizes speech and emotions using a combination of audio and video data. The uttered words and any accompanying acoustic characteristics, such as pitch, loudness, and time, make up the audio data. Facial movements are part of the video data and can reveal more about the speaker's emotional state. The system can better grasp the speaker's objectives and emotional state by merging these two kinds of information. The main applications of audio-visual speech recognition with emotions are improving speech recognition accuracy. Traditional speech recognition systems can struggle to recognize speech accurately in noisy or challenging environments. By incorporating visual information, such as lip movements, audio visual speech recognition with emotions can provide additional context and help to disambiguate ambiguous sounds. This can lead to more accurate speech recognition and better overall performance in challenging conditions. If the audio signal degrades, the system will switch to the visual mode. This study computes visual speech characteristics in a spatio-temporal domain that captures visual feature mobility and appearance. The co-occurrence matrix distinguishes lip movements. Illumination-invariant grayscale image attributes are generated for strong visual qualities. Thus, this study's visual and speech emotions features show frame co-relation, which is excellent for distinguishing word lip motions and emotions.

2. Related Work

Numerous researchers have developed a novel protocol for table-based data access in cloud computing. Xia et al. 2020 demonstrated significant information of visual communication is conveyed by the mobility of the lips, or dynamic characteristic. Dynamic feature extraction and correlation analysis of characteristics are additional crucial components for speech differentiation. Unaddressed by the researchers is the fact that co-relation analysis of visual elements gives discriminating information about the different types of speech. suggested a unique method for predicting residential building load. However, the co-occurrence values of frames have not been taken into account, which is crucial for distinguishing across frames. The Local binary pattern (LBP) and LBP-TOP appearance-based features are sensitive to light and stance. Therefore, these characteristics are not resistant to environmental changes. A very promising approach is the Convolutional Neural Network (CNN) approach for image classification using Long Short-Term Memory (LSTM).

Isobe et al. 2021 presented the input data is video and varying lighting conditions impact various frames, the visual characteristics should be illumination invariant. Numerous studies have employed colour characteristics for Region of Interest (ROI) identification and lip-reading. However, illumination change makes colour-changing characteristics less relevant for visual speech recognition. Occasionally, the colour models are inefficient owing to inadequate light. Variation in light and diverse facial postures complicate the interpretation of facial features. As the movement of the lip provides visual speech information, distinguishing dynamic aspects is vital. A technique for extracting visual speech characteristics utilizing appearance-based features and co-occurrence feature analysis is proposed.

Akçay et al. 2020 state that while neural networks were primarily used in industrial control and robotics in the past, more recent advancements have broadened their applications to include intelligent travel, health monitoring for precision medicine, home appliance automation, virtual online support, e-marketing, weather forecasting, natural disaster management, and other areas, leading to successful implementations in many facets of human life.

Shi et al. 2022 developed a new AVSR model through research which utilizes unsupervised data to outperform the previous state-of-the-art by 50%, even with limited labelled data. The AVSR model incorporates visual input to improve the precision of speech identification in environments with high levels of noise and is founded on the AV-HuBERT method for learning multimodal speech representation. The study emphasizes the integration of AVSR with resource-limited and multilingual settings, with the AV-HuBERT structure being the core of the self-supervised AVSR architecture.

Shi et al. 2022 outlines a novel AV-ASR system that uses a combination of connectionist temporal classification (CTC) and attention neural network architecture. On the Lip-Reading Sentences 3 (LRS3) dataset, this innovative methodology yields the most cutting-edge findings. By using a technique that integrates the encoded video and audio, the system resolves alignment regularization concerns and achieves enhanced performance when subjected to different kinds of noise. The method improves synchronization to make the AV-ASR system more precise and durable, and it works for offline as well as online systems.

Khalil et al. 2019 discussed various strategies that have been proposed in the literature for recognizing emotions in speech signals. These strategies include traditional speech analysis and classification techniques as well as newer deep learning approaches that have been suggested as an alternative. The authors provide an overview of deep learning techniques and review recent research that uses these approaches to identify emotions in speech. The paper examines the databases used in these studies, the emotions that were identified, the contributions of deep learning to speech emotion recognition, and the limitations of this approach.

Xu et al. 2019 propose a Spectral Regression model that combines Extreme Learning Machines (ELMs) and Subspace Learning (SL) to improve Speech Emotion Recognition (SER) by more accurately representing relationships among data using multiple embedded graphs. Their research found that this approach outperformed previous methods that used only ELM or SL techniques.

Huang et al. 2020 created a system for detecting depression in speech that uses a variety of tokens and is designed for use with heterogeneous data. Their hybrid system uses landmarks to extract information specific to individual types of articulation at a time, with LWs and AWs holding different types of information. The hybrid approach allows for the exploitation of various details, including articulatory dysfunction incorporated into conventional acoustic characteristics.

3. Proposed Work

3.1 Dataset

Visual

The dataset utilized in this study is the Grid Corpus dataset, which is a comprehensive audiovisual sentence corpus intended to facilitate joint computational-behavioural research in speech perception. The dataset comprises 34 talkers, including 18 males and 16 females, each of whom spoke 1000 sentences, leading to a total of 34000 numbers of male and female actors, who recite two corresponding statements with a sentence. The audio and video recordings are of high quality and aid in analyzing speech perception. The program is designed to detect and track the movement of a person's lips by utilizing a rectangular box. Once executed, the program will display the detected lip movement which is used to identify the text what a person is trying to speak.

Audio with Emotion

It uses both Grid Corpus and Ravedess dataset. The Ravedess database comprises of 24 skilled performers, consisting of equal neutral North American accent. The speech recordings cover a range of emotions, including calm, happiness, sadness, anger, fear, surprise, and disgust, while the song recordings feature calm, happy, sad, angry, and fearful emotions. Each emotion is recorded at two different levels of intensity - normal and strong - and a neutral expression is also included.

3.2 Pre-processing

Visual

The GRID corpus comprises of 34 participants, with each individual narrating 1000 sentences, resulting in a total of 34,000 videos. Unfortunately, the recordings of speaker 21 are not available, while a few others are either incomplete or corrupted. Therefore, only 32,746 videos can be utilized for analysis. To evaluate our model, two male (1 and 2) and two female (20 and 22) speakers were randomly selected, and withhold their data, resulting in a total of 3971 videos for evaluation. The remaining 28,775 videos are used for training, which includes all the other speakers. Each video is 3 seconds long and has a frame rate of 25fps. The initial stage (ROI) is the extraction of the mouth region of interest. As shown in Fig. 9.1, 80 x 90 fixed bounding boxes with height and breadth of 6 and 8, respectively, are used for all movies because the mouth ROIs are already centred. The frames are then converted to grayscale and adjusted according to the global mean and standard deviation.

Fig. 9.1 Mouth ROI extraction

Source: Filtered image from online dataset

Audio with Emotion

The speech signal undergoes preprocessing before its features are extracted. Preprocessing typically involves several steps, such as removing silent parts, applying pre-emphasis, normalization, and windowing. The removal of silent parts is essential to eliminate portions of the signal that do not contain any useful information. Techniques like zero-crossing rate (ZCR) and short time energy (STE) are commonly used to achieve this. ZCR counts how many times the speech signal crosses the zero-amplitude threshold in a predetermined amount of time. Pre-emphasis is another crucial step, particularly for high-frequency signals, which involves passing the speech signal through a high-pass filter (FIR) to obtain comparable amplitudes for all formants. Normalization adjusts the volume level of the signal to a standard level, typically by dividing the signal sequence by the highest value of the signal. Finally, windowing involves smoothing the edges and reducing the effect of side lobe by dividing the signal into small overlapping time frames, typically with a window time of 25 ms and overlapping every 10 ms.

3.3 Building the Models

Neural networks are defined as a series of layers in Kera's. The Sequential class is used to create a framework for these layers. The first step is to build an instance of the Sequential class, followed by stacking the layers in the desired sequence. The Dense layer is a fully connected layer that often comes before the LSTM stack of layers and produces the output. After building the network, it needs to be compiled, which is a time-saving process that optimizes the sequence of layers into a set of matrix transformations. Before compiling the model, certain parameters like optimizer and error functions need to be specified.

Once the network is trained, it needs to be evaluated on a separate set of training data to predict its performance. The accuracy of prediction is the metric used to evaluate the performance of the built model. Once the performance of the model is evaluated, it can be used to predict the data, and the output format will be the same as specified by the output layer.

The last step involves saving the model in the h5 format and generating plots to visualize the results and accuracy.

4. Implementation

First, the Grid Corpus dataset is obtained from a publicly available source. Before partitioning the video dataset into training and testing data, various pre-processing techniques such as filtering, shrinking frames, and normalizing data are applied. Many machines learning models, including MFCC and Bi-LSTM, were trained on the processed data. Characteristics are directly generated from the audio and image waveforms used as original input. A residual network that learns to automatically extract important features from unprocessed data and a two-layer Bi-LSTM that replicates the temporal dynamics of those features within each stream make up each stream. Finally, two Bi-LSTM layers are utilized on top of two streams to combine the information from the visual and audio streams which can be seen in Fig. 9.2.

The visual stream starts with a spatiotemporal convolution, then moves towards a 2-layer Bi-LSTM a 34-layer ResNet. Although recurrent networks can be employed for the back-end, the spatiotemporal convolution operation remains effective in capturing short-term fluctuations in the mouth area. The first layer in this system, a convolutional layer with 64 3D kernels, is used to carry out this procedure. Batch normalization and corrected linear units are the next two layers. The spatial dimensionality of the ResNet is gradually reduced until it produces a one-dimensional tensor for each time step. It is important to note that because pre-trained models are tuned for entirely different tasks, we did not employ them. Finally, a 2-layer Bi-LSTM with 512 cells within every layer is fed the output of ResNet-34.

An 18-layer ResNet and two Bi-LSTM layers are combined to process the audio stream. The audio waveform is a 1D signal, hence a spatiotemporal convolution front-end is not required. The ResNet-18 uses 1D kernels rather than 2D kernels for image data, but otherwise adheres to the standard design. To obtain fine-scale spectral information, the first convolutional layer employs a temporal kernel of 5 ms and a stride of 0.25 ms. The ResNet output is split into 29 frames, or windows, using average pooling to maintain a constant frame rate throughout the video.

To jointly capture the temporal dynamics of the audio and visual streams, the Bi-LSTM outputs of each stream are merged by concatenating them and passing them through a 2-layer Bi-LSTM. The resulting output is fed into a SoftMax layer that classifies each frame, and the sequence with the highest average probability is labelled.

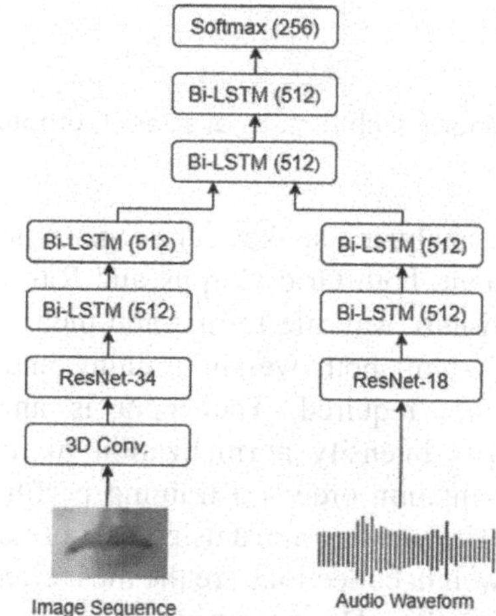

Fig. 9.2 General architecture of audio-visual model

Source: Author

The AV network is trained twice: once for each audio and video stream separately, and once for the entire network. Video sequences with mouth regions of interest (ROIs) are used for data augmentation during training. This is accomplished by randomly trimming and flipping each frame's horizontal orientation inside a video clip. Data augmentation can also be used in audio sequences. Clean audio is used in the original source sample to instruct the system. Each stream receives first instruction on its own.

SingleStreamTraining: A temporal convolutional backend is utilised in place of the standard 2-layer Bi-LSTM as a first step. A ResNet combined with temporal con-volution is trained until the validation set classification rate stops increasing (usually after 5 epochs of training). Then, detach the temporal convolutional backend and connect the Bi-LSTM backend. After each stream's ResNet and 2-layer Bi-LSTM have been individually pretrained, both individual streams are joined for end-to-end training. The Adam training method is used for full-sequence training, with an early learning rate of 0.0001 and a mini-batch size of 36 sequences. A five-epoch delay was also applied for early termination.

AudioVisual Training: The streams are used to first populate the multi-stream architecture with the appropriate streams once each stream has been trained separately. The individual Bi-LSTM outputs are then combined by building a 2-layer Bi-LSTM on top of each stream. It returns the anticipated result at the end of the sequence.

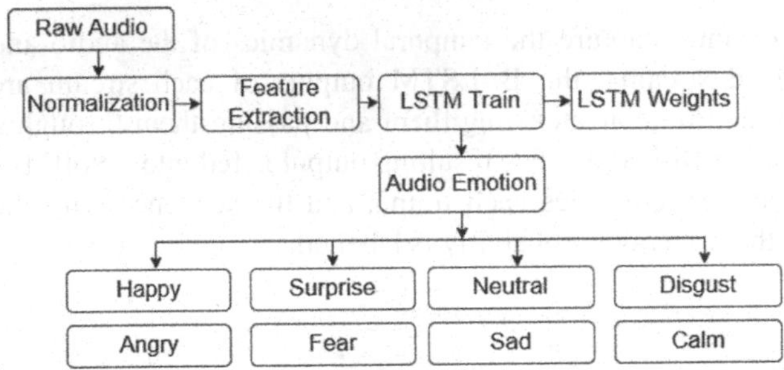

Fig. 9.3 General architecture of speech emotion model

Source: Author

In Fig. 9.3, for analyzing spoken language to determine the emotional content, both Grid Corpus and Ravedess dataset were converted into .wav file format and then were trained. To train the system, both weight training and expression labeling data are required. The input is an audio file, which undergoes intensity normalization to minimize the impact of presentation order on training performance. The Convolutional Network is trained using the normalized audio. The resulting weight collections are the most effective for use with the learning data. During testing, the system uses pitch and energy data from the dataset and learns from the final network weights to identify the corresponding emotion. Each of the eight expressions that make the result is represented as a numerical value in the output. Based on the individual's bpm value, eight emotions- calm, happiness, sadness, anger, fear, surprise, neutral and disgust are identified. The Adam training method is used for full-sequence training, with an early learning rate of 0.0001 and a batch size of 32 sequences. A two-epoch delay was also applied for early termination.

5. Result Analysis

The training and validation accuracy results have been computed and presented in the following manner. The training accuracy indicates the performance of the network during each epoch of the training process, which was set to 200 epochs for Audiovisual part and 100 epochs for emotions in this study. The training accuracy is represented by a blue line in the graph, with the x-axis showing the epoch number and the y-axis indicating the accuracy score, where 1 represents the highest accuracy and 0 indicates the need for improvement. On the other hand, the validation accuracy represents the model's ability to predict the output for a given input, as measured using the validation set. To ensure that the same set of images is not used for both training and validation, the data is shuffled before splitting it into training and validation datasets. This approach helps to improve the accuracy of the model with each training iteration.

When compare among in comparison to CNN, LSTM demonstrates marginally high-er accuracy and all other models like SVM and MLP Classifier. In general, the LSTM model outperforms other models due to its higher accuracy in the initial iterations.

The outcomes below are the output of executing multiple models:

5.1 Audio Visual Model

Based on the experimentation results depicted in Fig. 9.4, the Audiovisual network demonstrated a consistent accuracy of 85% throughout the training process. The training time for each epoch was 3-4 minutes.

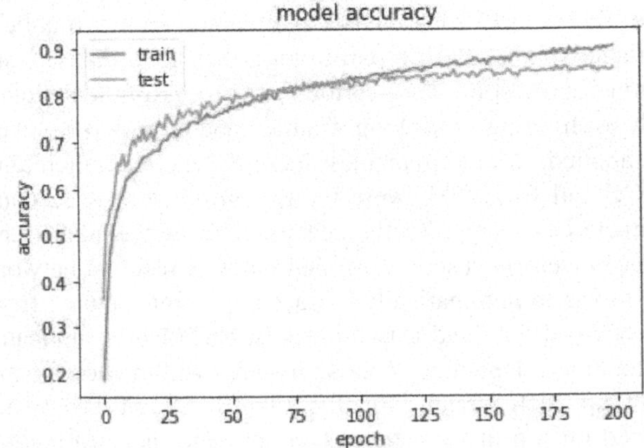

Fig. 9.4 Total accuracy vs total validation accuracy (A + V)

Source: Author

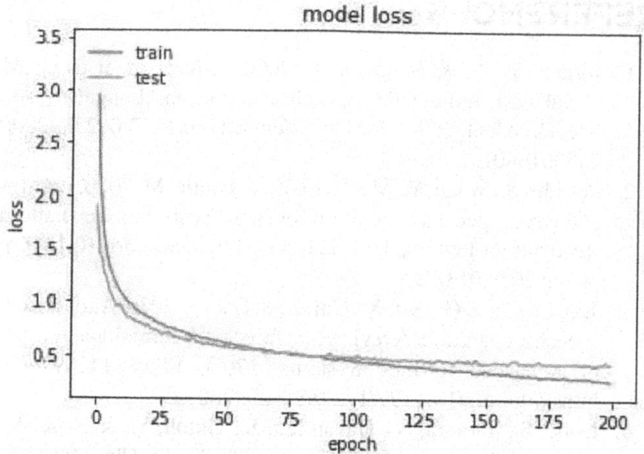

Fig. 9.5 Total loss vs total validation loss (A + V)

Source: Author

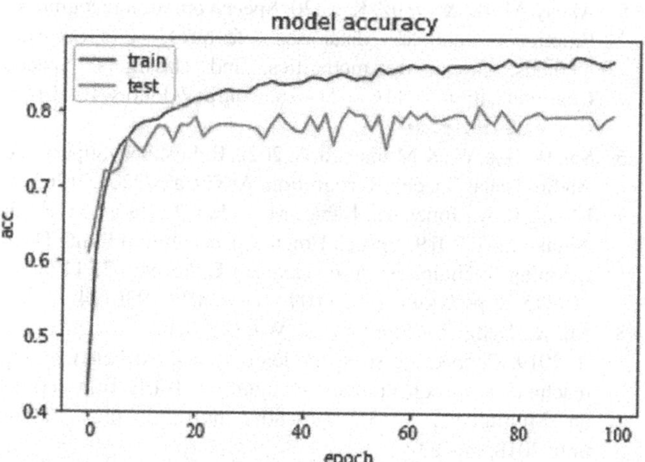

Fig. 9.6 Total Accuracy vs Total Validation Accuracy (MLP Classifier)

Source: Author

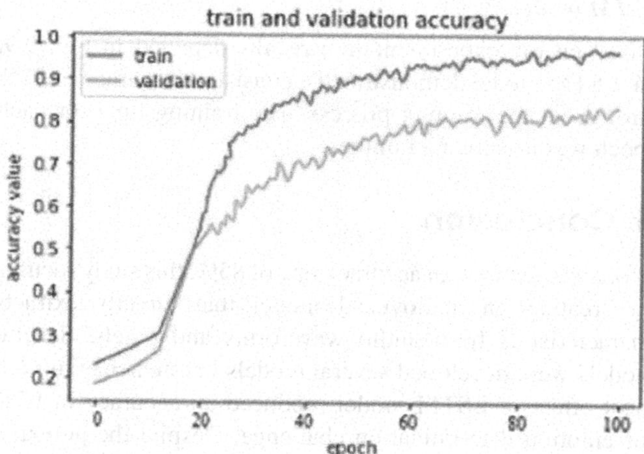

Fig. 9.7 Total accuracy vs total validation accuracy (SVM)

Source: Author

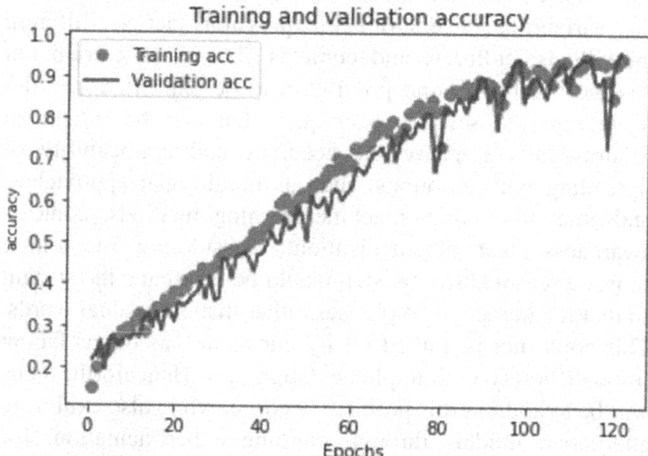

Fig. 9.8 Total accuracy vs total validation accuracy (CNN)

Source: Author

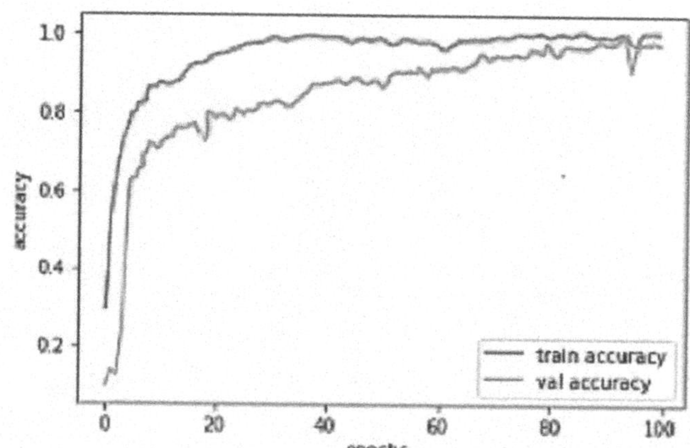

Fig. 9.9 Total accuracy vs total validation accuracy (LSTM)

Source: Author

5.2 Speech Emotion Models

MLP Classifier model

Based on the experimentation results depicted in Fig. 9.6, the MLP Classifier model demonstrated a consistent accuracy of 79% throughout the training pro-cess. The training time for each epoch was less than 2 minutes.

SVM model

Based on the experimentation results depicted in Fig. 9.7, the SVM model demonstrated a consistent accuracy of 83% throughout the training process. The training time for each epoch was less than 2 minutes.

CNN model

Based on the experimentation results depicted in Fig. 9.8, the CNN model demonstrated a consistent accuracy of 95% throughout the training process. The training time for each epoch was less than 1 minute.

LSTM model

Based on the experimentation results depicted in Fig. 9.9, the LSTM model demonstrated a consistent accuracy of 97% throughout the training process. The training time for each epoch was less than 2 minutes.

6. Conclusion

In order to achieve an accuracy rate of 85%, this study focuses on creating an audiovisual model that directly extracts characteristics from audio waveforms and pixels. Several models were developed several models before achieving our most effective LSTM model produced an accuracy of 97% for emotion discrimination challenge. Despite the potential benefits of lipreading with emotions, there are still significant hurdles that needs to be overcome for this technology to become widely adopted. One of the main challenges that has been faced, and should be addressed in the future, is the variability of emotional expressions across different individuals, cultures, and contexts. The work carried out has the bandwidth and possibility to be expanded in order to incorporate several techniques that can be integrated to drastically improve the accuracy and applicability of lipreading with emotions, such as multimodal approaches, real-time processing, machine learning methods, context-awareness, and personalization. Considering the future scope, a reasonable next step would be to expand the system so that it can recognize phrases rather than individual words. This could not be pulled off by our model, as it was facing some difficulty with implementation part. Henceforth, focus will be to address this problem head-on, while also exploring alternative models through ongoing experimentation. for lipreading with speech emotions to deliver effective results.

REFERENCES

1. Jordan, T. R., & Sergeant, P. 2000. Effects of distance on visual and audiovisual speech recognition. Language and Speech, 43(1), 107–124. https://doi.org/10.1177/00238309000430010401.
2. Petridis, S., Wang, Y., Ma, P., Li, Z., & Pantic, M. 2020. End-to-end visual speech recognition for small-scale datasets. Pattern Recognition Letters, 131, 421–427. https://doi.org/10.1016/j.patrec.2020.01.022.
3. Xia, L., Chen, G., Xu, X., Cui, J., & Gao, Y. 2020. Audiovisual speech recognition: A review and forecast. International Journal of Advanced Robotic Systems, 17(6), 172988142097608. https://doi.org/10.1177/1729881420976082.
4. Isobe, S., Tamura, S., Hayamizu, S., Gotoh, Y., & Nose, M. 2021. Multi-Angle Lipreading with Angle Classification-Based Feature Extraction and Its Application to Audio-Visual Speech Recognition. Future Internet, 13(7), 182. https://doi.org/10.3390/fi13070182.
5. Akçay, M. B., & Oguz, K. 2020. Speech emotion recognition: Emotional models, databases, features, preprocessing methods, supporting modalities, and classifiers. Speech Communication, 116, 56–76. https://doi.org/10.1016/j.specom.2019.12.001.
6. Shi, B., Hsu, W., & Mohamed, A. 2022. Robust Self-Supervised Audio-Visual Speech Recognition. ArXiv, abs/2201.01763.
7. Khalil, R. A., Jones, E., Babar, M. I., Jan, T., Zafar, M. H., & Alhussain, T. 2019. Speech Emotion Recognition Using Deep Learning Techniques: A review. IEEE Access, 7, 117327–117345. https://doi.org/10.1109/access.2019.2936124.
8. Xu, X., Deng, J., Coutinho, E., Wu, C., Zhao, L., & Schuller, B. 2019. Connecting subspace learning and extreme learning machine in speech emotion recognition. IEEE Transactions on Multimedia, 21(3), 795–808. https://doi.org/10.1109/tmm.2018.2865834.
9. Huang, Z., Epps, J., Joachim, D., & Sethu, V. 2020. Natural language processing methods for acoustic and landmark Event-Based features in Speech-Based Depression Detection. IEEE Journal of Selected Topics in Signal Processing, 14(2), 435–448. https://doi.org/10.1109/jstsp.2019.2949419.project

Advancement of Intelligent Computational Methods and Technologies (AICMT2023) – Dr. O. P. Verma et al. (eds)

10

Review: Machine Learning-Based Network Intrusion Detection System for Enhanced Cyber-security

Preeti Lakhani[1], Bhavya Alankar[2], Syed Shahabuddin Ashraf[3], Suraiya Parveen[4]
Department of Computer Science and Engineering, Jamia Hamdard, New Delhi, India

ABSTRACT: The rapid advancement of technology and communication systems presents new security challenges that require innovative approaches. This article explores the development of algorithms and techniques to prevent network attacks and improve threat detection mechanisms. Cyber-attacks such as DDoS, APT, insider threats, and ransomware pose a significant risk to governments and large enterprises worldwide. Traditional security measures like firewalls and antivirus software have limitations, prompting the need for advanced solutions. To swiftly identify cyberattacks, a network intrusion detection system (NIDS) must be effective. Solutions based on machine learning (ML) offer specialized and flexible methods for managing network security. By utilizing dynamic reconfiguration and AI/ML techniques, ML-based solutions outperform traditional algorithms by promptly responding to suspicious activities. An intrusion detection system's effectiveness is influenced by variables such as abnormality detection, accuracy, speed, false positive/negative rates, and reliability. ML-based solutions, integrated with software-defined controllers, enhance monitoring and security. IDS can be categorized into NIDS and host-based intrusion detection systems (HIDS), utilizing marked preference, anomaly-based, or hybrid detection mechanisms. This article emphasizes the progressions in ML-NIDS systems highlighting their effectiveness in combating modern cyber threats. By embracing these innovative approaches, recent systems can improve their cyber security posture and safeguard critical assets.

KEYWORDS: Network Security, Intrusion Detection System, Machine Learning, Cyber-Security, Threat Detection, Anomaly Detection, Software-Defined Security

1. Introduction

The advancement of technologies and changes in communication systems poses new challenges in terms of security. Various algorithms and techniques have been designed to prevent network attacks. Also, several threat detection mechanisms have been studied and developed rapidly to get rid of different attacks against enterprises that occur frequently nowadays. Recent cyber-attacks include Distributed Denial of Services (DDoS), Advanced Persistent Threats (APT), malicious insiders, and Ransomware software which targets government and large enterprises to impact on a global scale. One common mechanism to protect organizational data from cyber-attack is to deploy a firewall or antivirus but these techniques have limited capabilities. Attackers utilize intelligent mechanisms to increase the scalability of the damage which thereby escalates the need for advanced security solutions that can detect and respond to these attacks timely. An efficient network intrusion detection system (NIDS) needs to be placed to respond to increasing cyber-attacks (Kabir and Hartmann, 2018).

The major objective of NIDS is to detect cyber-attacks quickly. The systems integrated with NIDS are designed to detect any malicious activity as early as possible to reduce the spreading impact of any viruses, worms, and attacks (Khraisat and Alazab, 2021). Due to the growing resilience on software-defined security services in contrast to hardware-oriented approaches, there has been a development of ML-based solutions for security management of networking systems (Chaabouni et al. 2019). The ML-based security solutions provide customized solutions and adapt to

[1]preetilakhani123@gmail.com, [2]bhavya.alankar@gmail.com, [3]shahabash@gmail.com, [4]suraiya@jamiahamdard.ac.in

DOI: 10.1201/9781003487906-10

randomly changing network scenarios. The use of dynamic reconfiguration and AI/ML-based techniques to have a prompt response in case of any suspicious activity results in better performance as compared to traditional algorithms (Ridwan et al. 2021).

The performance of IDS depends upon several factors such as degree of abnormality detection, accuracy, speed, false positive/negative rate, time/space complexity, and reliability. The ML-based solutions are implemented using software-defined controllers to improve monitoring and security. The system is programmed to detect irregular and malevolent activities from intruders. The IDS is categorized as NIDS and HIDS. The NIDS mechanism is implemented by using one of the three detection techniques (Zhou et al. 2020) Malware detection using authentic signature masks, Outlier/anomaly identification and detection and amalgam detection mechanism.

The document is structured into different sections. In Section 2, an overview of the latest research conducted in the domain of NIDS is presented. Section 3 represents a comprehensive discussion and description of ML-based different techniques for intrusion detection. The details of datasets used in previous research are outlined in section 4. In section 5, various performance metrics are mathematically explained in detail. Finally, section 6 completes the article, discussing the key findings and brief contributions.

2. Related Work

The methodologies for ML-based intrusion detection are highlighted in this section. Various state-of-the-art techniques along with their suggested approaches, datasets, and implementation results are given in this section.

A hybrid ML-based intrusion detection technique was proposed in (Rincy and Gupta, 2021) in which a novel hybrid IDS (NIDS) is given to predict vulnerability using CAPPER feature selection. This algorithm uses UNSW-NB15 and NSL-KDD datasets. The authors (Li et al. 2019) carried out a detailed review of techniques for intrusion detection. This algorithm focused on fuzzy logic and ANN using the KDD dataset.

The intrusion detection-based techniques and their description are very well presented by the authors of (Ahmad et al. 2021). A wide variety of ML and DL-based (deep learning) techniques is studied in this article. The methodology, datasets, and performance metrics are tabulated in this work. Spark-Chi-SVM model (Othman et al. 2018) was proposed for ML-based intrusion detection which uses chi2 feature selection matrix using Apache spark data platform. The implementation is carried out over the KDD99 dataset where the results reflect that efficiency is improved and training time is reduced.

Various applications of ML-based intrusion techniques are studied by the authors (Saranya et al. 2020). This research work uses the KDD-CUP dataset using discriminant and classifier regression techniques. A few studied applications are depicted in Fig. 10.1.

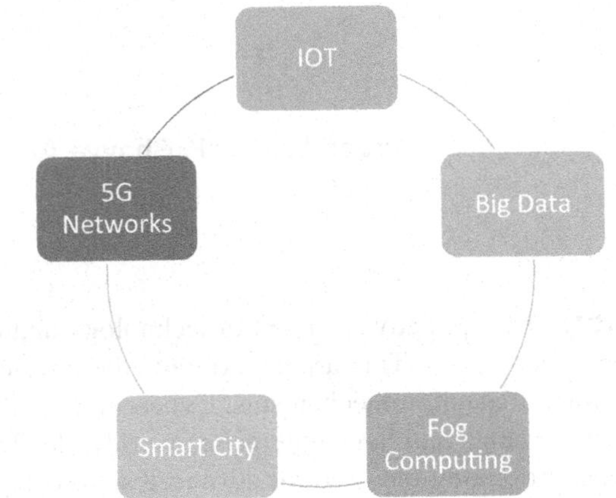

Fig. 10.1 Applications of ML-based intrusion techniques

A comparative analysis is carried out by the author in (Panda and Patra, 2018). The proposed work classifies three basic ML techniques commonly adopted for intrusion detect include ID3, J48, and Naïve Bayes. The KDDCuppsila99 IDS dataset is used. The accuracy and efficiency analysis is carried out in (Das et al. 2020). Different ML algorithms are experimented on UNSW-NB15 dataset along with the impact on different attacks. The findings of the given work indicate that the random forest method has the lowest time complexity and the highest accuracy thus making it a promising solution.

Entropy is calculated using 7 different ML models for the Kyoto dataset (Zaman and Lung, 2018) and the result reflects that the receiver operating performed radial basis function performs better as compared to others. AB-TRAP framework (Bertoli et al. 2021) is given to overcome the limitation of outdated and repetitive datasets. This is a five-step procedure that includes dataset generation, determining outstanding datasets, training, and implementation and performance evaluation.

Big Data-based Hierarchical Deep Learning System (BDHDLS) (Zhong et al. 2020) uses a big data approach to solve the limitation of linear ML models for intrusion detection. It utilizes parallel training and big data techniques for model construction which results in time complexity reduction for multiple simultaneous systems. A Boruta feature selection method is proposed with a random forest ML algorithm (Subbiah et al. 2022) to overcome the issues of inaccuracy and misclassification. Discriminant, classification, and regression tree techniques are used to contrast the performance of the recommended approach.

3. Machine Learning Based Intrusion Detection System Work

Machine learning models are used in every domain to enhance the system's capabilities and to improve performance metrics. Similarly, ML models are used wisely in intrusion detection systems to overcome the shortcomings of traditional detection methods such as lack of flexibility, increase of false detection, unable to handle multi-dimensional data, and lack of accuracy (Timčenko and Gajin, 2018). ML methods utilize data and existing patterns in data to develop intelligent systems which can classify between malicious and trusted traffic (Jain et al. 2022). There are three major techniques of implementation of ML methods that are used for intrusion detection. Figure 10.2 highlights fa ew approaches used in literature adopting one of the three ML techniques.

Supervised ML based IDS	Unsupervised ML based IDS	Semi-Supervised ML based IDS
• C4.5 • k-Nearest Neighbor • multi-layer perceptron • Regularized Discriminant Analysis • Fisher Linear Discriminant • Linear Programming Models and Support Vector Machine	• γ-algorithm • k-Means clustering • Single linkage clustering • quarter-sphere SVM	• Spectral Graph Transducer • Gaussian FieldsApproach • MPCK-means

Fig. 10.2 Example techniques implementing ML-based Intrusion detection system

In supervised ML-based IDS methods the algorithm learns from labeled input data to predict unknown cases. The ML-based classification techniques include SVM and random forest for regression models.

4. Dataset Description

This section includes the description of datasets (Table 10.1) available for design work-based-based. The state of artwork includes several datasets with classified features which may be further studied to implement advanced algorithms.

Table 10.1 Description of various datasets

Dataset	Features	Attack types	Remarks
KDD CUP 99	38 numeric and 3 categorical features	Denial of service (DOS), probing (PROBE), and User to Root (U2R) and Remote to Local (R2L).	This is an old dataset that is not according to the need for wireless communications.
NSL-KDD	41 features	DoS, U2R, R2L and probe	An extension of the KDD CUP 99 dataset. A reasonable size of data can be used for large-scale applications.
ISCX 2012	8 features	Brute force SSH, Infiltrating, HttpDoS, DDoS	The dataset does not contain traces of the wireless network.
UNSW NB 15	45 features	Analysis, backdoor, DoS, exploits, fuzzes, generic, Reconnaissance, shell code	Dataset with a wide range of modern and advanced attack types.
BoT-IoT	38 features	DDoS, DoS, Reconnaissance, theft	The Modern feature set applies to wireless networks.
IoT-DevNet	14 features	Wrong setup, DDoS, Data type probing, scan, MITM	The modern dataset contains modern attack types, applicable for designing IDS for wireless systems.

5. Performance Metrics

Performance evaluation is an important aspect of the validation of any proposed IDS by a researcher. The performance of any IDS depends on the application for which a particular IDS is designed.

Table 10.2 Confusion metrics for ml-based intrusion techniques

		Predicted	
		Positive (Anomaly)	Negative (Normal)
Actual	Positive (Anomaly)	TP	FN
	Negative (Normal)	FP	TN

Hence, in the literature, a number of performance evaluation and comparison metrics are used. Confusion metrics are the most widely used performance evaluation metric. The most popular performance evaluation metrics that are nothing but derived from confusion metrics are FP, FN, TP, and TN given in Table 10.2.

5.1 Accuracy

The performance metric "accuracy" in the context of ML-based NIDS technique refers to the measurement of how well the ML model can categorize network traffic occurrences as either normal or malicious.

As stated in Equation 1, accuracy is calculated by dividing the complete number of instances (both normal and malicious) correctly categorized by the overall dataset. The proportion used to express it ranges from 0% to 100%. The model is more successful at correctly predicting the class labels when the accuracy value is larger.

$$\text{Accuracy} = \frac{TP + TN}{TP + TN + FP + FN} \quad (1)$$

To assess a NIDS performance, accuracy might not be enough on its own. Due to the relative rarity of network intrusion events in comparison to other occurrences, uneven class distributions can produce overestimated accuracy results. Consequently, it is frequently required to take into account other performance parameters.

5.2 Precision

The performance metric "precision" represents the percentage of properly categorized malicious instances out of all instances predicted by the ML model to be malicious in the context of ML-based NIDS techniques.

Equation 2 can be used to calculate precision by dividing the complete number of true positive(TP) predictions (cases that were successfully categorized as malicious) by the sum of TP and FP predictions. The FP are false prediction instances that were wrongly classed as malicious. A greater value represents a higher proportion of accurate predictions for the malicious class, and it is given as a number between 0 and 1.

$$\text{Precision} = \frac{TP}{TP + FP} \quad (2)$$

Precision is a crucial metric in Network Intrusion Detection because it quantifies the reliability of the ML model in correctly identifying malicious instances. It helps to minimize the number of false positives, which are instances wrongly labeled as malicious, reducing unnecessary alarms and improving the overall effectiveness of the system.

5.3 Recall

The "recall" performance statistic, generally referred to as "sensitivity" or "TP rate," figures out what portion of the dataset's actual malicious occurrences are correctly classified as malicious.

Recall is calculated as shown in equation 3 by dividing the complete count of TP predictions (malicious instances correctly categorized) by the aggregate value of TP and FN predictions. Here the FN, false negative are the malicious instances wrongly classed as normal or overlooked by the model. It is stated as a number between 0 and 1, where a greater number denotes a larger percentage of harmful instances that were accurately identified.

$$TPR = \frac{TP}{TP + FN} \quad (3)$$

Recall is an important parameter in network intrusion detection since it measures how well the ML model can identify and capture malicious instances. A high recall value indicates a lower rate of false negatives, meaning the model is effectively detecting a larger proportion of actual malicious instances.

5.4 AURoC

A prominent evaluation metric in Network Intrusion Detection utilizing Machine Learning approaches is the "Area under the Receiver Operating Characteristic curve" (AUC-ROC). It provides a comprehensive assessment of the ML model's ability to differentiate among usual and unusual malicious instances across different classification thresholds.

Plotting the curve between TPR and FPR at various classification thresholds, the ROC curve is a graphical depiction of the performance of the ML model. By computing this area the AUC-ROC metric quantifies the model's overall performance.

A higher AUC-ROC score indicates greater performance; it goes from 0 to 1. AUC-ROC of 0.5 indicates a classifier that performs well when compared with the random chance, whereas AUC-ROC of 1 indicates a flawless classifier that can distinguish between normal and malevolent events.

AUC-ROC offers a more thorough assessment of the ML model's performance in Network Intrusion Detection by taking into account the whole range of potential categorization criteria. The model's capacity to strike a balance between detection accuracy and false alarm rate is revealed by considering both the TPR (sensitivity) and the FPR (1-specificity) simultaneously.

AUC-ROC metric evaluates the "Receiver Operating Characteristic curve" area to determine the overall discriminatory power of the ML model in Network Intrusion Detection. Better performance in terms of accurately differentiating between normal and malicious instances is indicated by a higher AUC-ROC score.

5.5 F-Score

Equation 4 describes the F-score, often known as the F1 score, which combines precision and recall to provide a fair assessment of the effectiveness of the ML model.

The harmonic mean of precision and recall, with equal weights for both measures, is used to produce the F-score. It offers a single value that sums up how well the model performs overall in identifying harmful occurrences while reducing FP and FN.

The F-score is between 0 and 1. A value of 1 represents the ideal performance, while a value of 0 represents the worst. A higher F-score indicates a better balance between precision and recall, meaning the model achieves both high accuracy in detecting malicious instances and low false alarm rates.

$$\text{F-score} = \frac{2 * \text{Precision} * \text{Recall}}{\text{Precision} + \text{Recall}} \quad (4)$$

The F-score is particularly useful when dealing with imbalanced datasets, where the number of normal instances significantly outweighs the number of malicious instances. It helps to overcome the bias that can be introduced by accuracy when the majority class dominates the evaluation.

6. Conclusion

In conclusion, the advancement of technology and the evolving landscape of communication systems have introduced new security challenges, particularly in terms of network attacks. This article has reviewed various algorithms and techniques designed to prevent such attacks and enhance threat detection mechanisms. Cyber-attacks such as DDoS, APT, malicious insiders, and ransomware pose a significant risk to governments and large enterprises on a global scale. Traditional security measures like firewalls and antivirus software have proven insufficient to mitigate these threats.

An effective NIDS is indispensable for addressing these issues since it can quickly identify and respond to cyberattacks. Machine learning (ML)-based solutions have become effective tools for managing network security because they offer tailored and adaptive strategies that can quickly react to changing network conditions. By leveraging dynamic reconfiguration and AI/ML techniques, ML-based solutions outperform traditional algorithms, enabling more accurate and timely detection of suspicious activities.

An intrusion detection system's performance relies on various factors, including abnormality detection, accuracy, speed, false positive/negative rates, and reliability. ML-based solutions, integrated with software-defined controllers, enhance monitoring and security capabilities. IDS can be categorized into NIDS and HIDS.

The review highlights the evolutiont in ML-based NIDS, emphasizing their effectiveness in combating modern cyber threats. By embracing these innovative approaches, organizations can enhance their cybersecurity posture and protect critical assets. However, further research is needed to address challenges such as scalability, real-time detection, and the ability to handle sophisticated attacks. Overall, ML-based NIDS holds great potential to mitigate the impact of cyber-attacks and safeguard network infrastructure in today's dynamic and evolving threat landscape.

REFERENCES

1. Kabir, M. Firoz, and Sven Hartmann. 2018. "Cyber security challenges: An efficient intrusion detection system design." In *2018 International Young Engineers Forum (YEF-ECE)*, pp. 19–24. IEEE.
6. Wong, Kevin, Craig Dillabaugh, Nabil Seddigh, and Biswajit Nandy. 2017. "Enhancing Suricata intrusion detection system for cyber security in SCADA networks." In *2017 IEEE 30th Canadian Conference on Electrical and Computer Engineering (CCECE)*, pp. 1–5. IEEE.
7. Khraisat, Ansam, and Ammar Alazab. 2021. "A critical review of intrusion detection systems in the internet of things: techniques, deployment strategy, validation strategy, attacks, public datasets and challenges." *Cybersecurity* 4: 1–27.
8. Kumar, Deepak, and Jawahar Thakur. 2022. "Handling Security Issues in Software-defined Networks (SDNs) Using Machine Learning." In *Computational Vision and Bio-Inspired Computing: Proceedings of ICCVBIC 2021*, pp. 263–277. Singapore: Springer Singapore.
9. Chaabouni, Nadia, Mohamed Mosbah, Akka Zemmari, Cyrille Sauvignac, and Parvez Faruki. 2019. "Network intrusion detection for IoT security based on learning techniques." *IEEE Communications Surveys & Tutorials* 21, no. 3: 2671–2701.
10. Ridwan, Mohammad Azmi, Nurul Asyikin Mohamed Radzi, Fairuz Abdullah, and Y. E. Jalil. 2021. "Applications of machine learning in networking: a survey of current issues and future challenges." *IEEE access* 9: 52523–52556.
11. Yao, Haipeng, Danyang Fu, Peiying Zhang, Maozhen Li, and Yunjie Liu. 2018. "MSML: A novel multilevel semi-supervised machine learning framework for intrusion detection system." *IEEE Internet of Things Journal* 6, no. 2: 1949–1959.
12. Al-Jarrah, Omar Y., Yousof Al-Hammdi, Paul D. Yoo, Sami Muhaidat, and Mahmoud Al-Qutayri. 2018. "Semi-supervised multi-layered clustering model for intrusion detection." *Digital Communications and Networks* 4, no. 4: 277–286.
13. Zhou, Yuyang, Guang Cheng, Shanqing Jiang, and Mian

Dai. 2020. "Building an efficient intrusion detection system based on feature selection and ensemble classifier." *Computer networks* 174: 107247.

14. Rincy N, Thomas, and Roopam Gupta. 2021. "Design and development of an efficient network intrusion detection system using machine learning techniques." *Wireless Communications and Mobile Computing* 2021: 1–35.
15. Li, Jie, Yanpeng Qu, Fei Chao, Hubert PH Shum, Edmond SL Ho, and Longzhi Yang. 2019. "Machine learning algorithms for network intrusion detection." *AI in Cybersecurity*: 151–179.
16. Ahmad, Zeeshan, Adnan Shahid Khan, Cheah Wai Shiang, Johari Abdullah, and Farhan Ahmad. 2021. "Network intrusion detection system: A systematic study of machine learning and deep learning approaches." *Transactions on Emerging Telecommunications Technologies* 32, no. 1: e4150.
17. Othman, Suad Mohammed, Fadl Mutaher Ba-Alwi, Nabeel T. Alsohybe, and Amal Y. Al-Hashida. 2018. "Intrusion detection model using machine learning algorithm on Big Data environment." *Journal of big data* 5, no. 1: 1–12.
18. Saranya, T., S. Sridevi, C. Deisy, Tran Duc Chung, and MKA Ahamed Khan. 2020. "Performance analysis of machine learning algorithms in intrusion detection system: A review." *Procedia Computer Science* 171: 1251–1260.
19. Panda, Mrutyunjaya, and Manas Ranjan Patra. 2008. "A comparative study of data mining algorithms for network intrusion detection." In *2008 First International Conference on Emerging Trends in Engineering and Technology*, pp. 504–507. IEEE.
20. Das, Anurag, Samuel A. Ajila, and Chung-Horng Lung. 2020. "A comprehensive analysis of accuracies of machine learning algorithms for network intrusion detection." In *Machine Learning for Networking: Second IFIP TC 6 International Conference, MLN 2019, Paris, France, December 3–5, 2019, Revised Selected Papers 2*, pp. 40-57. Springer International Publishing.
21. Zaman, Marzia, and Chung-Horng Lung. 2018. "Evaluation of machine learning techniques for network intrusion detection." In *NOMS 2018-2018 IEEE/IFIP Network Operations and Management Symposium*, pp. 1–5. IEEE.
22. Bertoli, Gustavo De Carvalho, Lourenço Alves Pereira Júnior, Osamu Saotome, Aldri L. Dos Santos, Filipe Alves Neto Verri, Cesar Augusto Cavalheiro Marcondes, Sidnei Barbieri, Moises S. Rodrigues, and José M. Parente De Oliveira. 2021. "An end-to-end framework for machine learning-based network intrusion detection system." *IEEE Access* 9: 106790–106805.
23. Zhong, Wei, Ning Yu, and Chunyu Ai. 2020. "Applying big data based deep learning system to intrusion detection." *Big Data Mining and Analytics* 3, no. 3: 181–195.
24. Subbiah, Sridevi, Kalaiarasi Sonai Muthu Anbananthen, Saranya Thangaraj, Subarmaniam Kannan, and Deisy Chelliah. 2022. "Intrusion detection technique in wireless sensor network using grid search random forest with Boruta feature selection algorithm." *Journal of Communications and Networks* 24, no. 2: 264–273.
25. Timčenko, Valentina, and Slavko Gajin. 2018. "Machine learning based network anomaly detection for IoT environments." In *ICIST-2018 conference*.
26. Jain, Khushboo, Akansha Singh, Poonam Singh, and Sanjana Yadav. 2022. "An improved supervised classification algorithm in healthcare diagnostics for predicting opioid habit disorder." *International Journal of Reliable and Quality E-Healthcare (IJRQEH)* 11, no. 1: 1–16.
27. Jain, Khushboo, Manali Gupta, Surabhi Patel, and Ajith Abraham. 2022. "Object Classification Using ECOC Multi-class SVM and HOG Characteristics." In *International Conference on Intelligent Systems Design and Applications*, pp. 23–33. Cham: Springer Nature Switzerland.
28. Jain, Khushboo, Manali Gupta, and Ajith Abraham. 2021. "A review on privacy and security assessment of cloud computing." *J. Inf. Assur. Secur* 16: 161–168.
29. Jain, Khushboo, Arun Agarwal, Ashima Jain, and Ajith Abraham. 2022. "A Multi-layer Deep Learning Model for ECG-Based Arrhythmia Classification." In *International Conference on Intelligent Systems Design and Applications*, pp. 44–52. Cham: Springer Nature Switzerland.
30. Raghuvanshi, Kamlesh Kumar, Arun Agarwal, Khushboo Jain, and V. B. Singh. 2022. "A generalized prediction model for improving software reliability using time-series modelling." *International Journal of System Assurance Engineering and Management* 13, no. 3: 1309–1320.
31. Jain, Khushboo, and Anoop Kumar. 2021. "ST-DAM: exploiting spatial and temporal correlation for energy-efficient data aggregation method in heterogeneous WSN." *International Journal of Wireless and Mobile Computing* 21, no. 3: 285–294.
32. Sarath Kumar, R., P. Sampath, and M. Ramkumar. 2023. "Enhanced Elman Spike Neural Network fostered intrusion detection framework for securing wireless sensor network." *Peer-to-Peer Networking and Applications*: 1–15.
33. Bahloul, Issam, Monia Bouzid, and Sejir Khojet El Khil. 2022. "Intelligent ITSC Fault Detection in PMSG Using the Machine Learning Technique." In *International Conference on Artificial Intelligence: Theories and Applications*, pp. 186–201. Cham: Springer Nature Switzerland.
34. Huy, Vo Trong Quang, and Chih-Min Lin. 2023. "An Improved Densenet Deep Neural Network Model for Tuberculosis Detection Using Chest X-Ray Images." *IEEE Access*.

Note: All the figures and tables in this chapter were made by the author.

Advancement of Intelligent Computational Methods and Technologies (AICMT2023) – Dr. O. P. Verma et al. (eds)

11

Bank Loan Approval Repayment Prediction System Using Machine Learning Models

Muskan Bali[1], Vansh Mehta[2], Anshul Bhatia[3], Nidhi Malik[4], Komal Jindal[5]
Department of Computer Science and Engineering, The NorthCap University, Gurugram, Haryana, India

ABSTRACT: The Bank Loan Approval Repayment Prediction System has been formulated to help financial institutions such as banks to predict the odds of loan repayment by analyzing historical loan data and making informed decisions. The system employs machine learning (ML) algorithms to analyze various parameters, such as credit score, income, credit status, and loan amount, to make accurate predictions. By analyzing this data, the system comes up with a comprehensive risk assessment for the financial institutions that assists in making informed loan giving decision making. This system could prove to be a vital tool for banks and other institutions carrying forward financial decision making in reducing risks and increasing profits alongside ensuring that loans are received by the re-payers well within their limits of repayment. ML algorithms like Random Forest, Decision Tree, XGBoost, and Logistic Regression were put into use for prediction. Results show that Random Forest is the most accurate amongst all the algorithms used for prediction with an accuracy of 95%.

KEYWORDS: Bank loan repayment prediction, Credit risk modelling, Default risk assessment, Loan delinquency, Probability of default, Machine learning

1. Introduction

Bank loan repayment forecasting is of one the of upmost importance area of research in the banking industry. Precisely predicting loan repayment helps banks to combat their risk and ensure the feasibility of their lending operations. Initially, banks have mostly relied only on credit scores and financial statements to predict loan defaulters. Nonetheless, now these methods have limitations, such as being backward-looking and not considering contextual factors that also determine their repayment behavior. Because of the continuous improvements in machine learning (ML) algorithms related researches, the development of a more accurate and dependable loan repayment prediction models has been made possible. Online behavior and social media interactions are now-a-days are being used as non-financial data in addition to considering a broad range of attributes due to the capabilities of the models for rate predictions. By using ML algorithms in loan defaulter forecasting, there is a possibility of improving the accuracy of loan approval process and the results it portrays. Studies have been conducted on the use of ML algorithms for loan defaulter predictions. For instance, a model based on a Logistic Regression (LR) model was developed by (Sheikh et al., 2020)to predict loan default, achieving an accuracy above 81.1%. Meanwhile, (Khan et al., 2021) put use the Random Forest (RF), LR and Decision Tree algorithm to predict loan default risk, obtaining the highest accuracy of 93.68% with Random Forest. In this paper, we aim to scout the use of ML algorithms for bank loan repayment prediction. Particularly, we will compare the performance of several popular algorithms, including XGBoost, RF, LR and Decision Tree. We will utilize the dataset of loan applications and repayment histories obtained to develop and assess the models. The results of this research have the potential to guide the formation of loan repayment prediction models that are more reliable and precise for financial institutions like banks.

2. Literature Survey

In the recent past, there has been a remarkable surge in the usage of ML techniques to predict loan repayment rates.

[1]muskan20csu174@ncuindia.edu, [2]vansh20csu177@ncuindia.edu, [3]anshulbhatia@ncuindia.edu, [4]nidhimalik@ncuindia.edu, [5]komaljindal@ncuindia.edu

DOI: 10.1201/9781003487906-11

Some of such studies are explained after. (Wei Li et al., 2018) proposed a different ML approach to detect loan defaulter by taking into consideration the data obtained from a Chinese peer-to-peer lending platform. The potency of algorithms such as XGBoost, LR and deep neural network was taken into consideration by authors using the feature engineering applied to extract relevant features from raw data. Furthermore, the research led by (Trivedi, 2020)explored the impact of feature selection on ML-based credit scoring prediction. The authors also analyzed the effect of different feature selection methods on the algorithms' effectiveness. Performances of several algorithms including naïve bayes, decision tree, RF, and SVM were compared and analyzed.

Different feature selection methods were also applied and assessed on the basis of the effectiveness of the algorithms by the authors. In the study, (Guerra et al., 2021) puts forward a big review for ML algorithms utilized for loan defaulter forecasting. The authors reviewed the benefits and disadvantages of various techniques such as decision tree, RF, SVM, and neural network. The challenges and future directions of research in this field were also discussed. Further, (Yang et al., 2021)employed a variety of ML techniques such a neural networks, Ridge Regression Models and Lasso Logistic Models to speculate the repayment rates for loans being given to small and medium-sized businesses (SMEs) in China. In accordance with their findings, the Lasso Logistic Model came out to be the most effective, with an accuracy rate of 96.5%, clearly above the other algorithms. Similarly, (Chen et al., 2021)et al. used the under sampling and cost sensitive algorithm to tackle the problem of an imbalanced data in Peer-to-Peer landing-based loan defaulter prediction. The authors analyzed the effectiveness of their approach against other different ML techniques, that included LR, RF and neural networks. Afterwards, (Lappas et al., 2021) proposed a novel ML framework that combines feature engineering, feature selection, optimization algorithms and ensemble learning for credit risk assessment. Further(Aditya Sai Srinivas et al., 2022), [3] applied LR, k-Nearest Neighbor, SVM and decision tree algorithms to predict loan defaulters. According to their predictions, the SVM exhibited a far better F1-Score of 90% in comparison to the other algorithms.

Subsequently, (Baodong Li, 2022)employed a Back propagation Neural Network (BPNN) model to predict the repayment rates of loans defaulters. The BPNN model was successful in obtaining an accuracy rate of 98%.

In conclusion, the unidentified potential of ML techniques in predicting loan repayment rates and defaulter identification came into light because of these studies. Moreover, model performance and interpretability can be made superior, and further research can help to resolve these issues.

3. Materials and Methods

This section identifies the methods and materials used in the current study.

3.1 Materials

A dataset that contains many different borrower and loan characteristics was employed by us from Kaggle, termed as BANK LOAN STATUS (ZAUR BEGIEV, 2020)in our study The Table 1 shows the attribute description of BANK LOAN STATUS Dataset. This analysis was enforced by using Python, generally used programming language for ML and data science. We used different Python libraries, such as scikit-learn for ML algorithms, pandas for data manipulation, and libraries like Matplotlib for data visualization. Jupyter Notebook, an interactive development environment, was employed for data analysis and report generation.

Table 11.1 Description of dataset

Attributes	Symbolizes
Loan ID	Application ID of Customer
Customer ID	Customer's Bank Id
Current Loan Amount	Loan Amount Undertaken by the Customer
Term	Loan Applied Whether for Short Term or Long Term
Credit Score	Determines the Paying Back Credibility of a Customer.
Annual Income	Depicts the Annual Income of the Applicant.
Years Spent in Present Job	Number of Years Spent in Recent Job
Home Ownership	Who has the Ownership of the House Resided by the Applicant
Purpose	Purpose of Loan
Tax Liens	If Any Tax Lien Issued
Monthly Debt	Monthly Debt of the Customer
Years of Credit History	For How Many Years the Applicant Has Been Using Credit.
Months since last delinquent	Last Time When the Applicant Was Unable to Make the Installment.
Number of Open Accounts	Number of Open Bank Accounts
Number of Credit Problems	If Faced Any Credit Problem in the Past
Current Credit Balance	Current Credit Balance that Needs to be Settled
Maximum Open Credit	Maximum Balance of The Credit of the Applicant
Bankruptcies	If Filed for Any Bankruptcy Over the Years

3.2 Methods

Data cleaning and pre-processing: To ensure the model's accuracy is not negatively impacted, any discrepancies, missing data, or outliers in the dataset must be removed. Missing value treatment has also been performed. Additionally, the dataset needs to be partitioned into training and testing sets to evaluate the model's effectiveness.

Feature Engineering: Here in feature selection, one chooses the most significant variables from the dataset that will be used to train the model. These variables could comprise the borrower's credit history, income, employment status, and loan amount, among others. In this study, Information Gain based feature selection has been done. After applying feature selection technique, we have obtained 16 best features out of 18.

Dataset Balancing: The dataset was imbalanced as in target variable 'Loan Status' there were 77361 samples of Fully Charged and 22369 samples of Charged off class. Therefore, we have applied Random Oversampling to balance the dataset and we have obtained 77361 samples in both the classes in modified dataset.

Model Selection: Various ML algorithms, including decision trees, logistic regression, random forest, and XGBoost Classifier, can be utilized on the pre- processed data to create a prediction model. The model's efficiency on the testing set should be used to determine which algorithm to choose.

Logistic Regression: It is a statistical method used to perform binary classification, which involves predicting the likelihood of an event taking place or not. When it comes to predicting bank loan repayment, logistic regression can be utilized to determine whether a borrower will repay the loan based on various input features, such as credit score, income, and employment status.

Random Forest: The random forest algorithm is a predictive modelling technique used in ML. It uses several decision trees to enhance prediction accuracy. In terms of bank loan repayment prediction, the procedure involves use of processed input features to predict whether the borrower will default on their loan or not. The features are borrower's credit score, income, and employment status.

Decision Tree: It is also another form of ML algorithm utilized in predictive modelling. It uses a tree-like structure to formulate decisions and its probable outcomes. In terms of bank loan repayment prediction, the procedure involves use of processed input features to predict whether the borrower will default on their loan or not. The features are borrower's credit score, income, and employment status.

XGBoost: Extreme Gradient Boosting, a forecasting technique forms a part of Machine Learning. It is an upgradation of the gradient boosting. In terms of bank loan repayment prediction, the procedure involves use of processed input features to predict whether the borrower will default on their loan or not. The features are borrower's credit score, income, and employment status.

Model Evaluation: To analyze the influence of our model in foreseeing loan approval predictions, its performance is measured by various metrics such as the F-1 Score, precision, recall, and accuracy. These metrics help in identifying how well our model is performing and the outcomes it is generating.

Interpretation of the model: The interpretation of the forecasting model is important for identifying the most crucial features and their effect on the created model's prediction. This information can be beneficial for banking professionals to make informed judgements when evaluating the loan applicants.

4. Proposed Approach

After providing an overview of the preparation phase, we present a detailed explanation of our proposed approach through a block diagram in Fig. 11.1. Initially, our dataset was in a raw form, and it contained inconsistencies and noise that needed cleaning. To achieve our objective of minimizing class-label noise in the Train Set, we divided the dataset into two subsets, Train Set and Test Set, in a 70:30 ratio. We performed various data wrangling activities, such as data exploration, validation, and enrichment, and we cleaned the data by removing outliers and filling missing values. The modified Train Set with minimized noise class labels was then used to build a prediction model, including XGBoost, Random Forest, decision tree, and logistic regression models. We selected the model with the highest accuracy for further predictions. The performance of each model was evaluated by testing them on the Test Set. We aimed to obtain the most accurate predictions possible.

5. Results

The results for bank loan repayment prediction system using random forest, decision tree, logistic regression, and XGBoost classifier with percentages might look something like the Table 11.2. In Table 11.2, each row represents one of the four algorithms being compared, and each column represents a performance metric.

The percentages in each cell represent the value of the corresponding metric for that algorithm. Table 11.2 presents the performance metrics of four different algorithms applied to the dataset. Based on the above table, it is observed that usage of Random Forest algorithm, accuracy level, precision,

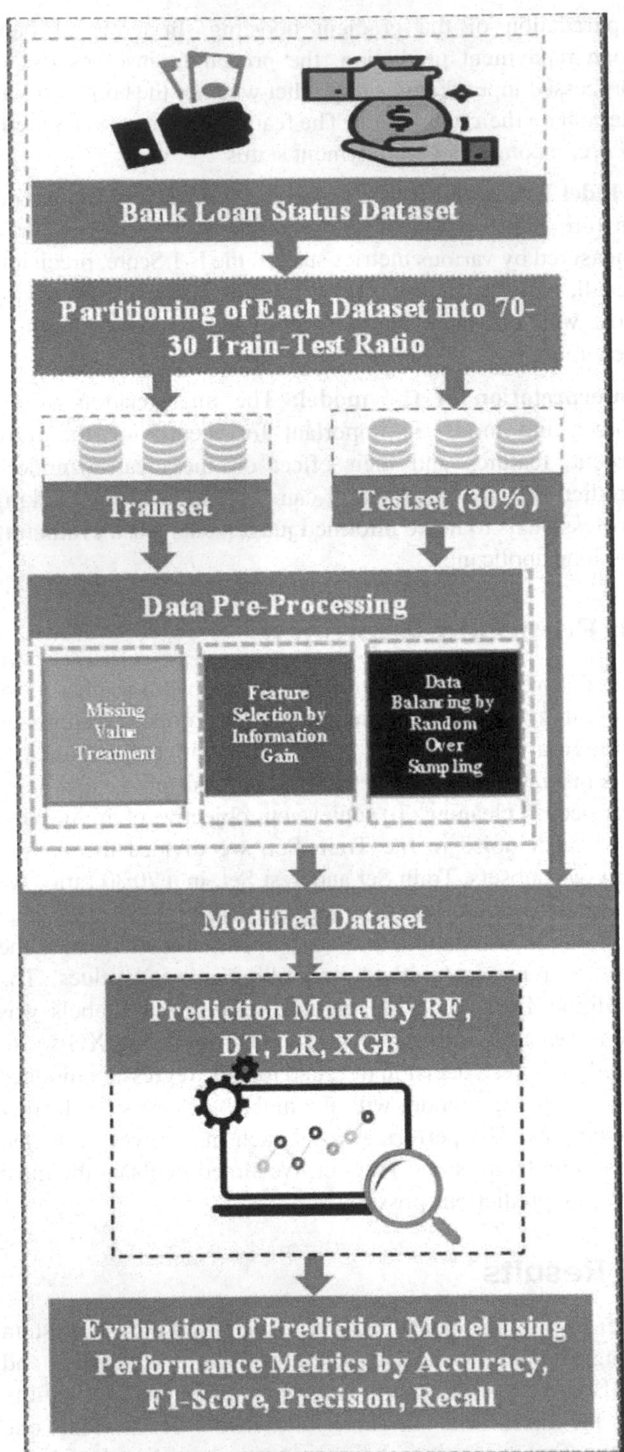

Fig. 11.1 Block diagram of proposed approach

recall and an F1 score all achieved a rate of 95.0%. The results obtained and portrayed in the table, shows that the XGBoost algorithm performed at the second position with the Logistic Regression algorithm performing at the last position with lowest performance.

Table 11.2 Experimental results

Algorithm	Accuracy	Precision	Recall	F1-Score
Decision Tree	0.82	0.82	0.82	0.82
Logistic Regression	0.90	0.90	0.90	0.90
Random Forest	0.95	0.95	0.95	0.95
XGBoost	0.91	0.91	0.91	0.91

6. Conclusion and Future Scope

In conclusion, the main objective of this paper is the creation of a prediction model for bank loan repayment for accurate prediction of defaulting i.e., to forecast whether an applicant would be able to repay the loan or not. Various ML algorithms were deployed to process and analyze bank repayment records, demographics of the borrower, and financial information. In terms of accuracy and efficiency it was found out that the Random Forest Classifier algorithm outperformed all the other algorithms in forecasting defaulters. The results of these analysis are of upmost importance for the financial institutions involved in loan lending business. With the ability to predict the chances of loan defaults, well-informed decisions can be made by the loan lending institutions regarding the rate at which loan is awarded, approval or denial of applications and to put into place risk minimizing strategies. The main aim for this research paper was to develop a ML model for predicting optimal bank loan repayment agendas. Nonetheless, the research was limited to assessing a dataset that only contained bank records of loan repayment, the borrower's demographics, and their financial information. The did not entail the consideration of other factors such as the alterations in the economy, the conduct of borrower and other external factors and their effect on the loan repayment.

Along with it the research paper did not delve into the ethical implications of using such computerized metrics in loan approvals and the potential biases that arises from such models. The scope of the research was limited only to the development and evaluation of a forecasting model using Ml algorithms.

REFERENCES

1. Aditya Sai Srinivas, T., Ramasubbareddy, S. and Govinda, K., Loan Default Prediction Using Machine Learning Techniques, in *Innovations in Computer Science and Engineering: Proceedings of the Ninth ICICSE, 2021*, Springer, pp. 529–35, 2022.
2. ZAUR BEGIEV, Bank Loan Status Dataset, 2020. https://www.kaggle.com/datasets/zaurbegiev/my-dataset. Accessed (July 22, 2023)
3. Chen, Y.-R., Leu, J.-S., Huang, S.-A., Wang, J.-T. and Takada, J.-I., Predicting Default Risk on Peer-to-Peer Lending Imbalanced Datasets, *IEEE Access*, vol. **9**, pp. 73103–9, 2021.

3. Guerra, P. and Castelli, M., Machine Learning Applied to Banking Supervision a Literature Review, *Risks*, vol. **9**, no. 7, p. 136, 2021.
4. Khan, A., Bhadola, E., Kumar, A. and Singh, N., Loan Approval Prediction Model a Comparative Analysis, *Advances and Applications in Mathematical Sciences*, vol. **20**, no. 3, 2021.
5. Lappas, P. Z. and Yannacopoulos, A. N., A Machine Learning Approach Combining Expert Knowledge with Genetic Algorithms in Feature Selection for Credit Risk Assessment, *Applied Soft Computing*, vol. **107**, p. 107391, 2021.
6. Li, B., Online Loan Default Prediction Model Based on Deep Learning Neural Network, *Computational Intelligence and Neuroscience*, vol. **2022**, 2022.
7. Li, W., Ding, S., Chen, Y. and Yang, S., Heterogeneous Ensemble for Default Prediction of Peer-to-Peer Lending in China, *Ieee Access*, vol. **6**, pp. 54396–406, 2018.
8. Sheikh, M. A., Goel, A. K., and Kumar, T., An Approach for Prediction of Loan Approval Using Machine Learning Algorithm, *2020 International Conference on Electronics and Sustainable Communication Systems (ICESC)*, pp. 490–94, 2020.
9. Trivedi, S. K., A Study on Credit Scoring Modeling with Different Feature Selection and Machine Learning Approaches, *Technology in Society*, vol. **63**, p. 101413, 2020.
10. Yang, Y., Chu, X., Pang, R., Liu, F. and Yang, P., Identifying and Predicting the Credit Risk of Small and Medium-Sized Enterprises in Sustainable Supply Chain Finance: Evidence from China, *Sustainability*, vol. **13**, no. 10, p. 5714, 2021.

Note: All the tables and figure in this chapter were made by the author.

Advancement of Intelligent Computational Methods and Technologies (AICMT2023) – Dr. O. P. Verma et al. (eds)
© 2024 Taylor & Francis Group, London, ISBN 978-1-032-78445-8

12

Machine Learning Model for Heart Disease Prediction with Consideration of Optimized Hyperparameters

Ramani Kant Jha[1], Nishtha Deep[2], Radha[3], Aridaman Kumar[4], Seema Verma[5]
Delhi Technical Campus (Affiliated to GGSIPU), Greater Noida, UP, India

ABSTRACT: Heart disease, a leading cause of global mortality, can be mitigated through early detection, highlighting the significance of prevention and treatment. Recently, machine learning (ML) algorithms have exhibited remarkable potential in predicting heart disease risk. This study's goal is to create an optimized heart disease prediction model using machine learning. The prediction model is developed using a dataset encompassing various cardiovascular risk factors. Here, the model is developed with five distinct machine-learning algorithms: Random Forest, LightGBM, SVC, XGBoost, and Logistic Regression. The hypermeters are tuned so as to optimize the accuracy of the model with various machine-learning algorithms. The accuracy rates of every method are compared with the existing model in tabular and graphical ways. The proposed model acquired an accuracy rate of 92.07% using a random forest algorithm, while the highest accuracy rate achieved by the model in the previous approach was 88.50%. Also, the proposed model outperformed every algorithm with the existing model.

KEYWORDS: ML, Logistic regression, Cardiovascular, Disease, Prediction, Random forests, XGBoost, LightGBM, Support vector machines

1. Introduction

Heart disease is considered to be a leading cause of global mortality. Heart disease may be accurately predicted and detected early, which can considerably improve patient outcomes and allow for earlier therapies. In recent years, machine learning techniques have gained substantial attention in the healthcare domain, enabling the development of robust predictive models. This paper gives a thorough investigation into the creation and assessment for predicting cardiac disease using several machine learning models, namely Random Forest (Breiman and Leo, 2001), LightGBM (Ke et al. 1970), Support Vector Classification (SVC) (Cortes & Vapnik, 1995), XGBoost (Chen & Guestrin, 2016), and Logistic Regression (Cox, 1958).

The predictive model leverages an extensiveness of cardiovascular risk factors, that includes age, gender, blood pressure, body mass index (BMI), cholesterol levels, habits of smoking, and lineage of the patient. By analyzing these factors, the model aims to identify patterns and associations that contribute to the onset and progression of heart disease. The machine learning sector has widely embraced the algorithmic techniques used in this work, which have shown promising outcomes in earlier medical research. Random Forest (Breiman and Leo, 2001) was first introduced by Leo Breiman in 2001. The work presents the concept of combining multiple decision trees to generate an ensemble model that can manage high-dimensional data and improve accuracy.

LightGBM (Ke et al. 1970) is a framework for gradient-boosting developed by Microsoft in 2017. The work outlines the design principles of LightGBM and highlights its efficiency and scalability.

Support Vector Machines (SVM) (Cortes & Vapnik, 1995), including the SVC variant, was introduced in 1995. Since then, SVMs have been extensively studied and applied in various classification tasks, including SVC.

XGBoost (Chen & Guestrin, 2016), or eXtreme Gradient Boosting, was introduced in 2016. The paper focuses on the scalability, flexibility, and handling of large-scale datasets offered by XGBoost.

[1]kantramani01@gmail.com, [2]nishthadeep3@gmail.com, [3]kradha83739@gmail.com, [4]aridaman.kumar99@gmail.com, [5]seemaknl@gmail.com

DOI: 10.1201/9781003487906-12

Logistic Regression (Cox, 1958) is a statistical model widely used in different fields, including machine learning.

In this work, extensive experimentation and evaluation have been conducted using a comprehensive dataset encompassing a large cohort of patients. The work's objective is to determine improvement in the accuracy of the various machine learning models that can help in providing early detection and proactive handling of heart disease, thereby improving patient outcomes and reducing the burden on healthcare systems.

The remaining workflow is as follows: related background is shown in the next section, and the method is proposed and shown in section 3 with implementation details and review. Finally, the paper is concluded in section 4.

2. Related Background

2.1 Random Forest

The notion of Random Forest was first introduced by Leo Breiman (Breiman and Leo, 2001) in his paper titled "Random Forests" published in 2001. The paper outlines the methodology (Fig. 12.1) of combining multiple decision trees to generate a robust ensemble model that can manage high-dimensional data and achieve improved accuracy.

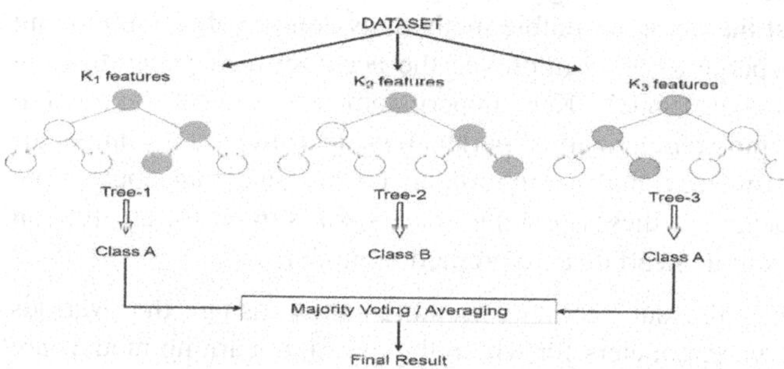

Fig. 12.1 Random forest technique

2.2 LightGBM

A gradient-boosting framework developed by Microsoft. The earliest research paper on LightGBM (Ke et al. 1970) presented at the in 2017 (Fig. 12.2). The paper introduces the algorithm's design principles and highlights its efficiency and scalability.

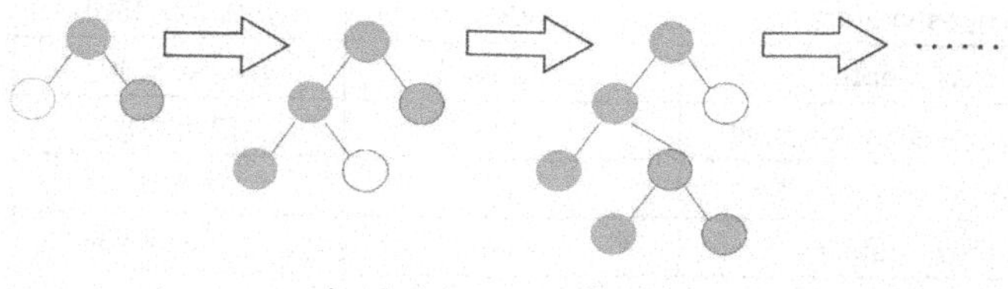

Fig. 12.2 Light GBM's working

2.3 Support Vector Classification (SVC)

The concept of Support Vector Machines (SVM), of which SVC is a variant, was introduced by Corinna Cortes & Vladimir Vapnik (Cortes & Vapnik, 1995) in their paper published in 1995. SVMs have since been widely studied and applied in various classification tasks, including SVC (Fig. 12.3).

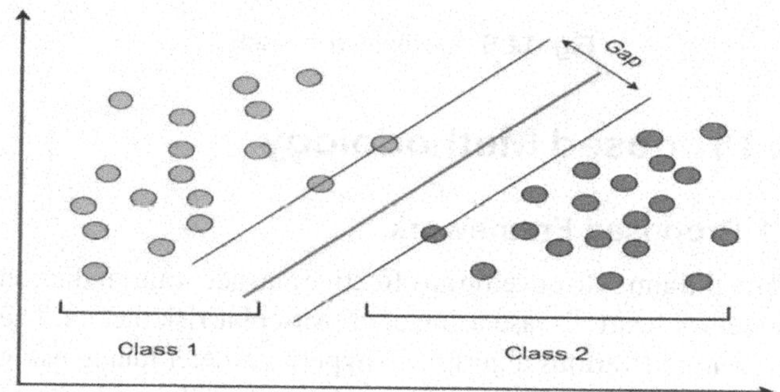

Fig. 12.3 Support vector machine classifier

2.4 XGBOOST

XGBoost or eXtreme Gradient Boosting, was introduced in 2016. The paper presents the XGBoost framework, emphasizing its scalability, flexibility, and ability to handle large-scale datasets (Fig. 12.4).

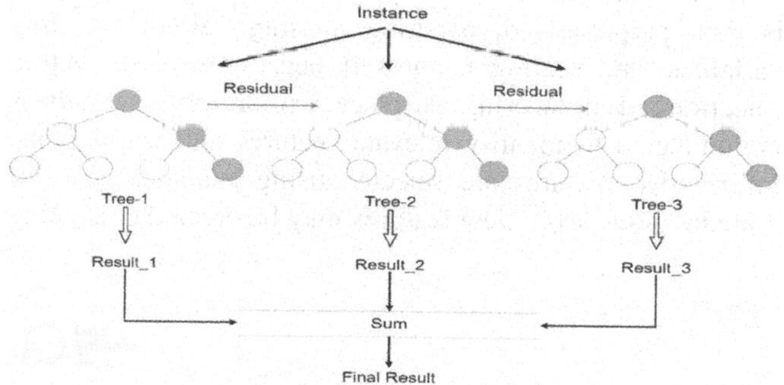

Fig. 12.4 XGBoost classifier

2.5 Logistic Regression

It is a statistical model that has been intensively used in various fields, including machine learning. The earliest research papers on logistic regression date back to the mid-20th century. One influential paper on logistic regression is "The Logistic Analysis of Contingency Tables" by David R. Cox (Cox, 1958) in 1958. This paper introduced the logistic regression model and discussed its applications in analyzing categorical data (Fig. 12.5).

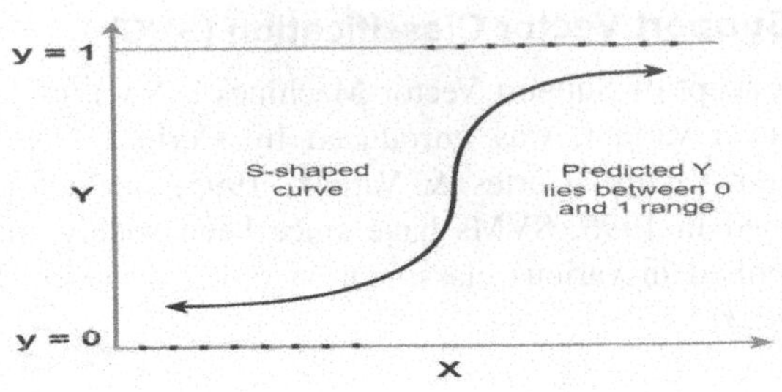

Fig. 12.5 Logistic regression

3. Proposed Methodology

3.1 Proposed Framework

Here, the aim is to develop an effective and accurate prediction model for heart disease using cardiovascular risk factors. The inclusion of various algorithms, hyperparameter tuning using GridSearchCV, and thorough evaluation will enable us to identify the finest-performing model for primitive detection and proactive handling of cardiac disease. The model's accuracy is improved based on the Hyperparameter tuning, details are presented in subsection A.

The framework as presented in Fig. 12.6 displays the various steps of the model. Firstly, data collection and preprocessing are performed. This includes gathering a dataset with cardiovascular risk factors and heart disease labels. The data is then preprocessed, handling missing values, encoding variables, and scaling features if necessary. Next, feature selection and engineering take place. Exploratory data analysis is conducted to identify relevant features and correlations. Informative features are selected using statistical tests or domain knowledge. New features may be created or existing

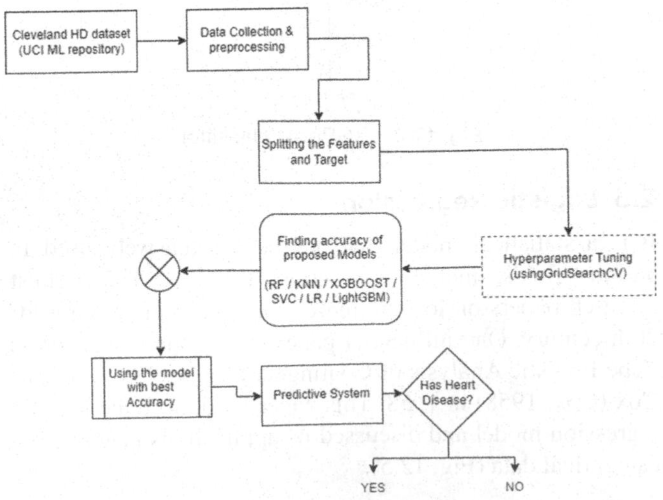

Fig. 12.6 Heart disease prediction model methodology

ones transformed. Then, model building and evaluation occur. Algorithms like Random Forest, LightGBM, SVC, XGBoost, KNN, and Logistic Regression are implemented separately for heart disease prediction. Models are developed using training data and assessed using testing data.

Hyperparameter tuning is performed using GridSearchCV. This involves searching over a grid of values for each algorithm's hyperparameters. Cross-validation is utilized to estimate model performance and bypass overfitting. The best hyperparameters are selected based on performance metrics.

The models' performance is compared, and the best-performing algorithm is determined for heart disease prediction. Once the best model is chosen, it is deployed in a real-world setting, and integrated with existing healthcare systems. Continuous monitoring and evaluation are done, collecting feedback for potential improvements. Additional techniques, such as ensemble methods or feature selection algorithms, may be explored for further enhancement.

3.2 Hyperparameters Tuning

Hyperparameters in heart disease prediction models have a major impact on model's performance. Control of the complexity of the model, regulate overfitting, determining the rate of learning, convergence speed, and the number of estimators in ensemble methods is done by this. Optimizing hyperparameters improves the accuracy and generalization of the model. Key hyperparameters include maximum depth, regularization parameters, learning rate, number of estimators, and neighborhood count. Selecting appropriate values for these hyperparameters is essential for creating an accurate heart disease prediction model.

In this sub-section, we are showcasing the various hyperparameters for which the machine learning models are optimized with better accuracy. The various parameters for Random Forest, LightGBM, Support Vector Classification, XGBoost, and Logistic Regression are shown in Tables (12.1 to 12.6) respectively.

Table 12.1 Hyperparameter comparison of random forest model

Parameter	Default value	Tuned value
n_estimators	100	[50, 100, 150]
max_depth	None	[None, 5, 10]
min_samples_split	2	[2, 5, 10]
min_samples_leaf	1	[1, 2, 4]
max_features	auto	['auto', 'sqrt', 'log2']

Table 12.2 Hyperparameter comparison of the LightGBM model

Parameter	Default value	Tuned value
learning_rate	0.1	[0.01, 0.1, 1]
n_estimators	100	[50, 100, 150]
max_depth	-1	[None, 5, 10]
num_leaves	31	[31, 63, 127]
min_child_samples	20	[1, 5, 10]

Table 12.3 Hyperparameter comparison of SVC model

Parameter	Default value	Tuned value
C	1	[0.1, 1, 10]
kernel	rbf	['linear', 'poly', 'rbf']
gamma	scale	['scale', 'auto']
degree	3	[2, 3, 4]
probability	False	[True]

Table 12.4 Hyperparameter comparison of the XGBoost model

Parameter	Default value	Tuned value
learning_rate	0.3	[0.05, 0.1, 0.3]
max_depth	6	[3, 5, 7]
min_child_weight	1	[1, 3, 5]
Gamma	0	[0, 0.1, 0.2]
Subsample	1	[0.8, 1]
colsample_bytree	1	[0.8, 1]
reg_alpha	0	[0, 0.1, 0.5]
reg_lambda	1	[1, 2, 5]

Table 12.5 Hyperparameter comparison of the KNN model

Parameter	Default value	Tuned value
n_neighbors	5	list(range(1, 21))

Table 12.6 Hyperparameter comparison of Logistic regression model

Parameter	Default value	Tuned value
C	100	[0.001, 0.01, 0.1, 1, 10, 100]

4. Implementation and Result

A dataset consisting of 303 patients and 14 cardiovascular risk factors is utilized in this study; Cleveland Heart disease dataset is processed which is collected from UCI ML. The set of data underwent preprocessing by removing redundant values and normalizing the data.

Here, various performance measures are used such as accuracy, precision, recall, and area under curve (AUC-ROC) have been employed to test and undermine the models' predictive capabilities. AUC is a measure used to gauge the potency of binary classification models. AUC evaluates the capacity of the model to discern between favorable and unfavorable cases. An optimal classifier has an AUC-ROC score of 1, while a random classifier has a score of 0.5. The AUC is computed by creating a ROC curve and calculating the area under it.

Here, training and evaluation of five machine learning algorithms are done: logistic regression (LR) in Fig. 12.7, support vector classifier (SVC) in Fig. 12.8, LightGBM (LGBM) in Fig. 12.9, random forest (RF) in Fig. 12.10, and gradient boosting (XGBOOST) in Fig. 12.11.

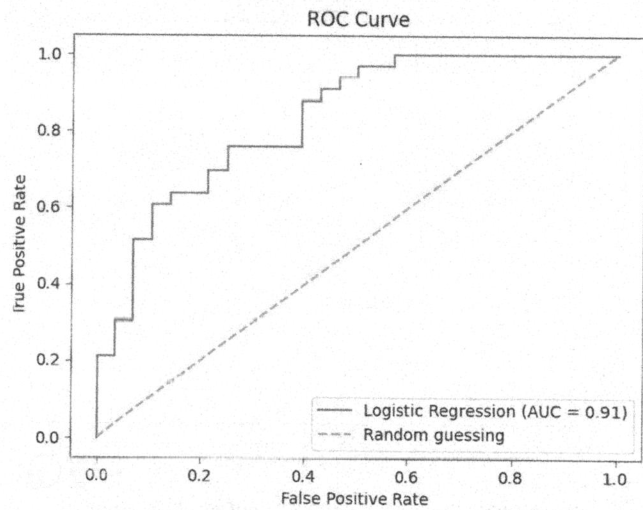

Fig. 12.7 Logistic Regression (AUC Score)

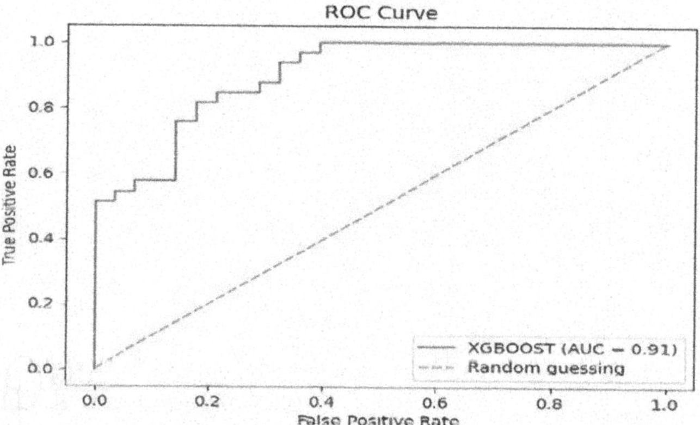

Fig. 12.8 XGBOOST (AUC Score)

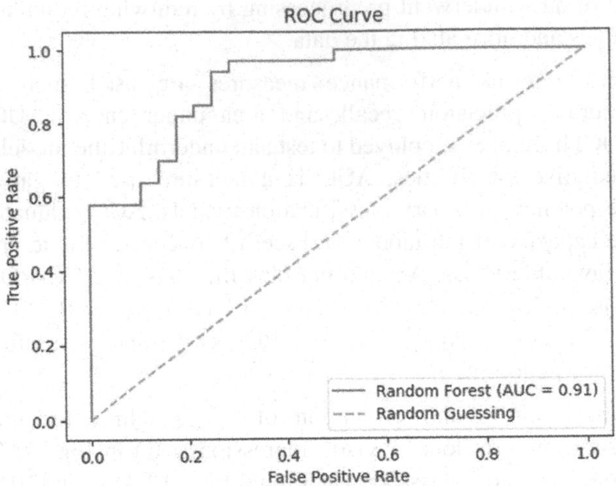

Fig. 12.9 Random Forest (AUC Score)

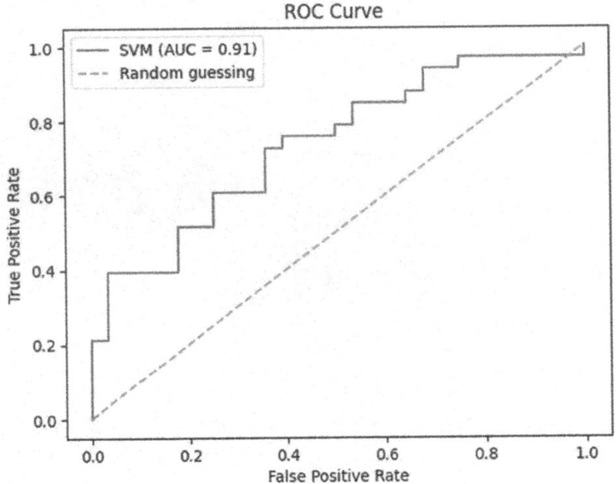

Fig. 12.10 Support Vector Classifier (AUC Score)

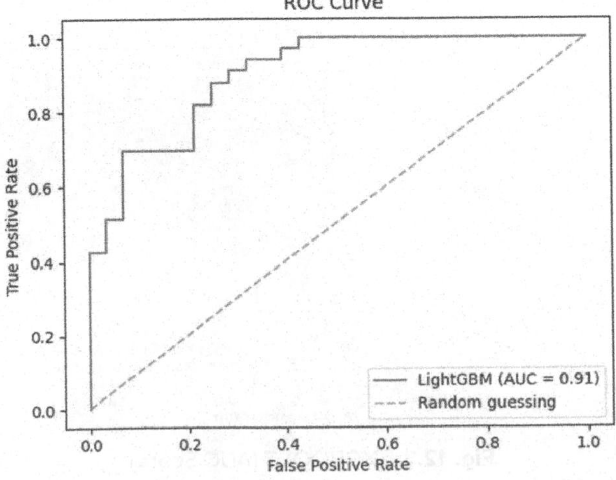

Fig. 12.11 LightGBM (AUC Score)

Analysis Of The Proposed Model

Here, the findings are contrasted with K. Karthick et al research on heart disease prediction (Karthick et al. 2022). Our ML-based heart disease prediction model outperformed the model presented by K. Karthick et al. in terms of accuracy, as demonstrated in Table 12.7.

Table 12.7 Accuracy comparison between the model proposed by K. Karthick et al. and our proposed model models

Model Name	Proposed model's accuracy	K. Karthick et al. model's accuracy
Logistic regression	85.14 %	80.32 %
Random Forest	92.07 %	88.50 %
XGBOOST	89.76 %	73.77 %
SVC	90.42 %	80.32 %
LightGBM	90.42 %	77.04 %

Our model acquired an accuracy rate of 92.07% using a random forest algorithm, while the highest accuracy rate achieved by the model in the previous approach was 88.50%. The comparison is shown in Fig. 12.12. Also, every algorithm is showing better accuracy as compared to the previous approach (Karthick et al. 2022).

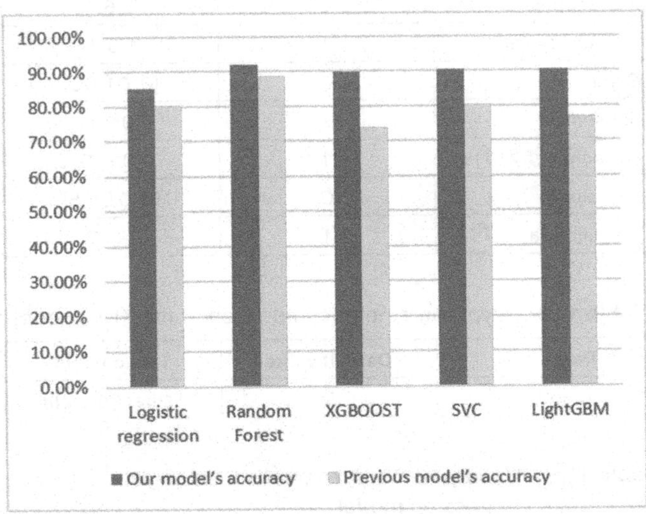

Fig. 12.12 Visual accuracy comparison of two models

5. Conclusion

Heart disease is a major cause of global mortality, but early detection can help mitigate its impact. In this work, an enhanced ML model is developed for heart disease prediction using a dataset containing various cardiovascular risk factors. The model utilizes five distinct ML algorithms; random forest, LightGBM, SVC, XGBoost, and Logistic

Regression. The hyperparameters of each algorithm are tuned to maximize model accuracy. The accuracy rates of all methods are compared with the existing model. The proposed model attains an impressive accuracy rate of 92.07% with the random forest algorithm, surpassing the previous approach's highest accuracy rate of 88.50%. Furthermore, the model proposed in this paper outperforms all other algorithms in the existing model. Our findings may have important implications for improving patient outcomes and reducing healthcare costs related to heart disease.

REFERENCES

1. Breiman, Leo. "Random forests." Machine learning 45 (2001): 5-32. https://doi.org/10.1023/A:1010933404324
2. Ke, Guolin, Qi Meng, Thomas Finley, Taifeng Wang, Wei Chen, Weidong Ma, Qiwei Ye, and Tie-Yan Liu. "LightGBM: A Highly Efficient Gradient Boosting Decision Tree." Advances in Neural Information Processing Systems, January 1, 1970. https://proceedings.neurips.cc/paper/2017/hash/6449f44a102fde848669bdd9eb6b76fa-Abstract.html.
3. Cortes, Corinna, and Vladimir Vapnik. 1995. "Support-Vector Networks." Machine Learning 20 (3): 273–97. https://doi.org/10.1007/bf00994018.
4. Chen, Tianqi, and Carlos Guestrin. 2016. "XGBoost." Proceedings of the 22nd ACM SIGKDD International Conference on Knowledge Discovery and Data Mining. https://doi.org/10.1145/2939672.2939785.
5. Cox, D. R. 1958. "The Regression Analysis of Binary Sequences." Journal of the Royal Statistical Society: Series B (Methodological) 20 (2): 215–32. https://doi.org/10.1111/j.2517-6161.1958.tb00292.x.
6. Aggrawal, Ritu, and Saurabh Pal. 2020. "Sequential Feature Selection and Machine Learning Algorithm-Based Patient's Death Events Prediction and Diagnosis in Heart Disease." SN Computer Science 1 (6). https://doi.org/10.1007/s42979-020-00370-1.
7. Chen, Si-Ding, Jia You, Xiao-Meng Yang, Hong-Qiu Gu, Xin-Ying Huang, Huan Liu, Jian-Feng Feng, Yong Jiang, and Yong-jun Wang. 2022. "Machine Learning Is an Effective Method to Predict the 90-Day Prognosis of Patients with Transient Ischemic Attack and Minor Stroke." BMC Medical Research Methodology 22 (1). https://doi.org/10.1186/s12874-022-01672-z.
8. Kanwal, Samina, Junaid Rashid, Muhammad Wasif Nisar, Jungeun Kim, and Amir Hussain. 2021. "An Effective Classification Algorithm for Heart Disease Prediction with Genetic Algorithm for Feature Selection." 2021 Mohammad Ali Jinnah University International Conference on Computing (MAJICC). https://doi.org/10.1109/majicc53071.2021.9526242.
9. Khourdifi, Youness, and Mohamed Bahaj. 2019. "Heart Disease Prediction and Classification Using Machine Learning Algorithms Optimized by Particle Swarm Optimization and Ant Colony Optimization." International Journal of Intelligent Engineering and Systems 12 (1): 242–52. https://doi.org/10.22266/ijies2019.0228.24.
10. Latha, C. Beulah, and S. Carolin Jeeva. 2019. "Improving the Accuracy of Prediction of Heart Disease Risk Based on Ensemble Classification Techniques." Informatics in Medicine Unlocked 16: 100203. https://doi.org/10.1016/j.imu.2019.100203.
11. Mohan, Senthilkumar, Chandrasegar Thirumalai, and Gautam Srivastava. 2019. "Effective Heart Disease Prediction Using Hybrid Machine Learning Techniques." IEEE Access 7: 81542–54. https://doi.org/10.1109/access.2019.2923707.
12. Spencer, Robinson, Fadi Thabtah, Neda Abdelhamid, and Michael Thompson. 2020. "Exploring Feature Selection and Classification Methods for Predicting Heart Disease." DIGITAL HEALTH 6: 205520762091477. https://doi.org/10.1177/2055207620914777.
13. Yuvaraj, N., and K. R. SriPreethaa. 2017. "Diabetes Prediction in Healthcare Systems Using Machine Learning Algorithms on Hadoop Cluster." Cluster Computing 22 (S1): 1–9. https://doi.org/10.1007/s10586-017-1532-x.
14. Zhenya, Qi, and Zuoru Zhang. 2021. "A Hybrid Cost-Sensitive Ensemble for Heart Disease Prediction." BMC Medical Informatics and Decision Making 21 (1). https://doi.org/10.1186/s12911-021-01436-7.
15. Karthick, K., S. K. Aruna, Ravi Samikannu, Ramya Kuppusamy, Yuvaraja Teekaraman, and Amruth Ramesh Thelkar. 2022. "Implementation of a Heart Disease Risk Prediction Model Using Machine Learning." Computational and Mathematical Methods in Medicine 2022: 1–14. https://doi.org/10.1155/2022/6517716.
16. Takci, Hidayet. "Improvement of heart attack prediction by the feature selection methods." Turkish Journal of Electrical Engineering and Computer Sciences 26, no. 1 (2018): 1-10. https://doi.org/10.3906/elk-1611-235.
17. Gao, Xiao-Yan, Abdelmegeid Amin Ali, Hassan Shaban Hassan, and Eman M. Anwar. "Improving the accuracy for analyzing heart diseases prediction based on the ensemble method." Complexity 2021 (2021): 1-10. https://doi.org/10.1155/2021/6663455.
18. Gárate-Escamila, Anna Karen, Amir Hajjam El Hassani, and Emmanuel Andrès. "Classification models for heart disease prediction using feature selection and PCA." Informatics in Medicine Unlocked 19 (2020): 100330. https://doi.org/10.1016/j.imu.2020.100330.

Note: All the figures and tables in this chapter were made by the author.

Advancement of Intelligent Computational Methods and Technologies (AICMT2023) – Dr. O. P. Verma et al. (eds)

13

Exploring Advanced Techniques for Enhancing Resolution of Images

Shivank Naruka[1], Shrey Gupta[2], Vinayak Saxena[3], Rishab Rana[4], Umnah[5]
Department of Computer Application, Delhi Technical Campus, UP, India

ABSTRACT: Image enhancement plays a very important act in various fields, such as computer technology, medical imaging, and different Multimedia Applications. The major aim of image enhancement technique is to improve the visual quality of an image by enhancing its various details, contrast, and overall appearance while preserving its essential features. It covers the modern approaches used to enhance images such as, histogram equalization, contrast stretching, spatial domain filtering, and adaptive enhancement methods. Each technique is briefly explained, highlighting its underlying principles and potential applications. These methods modify pixel intensities or apply filters directly to the image to enhance its overall appearance. While these techniques can be effective in certain scenarios, they may lack adaptability and fail to produce satisfactory results for complex images with diverse content. This paper is study on image enhancement techniques that have witnessed substantial advancements, combining traditional approaches with modern AI-based methods using 'MATLAB' Software. These techniques have found applications in Various fields and continue to evolve in future improvements in visual quality, object detection, and image analysis tasks.

KEYWORDS: Image enhancement, Spatial domain operations, MATLAB, Contrast stretching

1. Introduction

Image enhancement is a critical process in the field of image processing that aims to improve the visual quality of digital images. MATLAB, a widely-used software environment for technical computing, provides a comprehensive set of tools and functions for implementing image enhancement techniques. MATLAB's extensive image processing toolbox offers a wide range of functions and algorithms that enable researchers, engineers, and practitioners to enhance images efficiently and effectively.

The process of image enhancement using, MATLAB typically involves loading an image into the MATLAB environment and applying various enhancement operations and filters to modify the image's appearance (Parthasarathy et al. 2012). MATLAB's rich collection of functions allows users to adjust image properties such as brightness, contrast, and sharpness, as well as reduce noise and enhance fine details.

1.1 Image Enhancement

The critical thought perceived with the image improvement is to convey out component that isn't perceptible obviously or spotlight certain significant components of an image (Yahya et al. 2009). In like manner it is imperative to embellish the detectable quality of the picture by removing unfortunate upheaval, to find extra inconspicuous components and upgrade separate, etc.

The idea at the rear of this procedure is to update the photograph by utilizing controlling the substitute coefficients. The upsides of repeat basically based picture advancement comprises of low unconventionality of estimations, controlling the repeat structure of the photo, straight forwardness of diagram and the basic relevance of extraordinary changed territory properties.

2. Proposed Methods

The photos which have histogram compartments extra

[1]shivanknaruka@gmail.com, [2]guptashrey163@gmail.com, [3]vinayak092002saxena@gmail.com, [4]rishurana1515@gmail.com, [5]umnah@delhitechnicalcampus.ac.in

DOI: 10.1201/9781003487906-13

centered nearer to diminish part or the darker diminish levels have low power gentle while pictures having histogram containers moved toward better segment or the more brilliant part have high power illumination. Taking into account the vitality of illumination, pics might be radically appointed underneath or over lit up picture.

The proposed technique for HE is have to contain of 3 phases, to be specific Brightening limits estimation, Histogram Cutting and Histogram Sub division and Balance.

3. Equalization Histogram

The histogram is an estimate of the chance that a piece of data will be transported. An picture histogram is a kind of histogram which gives a graph representation of the tonal stream of the darkish qualities in a muddled picture. We can examine the repetition of the look of the adjusted reduction values in the image by assessing the histogram.

A technique known as Histogram Balance alters an image's histogram by redistributing all of the pixel highlights to be as close as is practical to a customer-unmistakably preferred histogram (wang et al. 2017). Histogram levelling achieves this by efficiently distributing the most common power esteems. Unquestionably, Histogram Night Out visits a preferred trade company aiming to create a yield image using a uniform Histogram.

3.1 Specific Brightening Limits Estimation

Brightening limits estimation is an essential aspect of image enhancement that aims to determine the optimal range for adjusting the brightness of an image (zhang et al. 2010). MATLAB provides powerful tools and techniques to estimate these limits accurately, enabling users to enhance image visibility while preserving details and avoiding overexposure.

3.2 Histogram Sub-Division

The histogram of an image is split up into smaller sections or subregions using a technique called histogram subdivision. A more localised study of the pixel intensity distribution is made possible by this subdivision, giving users more precise control over operations like contrast adjustment, brightness correction, and histogram equalisation .

4. Spatial Domain Filtering

A fundamental method in image processing called spatial domain filtering involves pixel-by-pixel manipulation of a picture in the spatial domain. Applying filters to the image's pixel values is a common technique for enhancing photos, eliminating noise, and extracting useful characteristics. The neighbourhood of each pixel is taken into account for filtering operations in this technique, which operates on the spatial domain representation of the image.

Spatial domain filters utilize a mathematical mask or kernel, which is typically a small matrix or window, to perform operations on the pixel values within the image. The size and shape of the kernel determine the scope and characteristics of the filtering process. The kernel is applied to each pixel in the image, and the resulting output pixel value is calculated based on the corresponding values in the neighbourhood defined by the kernel.

There are various types of spatial domain filters that serve different purposes. Some commonly used filters include:

- *Averaging filter:* Also known as a box filter, it substitutes the average value of each pixel's neighborhood for the value of each pixel. To lessen noise and blur the image, apply averaging filters.
- *The median filter:* replaces each pixel's value with the median value for its neighborhood. Edges and minute details are preserved while impulsive noise, such as salt-and-pepper noise, is effectively reduced.
- *Gaussian filter:* A Gaussian distribution-based weighted average of the nearby pixel values serves as the foundation for the Gaussian filter. It is frequently used to blur and smooth photos while keeping the edges sharp.

5. Contrast Stretching of Image

Contrast stretching is a well-liked method of image enhancement that raises an image's visual quality and dynamic range (Demirel et al. 2004). It seeks to make the image more visually appealing and understandable by enhancing the contrast between various intensity levels. In order to use the entire range of the image's intensity values, contrast stretching linearly scales them.

Using straightforward arithmetic operations on the picture pixel values, contrast stretching can be implemented in MATLAB. The following steps are often included in the process:

- Utilize MATLAB functions like min and max to determine the image's minimum and maximum pixel values.
- Set the stretched image's intended range, which is commonly 0 to 255 for an 8-bit image.
- Calculate the offset and scale factor needed to convert the original pixel values to the specified range.

To create the contrast-stretched image, apply the scale factor and offset to each and every pixel in the original image.

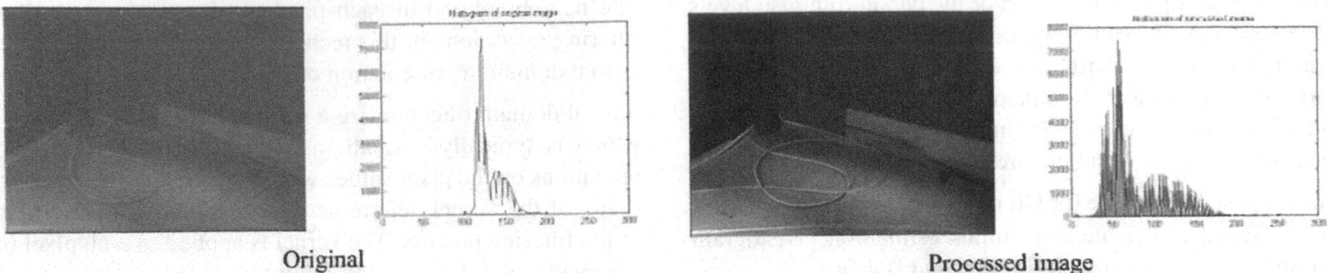

Fig. 13.1 Contrast stretching

Source: Author

6. Threshold Calculation

The normalized extent of creation regard is 0–1. In case the estimation of presentation for a specific picture is more prominent than zero.5 and slants more like 1, it implies that the photo has lion's level of overexposed district and if this regard is underneath 0.five and slanting toward 0 at that point photo is containing bigger piece of underneath uncovered areas. In the two cases photo comprises of horrendous separation and necessities separate improvement. Picture pressure introduction regard can be determined as

$$exposure = \frac{1}{L}\frac{\sum_{k=1}^{L} h(k)k}{\sum_{k=1}^{L} h(k)} \tag{1}$$

Where, $h(k)$ is a histogram of photos and L is included up to the quantity darkish level. Another parameter Xa (as ascertained in the equation, is identified with the creation of marked, which offers estimates of the partition-level restrictions dim picture below to open and sub pi is uncovered pictures.

7. Algorithm Design

- Create Gui (graphical User Inter Face)
- Calculate the histogram of the target image
- Calculate the edge parameter estimation Lighting
- Calculate histogram boundary and buckles for harness
- Divide cut into two sub histogram histogram utilizing the edge parameter.
- Apply HE sub histogram individuals.
- Integrating sub-images into single picture.

8. Methodology

The suggested method was evaluated using a dataset of frequently polluted previews of various scenes imprisoned in a harsh dusty environment. The dataset representations were obtained from a variety of online sources. To determine the state of development for treating images, it is advised to adopt an independent and explicit assessment technique for assessment purposes. In keeping with this, the method openly acknowledged having considered assessment to evaluate the accuracy, dependability, and separation hide dirty photo.

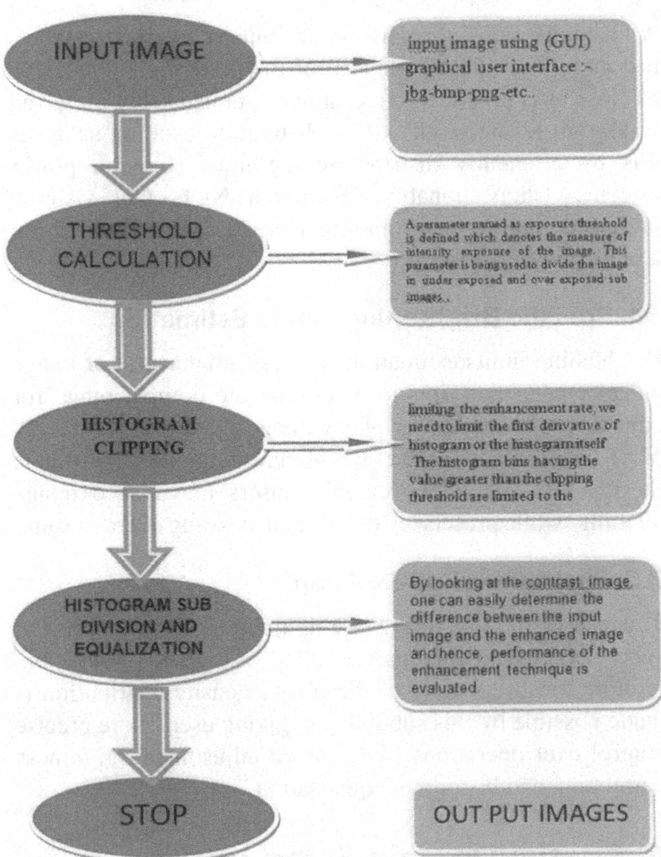

Fig. 13.2 Flowchart of image enhancement

Source: Author

9. Result Analysis

This modern technology of picture encasing is also used for picture demising. Three crucial steps are used to make the picture sing. It's them,

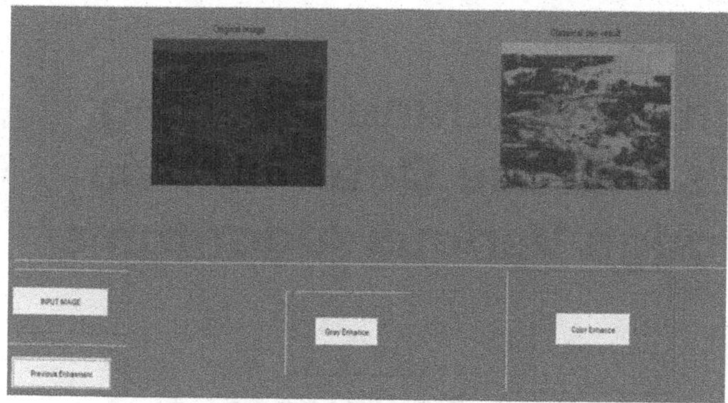

Fig. 13.3 Input satellite low resolution images

Source: Alexender Toet," Efficient contrast enhancement through log-power histogram modification",Image Enhancement,Dec 2014.

Fig. 13.4 After output Images

Source: Author

- The pixels are arranged in a picture's smooth and surface areas.
- After that, the smooth district evaluates the pixels to change each pixel's direction.
- The cross-breed modification is also used to lessen disturbance in some areas. The execution picture is improved using the mod-picture method.
- High-Throughput Computing Applications
- Create the code for your high-throughput computing programme.

10. Conclusion

This Paper Survey the most the techniques used in Image Enhancement Using 'MATLAB'. MATLAB provides a comprehensive environment for image enhancement, combining a wide range of functions, interactive visualization tools, and compatibility with advanced algorithms. Whether it is for research, development, or practical applications, MATLAB empowers users to enhance image quality, extract meaningful information, and improve the visual appeal of images effectively and efficiently.

11. Acknowledgement

The authors gratefully acknowledge the students, staff, and authority of Computer Science and Engineering department for their cooperation in the research.

REFERENCES

1. Yahya, Sitti Rachmawati, S. N. Abdullah, K. Omar, M. S. Zakaria, and C. Y. Liong. *2009*. "Review on Image Enhancement Methods of Old Manuscript with the Damaged Background." *International Conference on Electrical Engineering and Informatics*. https://doi.org/10.1109/iceei.2009.5254816.
2. Wang, Yang, and Zhibin Pan. 2017. "Image Contrast Enhancement Using Adjacent-Blocks-Based Modification for Local Histogram Equalization." *Infrared Physics & Technology* 86: 59–65. https://doi.org/10.1016/j.infrared.2017.08.005.
3. Yang, Miao, Jintong Hu, Chongyi Li, Gustavo Rohde, Yixiang Du, and Ke Hu.2019. "An In-Depth Survey of Underwater Image Enhancement and Restoration." *IEEE Access* 7: 123638–57.
4. Zhang, YuDong, LeNan Wu, ShuiHua Wang, and Geng Wei.2010. "Color Image Enhancement Based on HVS and PCNN." *Science China Information Sciences* 53, no. 10: 1963–76. https://doi.org/10.1007/s11432-010-4075-9.
5. Jin, Shang, Yang You, and Yang Huafen. *2010* ."A Scanned Document Image Processing Model for Information System." *Asia-Pacific Conference on Wearable Computing Systems*. https://doi.org/10.1109/apwcs.2010.56.
6. Ackar, Haris, Ali Abd Almisreb, and Mohamed A. Saleh. (2019). "A Review on Image Enhancement Techniques." *Southeast Europe Journal of Soft Computing* 8, no. 1. https://doi.org/10.21533/scjournal.v8i1.175.
7. Demirel, Hasan, and Gholamreza Anbarjafari. 2004. "Discrete Wavelet Transform-Based Satellite Image Resolution Enhancement." *IEEE Transactions on Geoscience and Remote Sensing* 49, no. 6 (2011): 1997–. https://doi.org/10.1109/tgrs.2010.2100401.
8. Ghimire, Sarala, Nagaraj Yamanakkanavar, and Bumshik Lee,2020."A No-Reference Image Quality Assessment Based on Reference Generating Network." *2020 IEEE International Conference on Consumer Electronics - Asia (ICCE-Asia)*. https://doi.org/10.1109/icce-asia49877.2020.9276916.
9. Parthasarathy, Sudharsan, and Praveen Sankaran.2012. "Fusion Based Multi Scale RETINEX with Color Restoration for Image Enhancement." *2012 International Conference on Computer Communication and Informatics*. https://doi.org/10.1109/iccci.2012.6158793.
10. Bronte, S., L. M. Bergasa, and P. F. Alcantarilla. *2009*."Fog Detection System Based on Computer Vision Techniques." *12th International IEEE Conference on Intelligent Transportation Systems*, 2009. https://doi.org/10.1109/itsc.2009.5309842.

Advancement of Intelligent Computational Methods and Technologies (AICMT2023) – Dr. O. P. Verma et al. (eds)

14

A Symphony of Signals: Machine Learning Enabled Parkinson's Disease Detection via Audio Analysis Through Various Algorithms

Shubham Tiwari[1], Kartikey Raghuvanshi[2], Sanand Mishra[3], Saakshi Srivastava[4]

Department of Computer Science and Engineering and Student of BCA Delhi Technical campus, affiliated by GGSIPU, Greater Noida, India

Ayasha Malik[5], Seema Verma[6]

Department of Computer Science and Engineering and Faculty of Computer, Science and Engineering, Delhi Technical campus, affiliated by GGSIPU, Greater Noida, India

ABSTRACT: The disease of Parkinson's is a neurological progressive disease which can affect anyone around the world and causes abnormalities in brain activity and motor function. For the early diagnosis of Parkinson's disease symptoms, medical research has recently used computational intelligence tools, notably machine learning and deep learning approaches. These methods make use of numerous medical measurements made using various medical equipment, such as voice volume, handwriting fluctuations, bodily motions, brain signal variations, and protein aggregations. The moderate nature of the earliest indicators, however, makes it difficult to recognize Parkinson's disease in its early stages. The algorithms of ML diagnose and predict with the help of audio data, is the main topic of this research study. Particularly, the examination of voice-related symptoms offers a potential route for practical and non-invasive screening methods. This problem is identified based on a combination of kinetic and other signs, including sluggishness, stiffness, balance problems, tremors, anxiety, breathing problems, sadness, etc. Our work intends to identify the most accurate diagnostic method/algorithm for early Parkinson's disease identification by taking into account speech characteristics and patient data.

KEYWORDS: Parkinson's disease, Model, Detection, SVM, Machine learning, Algorithms

1. Introduction

This neurological condition is very common nowadays that affects people of all ages, all around the world.[1] Disruptions in brain activity and bodily motion are its defining characteristics, which cause a variety of motor and non-motor symptoms. For successful care and intervention, Parkinson's disease must be recognized and detected early.[2] By using computational intelligence methods, notably machine learning and deep learning methodologies, to anticipate and diagnose Parkinson's disease symptoms, medical research has made considerable strides recently.[3] Parkinson's disease is categorized based on the specific anomalies seen in those who have it. The disorder mostly affects how the brain functions and how the body moves, and it shows up as symptoms including slowness of movement, stiffness, balance issues, tremors, altered speech, etc. The ultimate aim of this paper is to learn and implement various ML models for identification and prediction using auditory inputs and find the best among them. In summary, the goal of this study is to use machine learning and acoustic signal analysis to advance the area of Parkinson's disease identification.[4] Enhancing early detection skills and enabling prompt therapies are the ultimate goals in order to improve the lives of people with Parkinson's disease.

In order to better understand the pathophysiology of Parkinson's disease and pave the way for future developments in diagnostic procedures and therapeutic approaches, this

[1]shubhamtiwari0131@gmail.com, [2]kartikeyips302@gmail.com, [3]sanand4j@gmail.com, [4]Srivastava.saakshi1234@gmail.com, [5]a.malik@delhitechnicalcampus.ac.in, [6]seemaknl@gmail.com

DOI: 10.1201/9781003487906-14

project aims to get a deeper knowledge of the underlying processes of neurodegenerative illnesses.[5] The overall format/flow of the paper is as follows: The paper's introduction, which has previously been examined, is the first part. The literature review, or all the papers reviewed to produce this research study, is found in Section 2, which we will now go on to. Reviewing the previous research on the subject here aids in creating a better research report. The technique, which comprises of numerous modules and various functional and non-functional needs, is covered in Section 3 of the article. The necessary hardware and software are listed in the next section. Furthermore, outcomes that commonly displayed the application snapshots are discussed in Section 5 of this article. The study comes to a close with Section 6, which contains the recommendations.

2. Literature Review

A thorough summary of earlier studies on the subject is given in the literature review. We shall synthesise and summarise the results of relevant studies in the following table. The research papers that were read in order to effectively compose this one are shown in the table below:

Table 14.1 Literature review

S. No	Year	Contribution	Name
1	2011	Parkinson's disease is an irreversible neurological ailment that causes slowness of movement, tremor, and stiffness of the muscles.	Heisters D.
2	2012	With up to 97% accuracy in the top- performing classifier, a novel classification model based on support vector machine.	A. Ozcift
3	2013	This study classifies Parkinson's disease with great accuracy usingtwo types of artificial neural networks (MBFand MLP).	Farhad Soleimanian Gharehehopog h et al.
4	2016	The use of machine learning techniques to identify and categorise tremors, gait patterns, and voice dysfunction.	Dragana Miljkovic etal.
5	2018	In order to identify the most precise classification method, this research intends to identify Parkinson's Disease by data mining and statistical study of typical symptoms including gait, tremors, and micro-graphia.	Dr. Anupam bhatia et al.
6	2018	This study uses Parkinson's disease data from UCI to evaluate the diagnostic performance of SVM and Bayesian networks.	M. Abdar et al.
7	2019	Data mining can provide light on the small variations between Parkinson's disease and Progressive Supranuclear.	Carlo Ricciardi et al.
8	2020	The study proposes a unique method for accurately diagnosing this neurological condition with the help of neural networks.	Anila M et al.
9	2022	The existence of the beforehand made project is dependent on not only audio evaluation but also image evaluation. It shows how the old and new way to detect Parkinson's disease is change. It also shows us how the new technology work and what new libraries use to do that and In future there will be new methods will be evolved and that method will be used to detect the Parkinson's.	Shreevallabha datta at el
10	2023	The most feasible and desirable way is to apply algorithms based on machine learning to understand and evaluate if the person suffers from the disease	J Divya et al

3. Methodology

The research study discusses about the Parkinson's disease and how its detection is possible using a machine learning model. In this study, we discussed about various Machine Learning algorithms through which this disease can be detected and find the best amongst them.

3.1 Functional Requirements

In Parkinson's disease applications, functional criteria are crucial to ensure that the built system satisfies the demands of the intended users and stakeholders. Several crucial functional needs for Parkinson's disease applications are listed below:

(a) *Data collection:* In order to follow disease development, identify risk factors, and assess the efficacy of therapies, data collecting is a crucial part of research into Parkinson's disease. Data collection is done from Kaggle with 24 feature/characteristics of 195 people of different age groups. MDVP: Fo(Hz), MDVP: Fhi(Hz), MDVP: Flo(Hz), MDVP: Jitter(%), MDVP: Jitter(Abs), MDVP: RAP, MDVP: PPQ, Jitter: DDP, MDVP: Shimmer, MDVP: Shimmer (dB), Shimm er: APQ3, Shimmer: APQ5, MDVP: APQ, Shimm er: DDA, NHR, HNR, status, RPDE, D2, DFA, spread1, spread2, PPE are the features.

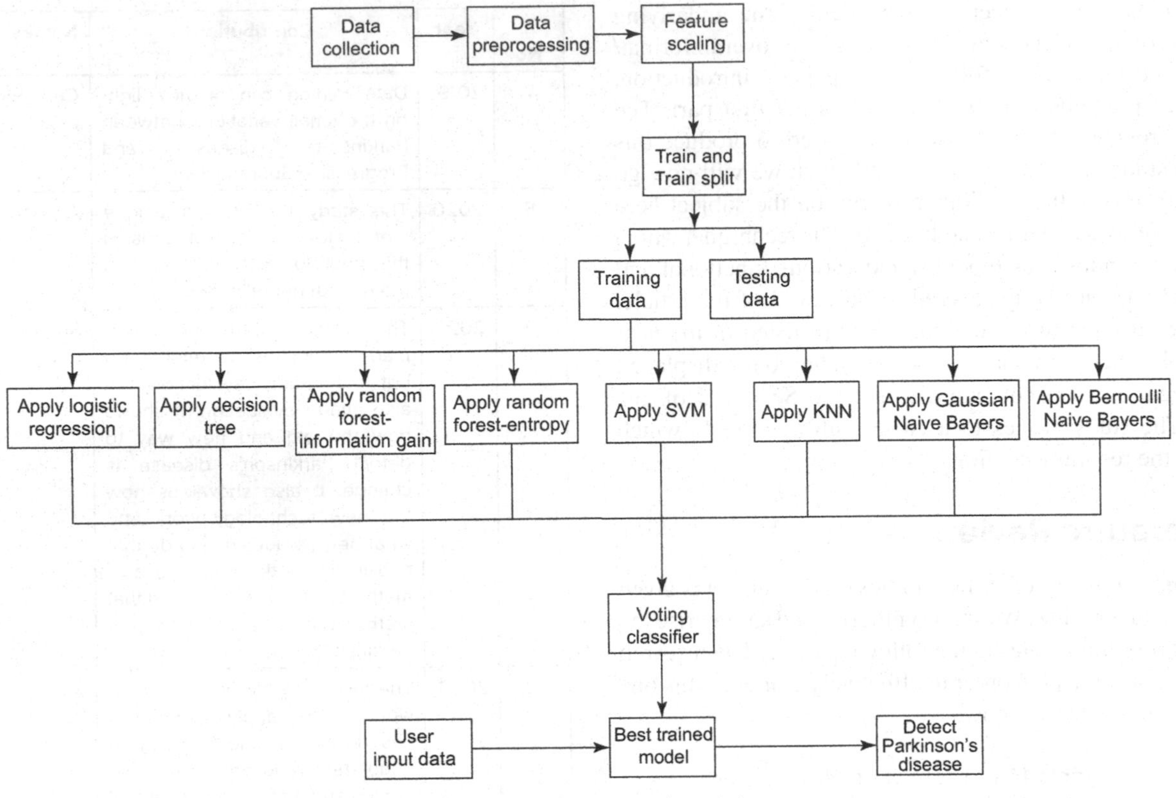

Fig. 14.1 Conceptual model

	MDVP:Fo(Hz)	MDVP:Fhi(Hz)	MDVP:Flo(Hz)	MDVP:Jitter(%)	MDVP:Jitter(Abs)	MDVP:RAP	MDVP:PPQ	Jitter:DDP	MDVP:Shimmer	MDVP:Shimmer(dB)
count	195.000000	195.000000	195.000000	195.000000	195.000000	195.000000	195.000000	195.000000	195.000000	195.000000
mean	154.228641	197.104918	116.324631	0.006220	0.000044	0.003306	0.003446	0.009920	0.029709	0.282251
std	41.390065	91.491548	43.521413	0.004848	0.000035	0.002968	0.002759	0.008903	0.018857	0.194877
min	88.333000	102.145000	65.476000	0.001680	0.000007	0.000680	0.000920	0.002040	0.009540	0.085000
25%	117.572000	134.862500	84.291000	0.003460	0.000020	0.001660	0.001860	0.004985	0.016505	0.148500
50%	148.790000	175.829000	104.315000	0.004940	0.000030	0.002500	0.002690	0.007490	0.022970	0.221000
75%	182.769000	224.205500	140.018500	0.007365	0.000060	0.003835	0.003955	0.011505	0.037885	0.350000
max	260.105000	592.030000	239.170000	0.033160	0.000260	0.021440	0.019580	0.064330	0.119080	1.302000

Fig. 14.2 Statistical description of data

(b) *Data processing and analysis:* For the purpose of creating ML model for this disease's research, data processing, analysis are crucial processes. The data is statistically analysed for the better understanding of the dataset.

Once a model has been chosen, it is trained using a dataset to show it how to spot patterns in the data.[9] From the dataset, a training set and a validation/test set are produced. The validation/test dataset is used to evaluate the model's performance after it has been trained using the training set. The split between the training and testing sets is 80:20

Table 14.2 Data after being split into test and train sets

No of people's data for training of model	156
No of people's data for testing of model	39

Until the model's performance is sufficient, this process is repeated.

(c) Model training through various algorithms

- Logistic regression

```
******** LogisticRegression(C=0.4, max_iter=1000, solver='liblinear') ********
              precision    recall  f1-score   support

           0       0.76      0.79      0.78        24
           1       0.85      0.83      0.84        35

    accuracy                           0.81        59
   macro avg       0.81      0.81      0.81        59
weighted avg       0.82      0.81      0.81        59

confusion matrix
[[24  0]
 [ 0 35]]
```

Fig. 14.3 Model results of logistics regression

- Decision tree

```
******** DecisionTreeClassifier(random_state=14) ********
              precision    recall  f1-score   support

           0       0.86      1.00      0.92        24
           1       1.00      0.89      0.94        35

    accuracy                           0.93        59
   macro avg       0.93      0.94      0.93        59
weighted avg       0.94      0.93      0.93        59

confusion matrix
[[24  0]
 [ 0 35]]
```

Fig. 14.4 Model results of decision tree

- Random forest- Information gain

```
******** RandomForestClassifier(random_state=14) ********
              precision    recall  f1-score   support

           0       1.00      1.00      1.00        24
           1       1.00      1.00      1.00        35

    accuracy                           1.00        59
   macro avg       1.00      1.00      1.00        59
weighted avg       1.00      1.00      1.00        59

confusion matrix
[[24  0]
 [ 0 35]]
```

Fig. 14.5 Model results of Rondom forest-information gain

- Random forest-entropy

```
******** RandomForestClassifier(criterion='entropy') ********
              precision    recall  f1-score   support

           0       1.00      1.00      1.00        24
           1       1.00      1.00      1.00        35

    accuracy                           1.00        59
   macro avg       1.00      1.00      1.00        59
weighted avg       1.00      1.00      1.00        59

confusion matrix
[[24  0]
 [ 0 35]]
```

Fig. 14.6 Model results of Rondom forest-entropy

- Support vector machine

```
******** SVC(cache_size=100) ********
              precision    recall  f1-score   support

           0       0.88      0.96      0.92        24
           1       0.97      0.91      0.94        35

    accuracy                           0.93        59
   macro avg       0.93      0.94      0.93        59
weighted avg       0.94      0.93      0.93        59

confusion matrix
[[24  0]
 [ 0 35]]
```

Fig. 14.7 Model results of SVM

- KNN

```
******** KNeighborsClassifier(n_neighbors=3) ********
              precision    recall  f1-score   support

           0       0.96      0.96      0.96        24
           1       0.97      0.97      0.97        35

    accuracy                           0.97        59
   macro avg       0.96      0.96      0.96        59
weighted avg       0.97      0.97      0.97        59

confusion matrix
[[24  0]
 [ 0 35]]
```

Fig. 14.8 Model results of KNN

- Gaussian Naïve Bayes

```
******** GaussianNB() ********
              precision    recall  f1-score   support

           0       0.81      0.88      0.84        24
           1       0.91      0.86      0.88        35

    accuracy                           0.86        59
   macro avg       0.86      0.87      0.86        59
weighted avg       0.87      0.86      0.87        59

confusion matrix
[[24  0]
 [ 0 35]]
```

Fig. 14.9 Model results of Gaussian Naïve Bayes

- Bernoulli Naïve Bayes

3.2 Non-functional Requirements

In Parkinson's disease, non-functional criteria are just as crucial as functional requirements since they guarantee that the system or application operates effectively, securely, and efficiently while delivering a great user experience. Usability, Performance, Security, Reliability, Accessibility, Compatibility are the non- functional requirements.

```
******** BernoulliNB() ********
              precision    recall  f1-score   support

           0       0.78      0.88      0.82        24
           1       0.91      0.83      0.87        35

    accuracy                           0.85        59
   macro avg       0.84      0.85      0.84        59
weighted avg       0.85      0.85      0.85        59

confusion matrix
[[24  0]
 [ 0 35]]
```

Fig. 14.10 Model results of Bernoulli Naïve Bayes

4. Software and Hardware Requirements

The minimal software prerequisites for launching our product are described below. Prior to scaling out, it is advised to observe the results of pilot projects as requirements may change depending on utilization. Python, Html, CSS, Flask, and Python libraries are the software requirements.

4.1 Hardware Requirements

The minimal hardware specifications for implementing:

- OS: Window7
- Installed RAM: 4 GB
- Processor: Intel i3 or above
- System type: 64-bit operating system

5. Result and Discussion

Parkinson's disease is a very dangerous condition for which there is no known cure. Since it impacts how the body's components work, the speech is also influenced.

5.1 Snapshots

```
                        Algorithm  Accuracy
0             Logistic Regression  0.813559
1                   Decision Tree  0.932203
2  Random Forest-Information Gain  1.000000
3            Random Forest-Entropy  1.000000
4          Support Vector Machine  0.932203
5                             KNN  0.966102
6            Gaussian Naive Bayes  0.864407
7           Bernoulli Naive Bayes  0.847458
AxesSubplot(0.125,0.11;0.775x0.77)
```

Fig. 14.11 ML mdoels accuracy

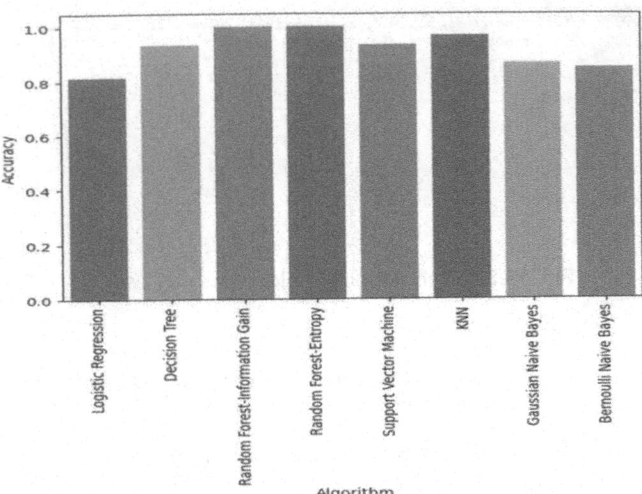

Fig. 14.12 ML models accuracy's graphical representation

6. Conclusion

The Random Forest Information Gain and Entropy has 100% accuracy. KNN following it has 96% accuracy. Decision Tree and SVM have accuracy score of 93%. Gaussian Naive Bayes stands with 86% whereas Bernoulli Naive Bayes stands with 84%. The minimum 81% Accuracy is of Logistic Regression. Random Forest Information Gain > Random Forest Entropy > KNN > Decision Tree > SVM > Gaussian Naive Bayes > Bernoulli Naive Bayes > Logistic Regression is the order of recommendation.

7. Future Scope

Machine Learning Based Parkinson's Disease Diagnosis offers numerous recommendations for future that will improve the process's precision, effectiveness and accessibility. Some of the potential future scopes are Dataset Expansion, Feature selection and engineering, Real-Time monitoring and mobile applications, External validation and clinical trials, User-friendly interfaces and user Experience.[10]

8. Acknowledgement

We extend our sincerest appreciation to Ayasha Malik, our esteemed project guide, for her priceless guidance, support, and motivation during our research endeavor. The dedicated college staff also deserves our gratitude for their valuable assistance and provision of resources that significantly contributed to the accomplishment of our project. Their unwavering commitment and expertise played a crucial role in shaping our academic pursuits. We would like to express our heartfelt thanks to everyone involved for their substantial contributions to our research paper.

REFERENCES

1. Heisters. D. (2011). Parkinson's: symptoms, treatments and research. British Journal of Nursing, 20(9), 548–554.
2. Ozcift. (2012). SVM feature selection-based rotation forest ensemble classifiers to improve computer aided diagnosis of Parkinson disease. Journal of medical systems. vol-36. no. 4. 2141–2147.
3. Farhad Soleimanian Gharehehopogh, Peymen Mohammadi. (2013). A Case Study of Parkinson's Disease Diagnosis Using Artificial Neural Networks. International Journal of Computer Applications. Vol-73. No.19.
4. Dragana Miljkovic. (2016). Machine Learning and Data Mining Methods for Managing Parkinson's Disease. LNAI 9605. 209–220.
5. Dr. Anupam Bhatia, Raunak Sulekh. (2017). Predictive Model for Parkinson's Disease through Naïve Bayes Classification. International Journal of Computer Science & Communication vol-9. 194–202.
6. M. Abdar, M. Zomorodi-Moghadam. (2018). Impact of Patients Gender on Parkinson's disease using Classification Algorithms. Journal of AI and Data Mining. vol-6.
7. Carlo Ricciardi. (2019). Using gait analysis parameters to classify Parkinsonism: A data mining approach. Computer Methods and Programs in Biomedicine. vol-180.
8. Anila M, Dr G Pradeepini. (2020). DIAGNOSIS OF PARKINSON'S DISEASE USING ARTIFICIAL NEURAL NETWORK. JCR. 7(19): 7260–7269.
9. Shreevallabhadatta, Suhas M, Vignesh, Manoj, RudramurthyV, Bhagyashri R Hanji. (2022). PARKINSON'S DISEASE DETECTION USING MACHINE LEARNING. International Research Journal of Engineering and Technology (IRJET). vol-9. issue 6. 1805–1811.
10. J Divya, P Radhakrishnan, G Pavithra, Anandbabu Gopatoti, D Baburao, R Krishnamoorthy. (2023). Detection of Parkinson Disease using Machine Learning. International Conference on Inventive Computation Technologies (ICICT). 53–57.

Note: All the figures and table in this chapter were made by the author.

Advancement of Intelligent Computational Methods and Technologies (AICMT2023) – Dr. O. P. Verma et al. (eds)
© 2024 Taylor & Francis Group, London, ISBN 978-1-032-78445-8

15

Exploring the Role of Machine Learning in Wine Quality Detection

Aditya Ranjan[1], Mayank Attrey[2], Gauransh Bhasin[3], Mohit Kumar[4] and Malik Nadeem[5]
Computer Science and Engineering, Delhi Technical Campus, Greater Noida, UP, India

ABSTRACT: The identification of wine quality is essential for assuring the production of high-quality wines. Traditional techniques of evaluating the quality of wine rely on expert subjective assessments, which can be time- consuming and vulnerable to human bias. Machine learning (Machine Learning) approaches have become a potential method for improving and automating wine quality identification. Research offers thorough examination of the implementation of the technology in determining wine quality. The purpose aims at creating precise and dependable models that can forecast wine quality based on its chemical and sensory characteristics. To ensure the quality and relevance of the incoming data, the study starts with data preparation, which includes data cleaning, normalization, and feature engineering. To find the most useful traits for predicting wine quality, feature selection approaches are used. By examining feature significance rankings, the research also examines the interpretability of the Machine Learning models. This investigation offers important new information about the chemical elements that strongly influence wine quality. The suggested Machine Learning based strategy has a number of benefits, including the ability for real-time monitoring, increased consistency, and a quicker and more accurate wine quality evaluation. By enabling producers to optimize their winemaking procedures and guarantee consistent quality across several batches, it has the potential to revolutionize the wine business. This study shows, in conclusion, how Machine Learning approaches may be used to identify wine quality. The results demonstrate the potential of Machine Learning algorithms to increase and automate the evaluation of wine quality, resulting in better production techniques and consumer satisfaction. To further enhance the precision and application of wine quality identification, future research might concentrate on extending the dataset and investigating cutting-edge Machine Learning models.

KEYWORDS: Wine Quality, Machine learning, Detection

1. Introduction

In the wine business, machine learning based wine quality prediction is a common use of data science and artificial intelligence. Machine learning algorithms may be trained to estimate the quality of a certain wine based on its properties by examining numerous traits and characteristics of wines. It's vital to remember that choosing the right features and methods, as well as employing a high-quality dataset, are critical to the success to evaluate the status. It also assists in improving model's accuracy and dependability over time to continuously monitor it and update it with fresh data. A specialized use of machine learning is wine quality prediction, which seeks to forecast the quality or rating of wines based on their numerous characteristics. The objective is to create models that can accurately analyses a wine's characteristics and determine its quality. A high quality and representative dataset must be available, and the machine learning model must be carefully chosen and tuned if wine quality prediction is to be successful. Over time, the model's prediction powers may be further improved by ongoing monitoring and updating with fresh data.

[1]ranjanaditya7277@gmail.com, [2]mayankattreybca@delhitechnicalcampus.ac.in, [3]gauranshbhasin5@gmail.com, [4]mohitkumarbca@delhitechnicalcamp us.ac.in, [5]n.malik@delhitechnicalcampus.ac.in

DOI: 10.1201/9781003487906-15

2. Literature Survey

Wine quality y certification is vital in every endeavour in this domain, and assessing wine necessitates human experts. (Vanmathi 2021)

In recent years, there has been an upward trend in interest in the wine market, which mandates diversification in this industry. As a consequence, wineries are investing in creative innovations to enhance wine sales and production. (Gupta 2018)

In addition, this helped in accumulating lots of data with various parameters such as quantity of different chemicals and temperature used during the production, and the quality of the wine produced. These data are available in various databases . (Dahal and Banjade et al. 2021)

Data mining is a blend of factual models and machine learning. The term data mining deals with the extraction of learning and models from huge dataset. (Kumar and Agrawal et al. 2020)

3. Functional and Non-functional Requirements

A specialized use of machine learning is wine quality prediction, which seeks to forecast the quality or rating of wines based on their numerous characteristics. The objective is to create models that can accurately analyses a wine's characteristics and determine its quality.

3.1 Functional Requirements

Data gathering, Data composing, Feature nomination, Decision tree ensemble, Model election, Model tutoring, Model assessment, Model optimization, Prediction and deployment are the functional requirements. A high-quality and representative dataset must be available, and the machine learning model must be carefully chosen and tuned if wine quality prediction is to be successful. Continuous monitoring and updating of the model with new data can further enhance its predictive capabilities over time.

3.2 Non-functional Requirements

Non-functional requirements are the qualities and restrictions that the system should display in terms of Performance, Reliability, Usability, Security, Accuracy, Scalability, Robustness, Maintainability, Compliance, and other areas in the context of wine quality detection using machine learning. These nonfunctional requirements are essential for creating a wine quality detection system that fulfils user expectations.

4. Software and Hardware Requirements

Hardware prerequisites for launching our model are described below.

4.1 Software Requirements

The minimal software specifications for implementation are:

- HTML
- CSS
- Flask
- Python
- Python libraries

4.2 Hardware Requirements

The minimal hardware specifications for implementation are:

- OS: Window7
- Installed RAM: 4 GB
- Processor: Intel i3 or above
- System type: 64-bit operating system

5. Result and Discussion

The outcome of wine quality detection using machine learning relies heavily on the criteria used by the dataset, keeping in record quality as well as volume of the data, selected machine learning algorithm, the feature selection and engineering approaches utilized, and the evaluation metrics used to gauge the model's effectiveness. The ideal outcome of wine quality detection is the creation of a machine learning model that can predict wines' quality scores with accuracy. The quality evaluations might be displayed as continuous values (such as a numerical score) or discrete groups (such as low, medium, and high). However, if the data set used for prediction does not uses correct parameters, then the whole exercise of prediction may result in inaccurate data. After a thorough study of the literature the authors have identified 7 criteria which should be essential for any wine dataset. Following are the list of identification criteria explored by the authors, which gives an indication on the quality of wines decided based on any ML technique fed with datasets having these criteria as the basepoint

Criteria 1

Fixed acidity: Acidity is a crucial component of wine that greatly influences its overall flavor, structure, and ability to age. In particular, tartaric, malic, and citric acids are the main organic acids present in wine. The balance and apparent freshness of a wine are greatly influenced by its amount of acidity. To achieve the ideal balance and taste of the wine, winemakers meticulously monitor and modify acidity levels during the winemaking process. The evaluation, appreciation, and creation of high-quality wines are all aided by an understanding of acidity and how it affects wine.

Criteria 2

Volatile acidity: A particular sort of acidity in wine known as volatile acidity is connected to the presence of volatile acids, especially acetic acid. It has a substantial influence on the sensory qualities and overall quality of the wine, making it a crucial parameter in wine analysis. Monitoring and controlling volatile acidity is a crucial part of the winemaking process to guarantee that wines have the desired sensory qualities and adhere to quality requirements. Winemakers may take the necessary steps to maintain wine quality and avert potential issues by comprehending volatile acidity and its effects.

Criteria 3:

Citric acid: Small amounts of the organic acid known as citric acid can be discovered in some wines. Citric acid, albeit not as significant an acid as tartaric or malic acid, can influence the overall acidity and flavor of some wines. The presence and effects of citric acid in wine might vary based on the grape variety, winemaking processes, and regional customs, it is crucial to remember. Citric acid is not normally the main acid in wine, but its presence can help to balance the wine's overall acidity and flavor profile, giving it a subtle depth.

Criteria 4:

Residual Sugar: The quantity of sugar left in wine after fermentation is complete is referred to as residual sugar. The natural grape sugars are used by yeast during fermentation, which turns them into alcohol. To attain a specific level of sweetness, winemakers may purposefully leave a certain quantity of sugar in the wine. It's crucial to understand that added sugar, which describes the addition of sugar or sweeteners during or after fermentation, is different from residual sugar. While added sugar is a purposeful addition by the winemaker, residual sugar happens naturally from the grape's sugars. The presence and amount of residual sugar in wine can have a significant influence on its flavor profile, perception of sweetness, and compatibility for certain meals or events. Remaining sugar levels are carefully managed and regulated by winemakers to produce the appropriate style and balance in the finished product.

Criteria 5:

Chlorides: In the context of wine, the term "chlorides" refers particularly to the presence of chloride ions (Cl-) in the wine. The soil where the grapes are cultivated, irrigation water, winemaking additives, and processing machinery are some of the sources of chlorides. In order to preserve the intended flavor profile, protect the wine's quality, and prevent any sensory flaws, it is crucial to keep an eye on the chloride levels in wine. The natural expression of chloride ions and their effect on the wine's overall sensory experience are two opposing forces that winemakers work to reconcile wine's overall acidity and flavor profile, giving it a subtle depth.

Criteria 6

Density: The mass of the wine per unit volume is referred to as density in wine. Typically, it is expressed in kilogrammes per litre (kg/L) or grammes per millilitre (g/mL). The wine's temperature, alcohol percentage, and sugar content are only a few of the variables that affect density. Although density does not directly affect the taste or aroma of wine, it is a crucial physical attribute that can provide essential details about the wine's composition, the status of the fermentation, and its general quality. Density measurements are a part of the analytical and quality assurance procedures used by winemakers and wine scientists.

Criteria 7

Citric acid: Small amounts of the organic acid known as citric acid can be discovered in some wines. Citric acid, albeit not as significant an acid as tartaric or malic acid, can influence the overall acidity and flavor of some wines. The presence and effects of citric acid in wine might vary based on the grape variety, winemaking processes, and regional customs, it is crucial to remember. Citric acid is not normally the main acid in wine, but its presence can help to balance the wine's overall acidity and flavor profile, giving it a subtle depth.

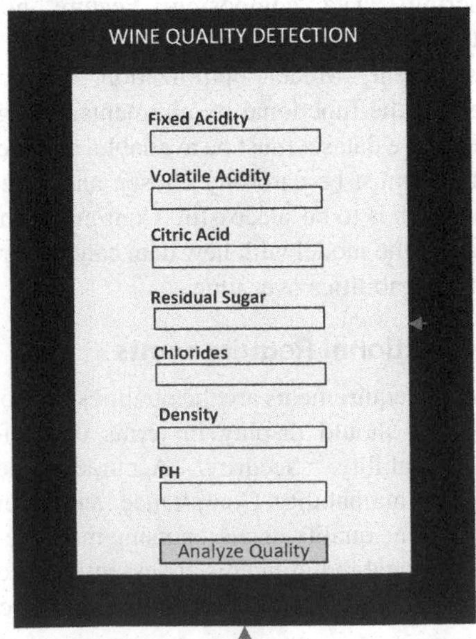

Fig. 15.1 Input data page

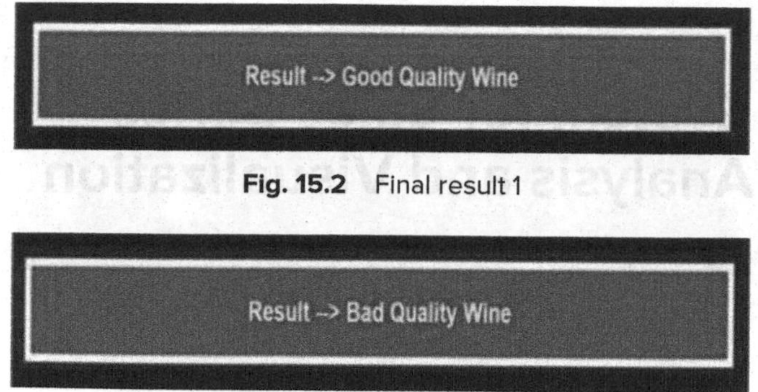

Fig. 15.2 Final result 1

Fig. 15.3 Final result 2

Figure 15.1 shows the interface of sample application that can use various criteria, as outlined by the authors crucial for determining the quality of the wine using various machine learning algorithms. The prototype of the application has a user interface which requires the user to fill various inputs like fixed acidity, volatile acidity, acidic content of the sample etc. Figures 15.2 and 15.3 depict the results of one of such a sample prototype toll showing the quality of the wine, classifying them as good or bad.

6. Conclusion

In conclusion, wineries, industry professionals, and consumers all stand to benefit greatly from machine learning-based wine quality identification. The characteristics of wines may be examined, and their quality ratings can be predicted, using ML algorithms like decision trees, random forests, or other complex models. Large datasets and strong computational methods are used by ML models to produce precise and unbiased evaluations of wine quality. However the quality of these ML models results depends largely on the criteria fixed for evaluating the wines. In this paper, the authors have identified 7 criteria which forms the backone of any such dataset on wine Quality prediction. The use of ML for wine quality identification has a number of advantages. It makes automated and uniform evaluations possible, minimizing the subjectivity and unpredictability that may result from human evaluations. The complexity of correlations between variables and wine quality may be captured by ML models, which can handle a large variety of attributes, including both numerical and categorical information.

7. Future Scope

In this section, we will discuss how to configure the ChatGPT API parameters to optimise the model's behaviour and acquire the desirable responses generated by AI. Understanding and effectively employing these parameters will enable us to create engaging and customised prompts, thereby elevating the quality of our AI-powered conversations to new heights (Qiu and Hongliang et al. 2023).

With a number of possible developments and applications in the works, the future potential of machine learning (ML) for wine quality identification is quite encouraging. The following are some areas where wine quality detection in ML shows promise in the future –

Hybrid Models: ML may be used in conjunction with other analytical methods like chemometrics and spectroscopy to produce ratings of wine quality that are more precise and thorough. Hybrid models, which combine several data sources and analytic techniques, can offer a comprehensive strategy for identifying wine quality.

Integration of Sensor Technology: Systems for real time wine quality monitoring may be created by combining ML with sensor technology. In order to anticipate wine quality in real time, IoT devices and smart sensors may gather data on a variety of characteristics, including temperature, humidity, pH levels, and chemical composition.

REFERENCES

1. Chawla, N.V., Data Mining for Imbalanced Datasets: An Overview, in: Maimon, O., Rokach, L. (Eds.), Data Mining and Knowledge Discovery Handbook. Springer US, Boston, MA, pp. (2005) 853–867.
2. Cortez, P., Cerdeira, A., Almeida, F., Matos, T., Reis, J., Modeling wine preferences by data mining from physicochemical properties. Decis. Support Syst. 47, (2009) 547–553.
3. Er, Y., Atasoy, A.,. The Classification of White Wine and Red Wine According to Their Physicochemical Qualities. Int. J. Intell. Syst. Appl. Eng. 4, (2016) 23–26.
4. Gupta, Yogesh. Selection of important features and predicting wine quality using machine learning techniques. Procedia Computer Science, 125, (2018) 305–312.
5. K. R. Dahal, J. N. Dahal, H. Banjade, S. Gaire "Prediction of Wine Quality Using Machine Learning Algorithms" published by Open Journal of Statistics, Vol.11 No.2, (2021).
6. Kumar, S., Agrawal, K., Mandan, N., 2020. Red Wine Quality Prediction Using Machine Learning Techniques, in: International (2020).
7. V. Preedy, and M. L. R. Mendez, "Wine Applications with Electronic Noses," in Electronic Noses and Tongues in Food Science, Cambridge, MA, USA: Academic Press, (2016), pp. 137–151.

Note: All the figures in this chapter were made by the author.

Advancement of Intelligent Computational Methods and Technologies (AICMT2023) – Dr. O. P. Verma et al. (eds)

16

Machine Learning System for Sales Series Forecasting: Data Analysis and Visualization Approach

Jhanvi Pathak[1], Vidhi Goel[2], Khushi Tanwar[3], Nidhi Sharma[4]
Department of Computer Science and Engineering, Delhi Technical Campus, Greater Noida, UP, India

ABSTRACT: Businesses use sales forecasting to make decisions about how to allocate resources and optimize their operations. This research paper presents a machine learning system that uses advanced data analysis and visualization techniques to forecast future sales trends. The system works by training machine learning models on historical sales data. These models use various machine learning algorithms to analyze the data, identify patterns, and generate accurate forecasts. The system also uses preprocessing techniques to handle data inconsistencies and improve the quality of the input data. Feature engineering is used to extract meaningful insights from the data, which further improves the predictive capabilities of the models. The system is designed to be easy to use and scalable, so that it can be used by businesses of all sizes.

KEYWORDS: Machine learning, Dataset collection, Data analysis, Future prediction, Data mining techniques, Feature extraction, Model building, etc.

1. Introduction

This research found that ml can be used to improve sales forecasting, which cam used to improve sales forecasting which can lead to increased profits. Python and Jupyter software were used to collect and analyze data, and different ML algorithms were evaluated to find the most accurate one.

The research also found that using ML can help businesses improve their resource planning. By collecting and analyzing data, businesses can better understand their customers and make more informed decisions about how to allocate resources.

The random forest regression model was found to be the most accurate model for predicting future sales. This model works by creating multiple decision trees and then averaging their predictions.

2. Dataset Preparation

Define the problem: Clearly understand the objective of your sales prediction. Are you trying to predict total sales, individual product sales, or sales for specific regions? Specify the target variable that you want to predict (Mann, A. K., & Kaur, N. 2013).

Gather data: Collect relevant data that can help in predicting sales. This may include historical sales data, product attributes, pricing information, marketing campaigns, customer demographics, and economic indicators. Obtain the data from internal databases, external sources, or through web scraping.

Clean the data: Data cleaning is essential to ensure the accuracy and quality of your dataset. Performs the following tasks: Handle missing values, remove duplicates, Resolve inconsistencies, and Feature engineering

Explore the data: Perform exploratory data analysis (EDA) to gain insights into your dataset. This step helps you understand the relationships between variables, detect patterns, and identify any potential issues or biases. Visualizations and statistical summaries can be useful for this purpose.

Splitting the dataset: The dataset is divided into two sets: training and testing sets. The training set and testing set is

[1]Jhanvipathak21@gmail.com, [2]imvidhigoel@gmail.comm [3]khushitanwar1209@gmail.com, [4]n.sharma@delhitechnicalcampus.ac.in

DOI: 10.1201/9781003487906-16

used to train the machine learning model and to evaluate its performance, respectively. It is common to allocate approximately 70-80% of the dataset for training and 20-30% for testing, although the specific proportions may vary depending on the dataset's size and characteristics.

Normalize or scale the data: If your dataset contains features with different scales, such as sales and product prices, it's important to normalize or scale them. This step ensures that all features are equally participating in the model training process. Min-max scaling, z-score normalization, and the use of robust scalers are all common strategies.

Features selection: Determine the most important features that have a major impact on sales forecasting. This step helps reduce noise, improve model performance, and avoid overfitting. You can use statistical tests, correlation analysis, or feature importance techniques (e.g., based on tree-based models) to determine which features to include.

Encode categorical variables: There is the need to encode the dataset if it contains categorical variables (e.g., product categories, customer segments), you need to encode them numerically. One-hot encoding, label encoding, or target encoding are commonly used methods for this purpose.

Build the Model: For sales prediction, suitable algorithm is selected, like linear regression, decision trees, random forests, gradient boosting, or neural networks. Train the model with the training dataset, making sure to tune the hyperparameters.

Model assessment or evaluation: Employ the testing dataset to assess the performance of the trained model. Standard evaluation metrics for regression tasks, like MSE (mean squared error), RMSE (root mean squared error), MAE (mean absolute error), and R-squared, can be utilized. The performance of model is compared against baseline models or alternative algorithms to verify its efficacy and validate its effectiveness.

3. Research Approach

This study's main goal is to evaluate and look into how data mining techniques are used in sales forecasting. The aim is to develop comprehensive and dependable models that can effectively predict sales outcomes. By evaluating the effectiveness of these techniques, the research seeks to enhance the accuracy and reliability of sales forecasting methods.

Preparation and Collection of Data: The initial step in machine learning involves gathering the dataset, and in our case, we obtained it from the Kaggle platform. Specifically, we utilized the sales data from the big Mart store spanning three consecutive years. Following data collection, we performed necessary preprocessing steps to ensure the dataset's quality and suitability for analysis and modelling purposes.

Exploratory Analysis: By conducting exploratory analysis, you can gain a deeper understanding of the dataset, identify important features, detect outliers, and uncover patterns and trends. This analysis provides valuable insights that inform the subsequent steps of data preprocessing, feature engineering, and model development for sales prediction using machine learning.

Outlier Detection: Outliers are data points that are different from the rest of the data. They can affect machine learning models, so it is important to detect and remove them. There are three ways to do this: visual inspection, statistical methods, and domain knowledge.

Once outliers have been detected, they can be removed or treated in some other way. Removing outliers can improve the performance of machine learning models.

Forecasting and Trends: Forecasting and trend analysis are essential for gaining insights into future demand and making informed business decisions. Machine learning plays crucial role in accurately predicting sales and uncovering underlying trends. The following approaches can be employed to forecast and identify trends in sales data for Big Mart using ML:

- **Time Series Analysis:** Utilize time series analysis techniques to convert sales data into a time-based format and uncover patterns, seasonality, & trends. Techniques like (ARIMA), (SARIMA), or Exponential Smoothing models can be applied for accurate sales forecasting. The performance of models can be assessed by employing various evaluation metrics, including mean absolute error, mean squared error, or root mean squared error. These metrics provide insights into the accuracy and precision of the models' prediction or forecast value.
- **Machine Learning Models:** Implement regression-based ML algorithms, including LR, RFR, or GBR , to develop predictive or forecasting models. To prepare the dataset, it is crucial to choose pertinent features, address missing values, encode categorical variables, and scale the data appropriately. After preparing the dataset, it must be separated into training and testing sets. The ML model is then fitted to the training data, and its performance is assessed using appropriate metrics. Finally, the trained model is used to anticipate future sales based on the data's learnt patterns and associations.
- **Feature Engineering:** Extract meaningful features from the dataset to capture seasonality, trends, and other relevant patterns. Generate lag variables to consider the impact of past sales on current sales. Incorporate external factors like holidays, promotions, or economic indicators that may influence sales.
- **Analyzing Trends:** Utilize data visualization techniques to analyze sales trends over time. Visualize the data using line charts or area charts to observe the overall

sales pattern. Apply techniques like moving averages or exponential smoothing to smooth the sales data and identify underlying trends. Explore seasonality patterns using seasonal decomposition methods such as seasonal subseries plots or seasonal boxplots.

It is crucial to consider that forecasting accuracy may be influenced by data quality, external events, and changes in market dynamics. Regularly reviewing and refining the forecasting approach based on performance can enhance the accuracy and reliability of sales predictions.

Prediction: Here two machine learning models; linear regression and random forest regression, are used to predict sales. The accuracy achieved with linear regression model 50.83% on the test set, and the accuracy achieved with random forest regression model is 94.05%. This means that the random forest regression model is more accurate at predicting sales.

The random forest regression model is a good choice for sales prediction because it is accurate and can be used with a variety of input features. Businesses that use this model can get insights into future sales trends and make informed decisions about their operations.

4. Objectives

We want to create a system that can accurately predict forecasted sales based on data from the past. We will use ml algorithms to analyze patterns, trends, and relationships in the data to make predictions. The model should be able to work with features like previous sales, establishment year, pricing, and other sales data to provide accurate sales results. Our main goal in building sales forecasting projects is to extract meaningful information from the datasets with the least possible error. We will use different algorithms to make more accurate predictions

5. Methodology

After gathering the necessary data, we can start the learning process. First, we preprocess the data to create the features we need and then split the data into three datasets. We run feature tests on the three datasets to find the optimal number of features for training, optimizing the Mean Absolute Error (MAE) score for all models.

To perform the final training, we use a train/test split, using all available data that was not included in the baseline test. We train the candidate models at this step by maximizing the MAE score. We then forecast the training datasets using the learned models, making it easier to compare the results using pre-defined measures.

The flowchart shows how to forecast sales. The data is scaled and the best number of features is chosen. The best models are tested. The process is the same even if the number of classes increases.

6. Implemented Tools

This section discusses the ml tools used for sales forecasting. Each tool is described, including its features, capabilities, and benefits. The tools are python libraries: Pandas, NumPy, scikit-learn, Klib, Dtale, Matplotlib, seaborn, Joblib, a specialized framework on Flask, and Python modules OS

Random Forest: Random Forest is a ML model that utilizes an ensemble approach, consisting of multiple decision trees. This model excels in capturing intricate relationships among variables and is applicable for both classification and regression tasks.

Linear Regression: For establishing the relationship between a dependent variable and one or more independent variables, (LR) is a frequently employed statistical modelling technique. It assumes that the variables are related linearly, with changes in the independent variables resulting in corresponding changes in the dependent variable (Sigrist, F., & Henschell, C. 2018).

7. Result and Analysis

Result: The results section summarizes the findings of the experiments. It includes the accuracy and performance metrics achieved by each ML algorithm tested. The predictions made by the models are compared to the actual sales figures, providing insights into the effectiveness of the ML techniques for sales prediction.

Analysis: We analyze and interpret the results. We discuss the strengths and weaknesses of each machine learning algorithm, and how they can be used for sales prediction in different situations. We also consider factors that affect the accuracy of the predictions.

Table 16.1 Result

Algorithm	Mean Absolute Error	Root Mean Squared Error	R2 Score	Accuracy
Linear Regression	880.99	1162.44	0.50	50.83
Random Forests	782.05	1108.37	0.54	94.05

Source: Author

8. Conclusion

This research shows that using the Machine Learning (ML) techniques can significantly improve the accuracy of sales predictions, which can lead to increased profits for businesses. Python and Jupyter software help business use data to improve sales. They make it easier to collect and make better prediction or forecasting about the future sales.

The research paper studies how ML can help businesses predict sales. Using a variety of software tools and algorithms, businesses can make significant improvements to their resource planning.

This research paper used data from other businesses to evaluate the impact of machine learning (ML) on sales prediction. The paper provides valuable insights into the field of sales prediction through its detailed findings and analysis.

The study found that the Random Forest Regression model was the most accurate in predicting future sales.

9. Acknowledgement

We would like to thank everyone who helped us with this research paper on ml for sales forecasting especially those who worked on data analysis and visualization. First and foremost, we would like to thank our project guide, Ms. Nidhi Sharma, for her essential guidance, support, and expertise in the project. She helped make this study better with her knowledge and insights. Their collaboration has significantly increased the richness and accuracy of the dataset used in this study.

We were grateful to our team and colleagues for their help and cooperation. Their insights and feedbacks were valuable in refining the research methodology and improving the analysis. Their support has been vital in the successful completion of this research.

We would like to thank all the researchers, scholars, and authors who helped us with our study. Their work was helpful in developing our theoretical framework and providing valuable insights. We are also grateful to everyone who contributed to the completion of this research paper

REFERENCES

1. Huang, Q., & Zhou, F. (2017, March). Research on retailer data clustering algorithm based on spark. In AIP Conference Proceedings (Vol. 1820, No. 1, p. 080022). AIP Publishing.
2. Saylı, A., Ozturk, I., & Ustunel, M. (2016). Brand loyalty analysis system using the K-Means algorithm. Journal of Engineering Technology and Applied Sciences, 1(3).
3. Maingi, M. N. A Survey on the Clustering Algorithms in Sales Data Mining.
4. Sastry, S. H., Babu, P., & Prasada, M. S. (2013). Analysis & Prediction of Sales Data in SAP-ERP System using Clustering Algorithms. arXiv preprint arXiv:1312.2678.
5. Shrivastava, V., & Arya, N. (2012). A study of various clustering algorithms on retail sales data. Int. J. Comput. Commun. Netw, 1(2).
6. Rajagopal, D. (2011). Customer data clustering using data mining technique. arXiv preprint arXiv:1112.2663.
7. Tsai, C. F., Wu, H. C., & Tsai, C. W. (2002). A new data clustering approach for data mining in large databases. In Parallel Architectures, Algorithms, and Networks, 2002. I-SPAN'02. Proceedings. International Symposium on (pp. 315-320). IEEE.
8. Mann, A. K., & Kaur, N. (2013). Review paper on clustering techniques. Global Journal of Computer Science and Technology.
9. Shah, N., Solanki, M., Tambe, A., & Dhangar, D. Sales Prediction Using Effective Mining Techniques.
10. Korolev, M., & Ruegg, K. (2015). Gradient Boosted Trees to Predict Store Sales.
11. Jain, A., Menon, M. N., & Chandra, S. Sales Forecasting for Retail Chains.
12. Rey, T. D., Wells, C., & Kauhl, J. (2013). Using data mining in forecasting problems. In SAS Global Forum 2013: Data Mining and Text Analytics.
13. Huang, W., Zhang, Q., Xu, W., Fu, H., Wang, M., & Liang, X. (2015).A Novel Trigger Model for Sales Prediction with Data Mining Techniques. Data Science Journal, 14.
14. Ethem Alpaydin. (2004). Introduction to Machine Learning (Adaptive Computation and Machine Learning), The MIT Press.
15. Lytvynenko, T. I. (2016). Problem of data analysis and forecasting using decision trees method.
16. Lazăr, C., & Lazăr, M. (2015). Using the Method of Decision Trees in the Forecasting Activity. Petroleum-Gas University of Ploiesti Bulletin, Technical Series, 67(1).
17. Flesch, B., Satrap, R., Mukkamala, R. R., & Hussain, A. (2015,October). Social set visualizer: A set theoretical approach to bigsocial data analytics of real-world events. In Big Data (Big Data),2015 IEEE International Conference on(pp. 2418–2427). IEEE.
18. Asooja, K., Bordea, G., Vulcu, G., & Buitelaar, P. (2016). ForecastingEmerging Trends from Scientific Literature. In LREC.
19. Stearns, B., Rangel, F., Rangel, F., de Faria, F. F., Oliveira, J., &Ramos, A. A. D. S. (2017). Scholar Performance Prediction usingBoosted Regression Trees Techniques. In European Symposium onArtificial Neural Networks, Computational Intelligence and Machine Learning (ESANN). Citeseer.
20. Sigrist, F., & Henschell, C. (2018). Gradient Tree-Boosted TobitModels for Default Prediction.

Advancement of Intelligent Computational Methods and Technologies (AICMT2023) – Dr. O. P. Verma et al. (eds)
© 2024 Taylor & Francis Group, London, ISBN 978-1-032-78445-8

17

Automating a Mobile Application Using Appium

Preeti Pandey[1], Nishchey Bhutani[2], Richa Thakur[3], Shubham Kr. Jha[4]
CSE Department, Delhi Technical Campus, Greater Noida,India

ABSTRACT: Testing is a crucial aspect of software engineering, especially in industries that rely on product development. It serves a critical role in various applications, and businesses today allocate substantial resources, including time and financial investments, to manual testing. The primary goal is to achieve comprehensive testing of applications, ensuring optimal performance and a smooth user experience. Regular testing is carried out to accurately assess the impact of daily updates. This research paper specifically explores automated testing methodologies designed for hybrid and web mobile applications.

KEYWORDS: Approaches, Appium, Automated testing, UI testing, Scripting mobile applications, iOS

1. Introduction

Automation testing has gained immense importance in the software development life cycle, transforming the approach to quality assurance and reliability assessment of software applications. This research paper aims to explore the significance, challenges, and benefits associated with automation testing.

Assessing the application during usage is sometimes considered a part of software testing. The two primary methods of software testing include manual testing and automated testing. Automated testing involves using separate software to manage the execution of tests on the system being tested. Our current challenge is to find ways to streamline these efforts without compromising the overall quality of the system under development. One effective and practical solution to address this issue is to automate the testing of repetitive tasks (I. Burnetein. 2013).

2. Manual Testing-Automated Testing

Through the analysis of industry trends and real-world case studies, this study aims to provide valuable insights to organizations seeking to optimize their testing processes and make informed decisions regarding the adoption and implementation of automation testing strategies (P. Ammann and J. Offutt. 2008). Manual testing, for instance, may not be effective in uncovering hidden faults or identifying missing information, unlike automated testing, which enables the creation of sophisticated tests (K. Karhu, T. Repo and K. Smolander 2009). Manual testing often becomes tedious, time-consuming, and slow. On the other hand, automation offers a solution to the growing number of mobile applications by executing repetitive actions through scripts, thus reducing the likelihood of errors. Moreover, automation allows for testing a broader range of options, thereby minimizing potential errors (Milad Hanna, Mostafa Sami, Nahla El-Haggar. 2014).

3. UI Automation Testing

The rapid advancement of mobile technology has brought about significant changes in company procedures and IT systems. This research paper aims to explore the impact of UI automation testing in the field of automation testing, specifically focusing on mobile applications. Additionally, there is a need for a solution that can effectively test mobile applications across multiple platforms.

[1]p.pandey@delhitechnicalcampus.ac.in, [2]nishchay.bhutani3010@gmail.com, [3]richathakur914@gmail.com, [4]shubhamkrjha04@gmail.com

DOI: 10.1201/9781003487906-17

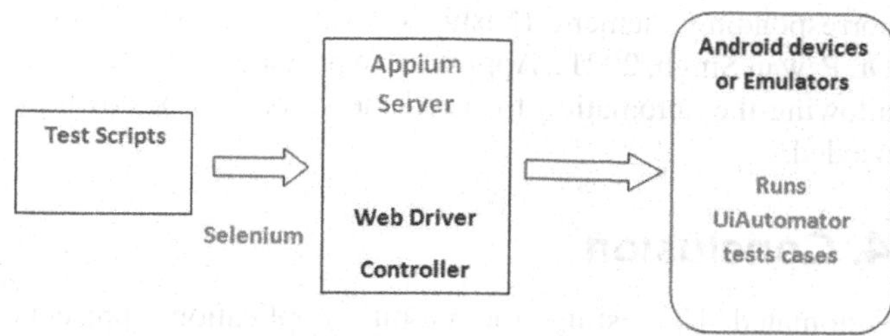

Fig. 17.1 The Appium framework

3.1 Types of Data Centric Applications

There are three types of data-centric applications that can be identified: native apps, mobile web apps, and hybrid apps. Appium is capable of supporting all three types, enabling the testing of modern applications that are frequently accessed online.

1. *Native apps:* Native apps refer to applications that are downloaded and executed directly on a mobile device.
2. *Mobile Web Apps:* These applications don't need to be downloaded. They must undergo testing on various mobile browsers.
3. *Hybrid Apps:* Hybrid apps represent a fusion of native apps and mobile web, incorporating the best elements from both. They combine the native app's familiar icon and interface with the versatility

3.2 Architecture of Appium

Appium, a popular automation framework, has greatly benefited from the widespread adoption of Selenium WebDrivers. Specifically, Figure 1 illustrates the framework specific to Android apps (Swati Hajela. 2020).

There are four main parts to Appium's architecture; scripts for Web Drivers (Monika Sharma and Rigzin Angmo. 2011):

(a) Selenium WebDriver

The test case scripts are created using libraries and APIs. These scripts are comparable for a certain event of a related application on both Android and iOS.

(b) Appium Server

The Web Driver sessions are managed and created by the HTTP server known as Appium Server. It initiates the execution of a test case that launches a server.

(c) Instruments or UiAutomator

For iOS apps, the Instruments Command Server, and for Android apps, the device-based UiAutomator, the Appium server listens to proxies for commands.

(d) Real devices or simulators and emulators

During app testing, simulators are used as replicas of genuine iOS devices, while emulators serve a similar purpose for Android.

3.3 Working of Appium

Appium offers support for a diverse range of programming languages, allowing developers to write scripts and implement desired functionalities using languages like Python, Perl, Java, Ruby, and C#. On the Windows platform, the Eclipse IDE is commonly used for script writing and defining capabilities (Marback Aaron, Do Hyunsook and Ehresmann Nathan. 2011).

Android app using an emulator, certain capabilities become essential. However, for testing an iOS app, specific modifications are required, such as changing the platform's name to iOS and the device's name to iPhone, while retaining other necessary features (I. Singh, B. Tarika, 2011).

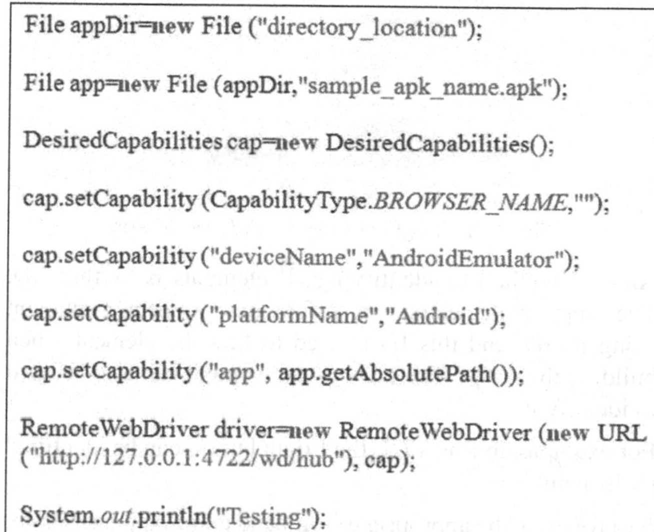

```
File appDir=new File ("directory_location");

File app=new File (appDir,"sample_apk_name.apk");

DesiredCapabilities cap=new DesiredCapabilities();

cap.setCapability (CapabilityType.BROWSER_NAME,"");

cap.setCapability ("deviceName","AndroidEmulator");

cap.setCapability ("platformName","Android");

cap.setCapability ("app", app.getAbsolutePath());

RemoteWebDriver driver=new RemoteWebDriver (new URL
("http://127.0.0.1:4722/wd/hub"), cap);

System.out.println("Testing");
```

Fig. 17.2 Desired features for testing Android Apps

Appium Inspector is an essential tool for automating the identification of elements within the graphical user interface (GUI) of apps.

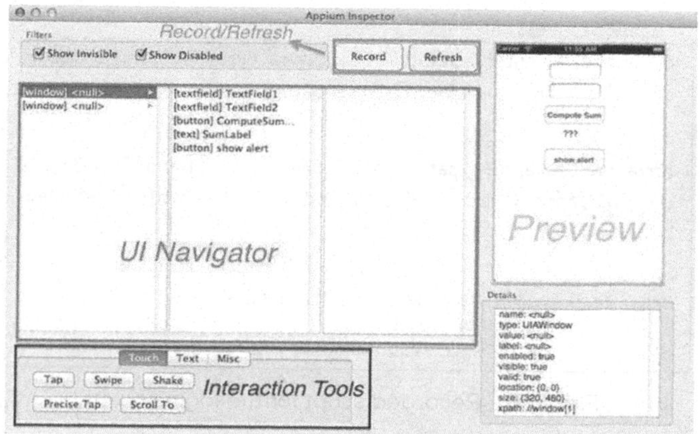

Fig. 17.3 Appium tool inspector

Locating an element within a user interface (UI) screenshot. In Fig. 17.4, the login and password items can be located by selecting them from the hierarchy of screen components (Y.C. Kulkarni 2011).

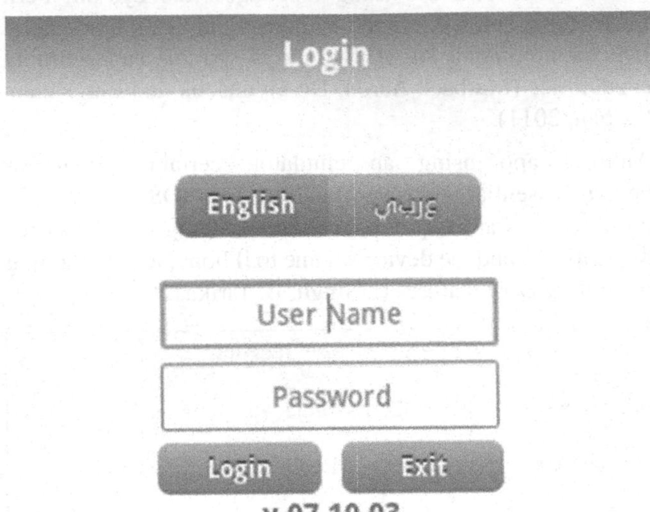

Fig. 17.4 Login screen of an Android app

Another method of identifying UI elements is by their ID. The Appium Inspector can differentiate a specific element using its ID, and this ID is used to find the element when building the script. The name of an element can also be used to identify it.

For example, in Fig. 17.4, the Login button can be identified by its name.

By providing the appropriate command to the Appium Server, the element can be interacted with accordingly.

The process of sending text to a textbox through automation is similar to a person manually entering text. In Fig. 17.4, the empty username textbox receives the text "username" by utilizing the sendKeys("username") method on the

```
driver.findElement(By.xpath("//android.view.View[1]/android.widget.ListView[1]/android.view.View[1]")).sendKeys("username");

driver.findElement(By.xpath("//android.view.View[1]/android.widget.ListView[1]/android.view.View[2]/android.widget.EditText[1]")).sendKeys("password");

driver.findElement(By.name("Login")).click();

System.out.println("Successfully logged in!");
```

Fig. 17.5 Recorded script for the login screen

corresponding element (Nishi Srivastava, Ujjwal Kumar, Dr. Pawan Singh, 2021). Appium also provides a scroll event, allowing the automation to scroll the screen up or down as needed.

4. Conclusion

Automated UI testing for mobile applications presents challenges and consumes significant time when conducted manually, particularly for intricate industrial applications. However, leveraging automated testing offers benefits in terms of platform independence, enabling flexibility in testing different application types, such as hybrid and online apps. The versatility of programming languages in automated testing empowers testers to use their preferred language, thereby enhancing productivity and user-friendliness.

REFERENCES

1. I. Burnetein. 2013. Practical Software Testing: process oriented approach. 2nd ed. Springer Professional Computing.
2. P. Ammann and J. Offutt, 2008. Introduction to Software Testing.1st ed. New York: Cambridge University Press.
3. K. Karhu, T. Repo and K. Smolander, 2009. Empirical Observations on Software Testing Automation, International Conference on Software Testing Verification and Validation.
4. Milad Hanna, Mostafa Sami, Nahla El- Haggar. 2014. A Review Of Scripting Techniques Used in Automated Software Testing. 3rd ed. International Journal of Advanced Computer Science and Applications, Vol. 5, No. 1.
5. Swati Hajela. 2020. Automation Testing in Mobile Applications. 4th ed. International SoftwareTesting Conference. http://appium. io/slate/en/master/?ruby#http://appium.io/s late/en/v1.0.0/#example
6. Monika Sharma and Rigzin Angmo. 2011. Mobile based Automation Testing and Tools, of Computer Science (IJCSIT), Vol. 5(1), ISSN:0975-9646, pp. 908–912.
7. Marback Aaron, Do Hyunsook and Ehresmann Nathan. 2011. An effective regression testing approach for php web applications
8. Boni García, and Michael Gallego. 2020. A Survey of the Selenium Ecosystem. 6th ed. Journals Electronics.
9. I. Singh, B. Tarika, 2011. "Comparative Analysis of Open Source Automated Software Testing Tools: Selenium, Sikuli and Watir" International Journal of Information & Computation Technology, vol 4, pp. 1507–1518.
10. Y.C. Kulkarni 2011, Automating the web applications using the selenium RC. 2011. ASM's International Journal of Ongoing Research in Management and IT e-ISSN-2320-0065.
11. Nishi Srivastava, Ujjwal Kumar,Dr. Pawan Singh. year 2021. Software and Performance Testing Tools. Volume 10.54060, jieee, 002.01.001

Note: All the figures in this chapter were made by the author.

Advancement of Intelligent Computational Methods and Technologies (AICMT2023) – Dr. O. P. Verma et al. (eds)
© 2024 Taylor & Francis Group, London, ISBN 978-1-032-78445-8

18

Discovering Generic Medicine Substitutes Using Machine Learning and Deep Learning

Karishma Arora[1], Karan Sharma[2], Sweta Kumari[3], Soodit Kumar[4], Udhay Kaul[5], Anshul[6]
Computer science and Engineering, Delhi Technical Campus, Greater Noida, India

ABSTRACT: The project "Discovering Generic Medication Substitutes with Machine Learning & Deep Learning" is a web-based application that utilizes React, Tailwind CSS, Node.js, and MySQL. It enables users to upload prescription lists, either as text or images, and provides cost-effective alternatives to expensive branded medications. By using OCR AI for accurate medicine detection and machine learning for error correction, the system ensures reliable results even if mistakes are made during data entry. This project aims to help individuals save money by suggesting affordable generic substitutes. With its user-friendly interface and advanced technologies, it empowers users to make informed decisions about their healthcare while alleviating financial burdens related to medication expenses.

KEYWORDS: Generic medicines, Deep learning, Machine learning, Image, Dataset, OCR AI, React, MySQL, Node JS, Branded medicines

1. Introduction

In the current healthcare landscape, the financial burden of prescription medications often poses significant challenges for individuals and families. Affordable generic substitutes for costly branded drugs present a potential solution to alleviate these economic pressures. However, identifying suitable alternatives can be a complex and time-consuming task, requiring extensive research and a deep understanding of the pharmaceutical industry. This research paper introduces an innovative web-based application named " Discovering Generic Medication Substitutes with Machine Learning & Deep Learning " that aims to address this issue.

The application leverages state-of-the-art technologies such as React, Tailwind CSS, Node.js, and MySQL to create a user-friendly interface that empowers individuals to make well-informed decisions about their healthcare while reducing expenses. By allowing users to upload prescription lists, whether in text or image format, the system utilizes Optical Character Recognition (OCR) AI to accurately detect and process medication information. Furthermore, advanced machine learning algorithms are employed to rectify any inaccuracies that may occur during the data entry process, ensuring reliable outcomes.

The primary objective of this project is to suggest affordable generic substitutes for expensive branded medications. By harnessing the power of machine learning, the application analyzes extensive pharmaceutical databases to identify alternative options that offer comparable effectiveness and safety profiles at a significantly lower cost.

This pioneering technology has the potential to revolutionize individuals' approach to medication selection, enabling access to economical alternatives without compromising health outcomes.

The application surpasses the mere suggestion of generic substitutes. It takes into consideration diverse factors such as dosage, frequency, and treatment duration, providing personalized recommendations tailored to each user's specific requirements. By accounting for individual preferences and healthcare needs, the application ensures that the proposed alternatives align with the unique circumstances of every user.

[1]k.arora@delhitechnicalcampus.ac.in, [2]ksks36781@gmail.com, [3]shwetakumari1811@gmail.com, [4]sooditkumarabc@gmail.com, [5]uday36481@gmail.com, [6]anshuleit@gmail.com

DOI: 10.1201/9781003487906-18

The implications of this project extend far beyond its immediate objectives, as it addresses a pressing global issue faced by numerous individuals. Escalating medication costs can deter adherence to prescribed treatment plans, leading to potential health risks and compromised well-being. By providing an accessible platform that facilitates the identification of affordable generic substitutes, this project aims to empower individuals to take control of their healthcare decisions and alleviate the financial burdens associated with medication expenses.

This research paper will delve into the technical aspects of the application, exploring the integration of React, Tailwind CSS, Node.js, and MySQL to develop a robust and scalable system. Additionally, it will provide insights into the implementation of OCR AI for precise medicine detection and the utilization of machine learning algorithms for error correction. By examining the project's architecture, functionality, and user experience, this research paper seeks to highlight the distinctive contributions and potential impact of the " Discovering Generic Medication Substitutes with Machine Learning & Deep Learning " application in the field of healthcare technology

2. Literature Review

The study examines the most recent advances in machine vision technology and the most advanced identification and sorting methods currently available.

Machine learning-based drug identification systems have demonstrated promising results.

Zhang et al. (2020) conducted a study where they developed a convolutional neural network (CNN) model capable of accurately identifying prescriptions

NLP-based recommendation systems have also been explored for medication alternatives. Yan et al. (2019) developed an NLP-based medication recommendation system that analyzed patient information and medication history to provide personalized recommendations for medications and dosages. Their system achieved high accuracy in predicting medication adherence, highlighting the potential of NLP in guiding medication choices.

Recent research has focused on deep learning-based drug identification and recommendation systems. Akhund et al. (2021) proposed a deep learning-based approach that utilized deep neural networks to analyze drug images and patient data. Their system achieved impressive accuracy in identifying prescription drugs and suggesting suitable generic alternatives, demonstrating the potential of deep learning techniques for more advanced applications in drug recommendation.

Furthermore, frameworks and algorithms have been proposed to enhance drug identification and recommendation systems. Gheiratmand et al. (2018) presented a comprehensive framework that integrated machine learning and NLP techniques for drug recommendation. This framework provided a systematic approach to guide the development of effective recommendation systems. Additionally, Gu et al. (2021) and Zhang et al. (2020) proposed novel algorithms and similarity measures for drug identification and the identification of generic alternatives.

These existing theoretical and methodological contributions pave the way for the development of a web application aimed at identifying cost-effective generic medication substitutes. By combining machine learning techniques for drug identification, NLP for personalized recommendation systems, and deep learning for advanced analysis, a comprehensive and efficient web application can be designed to help individuals make informed decisions about their healthcare while reducing medication expenses.

3. Proposed Methodology

The application has been constructed utilizing contemporary web development technologies, including React and Node.js. The backend follows a RESTful API architecture and employs a MySQL database to store comprehensive data on prescription drugs and their corresponding generic alternatives.

The application's development leverages cutting-edge web technologies, such as React and Node.js, to create a powerful and efficient platform. The backend is structured around a RESTful API architecture, allowing for seamless communication between different components. By utilizing a MySQL database, comprehensive information on prescription drugs and their generic alternatives can be securely stored and accessed.

The frontend of the application is designed to provide a seamless and visually pleasing user experience. NextJS, a popular frontend framework, is employed to ensure smooth navigation and enhanced performance. Tailwind CSS, a utility-first CSS framework, is used to style the interface and create a clean and modern look.

Overall, the application embraces modern web development technologies, with React and Node.js at its core. By utilizing a RESTful API architecture, a MySQL database for data storage, and employing NextJS and Tailwind CSS on the frontend, the application achieves a robust, responsive, and visually appealing user interface.

4. Implementation

Implementation of the "Discovering Generic Medication Substitutes with Machine Learning & Deep Learning" Project:

The project's implementation required the use of a variety of technologies and components to build a web-based application that could offer affordable substitutes for pricey branded medications. The implementation relied heavily on React, Tailwind CSS, Node.js, and MySQL as its main technologies. The use of each of these elements and the creation of the project are discussed in the sections that follow.

1. *React:* The front-end of the web application was made using React, a well-known JavaScript toolkit for creating user interfaces. It offered a quick and effective method for creating interactive UI elements. To manage user interactions, display prescription listings, and highlight the suggested generic drug alternatives, react components were created. The component-based design and declarative syntax of React were used to create the user-friendly interface.
2. *Tailwind CSS:* Tailwind CSS was used to guarantee a visually pleasing and responsive design. Using the utility-first CSS framework Tailwind CSS, programmers can quickly create unique user interfaces. It offered a broad variety of utility classes that had already been created and could be used to produce a special and reliable design system. The project's user interface is sleek and simple because to the usage of Tailwind CSS.
3. *Node.js:* The application's back-end was created with Node.js, a JavaScript runtime environment. Node.js made it possible to create a powerful server-side application that could manage user requests, conduct data processing, and communicate with the database. It offered an event-driven, scalable design that made it possible to handle several user requests concurrently.
4. MySQL to store and manage prescription data and pharmaceutical information, the project made use of MySQL, a well-known open-source relational database management system. The effective storing and retrieval of data was made possible using MySQL, guaranteeing the application's smooth integration. It allowed the system to save user-uploaded prescription lists and obtain pertinent pharmaceutical alternatives using the processed data.

A methodical implementation strategy brought the project to light. Creating a comprehensive database of pharmaceutical data, including both branded and generic medications, was the first stage. Deep learning and machine learning models were trained using this dataset.

Optical Character Recognition (OCR) AI algorithms were used for precise pharmaceutical detection. These methods gave the system the ability to precisely extract text information from prescription listings, whether they were presented as text or graphics. By minimizing potential data input mistakes, OCR AI plays a critical role in ensuring accurate findings.

The prescription data was then processed using machine learning algorithms to find possible generic alternatives to pricey branded drugs that could be more affordable. Using methods like natural language processing and pattern identification, these algorithms were trained on the collected information to find pertinent medication substitutes.

Error correcting techniques were built into the system to improve the results' precision and dependability. To find and fix any potential problems that could have happened during data entry or processing, machine learning techniques were used.

Overall, the project's implementation used the benefits of React, Tailwind CSS, Node.js, and MySQL to produce a web-based application that enabled users to make knowledgeable healthcare decisions while easing financial difficulties associated with pharmaceutical costs. The system offered trustworthy and affordable generic drug replacements to users, thereby assisting them in saving money and improving their healthcare results. It did this by utilizing OCR AI for accurate medicine recognition and machine learning for error correction.

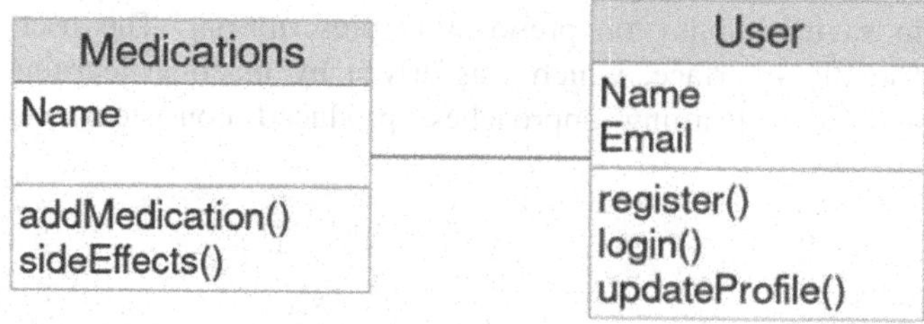

Fig. 18.1 Class diagram

5. Results

Results of the "Discovering Generic Medication Substitutes with Machine Learning & Deep Learning" Application:

The web-based application's results indicated that it had a good chance of reaching its goals of giving consumers easy access to generic versions of prescription drugs, allowing them to save money and enhance the standard of their healthcare. The outcomes attained in each of the application's primary aims are described in more detail in the following sections.

1. *Increasing Awareness of Generic Alternatives:*

   The online application met its purpose of educating patients about generic alternatives to their prescription drugs. Users could input their prescription lists as text or photos using the user-friendly interface. The programme used OCR AI algorithms to recognise and extract pharmaceutical information, guaranteeing trustworthy results even in the face of data entry mistakes. The prescription data was evaluated by machine learning algorithms, which provided customers with a full list of cost-effective generic alternatives. The application's straightforward display of these alternatives raised users' awareness and understanding of the availability of low-cost alternatives.

2. *Simplifying the Process of Finding Generic Alternatives:*
   The online tool excelled at making it easier to identify generic alternatives for prescription medications.
3. *Saving Money on Prescription Medication:*
   The online application's ultimate goal was to assist people save money on prescription medications while keeping the same quality of service. The results revealed that the application was successful in accomplishing this aim. The software enables consumers to explore more cheap solutions without sacrificing the quality of their healthcare by presenting them with cost-effective generic alternatives. Users were urged to explore these choices with their healthcare professionals, perhaps leading to a move to more cost-effective alternatives.

The online application's results indicated its usefulness in raising knowledge of generic alternatives, simplifying the process of locating them, and eventually assisting patients in saving money on prescription prescriptions. The user-friendly interface, which was driven by machine learning and deep learning approaches, produced consistent and accurate results. The programme serves as a significant aid in relieving financial pressures associated with prescription expenditures by educating users to make educated healthcare decisions. These findings demonstrate the favourable impact of using modern technology and intelligent algorithms in the healthcare sector, which ultimately benefits individuals and the healthcare system as a whole.

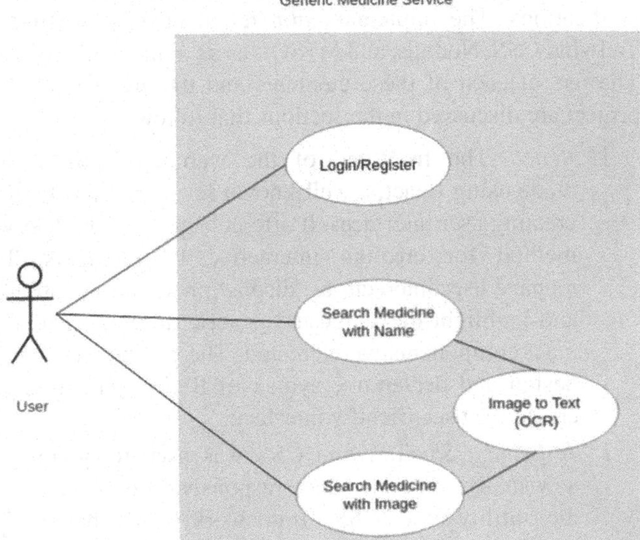

Fig. 18.2 UML diagram

6. Conclusion

Finally, the "Discovering Generic Medication Substitutes with Machine Learning & Deep Learning" project has successfully

	Task	Start	End	Dur	%	2023 Mar	Apr	May	Jun
	Generic Medicine Substitutes with Machine Learning and Deep Learning	11/3/23	14/6/23	68					
1	Collecting Generic Medicine Data with Company Name	11/3/23	9/4/23	20					
2	Creating User Interface with Figma and Frontend in NextJS	9/4/23	28/4/23	15					
3	Adding Medicine to Database with Connecting Frontend with Login Functionality	29/4/23	10/5/23	8					
4	Adding Image Recognition for Recognizing User Uploaded Image	11/5/23	25/5/23	11					
5	Adding Deep Learning, Correcting User Inputs	26/5/23	14/6/23	14					

Fig. 18.3 Gantt chart

created a web-based application that solves the problem of pricey branded pharmaceuticals by recommending affordable generic alternatives. The programme offers a user-friendly design and effective data processing capabilities thanks to the usage of React, Tailwind CSS, Node.js, and MySQL.

The project's outcomes show how effective it is in raising awareness of generic alternatives and streamlining the search for them. The programme offers consistent and accurate results, even in cases when data entry errors occur, by utilising OCR AI for precise medication recognition and machine learning for error correction. The idea successfully enables people to reduce their prescription drug costs while maintaining the standard of treatment.

The project has a bright future scope, to say the least. Some potential directions for future improvements include growing the pharmaceutical database, including real-time price data, putting in place a user feedback system, and interfacing with EHRs. These developments will enhance the application's capacity to empower users to make knowledgeable healthcare decisions while reducing financial pressures associated with drug costs.

The project "Discovering Generic Medication Substitutes with Machine Learning & Deep Learning" serves as an illustration of how the application of cutting-edge technology and clever algorithms may benefit the healthcare

REFERENCES

1. Gheiratmand, M., Hruby, G., Roy, P., & Davenport, M. (2018). A framework for personalized drug recommendation. Journal of Biomedical Informatics Rev. 51, 263–272. https://doi.org/10.1016/j.rser.2018.06.01006
2. Akhund, M. R., Perera, S., & Mendis, B. S. (2021). Deep learning-based drug identification and recommendation system. IEEE Access, 9, 35419–35427 https://doi.org/10.10416/j..
3. Disha Wang, Wenjun Liu, Zihao Shen, Lei Jiang, Jie Wang, Shiliang Li and Honglin Li(2020)- Deep Learning Based Drug Metabolites Prediction IEEE Access, 7, 76489-54367P. Nowakowski, K. Szwarc and U. Boryczka Transp. Res. Part Transp. Environ., 63 (2018), pp. 1–22, 10.1016/j.trd.2018.04.007
4. Alotaibi Gheiratmand, M., Hruby, G., Roy, P., & Davenport, M. (2018). A framework for personalized drug recommendation. Journal of Biomedical Informatics Reviews, 51, 263–272. doi:10.1016/j.rser.2018.06.01006
5. Akhtaruzzaman, M., Boubaker, S., and Sensoy, A. (2021). Financial contagion during COVID–19 crisis. Int. Financ. Res. Lett. 38(2):101604–101609.
6. Akhtaruzzaman, M., Boubaker, S., and Sensoy, A. (2021). Financial contagion during COVID–19 crisis. Int. Financ. Res. Lett. 38(2):101604–101609.

Note: All the figures in this chapter were made by the author.

Advancement of Intelligent Computational Methods and Technologies (AICMT2023) – Dr. O. P. Verma et al. (eds)
© 2024 Taylor & Francis Group, London, ISBN 978-1-032-78445-8

19

Deepfake Detection Using AI

Saurav[1], Dheeraj Azad[2]
Computer Science and Engineering, Delhi Technical Campus, (Affiliated to GGSIPU), Greater Noida, India
Preeti Pandey[3]
Assistant Professor, Computer Science and Engineering, Delhi Technical Campus, (Affiliated to GGSIPU), Greater Noida, India
Mohammad Sheihan Javaid[4], Utkarsh[5]
Computer Science and Engineering, Delhi Technical Campus, (Affiliated to GGSIPU), Greater Noida, India

ABSTRACT: The emergence of deepfake technology has raised concerns about the authenticity of digital media and therefore necessitated the development of deepfake detection techniques. In this research article, we present an in-depth research using artificial intelligence techniques, specifically Long Short Term Memory (LSTM) and ResNext models. Our approach focuses on the use of ResNext to remove facial features and preserve body expectations in videos using LSTMs. By combining these models, we aim to increase the accuracy and robustness of depth detection. Through extensive testing of deep datasets, our proposed method performs well in accurately distinguishing between real and fake videos. This research contributes to the advancement of deep learning and improves the integrity of multimedia content across different applications.

KEYWORDS: Deepfake detection, LSTM, ResNext, Computer vision

1. Introduction

Deepfake technology has become a growing concern in recent years, posing significant threats to various domains such as politics, entertainment, and personal privacy. Deepfakes are manipulated videos or images that use artificial intelligence (AI) algorithms to create realistic and convincing fake content. Detecting deepfakes is now an essential task such that to avoid the spread of wrong information and protect anyone from potential harm.

In this introduction, we will explore the concept of deepfake detection using two advanced techniques: LSTN (Long Short-Term Neural network) and DeepNext. These approaches leverage the power of deep learning algorithms to analyze and identify deepfake content with high accuracy internet world. The project focuses on identifying deep fakes with Renext and LSTMs and demonstrates the benefits of deep learning as a Django app.

Deepfake technology combines AI and machine learning to manipulate or generate realistic images, videos, or audio that appear authentic but are, in fact, artificially created. This technology utilizes deep neural networks, such as generative adversarial networks (GANs) or autoencoders, to generate and modify visual or auditory content with remarkable precision. Deepfakes have raised concerns due to their potential to spread misinformation, deceive people, and manipulate public opinion.

With the advancement of deepfake technology, the challenge to distinguish between real and fake content is getting increased (Li, Y., and Lyu, S. 2018). This creates a demand for robust and reliable deepfake detection methods. Detecting deepfakes is crucial for maintaining trust in media, protecting

[1]sauravgahlawat@gmail.com, [2]dheerajazad14@gmail.com, [3]p.pandey@delhitechnicalcampus.ac.in, [4]sheihanjd20@gmail.com, [5]utkarshg186@gmail.com

DOI: 10.1201/9781003487906-19

individuals from targeted attacks or harassment, and ensuring the integrity of digital evidence in various industries.

LSTN, or Long Short-Term Neural network, is a deep learning architecture designed to capture temporal dependencies in sequential data. LSTN models excel in analyzing time-series data, making them a suitable choice for detecting deepfake videos or audios. By processing frames or audio samples in a sequential manner, LSTN models can learn patterns and inconsistencies that are indicative of deepfake manipulations.

2. Literature Review

Deepfake technology, which enables the creation of highly realistic synthetic media, has emerged as a significant concern due to its potential for malicious use. Deepfakes refer to manipulated images, videos, or audio files that are generated using advanced machine learning algorithms, particularly deep neural networks. These synthetic media assets have the ability to deceive viewers, leading to various social, political, and security implications. Consequently, there is a growing need for robust deepfake detection techniques to counteract the spread of misinformation and protect the integrity of digital content.

2.1 Deepfake Generation Techniques

Deepfakes are often created using artificially distributed neural networks (GANs) or adaptive autoencoders (VAEs). GANs consist of two neural networks: a neural network that generates artificial intelligence and a separate neural network that tries to distinguish between real and fake news. Through iterative training, GANs learn to build greater trust. On the other hand, VAEs focus on encoding real information into the hidden space and decoding it to reconstruct the original information or create new models. (Liy, C. M., and InIctuOculi, L. Y. U. S. 2018).

2.2 Deepfake Detection Approaches

Many techniques have been proposed for deep search based on machine learning and deep learning. Traditional methods often rely on handcrafted features, such as facial landmarks, texture inconsistencies, or artifacts introduced during the manipulation process. Support vector machines (SVMs), random forests, and other classical classifiers are commonly employed to classify real and fake media based on these features.

In recent years, deep learning has made tremendous progress in deep learning; CNN (Convolutional neural networks) are used in many applications because of their ability to learn discrimination from image or video frames. This model is able to identify minor facial artifacts, inconsistencies, or differences in differences shown in deep media. Recurrent neural networks (RNNs), especially short-term temporal (LSTM) networks, are powerful products that have been used to capture moments of success in movies and allow deep visualization based on them.

2.3 Dataset Creation and Benchmarking

The availability of comprehensive and diverse datasets plays a crucial role in training and evaluating deepfake detection models. The researchers created a benchmarking database containing real and in-depth information, allowing research methods to be developed and compared. Notable examples include the DeepFake Detection Challenge (DFDC) dataset, the FaceForensics++ and Celeb-DF datasets (Nguyen, H.H., Yamagishi, J., and Echizen, I. 2019). This database contains thousands of videos that use various controls such as face swapping, expressive communication, and lip sync to simulate realistic deep fake scenarios (Kim, H., Garrido et al. 2018).

2.4 Limitations and Challenges

Deepfake detection still faces significant challenges. Adversarial attacks, where deepfakes are manipulated to deceive detection models, pose a major concern. Robustness against such attacks is crucial for reliable deepfake detection systems. Additionally, the rapid advancement of deepfake generation techniques necessitates continuous improvement and adaptation of detection methods to handle evolving deepfake variants. The interpretability of deep learning-based models also remains a challenge, as understanding the basis for their predictions is essential for building trust and identifying potential vulnerabilities.

The development of effective deepfake detection techniques is vital in combating the threats posed by synthetic media manipulation. While both traditional machine learning and deep learning approaches have shown promise, deep learning-based methods, such as CNNs and LSTMs, have demonstrated superior performance in detecting deepfakes. However, ongoing research is needed to address challenges related to adversarial attacks, model interpretability, and the evolution of deepfake generation techniques (Ciftci, U. A., Demir, I., & Yin, L. 2021). Robust deepfake detection methods will play a crucial role in preserving the trustworthiness and integrity of multimedia content in an era dominated by increasingly sophisticated synthetic media.

3. Methodology

Deep Literacy (occasionally appertained to as deep structured literacy) is a machine literacy approach grounded on artificial neural networks and representation literacy literacy can do under supervision, semi-supervision, or un supervision (Goodfellow, I. et al., 2014).

3.1 Convolutional Neural Networks

CNNs is greatly used in the field of computer vision and became the basis for many deep learning methods. CNNs are good at processing data such as images or video and have achieved significant results in tasks such as image classification, object detection and image segmentation.

3.2 Key Components of CNNs

1. **Convolutional Layers:** The basic building blocks of CNNs are convolutional layers. It applies a set of learnable filters (also called a kernel or feature detector) to the input data. CNN preserves spatial relationships by extracting local features by combining filters in the input. Convolutional layers help capture hierarchical patterns and enable the network to recognize complex representations.

2. **Pooling Layers**: Layers are usually placed behind layers to reduce the width of the map (Güera, D. and Delp, E. J. 2018). Pooling usually includes maximum pooling and average pooling. Convergence helps reduce computational complexity, maintain optimization, and achieve consistent interpretation while providing consistent data while preserving the most important features.

3. **Activation Functions:** The functionality brings nonlinearity to CNNs, allowing the network to learn the complexity of the input and output. Popular optimizations include the smoothed linear unit (ReLU) known for its simplicity and ability to solve the disappearing gradient problem, and many other optimizations such as Leaky ReLU and Parametric ReLU.

4. **Full connectivity:** After the convolution layer and pooling layer, use the full link method to combine learned features and make predictions. These layers connect all neurons in the previous layer to each neuron in the next layer, similar to neural network architectures. Full layers are often used for classification tasks and provide the final result of the CNN.

5. **Hierarchical Learning:** CNNs learn features hierarchically, starting from low-level features (e.g., edges, textures) and gradually progressing to high-level concepts (e.g., object shapes, semantics). This hierarchical learning facilitates the understanding of complex visual structures and enables the network to capture both local and global information (He, K., Zhang, X., Ren, S., and Sun, J. 2016).

3.3 LSTM

Long Short-term memory (LSTM) is a type of convolutional neural network (RNN) designed to process data models efficiently and effectively. Unlike traditional RNNs, which often suffer from fading or propagation problems, LSTMs overcome this limitation by combining cells and gating techniques.

The main components of basic LSTM cell are: an input gate, a memory gate, and an output gate. These gates control the data flow in the LSTM cell, allowing the relevant data to be selectively stored and retrieved at different times.

The input table determines where in the storage the new data should be placed. It examines the current input and previous cell state, using a sigmoid activation function to generate values between 0 and 1. Values close to 1 indicate important, allowable values for ideas stored in cell memory.

The memory gateway decides what data in the previous cell should be discarded. Similar to the input table, it combines the current input and the state of the previous cell, using the sigmoid function to create a forget gate. A value close to 0 indicates that the relevant data has been forgotten, and a value close to 1 indicates that it is important and stored.

The output gate regulates the output of the LSTM cell based on the input and the current cell state. It determines which information should be propagated to the next time step. By utilizing a sigmoid activation function, the output gate controls the level of influence from the current cell state, generating a gate value that filters the output accordingly.

Thanks to this technique, LSTM cells can be learned well and stored in the data array for a long time. The brain's memory allows information to flow over time, and the transition process allows the network to choose which information to remember and not to remember, allowing LSTMs to capture both short-term and long-term patterns.

4. Modules

4.1 Dataset

Obtain a diverse dataset containing both real and deepfake videos. It's important to have a balanced dataset with a significant number of deepfake and real examples. Various publicly available datasets, such as DeepFake Detection (DFDC) dataset, FaceForensics++, or Celeb-DF, can be used. For training and evaluation purposes, we divided the data as 70% training and 30% test.

4.2 Preprocessing

Dataset preparation entails dividing the movie into frames. Face detection is then performed, and the frame is cropped to include the identified face. Preprocess the videos to extract relevant features or frames. This may involve techniques like frame extraction, face alignment, and normalization. You can use existing libraries like OpenCV or facial recognition libraries like dlib or MTCNN for this step.

4.3 ResNext

To implement a ResNeXt model, you can start with a pre-trained ResNeXt model available in popular deep learning frameworks like PyTorch or TensorFlow. These frameworks provide pre-trained ResNeXt models that you can use as a base architecture and fine- tune on your specific task or dataset.

4.4 LSTM

LSTMs have been widely used and proven successful in various tasks, such as language modeling, machine translation, sentiment analysis, and speech recognition, where capturing long-term dependencies is crucial for accurate predictions.

4.5 Predict

In order to make predictions, the trained model receives a newly captured video as input, while the video undergoes preprocessing to match the required format for the model. The preprocessing step involves dividing the video into separate frames, where each frame consists of a cropped face region. Instead of storing the entire video locally, the cropped frames are promptly transmitted to the trained model for the purpose of identification.

5. Experimental Results

Fig. 19.1 Fake video output

Source: Author

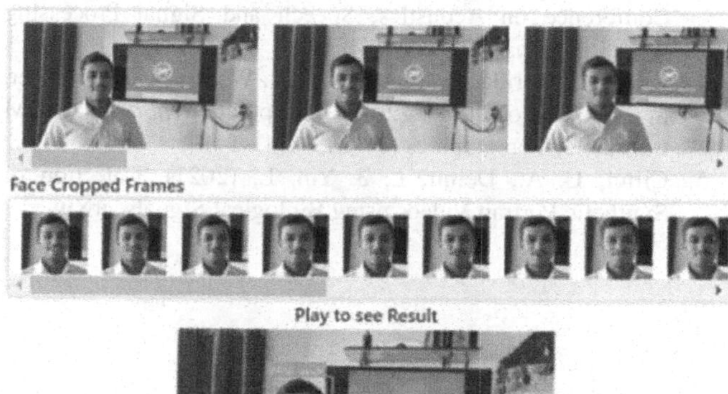

Fig. 19.2 Real video output

Source: Author

6. Conclusion

The emergence of deepfake technology has sparked doubts about the veracity of digital media, calling for the creation of effective deepfake detection techniques. In this study, we present a deep learning method using artificial intelligence, which is a combination of ResNext and Long Short-Term Memory (LSTM) models. Our strategy focuses on LSTM for capturing temporal correlations in video sequences and ResNext for extracting facial features from faces.

We hope to increase the precision and robustness of deepfake detection by merging these models. Our suggested approach shows promising results in reliably differentiating between real and fake videos after extensive experimentation on benchmark deepfake datasets. This study strengthens the integrity of multimedia content across a range of applications and advances deepfake detection algorithms.

REFERENCES

1. Li, Y., and Lyu, S. (2018). Exposing deepfake videos by detecting face warping artifacts. arXiv preprint arXiv:1811.00656.
2. Liy, C. M., and InIctuOculi, L. Y. U. S. (2018, December). Exposing ai created fake videos by detecting eye blinking. In Proceedings of the 2018 IEEE International workshop on information forensics and security (WIFS), Hong Kong, China (pp. 11–13).

3. Nguyen, H. H., Yamagishi, J., and Echizen, I. (2019, May). Capsule-forensics: Using capsule networks to detect forged images and videos. In ICASSP 2019-2019 IEEE International Conference on Acoustics, Speech and Signal Processing (ICASSP) (pp. 2307–2311). IEEE.
4. Kim, H., Garrido, P., Tewari, A., Xu, W., Thies, J., Niessner, M., and Theobalt, C. (2018). Deep video portraits. ACM transactions on graphics (TOG), 37(4), 1–14.
5. Ciftci, U. A., Demir, I., & Yin, L. (2021). Detection of Synthetic Portrait Videos using Biological Signals. arXiv.
6. Goodfellow, I., Pouget-Abadie, J., Mirza, M., Xu, B., Warde-Farley, D., Ozair, S., and Bengio, Y. (2014). Generative adversarial nets. Advances in neural information processing systems, 27.
7. Güera, D., and Delp, E. J. (2018, November). Deepfake video detection using recurrent neural networks. In 2018 15th IEEE international conference on advanced video and signal based surveillance (AVSS) (pp. 1–6). IEEE.
8. He, K., Zhang, X., Ren, S., and Sun, J. (2016). Deep residual learning for image recognition. In Proceedings of the IEEE conference on computer vision and pattern recognition (pp. 770–778).

Advancement of Intelligent Computational Methods and Technologies (AICMT2023) – Dr. O. P. Verma et al. (eds)
© 2024 Taylor & Francis Group, London, ISBN 978-1-032-78445-8

20

Comparative Analysis of Machine Learning Algorithms for High Electron Mobility Transistor (HEMT) Modeling

Neda[1], **Vandana Nath**[2]
University School of information communication and Technology, GGSIPU, Delhi, India

ABSTRACT: High Electron Mobility Transistors (HEMTs) are essential components in modern electronic devices, and accurate modeling of their behavior is crucial for the design and optimization of electronic circuits. In HEMT modeling, machine learning algorithms have shown progress by capturing complex relationships and improving modeling precision. This paper compares numerous machine learning algorithms for HEMT modeling. MLP, Decision Tree, and Random Forest were analyzed using MAE, RMSE, R2, RAE, RRSE, and MSE. The MLP model with the tanh activation function captured input feature-target variable interactions well. The Random Forest model performed well, but slightly behind the Decision Tree model. Decision Tree outperformed MLP and Random Forest models in predicting accuracy across all parameters. The Decision Tree model solved this problem well with an R2 of 0.9955 and an MAE of 0.00232.

KEYWORDS: Decision tree, GaN, HEMT, Machine learning, MLP, Random forest, Modeling

1. Introduction

High Electron Mobility Transistor is a field-effect transistor characterized by its high electron mobility. Due to its remarkable performance characteristics, it is commonly used in electronic devices and circuits. HEMTs are capable of operating at high frequencies, emit minimal levels of noise, and can withstand high levels of power. In applications such as amplifiers, oscillators, and switches, these transistors are particularly useful (Mishra et al. 2008).

GaN HEMTs (Gallium Nitride HEMTs) are common among HEMTs. GaN HEMTs are ideal for electronic circuit design due to their advantages. First, GaN's wide bandgap allows rapid electron transport (Mishra et al. 2002). This speeds up device switching and operation. Power amplifiers and converters use GaN HEMTs because they can handle high power. In addition to radar systems, wireless communications, and high-speed digital circuits, they have excellent high-frequency performance. GaN HEMTs save energy and are efficient (Nirmal et al. 2019).

HEMTs are modeled mathematically. For various reasons, accurate HEMT modeling is essential in electronic circuit design. Circuit designers can optimize gain, noise figure, linearity, and frequency response using HEMT models. Circuit designers can improve circuit performance by accurately modeling HEMT behavior (Ghosh et al. 2016).

Creating mathematical models of the device's behavior and electrical characteristics is the process of modeling HEMTs. Accurate HEMT modeling is essential for designing electronic circuits for a number of reasons. Circuit designers may predict and enhance the device's performance, including gain, noise figure, linearity, and frequency response, using HEMT models. Circuit designers are able to make wise design decisions and improve the overall performance of the devices by accurately capturing the behavior of HEMTs.

2. Background and Related Work

Due to the increasing demand for accurate transistor models in electronic circuit design, the field of HEMT modeling

[1]neda.216414219@ipu.ac.in, [2]Vandana.nath@ipu.ac.in

DOI: 10.1201/9781003487906-20

has been the subject of extensive research and development. Typically, empirical equations, analytical models, or physical simulations are used to characterize the behavior of HEMTs using conventional modeling techniques. Some of the noteworthy literature mentioned here are as follows, an analytical solution for calculating the intrinsic parameters was provided by Dambrine in 1988 and further enhanced by Berroth and Bosch. After that many extraction methods have been reported and applied to GaN and Gallium Arsenide devices by Berroth Bosch et al. 1990; Brady, Oxle et al. 2008; Cheng et al. 2012; Chen et al. 2006; Crupi et al. 2006; DiSanto Bolognesi et al. 2006; Jarndal et al. 2005; khusro et al. 2019. Although these are accurate but are often found to be highly complex and computationally inefficient. To extend the range of a model, it is generally necessary to use more complex models and extraction processes, which require additional time and effort. For instance, the EC-based technique gives more information about the physics of the device, and as a result, it makes it possible to directly extract the components of the lumped model by employing a simple and direct curve-fitting approach. This method works well for standard models that contain a limited number of circuit elements. However, in order to take into account, the parasitic effects at higher frequencies, the EC needs additional elements, and this is especially true for large device peripheries. In such a case, the direct extraction procedure is replaced by optimization or a combination of direct and optimization techniques (Zhou et al. 2021).

Due to their quick turnaround and high level of accuracy, alternative machine learning (ML) based modeling Several studies have investigated the use of machine learning algorithms to overcome the limitations of conventional techniques in HEMT modeling. Various aspects of HEMT modeling, including parameter extraction, model calibration, and performance prediction, have been the focus of these studies. Table 20.1 shows some notable research publications in this field:

Table 20.1 Noteworthy research on the Modelling of FETs based on machine learning

Type of ML technique	Type of Work & Technique	Reference
ANN	In this paper cryogenic modeling of HEMT using ANN.	A. Caddemi et al. 2007
ANN	This paper is based on the modeling of different FET devices based on ANN.	Zlatica Marinkovic et al. 2018
TDNN	The paper is based on DC, Small signal, and large signal modeling of MESFET and GaAs HEMT using TDNN	Wenyuan Liu et al. 2020
Hybrid ANN	This paper proposes two models: A hybrid neural network model uses equivalent circuit parameters and a neural network, while the other model is a black box. 6-18 GHz.	Zlatica D. Marinkovic et al. 2005
ANN	The paper is based on modeling of the S-parameter and noise parameter of HEMT using MLP -ANN.	Zlatica D. Marinkovic et al. 2006
Analytical and ANN	The paper makes a comparative study of modeling through the Analytical model and ANN-based model. And the proposed model is an improvement of the above paper.	Zlatica Marinkovic et al. 2009
ANN, SVM, DT	The paper proposes nonlinear modeling of GaN150 HEMT for I-V characteristics based on input parameters Vds, Vgs, and temperature ranging from (25-250 Celsius). Three models were built using ANN, SVR, and DT.	Ahmed Abubakr et al. 2018
ANN-GA, PSO, GWO	This paper focuses on optimization techniques used with ANN namely GA, PSO, and GWO. And comparing the optimized results with the measured data and moreover comparing different optimization techniques	Anwar Jarndal et al. 2019
Hybrid SVR	The article models GaN HEMT utilizing SVR and error correction. The model is accurate for 1GHz–10GHz frequencies.	MingQiang Geng et al. 2021

Source: Author

2. Machine Learning Algorithms for HEMT Modelling

In this section of the paper, we will be discussing some important Machine Learning techniques which we have used on our data set. They are as follows:

2.1 Multilayer Perceptron

MLP is an artificial neural network (ANN) with multiple layers of interconnected neurons as shown in Fig. 20.1. It utilizes feedforward architecture, with information flowing

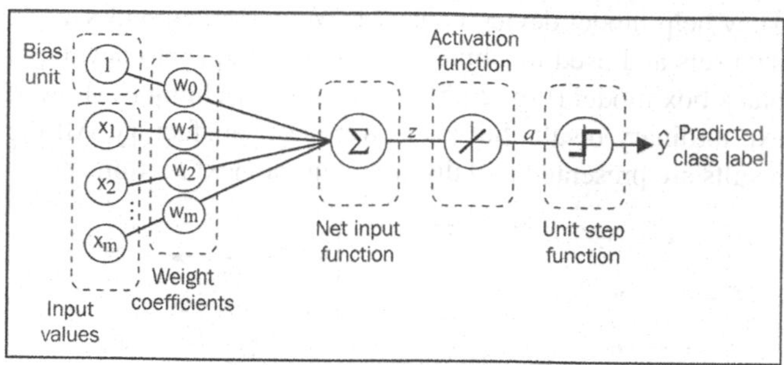

Fig. 20.1 Structure of MLP

Source: Python Machine Learning, S. Raschka (https://www.simplilearn.com/tutorials/deep-learning-tutorial/multilayer-perceptron)

from the input layer to the output layer via concealed layers. MLPs are commonly employed for classification, regression, and pattern recognition tasks. Nonlinearity is introduced by the application of an activation function to the weighted sum of inputs by each neuron.

Minimizing the difference between predicted and actual outputs, MLPs learn by modifying weights using optimization algorithms such as gradient descent. They are capable of learning complex patterns, but they may overfit. Regularization strategies reduce overfitting. MLPs are robust models capable of capturing complex relationships, making them useful for a variety of machine-learning applications.

2.2 Decision Tree

Decision trees are supervised machine learning algorithms for classification and regression. It predicts target values from input features using binary judgments' root node, representing the dataset, and starts the decision tree. Each internal node of the tree selects a feature based on information gain or Gini impurity to partition the data into subsets. Recursively splitting until a stopping requirement is met, such as reaching a maximum depth, a minimum quantity of samples per leaf, or when additional splitting does not increase predictive performance. The decision tree divides data by feature value or range, forming branches as shown in Fig. 20.2. Class labels are the tree's leaf nodes. To create accurate predictions, the decision tree learns the ideal feature splits that minimize impurity or maximize information gain during training.

As flowcharts, decision trees are straightforward to understand and visualize. Decision trees handle numerical, categorical, and missing data. They can handle outliers and non-linear relationships. When deep or complex, decision trees can overfit. When the tree collects noise or irrelevant patterns in training data, it overfits and generalizes poorly.

2.3 Random Forest

Random Forest predicts by combining many decision trees as shown in Fig. 20.3. It is used for classification and regression problems. Each decision tree in a Random Forest is constructed independently and operates on a random subset of features. Randomness reduces overfitting and increases tree diversity. The Random Forest trains each tree using a bootstrap sample from the original dataset. Instead of analyzing all features at each decision tree node, a random portion is split. The Random Forest predicts by aggregating all decision tree predictions. It employs majority voting to predict class labels for classification problems and the average or weighted average of predicted outcomes for regression tasks. Random Forests are advantageous. They handle high-dimensional datasets and complex feature connections with accuracy and reliability. They overfit less than decision trees. Random Forests also quantify feature relevance for variable selection and interpretability.

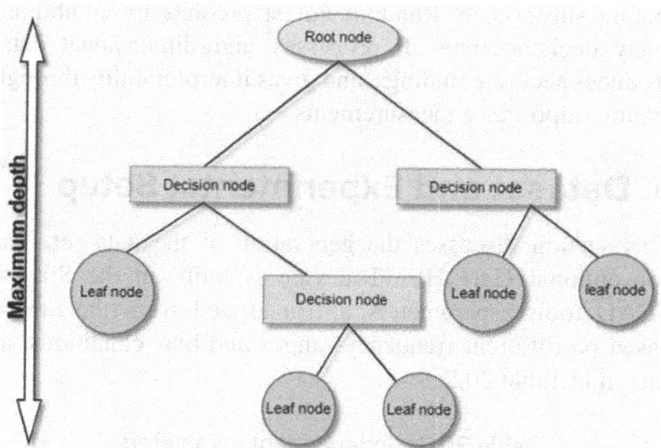

Fig. 20.2 Structure of decision tree

Source: Author

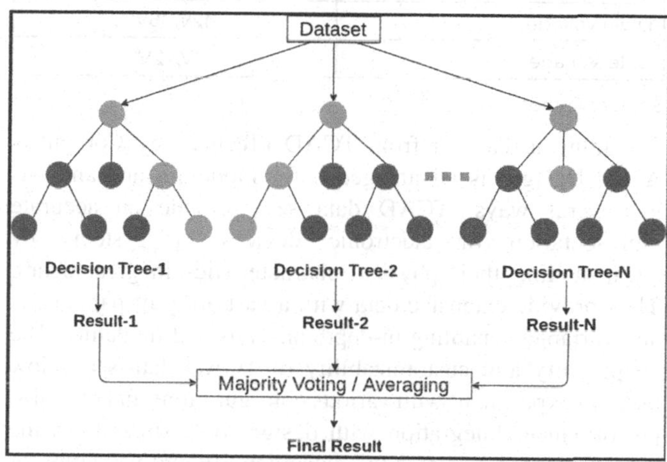

Fig. 20.3 Structure of random forest

Source: https://cdn.analyticsvidhya.com/wp-content/uploads/2020/02/rfc_vs_dt1.png

Due to multiple decision tree training and inference, Random Forests require computational overhead. They may need hyperparameter adjustment for tree numbers and random feature subset size. Random Forest predicts by combining many decision trees. It processes high-dimensional data, produces accurate findings, and gives interpretability through feature importance measurements.

3. Dataset and Experimental Setup

This section discusses the generation of the data set. The conventional GaN HEMT device is built on the Silvaco TCAD tool. S-parameters are generated from the device based on different frequency ranges and bias conditions, as shown in Table 20.2.

Table 20.2 Independent parameters

Parameter	Range
Frequency	10Hz -60GHz
Drain voltage	12V, 15V
Gate Voltage	-1V, -2V

Source: Author

Obtaining a data set from TCAD (Technology Computer-Aided Design) is advantageous for modeling and analysis in several ways. TCAD data sets provide an accurate representation of electronic devices or systems by encapsulating their physical characteristics in great detail. They provide extensive data with a vast array of parameters and variables, enabling in-depth analysis and modeling. The adaptability and customizability of TCAD data sets allow users to experiment with various configurations and optimize performance. Integration with design tools streamlines the design process, whereas the dependability and validation of TCAD data ensure accurate results. As shown in Fig. 20.4 GaN HEMT was designed and simulated in TCAD and a set of data was extracted.

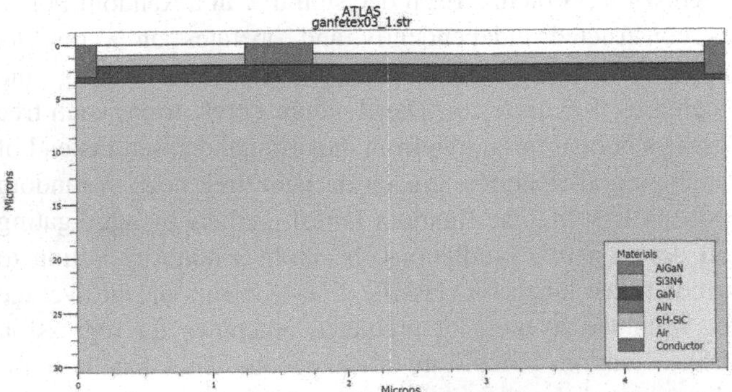

Fig. 20.4 Conventional GaN HEMT built on Silvaco TCAD

Source: Author

According to Table 20.2's input parameter combinations. Frequency and biases were input, and 8 S-parameters (S11, S12, S21, S22, both real and imaginary) were produced. They help model device behavior. We generated 343 sample data sets and used machine-learning techniques to develop a black box model (Fig. 20.5). Some of the techniques showed extraordinary results but some were not satisfactory. All the results are presented and discussed in the next section.

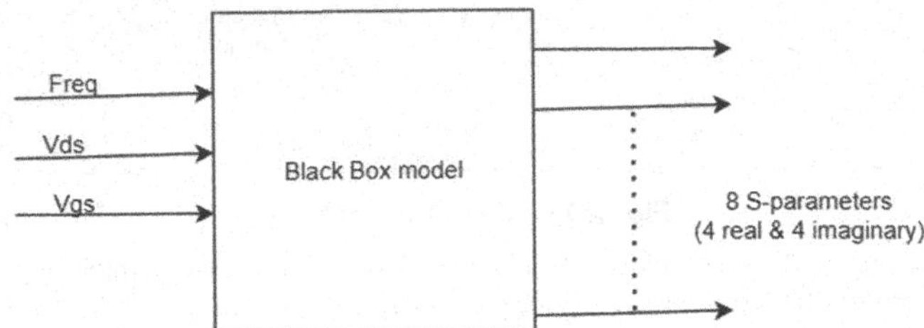

Fig. 20.5 Black box model created using supervised learning

Source: Author

4. Results and Discussion

The data set generated from the GaN HEMT device is fed to different machine learning algorithms and their results are as shown in Table 20.3.

Table 20.3 Results of Various evaluation metrics

ML Technique	Multilayer perceptron		Decision Tree	Random Forest
	tanh	logistic		
MAE	0.07798	0.09024	0.00232	0.00698
RMSE	0.5286	0.636	0.0149	0.08496
R2	0.4103	0.4974	0.9925	0.9861
RAE	0.1826	0.2113	0.0054	0.0163
RRSE	0.5331	0.6414	0.0151	0.08569
MSE	0.2795	0.4046	0.000224	0.00721

Source: Author

Based on the results obtained from the evaluation metrics, including MAE, RMSE, R2, RAE, RRSE, and MSE, the performance of different machine learning techniques, namely Multilayer Perceptron (MLP), Decision Tree, and Random Forest, was compared.

The Multilayer Perceptron model with the tanh activation function achieved an MAE of 0.07798 and an RMSE of 0.5286, indicating that it provided relatively accurate predictions with a moderate level of error. The R2 score of 0.4103 suggests that the MLP model explained approximately 41% of the variance in the target variable. The RAE and RRSE values of 0.1826 and 0.5331, respectively, further indicate the model's ability to capture the relative errors compared to the mean of the true values. The MSE value of 0.2795 demonstrates the average squared difference between the predicted and true values. So, we can say tanh is a better activation function than logistic.

In comparison, the Decision Tree model with the MLP and Random Forest showed better error metrics across the board, including MAE, RMSE, R2, RAE, RRSE, and MSE. The decision Tree model had a relatively higher R2 score of 0.9925 compared to the MLP model and nearer to 1 which concludes it's the best technique of all.

The Random Forest model outperformed the MLP and was slightly inferior to Decision Tree models in terms of all evaluation metrics. With an extremely low MAE, RMSE, R2, RAE, RRSE, and MSE, the Random Forest model demonstrated highly accurate predictions and a high level of variance explanation (R2 score of 0.9861). The model's low error metrics indicate that it captured the relationships and patterns in the data more effectively. Overall, based on the comparison of these three machine learning techniques, it can be concluded that the Decision tree model outperformed both the MLP and Random Forest models in terms of prediction accuracy and variance explanation. The Decision tree model's superior performance suggests its suitability for the given problem and dataset, making it a strong candidate for further analysis and implementation.

5. Conclusion

Multiple metrics, including MAE, RMSE, R2, RAE, RRSE, and MSE, were used to evaluate the performance of three machine learning (ML) techniques: Multilayer Perceptron (MLP), Decision Tree, and Random Forest. The MLP model with the tanh activation function performed better, accurately capturing the relationships between the input features and the target variable. Although marginally inferior to Decision Tree model the Random Forest model yielded relatively positive results. In contrast, Decision Tree outperformed both MLP and Random Forest models across all evaluation metrics, demonstrating its superior predictive accuracy. With an R2 of 0.9955 and an MAE of 0.00232, the decision tree proved to be the most effective technique for this particular problem.

6. Acknowledgment

The All-India Council for Technical Education (AICTE) funded the work under the AICTE Doctoral Fellowship PhD scheme.

REFERENCES

1. Mishra, Umesh K., Likun Shen, Thomas E. Kazior, and Yi-Feng Wu. "GaN-based RF power devices and amplifiers." Proceedings of the IEEE 96, no. 2 (2008): 287–305.
2. Mishra, Umesh K., Primit Parikh, and Yi-Feng Wu. "AlGaN/GaN HEMTs-an overview of device operation and applications." Proceedings of the IEEE 90, no. 6 (2002): 1022–1031.
3. Nirmal, D., and J. Ajayan, eds. Handbook for III-V high electron mobility transistor technologies. CRC Press, 2019.
4. Ghosh, Sudip, Sheikh Aamir Ahsan, Avirup Dasgupta, Sourabh Khandelwal, and Yogesh Singh Chauhan. "GaN HEMT modeling for power and RF applications using ASM-HEMT." In 2016 3rd International Conference on Emerging Electronics (ICEE), pp. 1–4. IEEE, 2016.
5. Dambrine, Gilles, Alain Cappy, Frederic Heliodore, and Edouard Playez. "A new method for determining the FET small-signal equivalent circuit." IEEE Transactions on microwave theory and techniques 36, no. 7 (1988): 1151–1159.
6. Berroth, Manfred, and Roland Bosch. "Broad-band determination of the FET small-signal equivalent circuit." IEEE Transactions on Microwave Theory and techniques 38, no. 7 (1990): 891–895.
7. Brady, Ronan G., Christopher H. Oxley, and Thomas J. Brazil. "An improved small-signal parameter-extraction algorithm for GaN HEMT devices." IEEE Transactions on Microwave Theory and Techniques 56, no. 7 (2008): 1535–1544.
8. Cheng, Jiali, Bo Han, Shoulin Li, Guohua Zhai, Ling Sun, and Jianjun Gao. "An improved and simple parameter extraction method and scaling model for RF MOSFETs up to 40 GHz." International Journal of Electronics 99, no. 5 (2012): 707–718.
9. Chen, Guang, Vipan Kumar, Randal S. Schwindt, and Ilesanmi Adesida. "A low gate bias model extraction technique for AlGaN/GaN HEMTs." IEEE Transactions on microwave theory and techniques 54, no. 7 (2006): 2949–2953.
10. Crupi, Giovanni, Dongping Xiao, DMM-P. Schreurs, Ernesto Limiti, Alina Caddemi, Walter De Raedt, and Marianne Germain. "Accurate multibias equivalent-circuit extraction for GaN HEMTs." IEEE transactions on microwave theory and techniques 54, no. 10 (2006): 3616–3622.
11. DiSanto, David W., and Colombo R. Bolognesi. "At-bias extraction of access parasitic resistances in AlGaN/GaN HEMTs: Impact on device linearity and channel electron velocity." IEEE transactions on electron devices 53, no. 12 (2006): 2914–2919.
12. Jarndal, Anwar, and Günter Kompa. "A new small-signal modeling approach applied to GaN devices." IEEE Transactions on Microwave Theory and Techniques 53, no. 11 (2005): 3440–3448.
13. Khusro, Ahmad, Mohammad S. Hashmi, Abdul Quaiyum Ansari, Aditya Mishra, and Mohammad Tarique. "An accurate and simplified small signal parameter extraction method for GaN HEMT." International Journal of Circuit Theory and Applications 47, no. 6 (2019): 941–953.
13. Zhou, Zhi-Hua. Machine learning. Springer Nature, 2021.
14. Caddemi, A., F. Catalfamo, and N. Donato. "A neural network approach for compact cryogenic modelling of HEMTs." International journal of electronics 94, no. 9 (2007): 877-887.
15. Marinković, Zlatica, Giovanni Crupi, Alina Caddemi, Vera Marković, and Dominique MM-P. Schreurs. "A review on the artificial neural network applications for small-signal modeling of microwave FETs." International Journal of Numerical Modelling: Electronic Networks, Devices and Fields 33, no. 3 (2020): e2668.

16. Liu, Wenyuan, Lin Zhu, Feng Feng, Wei Zhang, Qi-Jun Zhang, Qian Lin, and Gaohua Liu. "A time delay neural network based technique for nonlinear microwave device modeling." Micromachines 11, no. 9 (2020): 831.
17. Marinković, Zlatica D., and Vera V. Marković. "Temperature-dependent models of low-noise microwave transistors based on neural networks." International Journal of RF and Microwave Computer-Aided Engineering: Co-sponsored by the Center for Advanced Manufacturing and Packaging of Microwave, Optical, and Digital Electronics (CAMPmode) at the University of Colorado at Boulder 15, no. 6 (2005): 567-577.
18. Zlatica D Marinkoví c, Olivera R Proní c, and Vera V Markovíc. Bias-dependent scalable modeling of microwave fetsbased on artificial neural networks. Microwave and Optical Technology Letters, 48(10):1932–1936, 2006
19. Abubakr, Ahmed, Ahmad Hassan, Ahmed Ragab, Soumaya Yacout, Yvon Savaria, and Mohamad Sawan. "High-Temperature Modeling of the IV Characteristics of GaN150 HEMT Using Machine Learning Techniques." In 2018 IEEE International Symposium on Circuits and Systems (ISCAS), pp. 1-5. IEEE, 2018.
20. Jarndal, Anwar. "On neural networks based electrothermal modeling of GaN devices." IEEE Access 7 (2019): 94205–94214.
21. Geng, MingQiang, Jialin Cai, Justin King, Bin You, Jiangtao Su, Jun Liu, Lingling Sun, Wenhui Cao, and Mian Pan. "Modified small-signal behavioral model for GaN HEMTs based on support vector regression." International Journal of RF and Microwave Computer-Aided Engineering 31, no. 9 (2021): e22774.

Advancement of Intelligent Computational Methods and Technologies (AICMT2023) – Dr. O. P. Verma et al. (eds)
© 2024 Taylor & Francis Group, London, ISBN 978-1-032-78445-8

21

Real-time Sentiment Analysis

Archit Sarna, Devyanki Sokhal, Manan Taneja, Yashi Rai
Delhi Technical Campus, Greater Noida

ABSTRACT: This research paper focuses on analysis of sentiments in tweets, comparing the performance of logistic regression, recurrent neural networks (RNN), convolutional neural networks (CNN), and long short-term memory (LSTM) models. Both deep learning and traditional machine learning approaches are used. Additionally, the paper explores integrating optical character recognition (OCR) for sentiment analysis of text within images. Real-time sentiment analysis is implemented to capture and interpret sentiments in tweets as they are posted. Through comprehensive evaluations, this research provides insights into the effectiveness and limitations of sentiment analysis methods in real-world scenarios.

KEYWORDS: Sentiment analysis, Tweets, Logistic regression, RNN, CNN, LSTM, Deep learning, Machine learning, OCR, Real-time sentiment analysis

1. Introduction

It is very important to understand the emotions conveyed in a text, by a customer response by understanding the message conveyed. It helps businesses to gain insights into customer view and track online conversations. By evaluating opinion through surveys and social media, companies can identify areas of satisfaction and discontent. This analysis helps businesses to refine their products and services, which leads to business growth.

In addition, we use sentiment analysis on surveys, polls and social media to gather information on our products and services. Opinions, emotions and feelings stated in text are studied through this process. Sentiment analysis is widely used as it has the ability to provide us key information for of our products and services. For example, large numbers of reviews to determine customer satisfaction with rate plans and customer service can be analyzed using this. Therefore, the applications of sentiment analysis are infinite. A big role of peoples opinion is played in decision making whether it be buying a smartphone or investing to choosing a school.

Sentiment analysis has become a very important tool for measuring feelings and to understand the opinion of public. People's opinions of others influence our decision-making processes greatly. The decision making ranges from purchasing any product such as a phone, to make any investment, or to choose a school desired, and every decision affect different aspects of our lives.

2. Problem Definition

The process of analyzing text to identify sentiment or opinion expressed by the speaker or writer is sentiment analysis . Any positive or negative feeling expressed in a text or in a sentence or a document can be determined by this. The aim of this is to automatically classify text data into one of the determined sentiment categories to understand the feeling conveyed. The categories may include positive, negative, or neutral sentiment.

This system should be able to provide important insights to the users, such as identifying the most relevant topics, trends, and opinions, and visualizing the results in an intuitive and user-

[1]architsarna94@gmail.com, [2]devyanisokhal@gmail.com, [3]tanejamanan141@gmail.com, [4]yashirai3929@gmail.com

DOI: 10.1201/9781003487906-21

friendly interface. The system should also be customizable, which allows the users to configure the sentiment analyzing models, parameters, and visualize option to be taken according to their specific requirements and preferences.

3. Need and Significance

Sentiment analysis can be a powerful tool to understand customer sentiment and feedback, which provide insights into customer experience and feedback on products and services in order to improve them . With this businesses can get a big help to understand the customer needs better, also identify which opportunity will provide more improvement and will suit the marketing strategies to be taken accordingly. Companies can improve customer experience, perfect customer service which can increase customer loyalty by gaining a better understanding of customer sentiment and feelings.

In today's world, sentiment analysis has become increasingly essential. Understanding customer sentiment is essential for businesses to remain competitive as more and more people are turning to online reviews and social media to help inform purchasing decisions and get better products. Sentiment analysis can help a company to better understand the customer experience and identify potential possibility for making improvements in a product, and adjust their strategy according to what people need. It is an priceless tool for understanding customers feeling and reviews on something and to stay ahead of the competition which helps to cater the needs of customer and make better opportunity for oneself.

4. Existing System

In a research study by Akana Chandra Mouli Venkata Srinivas, Ch. Satyanarayana, Ch. Divakar and Katiki Reddy, Phani Sirisha conducted sentiment analysis using data from Twitter, in 2021 using deep learning techniques (Akana Chandra Mouli Venkata Srinivas , Ch.Satyanarayana , Ch.Divakar , Katikireddy Phani Sirisha 2021). Simple neural network, LSTM, and CNN techniques were used for analysis of the sentiments and their performance was assessed. LSTM performed first among all the proposed methods and had the highest accuracy of 87%. They collected Kaggle's Twitter records to conduct an experiment (Apoorv Agarwal, BoyiXie, Ilia Vovsha, Owen Rambow, Rebecca Passonneau).

Another study conducted by (Mounika Bagadi and Mounika Belusonti 2020) proposed LSTM-based sentiment classification approach for text data. Reviews and social media posts are one of the most interesting sections of text documents for sentiment analysis and customer review. The techniques such as LSTM perform better for sentiment classification with an accuracy of 85% when training data sets are large.

5. Proposed System

Depending on whether you choose a classical approach or a more sophisticated end-to-end solution the opinion mining model may change the result to cater the needs of user and to provide a better information to the user.

It is a field of classification action that exists in NLP. It's also called opinion mining, which transforms the opinion of people contained in written and spoken data into insights that the user need. For the first task that many people new to machine learning attempt is NLP as it is one the most straightforward and convenient technique which already has a lot of solutions to it in existence from which people can learn and adapt to achieve new improvements.

One of the main ability of deep learning is that it can automatically understand complex pattern and ideas from the existing data which has the ability to transform opinion mining. Modern models are the ones that capture refined sentiments which includes model like recurrent neural networks (RNNs), convolutional neural networks (CNNs), and transformer-based architectures which enhances the model and make it more efficient. Using deep learning, sentiment analysis models can become more effective and effectively understand and classify emotions expressed in text with much higher accuracy, which enables businesses and researchers to gain more valuable information into public opinion, consumer feeling, and social media sentiment to better understand the data. The accuracy and efficiency of sentiment classification tasks have significantly improved with the use of deep learning in sentiment analysis.

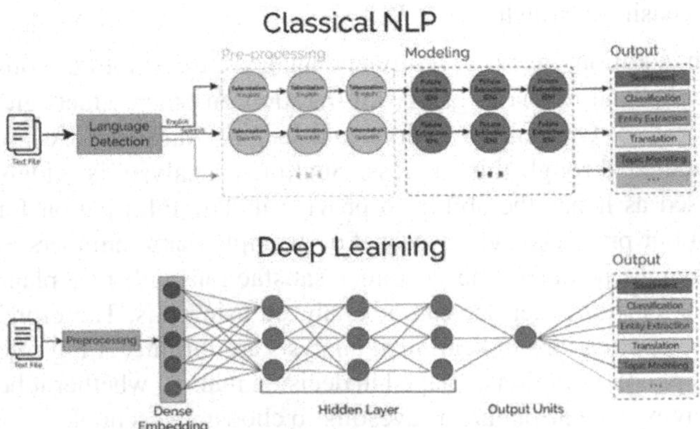

Fig. 21.1 Statistical NLP vs deep learning

6. Proposed Methodology

6.1 Data Collection

Gather a diverse dataset of textual data for sentiment analysis. Here, we have used the sentiment140 dataset from Kaggle which contains user tweets from Twitter. It is composed of 1.6 million tweets that are taken from Twitter.

6.2 Data Preprocessing

Clean and preprocess the data by discarding noise, punctuation, and exceptional characters. Convert text to lowercase, handle contractions, eliminate stop words, and perform tokenization, stemming, or lemmatization (Alantari HJ, Currim IS, Deng Y, Singh S .2022).

6.3 Feature Extraction

Feature Extraction: Extract meaningful features from the preprocessed text to represent the sentiment-bearing information. This can be achieved through techniques such as bag-of-words, which represent the frequency of words in the text; TF-IDF, which measures the importance of words in the text; or word set, which acquires linguistics relationships of the words. These features serve as input to the sentiment analysis models.

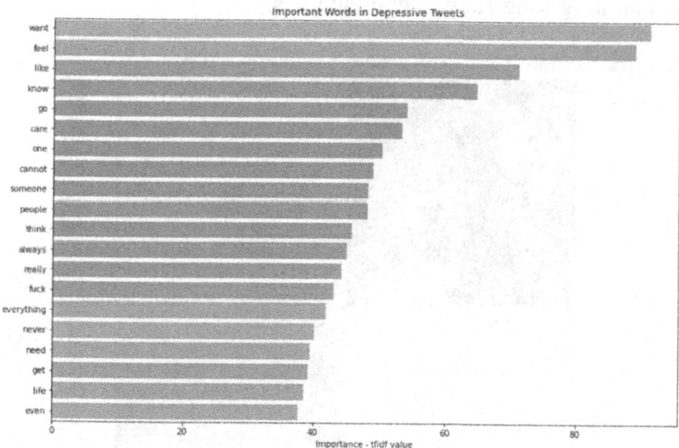

Fig. 21.2 Important words in depressive tweets

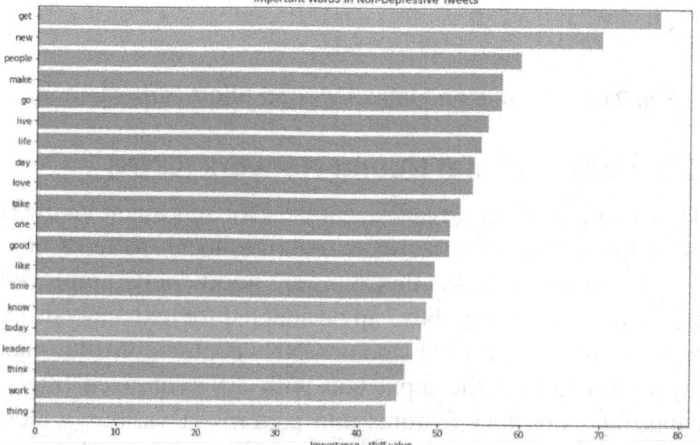

Fig. 21.3 Important words in Non-Depressive Tweets

6.4 Model Selection and Training

Choosing the appropriate models for sentiment analysis, including the ones which are traditional machine learning algorithms or deep learning architectures. We have the following models- Logistic Regression, Recurrant Neural Network (RNN), Long Short-Term Memory(LSTM) and Convolutional Neural Network(CNN). The Divided datasets were used into preparation and validation sets, training the models were done using labeled data, and fine-tune hyperparameters while experimenting with different architectures.

6.5 Model Evaluation and Optimization

Evaluating the trained models using metrics like accuracy, precision, recall, and F1-score. Compare the performance of different models and fine-tune the chosen model by adjusting hyperparameters and exploring different feature representations.

6.6 Real-time Sentiment Analysis

Implementing real-time sentiment analysis was done by integrating the trained models into a system that is capable of processing incoming textual data streams, enabling timely analysis of sentiments on text.

6.7 Functioning of Algorithm

This project focuses on extracting sentiment analysis information of tweets using various algorithms like: logistic regression, RNN, CNN, and LSTM. These algorithms are used to analyze public sentiment based on social media platforms. The goal is to compare the performances and determine the most efficient way to build a model for sentiment classification on tweets.

6.8 Logistic Regression

This is one the most popular algorithm in sentiment analysis due to its simplicity and effectiveness. It is implemented by modeling the relationship between text features and sentiment using a logistic function. By calculating probability of each tweet, it assigns that particular tweet to a positive or a negative sentiment class. Logistic regression is computationally efficient, easy to interpret, and suitable for datasets with limited features. However, it may struggle with difficult patterns when compared to deep learning models. It relies on hand-crafted features in the model and may not capture refined relationships between the tweets. Nevertheless, logistic regression remains irreplaceable in sentiment analysis, especially when it comes interpretability and efficiency are key considerations.

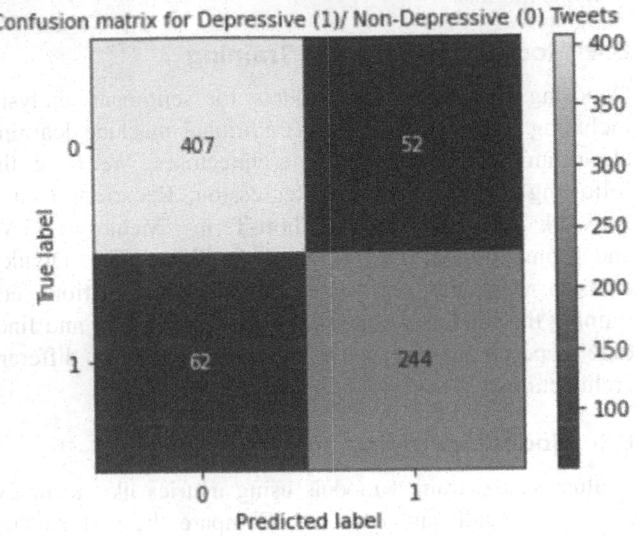

Fig. 21.4 Confusion Matrix for Logistic Regression

6.9 Recurrent Neural Network (RNN)

These are advanced models that are widely used in sentiment analysis because of their ability to acquire sequential state in text data. Different to the traditional models, RNNs have the ability to consider the context of words by understanding the hidden states, and making them more suitable for analyzing the sequential nature of sentences. RNNs process takes input text sequentially, while constantly updating their hidden states at each step and using the gathered information to make appropraite predictions (Parveen, N., Chakrabarti, P., Hung, B.T. et al.2023). This helps them to enable and capture long-term dependencies and contextual nuances in sentiment analysis tasks. RNNs have shown promising results in sentiment classification, while demonstrating their effectiveness in understanding and analyzing sentiment in text data.

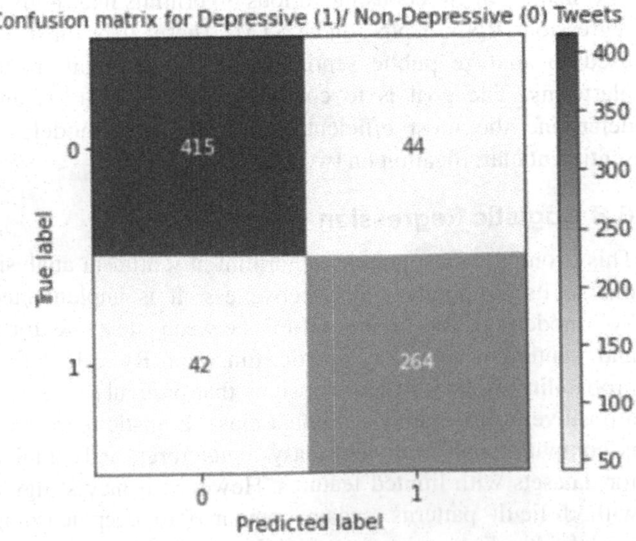

Fig. 21.5 Confusion matrix for recurrent neural network

6.10 Long Short-Term Memory (LSTM)

Text data used in this model can effectively capture the long-term dependencies and contextual information that are hidden,by making it an advanced updated models widely used. Unlike traditional models, LSTM tends to apply memory cells and gating mechanisms to recall and selectively omit data over time. This allows LSTM to handle sequences that are of differing lengths and capture the nuanced relationships between words in sentiment analysis tasks. LSTM has shown superior performance in sentiment classification by modeling the sequential nature of text and capturing the contextual dependencies that impact sentiment. Its ability to overcome the vanishing gradient problem makes it particularly effective in handling long-range dependencies.

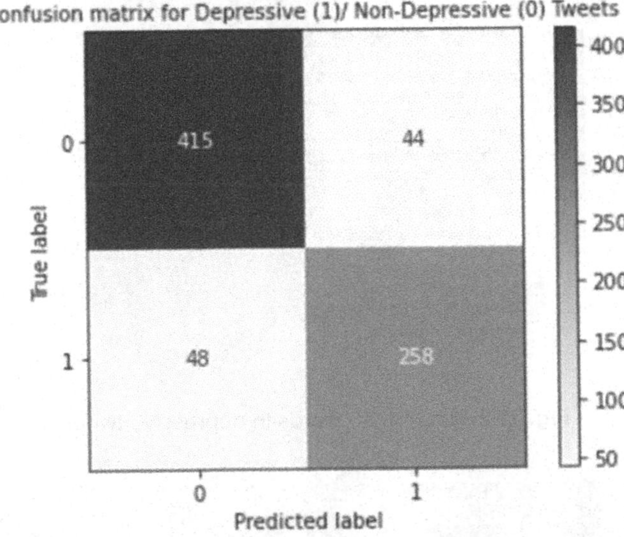

Fig. 21.6 Confusion Matrix for Long Short-Term Memory

6.11 Convolutional Neural Network (CNN)

They came forth as advanced models for sentiment analysis as their ability to effectively capture local patterns and features in text data. While CNNs are traditionally employed for image processing, they can be adapted for text analysis by treating the text as a 1D signal. CNNs deploy convolutional layers to examine the input text with different-sized filters, capturing important features and patterns at various scales. These features are then catered to fully connected layers for sentiment classification. CNNs excel at acquiring local relationships and detecting significant n-gram features, making them efficient in sentiment analysis tasks where context and local patterns play an importsnt role.

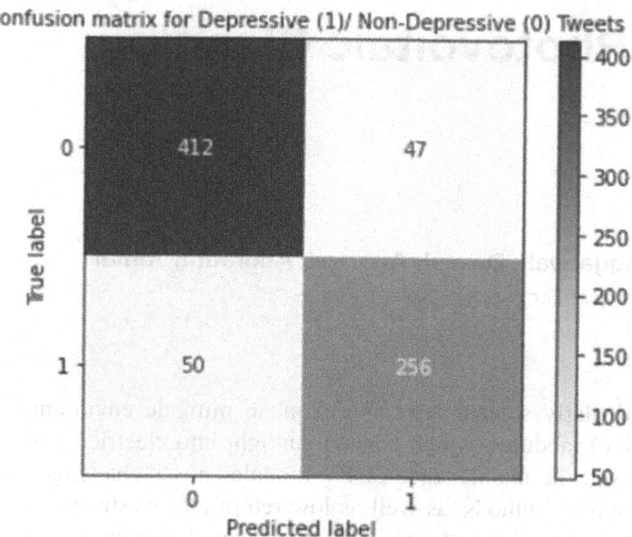

Fig. 21.7 Confusion matrix for convolutional neural network

7. Conclusion

In conclusion, this study examined different sentiment analysis methods, including logistic regression, RNN, CNN, and LSTM, for analyzing tweets. LSTM, a type of recurrent neural network, achieved the highest accuracy of 90%, outdoing logistic regression, RNN, and CNN. LSTM effectively captured the sequential nature and contextual dependencies in tweets, improving sentiment classification. The research shows the importance of sentiment analysis in understanding customer sentiments on social media, particularly Twitter. The findings suggest that LSTM is a promising method for sentiment analysis on tweets. Future research can explore enhancements like domain-specific knowledge and ensemble methods to further improve sentiment analysis in real-world scenarios.

Table 21.1 Accuracy and F-1 score of algorithms

S. No	Algorithms Used	Accuracy	F-1 Score
1	Logistic Regression	87%	0.88
2	Recurrent Neural Network	86%	0.86
3	Long Short-Term Memory	90%	0.90
4	Convolutional Neural Network	89%	0.89

REFERENCES

1. Maas, A. L., Daly, R. E., Pham, P. T., Huang, D., Ng, A. Y., and Potts,C. .2011, June. Learning word vectors for sentiment analysis. In Proceedings of the 49th Annual Meeting of the Association for Computational Linguistics: Human Language Technologies-Volume 1 (pp. 142-150). Association for Computational Linguistics.
2. ApoorvAgarwal, BoyiXie, Ilia Vovsha, Owen Rambow, Rebecca Passonneau. Sentiment Analysis on twitter data. Department of Computer Science, Columbia University, New York, NY 10027 USA.
3. Parveen, N., Chakrabarti, P., Hung, B.T. et al.2023.Twitter sentiment analysis using hybrid gated attention recurrent network. J Big Data10, 50. https://doi.org/10.1186/s40537-023-00726-3.
4. Akana Chandra Mouli Venkata Srinivas , Ch.Satyanarayana , Ch.Divakar , Katikireddy Phani Sirisha 2021 Sentiment Analysis using Neural Network and LSTM Akana Chandra Mouli Venkata Srinivas et al 2021 IOP Conf. Ser.: Mater. Sci. Eng. 1074 012007.
5. Dr. G. S. N. Murthy,Shanmukha Rao Allu, Bhargavi Andhavarapu, Mounika Belusonti Mounika Bagadi 2020 Text based Sentiment Analysis using LSTM DOI:10.17577/IJERTV9IS050290.
6. Alan Akbik, Duncan Blythe, and Roland Vollgraf. 2018. Contextual string embeddings for sequencelabeling. InProceedings of the 27th International Conference on Computational Linguistics, pages 1638–1649.
7. Rami Al-Rfou, Dokook Choe, Noah Constant, Mandy Guo, and Llion Jones. 2018. Character-level languagemodelingwith deeper self-attention. arXiv preprint arXiv:1808.04444.
8. Alantari HJ, Currim IS, Deng Y, Singh S .2022 An empirical comparison of machine learning methods fortext-basedsentiment analysis of online consumer reviews. Int J Res Mark 39(1): 1–19.
9. Benghuzzi H, Elsheh MM .2020. An investigation of keywords extraction from textual documents usingword2vecand decision tree. Int J Comput Sci Inf Secur 18.
10. Monali Bordoloi, Saroj Kumar Biswas .2023. Sentiment analysis: A survey on design framework, applications and future scopes doi.org/10.1007/s10462-023-10442-2.

Note: All the figures and table in this chapter were made by the author.

Advancement of Intelligent Computational Methods and Technologies (AICMT2023) – Dr. O. P. Verma et al. (eds)

22

Review of Various Photovoltaic Cleaning Methods

Mayank Kumar, Dhruv Verma, Yash Aggarwal*, Devesh Agarwal, Anuradha Tomar
Electrical EngineeringNetaji Subhas University of Technology Delhi, India

ABSTRACT: The transition to renewable energy resources, particularly solar energy, is crucial to mitigate environmental problems caused by conventional energy sources Photovoltaic (PV) modules, which convert sunlight into electricity, play a crucial role in achieving a clean and green energy future. However, the maintenance of PV modules poses challenges that hinder their widespread adoption. Insufficient and inefficient cleaning methods, as well as low return on investment (ROI), have hindered the efficient utilization of solar energy in both urban and rural installations. The benefits and drawbacks of these methods are examined, along with their suitability for different applications. Active cleaning as well as passive methods are evaluated. The research highlights the importance of efficient cleaning methods to maintain the implementation and longevity of PV modules. The benefits, drawbacks, and suitability of these methods for different applications are examined. The findings emphasize the significance of efficient PV cleaning to maximise energy output and return on investment.

KEYWORDS: Active, Mechanised, Nanotech, Passive, Photovoltaic, Robotic, Solar panel

1. Introduction

Power generation using Photovoltaic modules can be our key towards a green future. The amount of sunlight that strikes the earth's surface in an hour and a half is enough to cater for the total energy consumption of the world for one year, making solar energy a very plausible option for a sustainable and robust development. The technology that we use today to generate electricity from solar energy has come a long way and various researchers are still working to further improve the efficiency of the panels/ modules that we use.

But a major drawback leading to slow adoption of PV are the insufficient & inefficient cleaning methods. This is the case for both urban as well as rural installations. On practical grounds, it doesn't matter whether the energy is green or non-polluting, what matters most is low capital cost and higher Return on investment.

Power generation by Photo-Voltaic (PV) has gathered attention in recent times because of its eco-friendly nature. However, as a problem, research regarding maintenance is a great issue in this context. If the performance isn't maintained, power generation will be reduced. Therefore, it is necessary to develop solutions for cleaning and maintaining PV modules. Solar panels work on the principle of converting light energy into electrical energy. Dirt accumulation on the module/panel surface results in reduced amount of light being absorbed by the panel, thus resulting in reduced efficiency. This is where cleaning of solar panels comes into play (Patil, Bagi, and Wagh 2017). Cleaning of panels removes dirt and other contaminants from getting accumulated onto the surface. This has been very promising in improving the efficiency of modules and studies have shown that it can lead to up to 21% increase in efficiency in residential arrays and up to 60% in commercial ones. This in turn provides an improved ROI.

Cleaning solar panel becomes essential firstly because it maximises energy. Secondly, clean solar panels increase longevity. Lastly, efficiently cleaned solar panels operate at higher efficiency, translating into increased energy production. This leads to better Financial Returns for solar energy system owners.

*Corresponding author: yash.aggarwal.ug20@nsut.ac.in

DOI: 10.1201/9781003487906-22

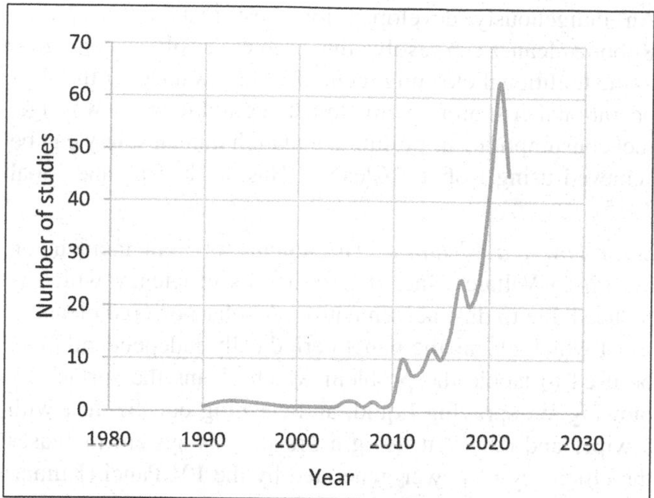

Fig. 22.1 Growth in number of studies studying the influence of dust on solar panel [9]

There are some considerations that need to be taken care of while cleaning solar panels such as safety measures of workers, water availability and environmental impact of chemicals used in the cleaning process. To overcome these, we can make use of some techniques to optimise the cleaning process—understanding weather patterns, finding ideal cleaning frequency, using self-cleaning technologies and monitoring using real time systems (Zahedi, Rafi and Ranjbaran 2021).

2. Classification of Cleaning Methods

Today there are various processes at hand in the market for cleaning PV- array many of which are still being developed for large scale usage at lower costs. In this paper we will look at methods such as Electrostatic cleaning, Manual cleaning, Natural cleaning, Robotic cleaning, cleaning using Wind, Automatic cleaning and new age methods like Nanotechnology cleaning.

3. Description of Various Cleaning Methods

3.1 Active Cleaning Methods

Manual Cleaning: These techniques are widely used to reduce the cost of cleaning as it includes use of soaps, water and cloth only. This applies specially for small installations, residential or commercial scale, as well as special structures and installations such as agri-voltaics. This method helps to reduce the economic losses by 7%.

Electro-Dynamic Dust Shield: Electrodynamic dust shield is a dust alleviation technique for an open-air PV system and spacious enough to be used for commercial size systems. It

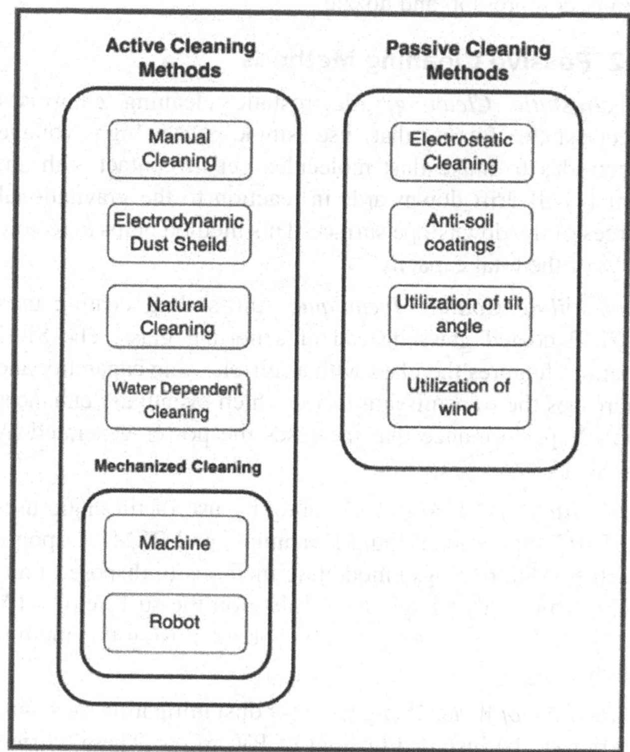

Fig. 22.2 Block diagram of solar panel cleaning methods

Source: https://www.tandfonline.com/doi/full/10.1080/19397038.2022.2140222?scroll=top&needAccess=true"

Fig. 22.3 Manual cleaning of panels installed at NSUT, Delhi

Source: https://soilar.tech/solar-panel-cleaning-systems-and-their-pros-and-cons/

consists of PET (Polyethylene terephthalate) covered sheet, silver electrodes and PET substrate.

Natural Cleaning: Natural cleaning includes natural factors like precipitation, air current and gravitational forces that make the Photo Voltaic system get rid of dust soiling. It is also a cost-efficient method of cleaning.

Water-Dependent Cleaning Method: This method includes the use of high-speed spraying water on the PV arrays parts.

The high speed of water is obtained using a high-pressure pump, compressor, and nozzle.

3.2 Passive Cleaning Methods

Electrostatic Cleaning: Electrostatic cleaning comprises electrostatic forces that use single-phase high voltage electrodes to make dust molecules get in contact with air, which will drift downwards in reaction to the gravitational forces of the downslope surface. This method helps to restore 90% of the total capacity.

Anti-Soiling Coating Technique: Anti-soiling coating uses a SiO2 coated glass instead of a normal glass. The SiO2 coating, features the glass with a self-cleaning capability and increases the transmission factor which eventually enhances the PV performance that increases the power generated by 5% to 15%.

Utilisation of Tilt Angle: Cleaning by use of tilt angle uses CFD (Computational Fluid Dynamics) and RSM (Response Surface Methodology) modelling methods to dispose of any dust particles that might accumulate on the surface of a PV array. 4.3% more energy can be obtained using this method of cleaning.

Utilisation of Wind: Using wind for dust mitigation uses wind barriers to be installed in front of PV arrays. These barriers block the dust particles to accumulate on the PV array.

3.4 Mechanised and Robotic Cleaning Methods

Robotic Cleaning: Energy production of Rooftop PV is influenced by its cleanliness directly. Electricity generation is hampered due to dust accrual on its surface. For the cleaning of panels in a vast land like deserts or farms, we can use a Cleaning Robot – equipped with navigation, brush, water spray & be able to send images and video wirelessly. This will enable the owner to keep the PV in good and clean condition (Riawan, Kumara, Partha, Setiawan and Santiari 2018).

Fig. 22.4 Mechanized cleaning of modules

Source: https://soilar.tech/solar-panel-cleaning-systems-and-their-pros-and-cons/

An indigenously developed low cost and simple design Robotic cleaner can resolve this problem easily as compared to the traditional cleaning methods. Studies uncover that low operational cost along with almost negligible water wastage, fuel consumption, air pollution and high human safety can be achieved using Robotic Cleaner (Hassan, Nawaz and Iqbal 2015).

Solar Powered Cleaning: The amount of light incident on the Photo Voltaic Panel determines its efficiency which is reduced due to dust accumulation. A solar powered cleaning robot which cleans the panel periodically independently can be used to tackle the problem which cleans the surface by blowing air, spraying liquid, and cleaning out the dust with a wiper and drying it using a brush. This system increases the efficiency of power generated by the PV Panel (Kumar, Shankar and Murthy 2020).

PV Cleaning Optimisation Methods: An intelligent cleaning robot and cleaning cycle optimisation helps in achieving an automated & low-cost Cleaning System. Experiments show that dust accumulation of 4 g/m^2, 6 g/m^2, 8 g/m^2 on PV Panel are cleaned with efficiencies of 92.14%, 91.04% and 90.09% respectively with a reduced cleansing cycle (from 48.3 days to 26.5 days – compared to manual cleansing of 2 MW PV system). Cleaning costs are greatly reduced, and power generation is improved (Jiang, Zhao, Cao, Fan and Sun 2021).

Fig. 22.5 Robotic cleaning of modules

Source: https://blog.africancorporatecleaning.co.za/2020/10/06/the-advantages-of-manual-mechanised-and-robotic-solar-panel-cleaning-solutions/"

For the economic operation decision of a PV power station, an optimization model can be developed. With the help of Adaptive Dynamic Programming (ADP) a method developed with the aim to maximise output power & minimise economic loss. It is found that for a 12 MW plant, the maintenance cost is the lowest for every 17 days (Fan, Yao, Cao and Zhao 2020).

Automatic Cleaning: In tropical countries such as India, PV modules are mainly operated in dusty conditions. The dust accumulated obstruct the incident light from the sun. If PV panels are not cleaned for a month, the power output diminishes by as much as by 50%. A sun tracking-cum-cleaning system can be developed to tackle the problem which would clean the panels twice daily. The daily output power is increased by 15-30% by employing the given method (Tejwani and Solanki 2010).

A low-cost Automated Cleaning System can be developed for cleaning of PV Panels which can provide an on-demand cleaning. Data can be collected from the panels using wireless sensors and the data hence collected can be monitored to trigger the system to clean the panels. It can immediately clean the panels whenever the generated current falls below the threshold value due to dust, dirt build-up (Gheitasi, Almaliky and Albaqawi 2015).

Miscellaneous Methods: By determining the cleansing frequency of grid-connected PV modules, we can overcome the present limitations of cleaning. Coefficient of Cleaning-Tolerance of the PV Power Plants can be calculated to determine the dynamic cleaning frequency to form a basis whether to execute out the cleaning work. The efficiency of PV plants can be significantly improved using this method (Mei, Shen and Zeng 2016).

Environmental factors such as soiling affect the performance of Solar Power Plant and reduce the efficiency of the plant. Dust deposition leads to a lower solar energy absorption. By studying the impact of soiling & periodic cleaning, we can analyze the financial benefits linked to it. Studies reveal that a cleaning frequency of 3 per month increases the plant performance by 12% (Alam, Aziz, Karim and Chowdhury 2021).

The accumulation of dust on PV surface is a major obstacle in its utilisation as it significantly lowers its efficiency. Experiment results of grid connected PV systems show that dust accumulation reduces AC/DC output power and energy which affects PV efficiencies therefore periodic cleaning is recommended especially in the dry desert areas (Mostefaoui, Neçaibia and Ziane 2018).

Nanotechnology Cleaning: A highly durable repellent coating is developed for deposition onto PV panels which gets rid of accumulated surface contamination. The coating is only a few microns thick, anti-reflective, resistant to high temperatures as well as changing weather conditions. Also, the coating is hydrophobic – silica-based network which readily repels water and related contamination, therefore rather than wetting the surface, water droplets form beads on the coatings and roll-off at low angles. This also eliminates the inefficient usage of clean water and reduces risk of cleaning related damages.

4. Comparative Study of Methods

In Table 22.1, we look at various new age cleaning methods based upon the various factors that influence them like increase in efficiency, time, cost and their feasibility.

Table 22.1 Parametric comparison of various solar cleaning methods (ACC 2020) (Solar Cleano)

Cleaning Method	Manual Cleaning	Robot Cleaning	Mechanised Cleaning
Time	100 Panels a day	Can clear entire installations in a day	800-1500 panels per hour
Cost	High Cost	Expensive installations	Cost effective
Labour Requirement	Cleaning Team/Staff	Autonomous working	Driver operator needed
Water (Per 500-1000 Panels)	500L	<10L	500L
Maintenance	Twice or thrice a year	Daily	Once in 6 weeks
Commercial Availability	Various companies offer this	Not available at all locations	Available for large farms having >5000 panels
Advantages	Cost Effective	Precise & thorough cleaning	Time-saving and efficient
Disadvantage	Labour Intensive process	High initial investment cost and specialized maintenance	Initial installation cost & regular maintenance requirements

Source: Author

Table 22.2 Broad comparison of solar cleaning methods (ACC 2020)(Sharma and Tripathi 2013)(Tyagi and Sharma 2015)(Das and Sahoo 2019)(Borah, Gogoi, and Sharma 2014)(Arumugam and Kumar 2015)(Lau, Ahmad, and Azman 2017)

Cleaning System	Efficiency (% increase in energy output)	Time (per panel)	Cost (per panel)	Feasibility
Water only	3-5 %	5-10 minutes	Low	Highly feasible
Water with Detergents	5-7 %	10-15 minutes	Low to moderate	Highly feasible

Cleaning System	Efficiency (% increase in energy output)	Time (per panel)	Cost (per panel)	Feasibility
Dry Cleaning (microfiber cloth)	2-3%	5-10 minutes	Low to moderate	Highly feasible
Automated cleaning (water or air)	7-10%	1-2 minutes	High	Moderately feasible
Robotic cleaning (water or air)	10-15%	1-2 minutes	Very high	Less feasible due to high cost

Source: Author

5. Discussion

The paper discusses the importance of solar energy as a key renewable resource and emphasizes the need for efficient cleaning methods to maintain the performance and maximize the return on investment (ROI) of photovoltaic (PV) modules. The paper provides an overview of various active and passive cleaning methods. Each method is described along with its advantages and limitations, addressing factors such as cost, efficiency, durability, and aesthetic appeal.

The research paper emphasizes the significance of cleaning PV modules to remove dirt and contaminants, which can reduce efficiency and hinder power generation. The paper concludes by highlighting the potential of nanotechnology cleaning as a promising solution for surface contamination, as it offers durability, hydrophobicity, and reduced water usage. Overall, this research paper sheds light on the importance of maintaining clean PV modules and explores various cleaning methods to enhance the efficiency and longevity of solar energy systems.

6. Conclusion

In this report regarding the importance of cleaning and maintenance of PV modules, we learnt about the various methods that are and/or being developed, their cost, commercial availability and maintenance requirements, to improve performance of the PV-arrays. Some of the methods discussed above - robotic cleaning, self-cleaning, nanotechnology, and cleaning panels via solar powered machines, highlight the importance of PV cleaning and change in the global scenario of solar-power generation and renewable energy generation as a whole.

These methods all have multiple applications depending upon the area of the site, number of panels, cost efficiency, nature of the surroundings (like sunny, rainy, snowy or dry), angle of tilt of the panels and material used. All these factors can be used to find the perfect method for any given PV plant.

REFERENCES

1. African Corporate Cleaning (ACC) (2020, October 6). The advantages of manual, mechanized, and robotic solar panel cleaning solutions (Blog post). Retrieved from https://blog.africancorporatecleaning.co.za/2020/10/06/the-advantages-of-manual-mechanised-and-robotic-solar-panel-cleaning-solutions/.
2. I. P. G. Riawan, I. N. S. Kumara, C. G. I. Partha, I. N. Setiawan and D. A. S. Santiari, "Robot for Cleaning Solar PV Module to Support Rooftop PV Development," 2018 International Conference on Smart Green Technology in Electrical and Information Systems (ICSGTEIS), Bali, Indonesia, 2018, pp. 132–137, doi: 10.1109/ICSGTEIS.2018.8709138.
3. M. Mostefaoui et al., "Importance cleaning of PV modules for grid-connected PV systems in a desert environment," 2018 4th International Conference on Optimization and Applications (ICOA), Mohammedia, Morocco, 2018, pp. 1–6, doi: 10.1109/ICOA.2018.8370518.
4. Huawei Mei, Zheji Shen and Chujie Zeng, "Study on cleaning frequency of grid-connected PV modules based on Related Data Model," 2016 IEEE International Conference on Power and Renewable Energy (ICPRE), Shanghai, China, 2016, pp. 621–624, doi: 10.1109/ICPRE.2016.7871152.
5. Zahedi, Rafi, Parisa Ranjbaran, Gevork B. Gharehpetian, Fazel Mohammadi, and Roya Ahmadiahangar. 2021. "Cleaning of Floating Photovoltaic Systems: A Critical Review on Approaches from Technical and Economic Perspectives" *Energies* 14, no. 7: 2018. https://doi.org/10.3390/en14072018S.
6. A. Gheitasi, A. Almaliky and N. Albaqawi, "Development of an automatic cleaning system for photovoltaic plants," 2015 IEEE PES Asia-Pacific Power and Energy Engineering Conference (APPEEC), Brisbane, QLD, Australia, 2015, pp. 1–4, doi: 10.1109/APPEEC.2015.7380938.
7. Soilar Tech. (n.d.). Solar Panel Cleaning Systems and Their Pros and Cons. Retrieved from https://soilar.tech/solar-panel-cleaning-systems-and-their-pros-and-cons/.
8. Solar Cleano FAQs. Retrieved from https://solarcleano.com/en/faqs.
9. Abuzaid, Haneen, Mahmoud Awad, and Abdulrahim Shamayleh. "Impact of Dust Accumulation on Photovoltaic Panels: A Review Paper." International Journal of Sustainable Engineering 15, no. 1 (2022): 264–285. doi:10.1080/19397038.2022.2140222.
10. P. A. Patil, J. S. Bagi and M. M. Wagh, "A review on cleaning mechanism of solar photovoltaic panel," 2017 International Conference on Energy, Communication, Data Analytics and Soft Computing (ICECDS), Chennai, India, 2017, pp. 250–256, doi: 10.1109/ICECDS.2017.8389895.
11. R. Tejwani and C. S. Solanki, "360° sun tracking with automated cleaning system for solar PV modules," 2010

35th IEEE Photovoltaic Specialists Conference, Honolulu, HI, USA, 2010, pp. 002895-002898, doi: 10.1109/PVSC.2010.5614475.

12. B. Sharma and G. C. Tripathi, "Efficiency enhancement of solar panel by cleaning dust particles," International Journal of Advanced Research in Electrical, Electronics and Instrumentation Engineering, vol. 2, no. 7, pp. 3227–3233, July 2013.
13. G. Tyagi and K. Sharma, "Performance analysis of a solar PV module under dust conditions for cleaning frequency," International Journal of Energy and Environmental Engineering, vol. 6, no. 3, pp. 277–285, June 2015.
14. P. Das and S. K. Sahoo, "Optimization of automated robotic solar panel cleaning system," International Journal of Engineering and Advanced Technology, vol. 8, no. 3, pp. 2139–2142, February 2019.
15. A. Borah, M. K. Gogoi, and A. Sharma, "Design and fabrication of autonomous solar panel cleaning system using programmable logic controller (PLC)," International Journal of Emerging Technology and Advanced Engineering, vol. 4, no. 4, pp. 111–117, April 2014.
16. M. Arumugam and R. P. Kumar, "Solar panel cleaning robot," International Journal of Innovative Research in Science, Engineering and Technology, vol. 4, no. 7, pp. 6586–6589, July 2015.
17. K. H. Lau, M. H. Ahmad, and A. Azman, "Design and development of automatic solar panel cleaning system," Journal of Automation and Control Engineering, vol. 5, no. 4, pp. 333–336, August 2017.
18. L. Jiang, B. Zhao, S. Cao, S. Fan and T. Sun, "Development and Cleaning Cycle Optimization of Photovoltaic Module Cleaning Robot," 2021 40th Chinese Control Conference (CCC), Shanghai, China, 2021, pp. 4108–4113, doi: 10.23919/CCC52363.2021.9550619.
19. S. Fan, X. Yao, S. Cao and B. Zhao, "An Optimization Method Based on Adaptive Dynamic Programming for Cleaning Photovoltaic Panels," 2020 39th Chinese Control Conference (CCC), Shenyang, China, 2020, pp. 1565–1568, doi: 10.23919/CCC50068.2020.9189437.
20. M. N. Alam, S. Aziz, R. Karim and S. A. Chowdhury, "Impact of Solar PV Panel Cleaning Frequency on the Performance of a Rooftop Solar PV Plant," 2021 6th International Conference on Development in Renewable Energy Technology (ICDRET), Dhaka, Bangladesh, 2021, pp. 1–4, doi: 10.1109/ICDRET54330.2021.9752681.
21. M. U. Hassan, M. I. Nawaz and J. Iqbal, "Towards autonomous cleaning of photovoltaic modules: Design and realization of a robotic cleaner," 2017 First International Conference on Latest trends in Electrical Engineering and Computing Technologies (INTELLECT), Karachi, Pakistan, 2017, pp. 1–6, doi: 10.1109/INTELLECT.2017.827763.
22. Santosh Kumar, S. shankar and K. Murthy, "Solar Powered PV Panel Cleaning Robot," 2020 International Conference on Recent Trends on Electronics, Information, Communication & Technology (RTEICT), Bangalore, India, 2020, pp. 169–172, doi: 10.1109/RTEICT49044.2020.9315548.

Advancement of Intelligent Computational Methods and Technologies (AICMT2023) – Dr. O. P. Verma et al. (eds)
© 2024 Taylor & Francis Group, London, ISBN 978-1-032-78445-8

23

Biometric Based Attendance System with Machine Learning Integrated Face Modelling and Recognition

Ritik[1], Sanidhya Gaur[2], Ashish Kumar[3], Rithik Nirwan[4], Chaitali Bhowmik[5], Neha Jain[6]
Delhi Technical Campus (Affiliated to GGSIPU), Greater Noida, UP, India

ABSTRACT: Managing attendance records is a very important and tedious task even today and took time. Technological advancement developed record-keeping techniques like RFID (Radio Frequency Identification) and biometric fingerprint scanning, but all these technologies consume some time while marking attendance and also have chances of proxy and security issues. A real-time face recognition system is a practical method to deal with all these issues faced by traditional or modern methods, due to the advancement in face recognition algorithms and low-cost and effective hardware that can possibly low-cost face recognition-based attendance systems. In this proposed model we use the Haar-cascade classifier to identify different faces, it determines the positive and negative characteristics of faces and also uses LBPH (Local Binary Pattern Histogram) algorithm for face recognition.

KEYWORDS: LBPH, Face recognition, Haar-cascade classifier, RFID (Radio frequency identification)

1. Introduction

In today's fast-paced world, attendance management systems play a crucial role in various organizations, schools and institutions. Traditional, manual attendance systems involving sign-in-sheet, time clock, or ID cards swipes have been prevalent. However, with advancements in technology, face recognition-based attendance system have emerged as a more efficient and accurate alternative. Leveraging the power of artificial intelligence and computer vision, these systems offer numerous advantages over their traditional counterparts.

1.1 Accuracy and Reliability

One of the significant benefits of face recognition-based attendance system is their accuracy and reliability. Unlike manual system that are prone to errors and can be manipulated, face recognition systems utilizes biometric data to uniquely identify individuals. By analyzing facial features, such as eye arrangement, nose and mouth these systems can accurately match individuals with their respective identities, minimizing the risk of errors of fraudulent activities.

1.2 Time Efficiency

Automated face recognition-based attendance system significantly reduce the time required to record attendance compared to manual method. Employee of student can simply stand in front of camera, and their attendance is automatically records within seconds. This eliminates the need for manual data entry, reducing administrative burdens ad saving valuable time for both staff and attendees.

1.3 Scalability

Traditional attendance systems often struggle to handle large volume of data efficiently, especially in organizational with numerous employees or education institutions with a large students population. In contrast, face recognition-based attendance systems are highly scalable. They can process and image a vast number of faces in real-time without compromising performance or accuracy. This scalability makes these systems suitable for organizations of all sizes, ensuring seamless attendance management.

[1]ritik2k01@gmail.com, [2]Sanusingh8209@gmail.com, [3]akashish078@gmail.com, [4]rithiknirwan0001@gmail.com, [5]c.bhowmik@delhitechnicalcampus.ac.in, [6]nehajain312@gmail.com

DOI: 10.1201/9781003487906-23

1.4 Enhance Security

Face recognition technology provides an additional layer of security compared to traditional attendance systems. Since it relies on unique biometric data, such as facial features, it becomes extremely difficult for individual to manipulate or incorporate or impersonate others. This prevents unauthorized access to restricted areas and ensures that attendance records are more reliable and tamper-proof.

1.5 Contactless and Hygienic

During COVID-19 pandemic, maintaining a contactless and hygienic environment has become a top priority for organizations. Face recognition-based attendance systems eliminate the need for physical contact, such as touching ID cards or fingerprint scanners, which can be potential sources of infection transmission. By utilizing non-intrusive facial recognition technology, these systems promote a safer and more hygienic attendance management process.

2. Literature Survey

This pioneering work by Bledsoe (Bledsoe, W. W. (1964) focused on facial recognition and lays the foundation for subsequent research in the field. The report early experiments and algorithms for facial recognition, providing insights into the historical development of the technology. This influential paper (Pantland,A., Truk,M. (1991)) introduces the concept of Eigenfaces, a popular technique for facial recognition. The author proposes using principle analysis (PCA) to extract facial features and demonstrate its effectiveness in face recognition task. This paper (Phillips, P.J.; Wechsler, H.; Huang, J.; Rauss, P. (1998) describes the FRET (facial recognition Technology) database a widely used benchmark dataset for the evaluation of face recognition algorithms. It provides details about data collection protocols, including variations in pose, illumination, and expression which are crucial for assessing algorithms performace. This paper (Phillips, P.J, et al. (2005)) presents the Face Recognition Grand Challenge (FRGC), a benchmark evaluation for face recognition algorithms. It discusses the dataset, evaluation protocols, and results from various algorithms, providing insights into the state of the art in face recognition at the time. This comprehensive survey Guo, G.; Zhang, N. (2019) shows the advancements in face recognition methods based on deep learning-based. It covers various deep learning architectures, loss functions, data augmentation techniques, and domain adaptation approaches used in face recognition of the field. This influential paper (Taigman, Y, et al., 2014) presents the Deep Face model, which achieves impressive face verification performance by leveraging deep convolutional neural networks (CNNs). The authors introduce novel architectural design choices and training procedures, pushing the performance boundaries in face recognition. This research paper (Pavithra, S., Hegde, S., Afshin (2020). focuses on the implementation of a face recognition-based attendance management system. It discusses the system's architecture, data collection methodology, and the use of machine learning algorithms for face recognition in an attendance context. This paper (Gowda, D., 2020) presents a face recognition-based attendance system, high lighting the use of Haar cascade classifiers for face detection and recognition. It provides insights into the design and implementation of such a system, focusing on its applicability in an attendance management context. The comprehensive review paper (Adjabi,I., 2020) provides an overview of the past, present, and future trends in face recognition technology. It covers various techniques, datasets, evaluation metrics, and future directions of the fields. This paper (Padilla,R., Costa,C.F.F, Costa, M.G.F. 2012) evaluates the performance of Haar cascade classifier for face detection. It discusses the methodology used for evaluation, analyzes the result, and provides insights into the strengths and limitations of Haar cascade classifier in the context of face detection. This paper (Senthamizh S.R , 2019) explores the use of Haar cascade classifies for face recognition in the context of criminal identification. Presents the implementation details, and evaluates the performance of the proposed system. This research paper (Bazith, S., Savant, P. 2022) focuses on the development of a face recognition-based-attendance system. It presents the system architecture, data collection methodology, and the integration of machine learning for face recognition. The paper provides insights into the design and implementation of such a system for attendance management purposes.

3. Methodology

In this work, a method is proposed to mark the attendance of a student using face recognition techniques. The framework of the proposed method is shown in the figure below (Fig. 23.1).

3.1 Haar-Cascade Classifier for Face Detection

In 2001, Paul Viola and Michael Jones in 2001, proposed this method; in this methodology machine learning approach is used to train a cascade function from a large dataset of positive and negative images. It enables the identification of objects in both images and videos, and can subsequently be applied to detect objects in new images. The algorithm's training process primarily relies on an abundant supply of positive and negative images. Following the acquisition of such data, feature extraction becomes essential.

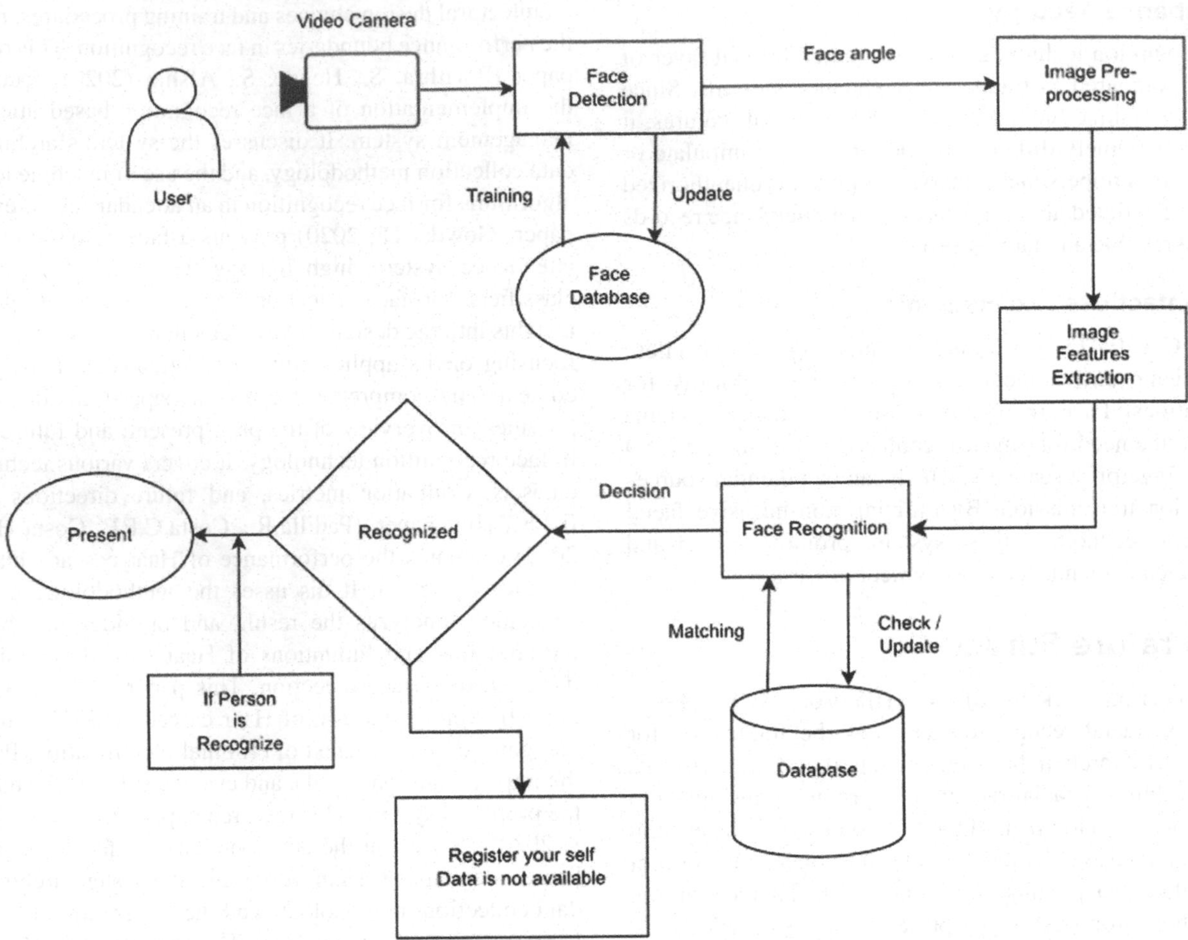

Fig. 23.1 Framework of proposed method [13]

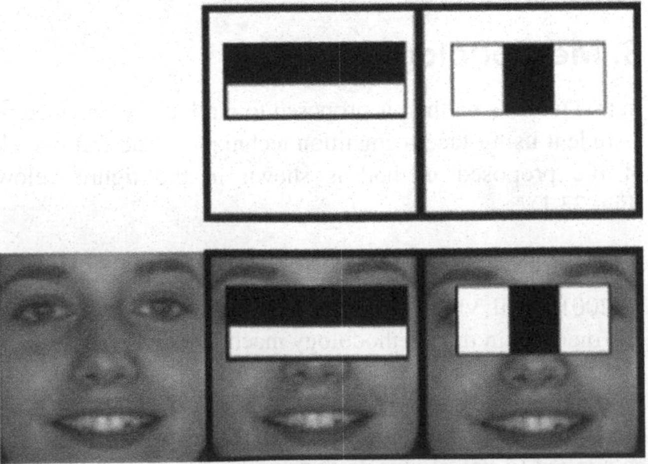

Fig. 23.2 Haar features applied on an image [13]

3.2 Algorithm Training

The algorithm is already trained on 35000 image samples, but for more accurate result algorithm is further trained on images of student that was captured by the system while detecting the face. System took 50 images of each student and store it, these images can further use for algorithm training. We also required a unique identification number for student images.

3.3 Local Binary Pattern Histogram (LBPH) for Face Recognition

The first procedural step of the LBPH algorithm involves creating an intermediate image that effectively emphasizes the facial features found in the original images. This is achieved through the utilization of the sliding window concept, which relies on the radius and neighbours parameters:

Below is the simple explanation for the concept:

- A pice of image is analyzed by matrix representation (Fig. 23.3). In this figure the image is represented by 3 rows and 3 columns, thus total nine pixels.
- Here, filter is applied considering central pixel, '8'. All the neighbouring cell greater than or equal to middle pixel will be reset to '1' and all others will be reset to '0'.

12	15	18
5	8	3
8	1	2

Fig. 23.3 LBHP example

Source: Author

1	1	1
0	8	0
1	0	0

Fig. 23.4 Binary values

Source: Author

- After imposing the condition, the matrix will be like this.
- Binary value is generated as per the matrix, i.e., 11100010.
- This algorithm will start applying the condition from the top left corner element goes up to the 1 element of the 2nd row making a circle.
- Then the binary value is converted to decimal value, i.e 216.

3.4 Performing the Face Recognition

- At this stage, training phase has already been completed. All images in the training dataset is represented by a unique histogram, allowing to apply the same process to a new input image, resulting in a histogram that represents the image.
- To find the most fitting image for the input image, two histograms are compared and image is selected closest to the histogram.
- Here for comparing the histograms, well-known Euclidean distance method is used.
- Consequently, the algorithm returns the ID of the images the closest histogram. Additionally, it provides the calculated distance, which can serve as an indicator of "confidence"
- Subsequently, one can utilize a threshold along with the "confidence" to determine if the algorithm correctly identified the image. If the confidence falls below the specified threshold, we can infer that the algorithm successfully recognized it.

4. Experimental Result

Here, for authentication system, both faculty as well as students are considered. When students are going to register itself there are few steps they need to perform:

First the student should have to fill their name and enrolment no/ID into the name and ID fields and then click into register.

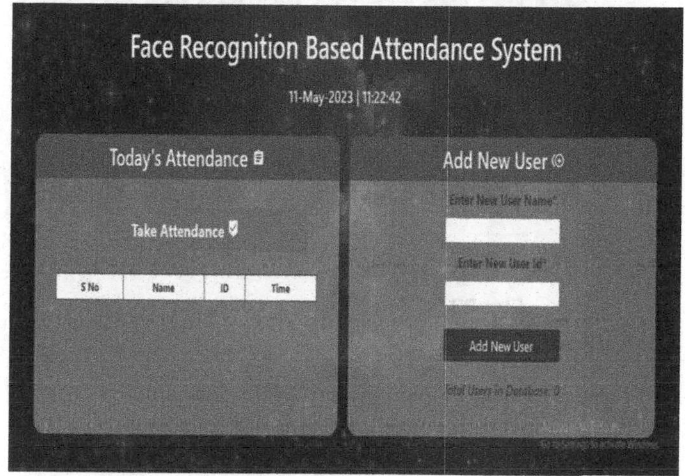

Fig. 23.5 Main screen

Source: Author

After clicking register web cam will open and a small screen will appear which detect the face and recognize it. Web will take 50 images of student face and store them into a separate file this face images are further use for training the model to increase its accuracy.

Fig. 23.6 Face detection

Source: Author

When students will came to mark the attendance first they need to enter their name and ID into the system and then click

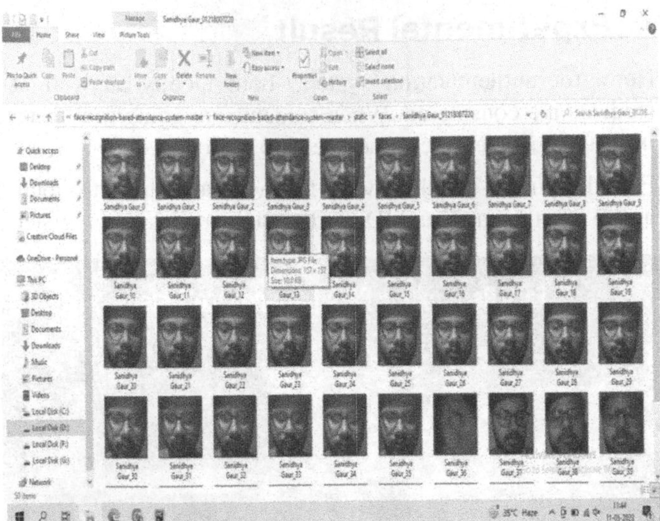

Fig. 23.7 Face images collection

Source: Author

on capture button to recognize it. The data entered by the student is appear on image capturing screen that cross check the image and data entered by student with the data inside database. If data is matched the attendance will mark present else it give a message "Credential is not matching" and will not marked.

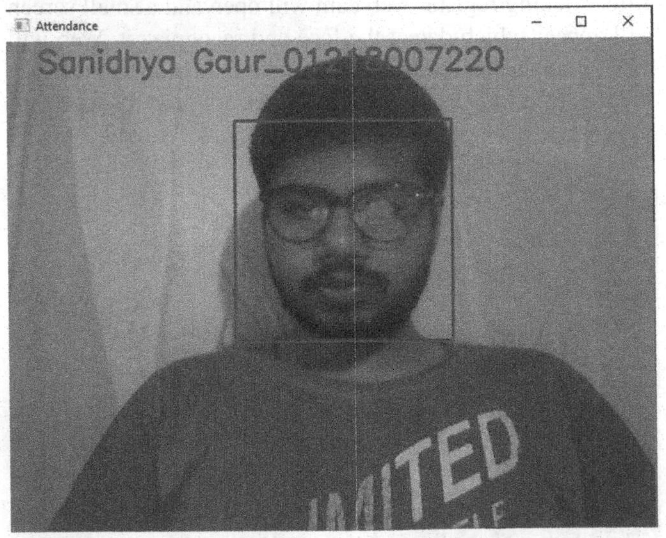

Fig. 23.8 Face recognition

Source: Author

After the recognition of the face, the system automatically mark the attendance into the excel sheet including day, date and system time.

5. Conclusion

The biometrics-based attendance system with machine learning integrated face modelling and recognition offers a powerful and efficient solution for attendance management in various domains. This system leverages the capabilities of machine learning algorithms and facial recognition technology to accurately identify individuals and record their attendance. By combining data collection, preprocessing, feature extraction, and model training, the system achieves reliable and automated attendance tracking.

With the utilization of hardware components such as cameras or sensors, the system captures facial images, ensuring a diverse and representative dataset. Consent and privacy measures are implemented to protect individuals' rights and comply with data protection regulations. Preprocessing techniques are applied to enhance the quality of facial images, and facial features are extracted using advanced modelling methods.

The training of a machine learning model enables accurate recognition and matching of captured faces with enrolled individuals in the database. Evaluation metrics such as accuracy, precision, recall, and F1 score assess the performance of the trained model, ensuring its effectiveness and generalization ability. The integration and deployment of the model into the attendance system facilitate real-time facial recognition during attendance recording.

Continuous monitoring, user feedback, and refinement processes are essential to optimize the system's performance, accuracy, and user experience. Adhering to ethical guidelines and privacy regulations throughout the implementation ensures that the system operates in a responsible and trustworthy manner.

In conclusion, the biometrics-based attendance system with machine learning integrated face modelling and recognition offers a robust and automated solution for attendance management. It streamlines the attendance tracking process, eliminates manual errors, and enhances overall efficiency. By leveraging the power of machine learning and facial recognition, this system contributes to improved accuracy, reliability, and convenience in attendance management across various industries and applications.

REFERENCES

1. Bledsoe, W. W. (1964). Facial Recognition project Report. Technical report PRI 10, Panoramic Research, Inc., Palo Alto, California.
2. Pantland,A., Truk,M. (1991): "Eigenface for Recognition" Journal of Cognitive Neuroscience, volume 3, Massachusetts Institute of Technology
3. Phillips, P.J.; Wechsler, H.; Huang, J.; Rauss, P. (1998). The FERET database and evaluation procedure for face recognition algorithms. Image Vis. Comput. 16, 295–306.
4. Phillips, P.J.; Flynn, P.J.; Scruggs, T.; Bowyer, K.W.; Chang, J.; Hoffman, K.; Marques, J.; Min, J.; Worek, W.(2005). Overview of the face recognition grand challenge. In

Proceedings of the 2005 IEEE Computer Society Conference on Computer Vision and Pattern Recognition (CVPR'05), San Diego, CA, USA, 20–26 June 2005; pp. 947–954.

5. Guo, G.; Zhang, N. (2019). A survey on deep learning based face recognition. Comput. Vis. Image Underst. 2019,189,10285.
6. Taigman, Y.; Yang, M.; Ranzato, M.; Wolf, L. (2014). Deepface: Closing the gap to human-level performance in face verification. In Proceedings of the 2014 IEEE Conference on Computer Vision and Pattern Recognition, Columbus, OH, USA, 23–28 June 2014; pp. 1701–1708.
7. Pavithra,S., Hegde, S., Afshin (2020). Face Recognition Based Attendance Management System of International journal of Engineering Research & Technology (IJERT), ISSN: 2778-0181, Volume 9, Issue 5, 2020, pp 1190–1191.
8. Gowda, D., Vishal, H.L.K., Keertiraj B. R, Dubey,N,K,, Pooja, M.R. (2020). Face Recognition based Attendance System of the International Journal of Engineering Research & Technology (IJERT), ISSN: 2278-0181, Volume 9, Issue 6, 2020, pp 761–762.
9. Adjabi,I., Ouahabi, A., Benzaoui, A. and Taleb, A. (2020). Past, Present, and Future of Face Recognition: A Review electronics MDPI, 2020, pp. 3–4.
10. Padilla,R., Costa,C.F.F, Costa, m.G.F. (2012). Evaluation of Haar Cascade Classifiers Designed for Face Detection of International Journal of Computer, Electrical, Automation, Control and Information Engineering Vol: 6, No: 4, 2012.
11. Senthamizh S.R , Sivakumar,D., Sandhya.J.S, Sowmiya.S.S., Ramya.S , Suba,K., Raja.S. (2019). Face Recognition Using Haar-Cascade Classifier for Criminal Identification of International Journal of Recent Technology and Engineering (IJRTE) ISSN: 2277-3878, Volume-7, Issue-6S5.
12. Bazith, S., Savant,P. (2022). Face Recognition Based Attendance System. International Journal for Research Trends and Innovation (IJRT), 2022, Volume 7, Issue 4.
13. Shetty, A. B., & Rebeiro, J. (2021). Facial recognition using Haar cascade and LBP classifiers. Global Transitions Proceedings, 2(2), 330–335.

Advancement of Intelligent Computational Methods and Technologies (AICMT2023) – Dr. O. P. Verma et al. (eds)

24

Plant Disease Detection Using Deep Learning

Devesh Bisht[1], Akhilesh[2], Aditya Rawat[3], Ishant Bhatt[4]
Dept. of CSE Delhi Technical Campus, Delhi, India
Kimmi Verma[5]
Associate Professor, Dept. of CSE, Delhi Technical Campus, Delhi, India

ABSTRACT: Plants have emerged as a significant renewable energy source and play a crucial role in addressing the urgent challenge of global warming. However, they are susceptible to various diseases that can severely impact their health and productivity. Leaf diseases, caused by microscopic organisms, are particularly difficult to detect with the naked eye. Nevertheless, leaves possess distinct visual characteristics that change when they are affected by diseases, making them valuable indicators for disease identification. This innovative approach enhances agricultural practices and contributes to combating the global warming crisis.

KEYWORDS: CNN (Convolutional Network), ResNet (Residual Network)

1. Introduction

In recent years, the agriculture industry has faced numerous challenges due to the increasing occurrence of plant diseases. These diseases not only cause significant crop losses but also pose a threat to global food security. Almost 5600 farmers have died because of crop losses due to plant diseases from 2014 to 2020. To combat this issue, advanced technologies like image recognition have emerged as powerful tools for early detection and accurate diagnosis of plant diseases.

The aim of this study is to introduce a novel web application utilizing ResNet50 image recognition technology to help farmers, agronomists, and crop disease experts to effectively identify and treat crop diseases. The app aims to revolutionize the way plant diseases are diagnosed and enable rapid action to mitigate their impact and prevent further spread.

By integrating ResNet50 into an easy-to-use web interface, the application provides farmers and experts with a convenient and accessible platform to identify crop diseases by simply uploading images of affected plants. The ResNet50 model quickly processes uploaded images, accurately identifies the current disease, and provides disease-specific information and recommended treatment strategies.

One of the significant advantages of image recognition, especially ResNet50, for plant disease detection is the ability to analyze plant images in a non-invasive manner. Traditional methods of diagnosing disease often require physical sampling, laboratory testing, and a time-consuming process. The web app allows users to quickly capture images of affected plants using a smartphone or camera, eliminating the need for invasive intervention, and enabling rapid disease detection.

Additionally, the Plant Disease Detection web application contains a comprehensive database of various plant diseases and their associated symptoms. The database is an invaluable resource for users, providing them with detailed information about each disease, its causes, and possible treatments.

[1]05118002719@delhitechnicalcampus.ac.in, [2]00318002719@delhitechnicalcampus.ac.in, [3]00918002719@delhitechnicalcampus.ac.in, [4]01218002719@delhitechnicalcampus.ac.in, [5]k.verma@delhitechnicalcampus.ac.in

DOI: 10.1201/9781003487906-24

2. Methodology

In this paper, the work is divided into four different modules such as preprocessing stage, image segmentation stage, feature extraction stage, and disease detection and classification.

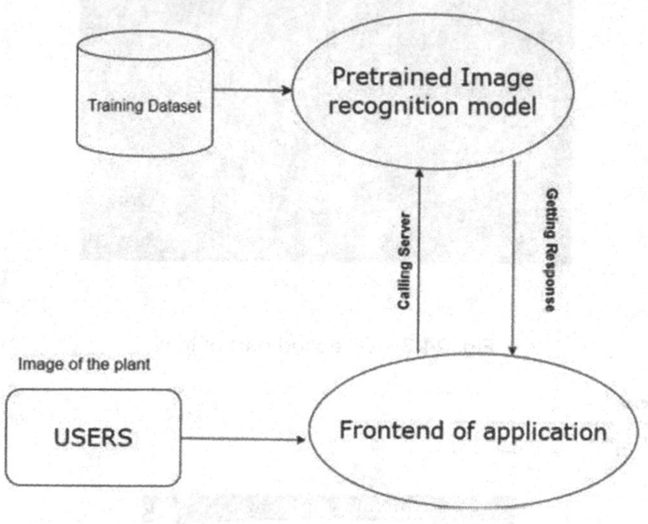

Fig. 24.1 Working model

2. Leaf Diseases

Leaf diseases can be detected using various methods, with the help pf technical aids such as image processing, visual analysis, and optical wireless sensors. For the production of outstanding results and to overcome limitations, a hybrid approachI can be implemented. Comparing the different methods, visual disease detection may not provide accurate output, while the use of optical sensors can be challenging and costly to implement. Consequently, image processing stands out as the most suitable option for developing a simple, reliable, and precise disease detection system [Fuentes & Yoon, 2010].

However, when working with image processing, building a comprehensive database becomes a challenging task. The gathering of essential information about the crops and their associated illnesses is crucial. A thorough investigation of disease types, symptoms on crops, and patterns of diseases is necessary to ensure accurate detection. By observing these disease patterns, the system can be effectively designed.

The most prevalent leaf diseases include bacterial illnesses, fungal diseases, viral diseases, and those transmitted by insects. A detailed exploration of these disorders is extensively covered in the study [Ferentinos, 2018]. By considering the characteristics and patterns of these diseases, the designed system can successfully identify and diagnose them, contributing to effective disease management in the agricultural sector.

2.1 Disease Recognition of Plants Using Image Dataset

Aduwo et al. produced one of the earliest pieces of reaserch in this area [Fuentes & Yoon, 2010; Ferentinos, 2018]. They used leaf photos of cassava plants obtained in a lab with consistent illumination and uniform background. A two-class algorithm was created to determine if a leaf image belongs to a damaged or healthy plant. They used leaf photos of cassava plants obtained in a lab with consistent illumination and uniform background. A two-class algorithm was created to determine if a leaf image belongs to a damaged or healthy plant.In future research, the categorization systems employed were enhanced, [Ferentinos, 2018; Sladojevic et al., 2016; Mehmood et al., 2017] .Deep learning is used in more recent image-based techniques for cassava disease identification, such as Ramcharan et al [Sladojevic et al., 2016; Mehmood et al., 2017; Ferentinos, 2018].In the literature, several more image-based techniques to crop disease identification have been proposed, such as [Sladojevic et al., 2016; Mehmood et al., 2017; Ferentinos, 2018;].Obviously, every image-based technique relies on the presence of visual symptoms, whether or not it is integrated with machine learning. The importance of detecting illness early, before the plant becomes symptomatic, cannot be overstated. The usage of spectrometry is one of the topics we look into in this paper. We believe that obtaining a leaf's spectral signature will be more informative of the plant's disease state than image data, especially if we wish to diagnose disease before the plant becomes obviously unwell.

2.2 Validation

To ensure the accuracy and reliability of the leaf dataset, a robust validation process is essential. Validating the dataset involves several crucial steps that help verify its quality and suitability for further analysis and research.

The first step in the validation process is to carefully examine the data collection methodology. This involves reviewing the protocols and procedures followed during the acquisition of leaf samples and recording relevant information about the plants and their associated diseases. Any inconsistencies or errors in data collection need to be addressed and rectified to maintain the integrity of the dataset.

2.3 ResNet50

ResNet50 is a convolutional neural network (CNN) model that was introducedin 2015 by researchers at Microsoft Research Asia. It is a deep residual network. The convolutional layers are arranged in a series of blocks, with each block containing several layers. One key feature of ResNet50 is the use of skip connections, also called identity mappings or shortcut connections. These connections allow the output of one layerto be added to the output of a later layer, effectively bypassing one or more layers in between. This helps to alleviate the vanishing gradient problem and allows the network to be trained to greater depths.

3. Experimental Results

For executing the algorithm two types of datasets are evaluated. First data set consist of mutiple images and this dataset will be put into the folder named as training dataset and other folder is named as train dataset which consist of images that will match the images of the trained folder for the feature matching SIFT algorithm.

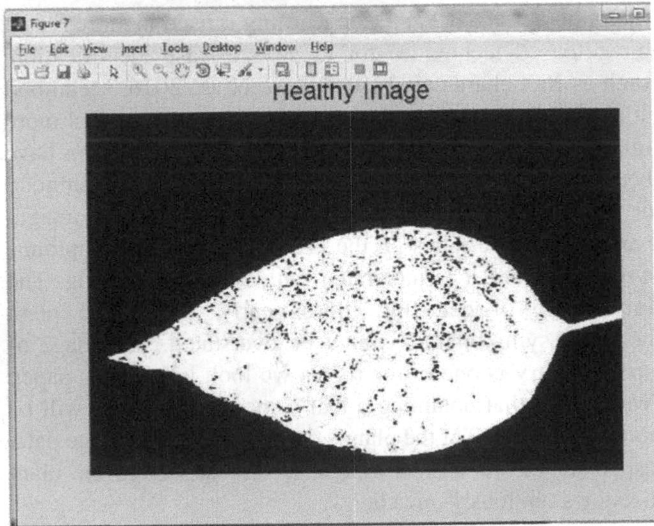

Fig. 24.2 Healthy part of leaf

Figure 24.2 indicates the part of the leaf which has been detected .The images in the trained folder will be matched with the images in the train folder, for feature matching the SIFT algorithm will be applied. Leaf with matching traits will be extracted and diseases will be diagnosed using enhanced SVM on those leaves, as shown in the diagram.

The black background from the leaf will be extracted to know how much portion of the leaf will be cut.

Figure 24.3 indicates the region of diseases. The SATURATION value of the contaminated leaf will be calculated, which will help to improve the accuracy of the detection. The upgraded SVM technique will be used in this figure to differentiate the diseased and uninfected portions of the leaf. The contaminated section of the leaf will be separated using the upgraded SVM technique. The SVM displays the percentage of infected tissue, which is 5.54 percent.

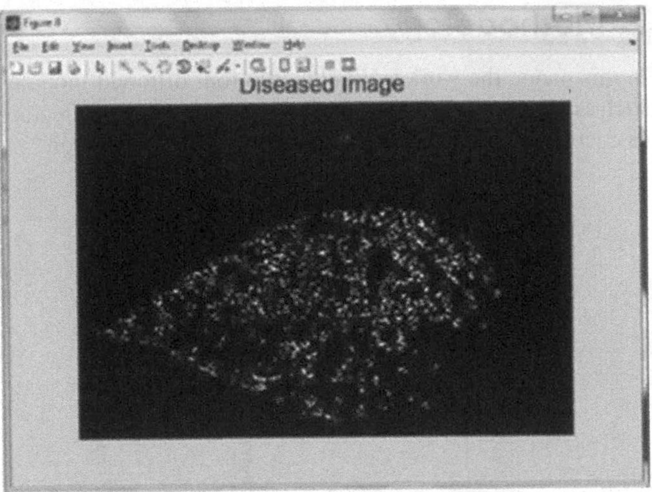

Fig. 24.3 Diseased part of leaf

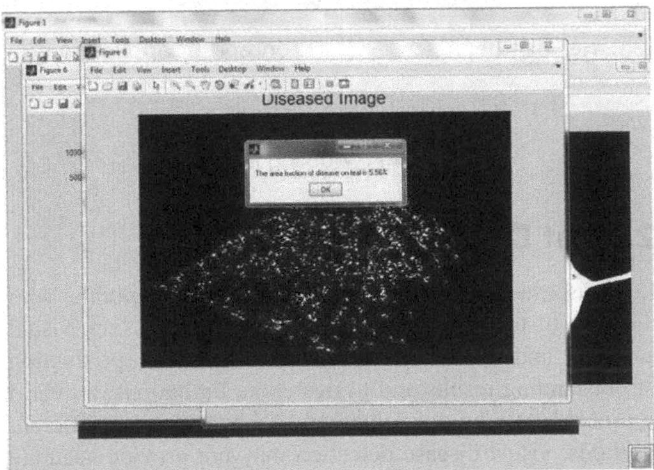

Fig. 24.4 Region of disease

4. Conclusion

This research concludes that the ResNet50 model is quite good for finding the Diseases in the plants using the images dataset. We have used almost 38 classes of the dataset in this research and the accuracy achieved by the ResNet50 model was around 99.5%.

Farmers can use this web application or the Image recognition model to find out that what kind of the disease is in the plant and the can be able to rectify the disease easily or as soon as possible so that the loss of corps would be less.

The significance of this research lies in its potential impact on agriculture and food security. Early detection and diagnosis of plant diseases are crucial for effective disease management and crop protection.

In conclusion, this research highlights the potential of the ResNet50 model for plant disease recognition, contributing to the field of agriculture and paving the way for further advancements in automated disease diagnosis.

REFERENCES

1. Mohanty, S. P., Hughes, D. P., and Salathé, M. (2016). *Deep Learning-Based Plant Disease Detection Using Convolutional Neural Networks.* Computers and Electronics in Agriculture. Vol: 125 125, 1-13.
2. Fuentes, A., and Yoon, S. (2020). *Plant Pathology 2020: AI, Multispectral Imaging, and Digital Platforms for Sustainable Crop Disease Management.* Annual Review of Phytopathology. Vol 58.
3. Ferentinos, K. P. (2018). *Deep Learning for Plant Disease Diagnosis: A Study on Recognition of Healthy and Infected Individual Tomato Leaves.* Computers and Electronics in Agriculture. Vol: 145.
4. Sladojevic, S., Arsenovic, M., Anderla, A., Culibrk, D., and Stefanovic, D. (2016). *Using Deep Convolutional Neural Networks for Multi-classification of Tomato Diseases.* Computers and Electronics in Agriculture). Vol: 127.
5. Mehmood, A., Shabbir, A., and Khurshid, K. (2017). *Automatic Detection of Plant Diseases: A Brief Survey and Its Experimental Study.* Computers and Electronics in Agriculture. Vol 145.

Note: All the figures in this chapter were made by the author.

Advancement of Intelligent Computational Methods and Technologies (AICMT2023) – Dr. O. P. Verma et al. (eds)
© 2024 Taylor & Francis Group, London, ISBN 978-1-032-78445-8

25

Autonomous Driving Using Deep Learning

Uttam Sharma[1], Rohan Pal[2], Gaurav Sarosha[3], Pulkit Mathur[4], Yashu Shanker[5], Md Shamsuzzama Siddiqui[6]
Delhi Technical Campus, Greater Noida, U.P

ABSTRACT: The largest undertaking of a self-driving car is self-sufficient lateral motion so the primary goal of this paper is to clone drives for higher performance of the self-reliant car for which we're using multilayer neural networks and deep studying strategies. We are able to recognition to attain autonomous automobiles riding in stimulator conditions. Within the simulator, pre-processing the image received from the digicam placed inside the car imitate the driver's imaginative and prescient and then the response, which is the steerage perspective of the auto. The neural network trains the deep gaining knowledge of technique on the idea of pix taken from a camera in guide mode which provides a situation for running the automobile in self-reliant mode, utilizing the skilled multilayered neural network. The driver imitation set of rules fabricated and characterized inside the paper is all about the profound learning approach this is centered across the NVIDIA CNN version.

KEYWORDS: Self-driving car, Lateral motion, Multilayer neural networks, Deep learning, Simulation, Image recognition, Steering angle, NVIDIA CNN architecture

1. Introduction

Traveling by car is now one of the deadliest modes of transport, killing more than a million people worldwide each year. Driving mistakes are the cause of most car accidents, especially fatal ones. The introduction of self-driving cars has the potential to eliminate many of the risks associated with driving, including driver deaths, safety issues, access and injury to everyone. (Nicolas Gallardo.2017) The concept of the self-driving car offers revolutionary promise. Such vehicles are equipped with automatic driving, which allows them to work without human intervention. Although it was originally developed from self-directed methods, advances in computer vision and artificial intelligence have led to the use of deep learning methods. Still, there are still some challenges to overcome before self-driving cars become a reality.

One crucial capability of self-driving vehicles is autonomous Lateral control always depends on imaging techniques. The process includes tasks such as determining the route, determining the centerline, planning and monitoring the route, and implementing management strategies (S. Liu et al.2019). The accuracy of these systems depends on the accuracy of the image processing filters. However, these methods are very sensitive to changes in lighting conditions and result in poor performance. Algorithms optimized for observing lines in bright and sunny conditions may not perform well in dark and cloudy conditions. To address this, the framework uses a convolutional neural network to generate checkpoints from the road image that essentially simulates human driving behavior. Because this end-to-end model is not based on quality guidelines, it rarely changes in lighting conditions.

Deep learning has proven to be an effective tool for self-driving and is gradually improving driverless cars. However, there are challenges to overcome before deep learning can be integrated into autonomous vehicles. These issues include data collection, algorithm development, and security.

This article ends with an in-depth review of vehicle control. This includes developing a model of the vehicle's motion and then evaluating the control design in a simulator environment.

[1]sharmauttam1610@gmail.com, [2]Rohanpal3232@gmail.com, [3]gouravsaroha@gmail.com, [4]Pulkitmathur4u@gmail.com, [5]yashu.shanker@gmail.com, [6]mdshamsuzzama19@gmail.com

DOI: 10.1201/9781003487906-25

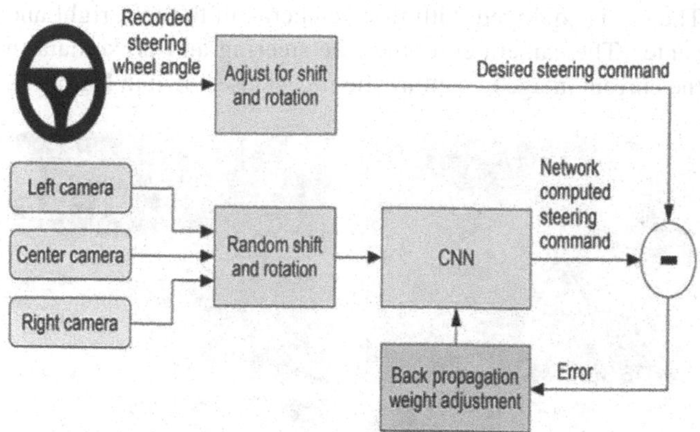

Fig. 25.1 Schematic representation autonomous driving

2. Literature Survey

Autonomous vehicles represent a rapidly evolving technology poised to revolutionize the transportation landscape. Deep learning, a potent machine learning approach, has proven its effectiveness across diverse tasks, encompassing image recognition, object detection, and natural language processing. These capabilities render deep learning a logical fit for numerous challenges entailed in constructing autonomous vehicles. Recent years have witnessed extensive research in employing deep learning for automated vehicles. (D. Bemstcin and A. Kamhauser 2012) Somc prcvalent applications of deep learning in this domain encompass:

- *Environmental perception:* Dccp lcarning can identify objects in the surroundings like cars, pedestrians, and cyclists, pivotal for safe navigation by autonomous vehicles (Joshi and M. R. James.2014).
- *Path planning:* Utilizing deep learning, autonomous vehicles can chart secure and efficient routes, accounting for the environment's current state, the vehicle's objectives, and constraints (Qudsia Memon, Shahzeb Ali, Wajiha Shah.2016).
- *Decision-making:* Deep learning can facilitate real-time decisions in response to unforeseen events, such as pedestrians crossing roads, necessitating the ability to comprehend situations and take suitable actions (Naveen S Yeshodara, Nikhitha Kishore.2014).

Although deep learning holds significant promise for autonomous vehicle development, several challenges need resolution before its full integration for creating entirely self-sufficient vehicles. Continuous research endeavors are likely to define a pivotal role for deep learning in the future of autonomous driving.

2.1 Issue at Hand

The field of autonomous vehicles remains in its embryonic phase, marked by a multitude of challenges that require resolution before their safe integration onto public roads. One substantial hurdle revolves around developing robust and dependable deep learning algorithms capable of comprehending the environment and making informed navigational choices.

Deep learning is a branch of machine learning that uses neural networks to extract insights from data. Neural networks originating from the human brain are good at recognizing complex patterns in data, making them suitable for tasks such as object detection, image classification, and natural language processing. Within the context of autonomous vehicles, the potential applications of deep learning include:

- Accurate environmental perception in the proximity of autonomous vehicles.
- Cognizant and reliable decision-making concerning navigation within the environment.
- Assessment of deep learning algorithm performance within simulated scenarios.

The development of robust and dependable deep learning algorithms for autonomous vehicles possesses the potential to substantially enhance road safety and pave the way for the realization of autonomous vehicles as a tangible and safe reality.

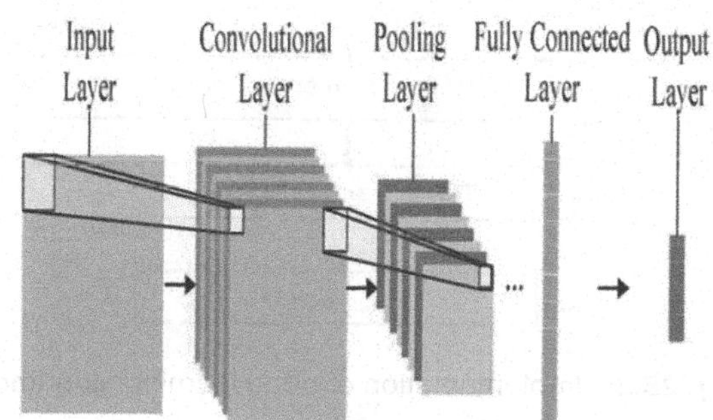

Fig. 25.2 Development of robust and dependable deep learning algorithms

2.2 Implementation and Algorithm

The algorithm consists of components that begin with data collection, encompassing images, steering angles, and speed. Subsequently, there is a phase dedicated to achieving data balance, followed by essential data processing to appropriately ready the input for the neural network.

Our process is used to process the data first:

1. Normalization
2. Enhancement
3. Image cropping to remove unnecessary areas such as sky and car hoods. At the heart of the

Deep learning is a branch of machine learning that uses neural networks to extract insights from data. Neural networks originating from the human brain are good at recognizing

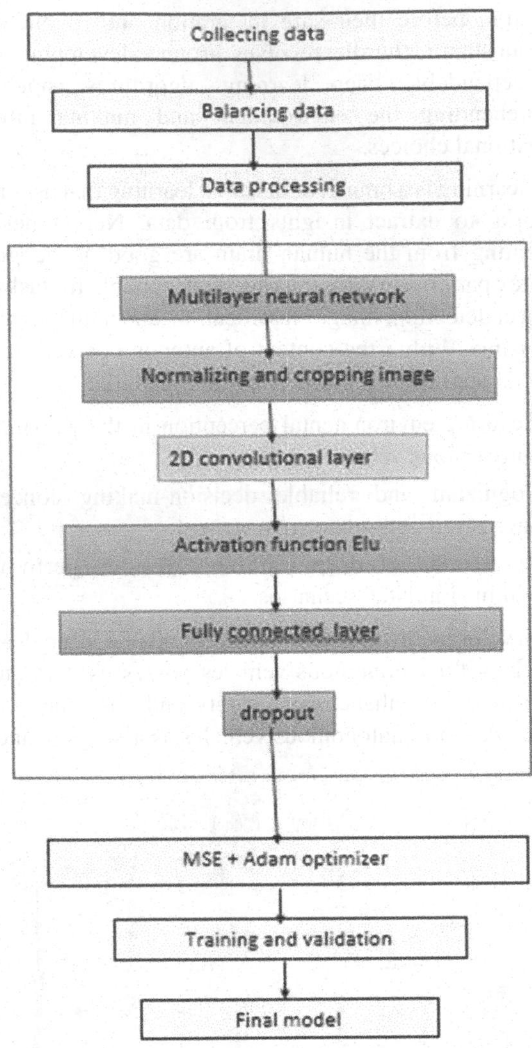

Fig. 25.3 Implementation of deep learning alogrithm

complex patterns in data, making them suitable for tasks such as object detection, image classification, and natural language processing.

2.3 Collection of Data

The datastore must control the vehicle in the simulator using keyboard commands. More driving led to better models than true mirroring behavior simulation or "behavior cloning". For this, the open source emulator provided by Udacity was used. Alternatively, the Unreal Engine-based Air simulator can be used as an alternative.

Training models involve driving a vehicle with keyboard input, similar to controlling behavior in a video game. The path layout is designed according to the neural network, especially when using smart rails. The aim is to control the central driving system to provide equal information.

The car is equipped with three cameras in the left, right and center. The camera combines the steering and brake data in the current image to capture the image. as shown in Fig. 25.4.

Fig. 25.4 Example image captured

```
model.compile(optimizer= Adam(learning_rate=0.0001),metrics=['accuracy'],los
history=model.fit(train_data,epochs=20,steps_per_epoch=len(train_data),valid

Epoch 1/20
201/201 [==============================] - 14s 68ms/step - loss: 1.2697 - a
ccuracy: 0.6318 - val_loss: 0.7773 - val_accuracy: 0.6102
Epoch 2/20
201/201 [==============================] - 14s 69ms/step - loss: 0.5029 - a
ccuracy: 0.7910 - val_loss: 0.6609 - val_accuracy: 0.6949
Epoch 3/20
201/201 [==============================] - 14s 68ms/step - loss: 0.4033 - a
ccuracy: 0.8358 - val_loss: 0.6414 - val_accuracy: 0.7119
Epoch 4/20
201/201 [==============================] - 14s 68ms/step - loss: 0.3500 - a
ccuracy: 0.8557 - val_loss: 0.5641 - val_accuracy: 0.7119
Epoch 5/20
201/201 [==============================] - 14s 69ms/step - loss: 0.3181 - a
ccuracy: 0.8706 - val_loss: 0.6843 - val_accuracy: 0.7288
Epoch 6/20
201/201 [==============================] - 14s 69ms/step - loss: 0.2770 - a
ccuracy: 0.8856 - val_loss: 0.5476 - val_accuracy: 0.7627
Epoch 7/20
201/201 [==============================] - 14s 70ms/step - loss: 0.2611 - a
ccuracy: 0.9005 - val_loss: 0.6403 - val_accuracy: 0.7288
Epoch 8/20
201/201 [==============================] - 14s 70ms/step - loss: 0.2520 - a
ccuracy: 0.8955 - val_loss: 0.6501 - val_accuracy: 0.7119
Epoch 9/20
201/201 [==============================] - 14s 68ms/step - loss: 0.2398 - a
ccuracy: 0.9104 - val_loss: 0.4683 - val_accuracy: 0.7458
Epoch 10/20
201/201 [==============================] - 14s 70ms/step - loss: 0.2257 - a
ccuracy: 0.9104 - val_loss: 0.6027 - val_accuracy: 0.6780
Epoch 11/20
201/201 [==============================] - 14s 69ms/step - loss: 0.1974 - a
ccuracy: 0.9005 - val_loss: 0.4862 - val_accuracy: 0.7627
Epoch 12/20
201/201 [==============================] - 14s 68ms/step - loss: 0.1969 - a
ccuracy: 0.9254 - val_loss: 0.5088 - val_accuracy: 0.7627
Epoch 13/20
201/201 [==============================] - 14s 69ms/step - loss: 0.1814 - a
ccuracy: 0.9303 - val_loss: 0.5013 - val_accuracy: 0.7288
Epoch 14/20
201/201 [==============================] - 14s 68ms/step - loss: 0.1853 - a
ccuracy: 0.9204 - val_loss: 0.5855 - val_accuracy: 0.7797
Epoch 15/20
201/201 [==============================] - 14s 69ms/step - loss: 0.1700 - a
ccuracy: 0.9353 - val_loss: 0.8720 - val_accuracy: 0.7797
Epoch 16/20
201/201 [==============================] - 14s 69ms/step - loss: 0.1955 - a
ccuracy: 0.9353 - val_loss: 0.5737 - val_accuracy: 0.7288
Epoch 17/20
201/201 [==============================] - 14s 70ms/step - loss: 0.1612 - a
ccuracy: 0.9403 - val_loss: 0.6432 - val_accuracy: 0.7797
Epoch 18/20
201/201 [==============================] - 15s 73ms/step - loss: 0.1424 - a
ccuracy: 0.9602 - val_loss: 0.6478 - val_accuracy: 0.7627
Epoch 19/20
201/201 [==============================] - 15s 74ms/step - loss: 0.1410 - a
ccuracy: 0.9602 - val_loss: 0.4513 - val_accuracy: 0.7797
Epoch 20/20
```

Fig. 25.5 Example CSV file

Steering angles are ponds from 1 to right and left, 0 indicates the car is going straight.

In this case, the vertical axis represents the histogram values, taking into account the frequency distribution of each angle during simulation.

2.4 Equivalent Data

is graph shows that the angle occurs most often at 0 and shows the actual frequency of this value. This can cause the model to run mostly along a straight line, resulting in inconsistent data. To mitigate this concern, these solutions include filtering out samples that exceed a predefined threshold. This feedback filter corrects the error by ensuring that data cannot be followed in a straight driving line.

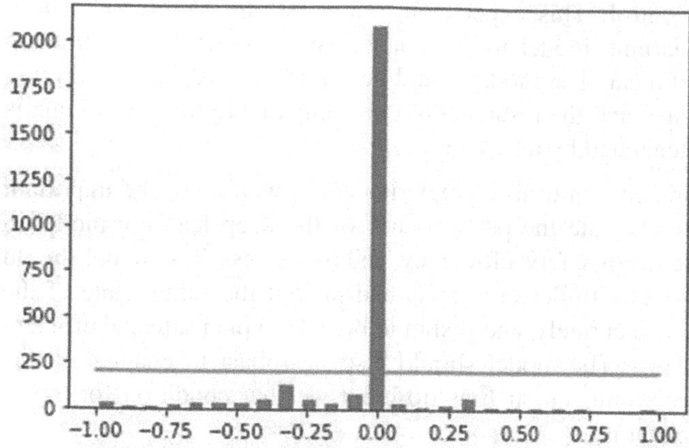

Fig. 25.6 Bar graph of orientation angle

2.5 Data Reprocessing

This is an important step as it expresses the need to remove redundant areas from the image. In our images, some of them are meaningless or irrelevant to our purpose, so they should be excluded. This clipping allows for a more focused analysis of relevant feature.

Fig. 25.7 Cropped image

Next step is to change the color space of the image, it is important to do this first because the model we are using tells us to use YUV color where Y represents the brightness or brightness of the image and UV rose for Chrome can add color. We show the finished image by adding a Gaussian Blur operation that helps soften the image and reduce noise.

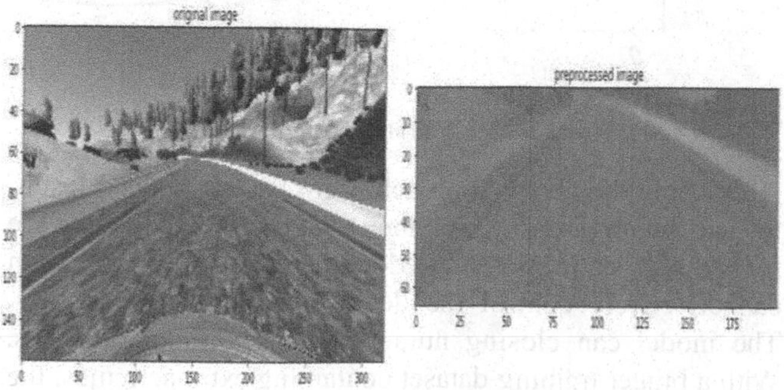

Fig. 25.8 Pre-processed image

2.6 Blue Print

In behavior our dataset is more complex than other datasets because we are now dealing with 200x66 images. A popular model that uses behavior cloning is the NVIDIA model, which should be used during personal driving.

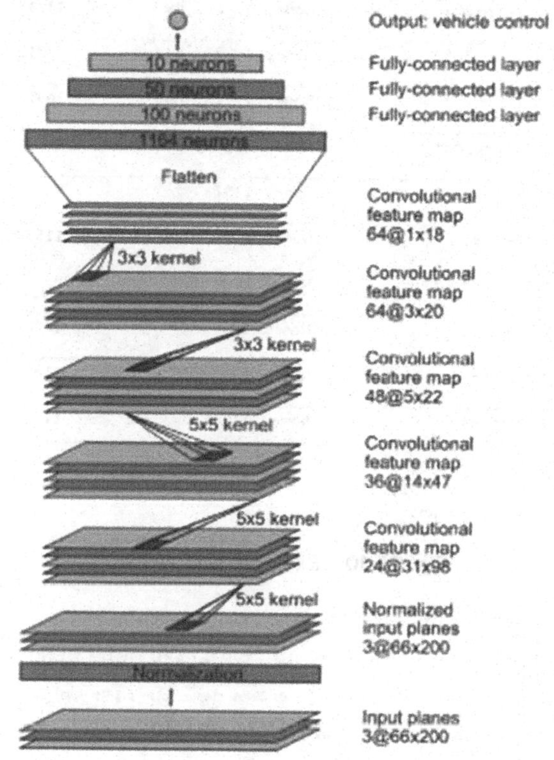

Fig. 25.9 Three-character cloning pattern

This pattern will work as follows.

Step 1: Normalization layer (hard coded)

is split through 127.five and subtracted from 1.

Step 2: Convolution layer with 24, 36, 48 filters and 5x5 cores with step 2.

Step 3: 64, 3x3 2-convolution layer filter core and step 1.

Step 4: Align the layers.

Step 5: 3 total layers with output sizes 100, 50, 10.

Step 6: Put the last output layer on the control layer.

Next, we use epochs for the training and validation process. Here we loop 30 times and each group has 100 points to help reduce loss as shown in Figure 2.

3. Experiments

Object detection: This experiment could test the accuracy of a deep learning model for object detection in a variety of environments. The model could be tested on a dataset of

```
Model: "sequential_1"
_________________________________________________________________
Layer (type)                 Output Shape              Param #
=================================================================
conv2d_1 (Conv2D)            (None, 31, 98, 24)        1824
_________________________________________________________________
conv2d_2 (Conv2D)            (None, 14, 47, 36)        21636
_________________________________________________________________
conv2d_3 (Conv2D)            (None, 5, 22, 48)         43248
_________________________________________________________________
conv2d_4 (Conv2D)            (None, 3, 20, 64)         27712
_________________________________________________________________
conv2d_5 (Conv2D)            (None, 1, 18, 64)         36928
_________________________________________________________________
dropout_1 (Dropout)          (None, 1, 18, 64)         0
_________________________________________________________________
flatten_1 (Flatten)          (None, 1152)              0
_________________________________________________________________
dense_1 (Dense)              (None, 100)               115300
_________________________________________________________________
dropout_2 (Dropout)          (None, 100)               0
_________________________________________________________________
dense_2 (Dense)              (None, 50)                5050
_________________________________________________________________
dense_3 (Dense)              (None, 10)                510
_________________________________________________________________
dense_4 (Dense)              (None, 1)                 11
=================================================================
Total params: 252,219
Trainable params: 252,219
Non-trainable params: 0
```

Fig. 25.10 Example sequence

```
Train on 662 samples, validate on 166 samples
Epoch 1/10
662/662 [==============================] - 7s 10ms/step - loss: 0.6617 - val_loss: 0.2204
Epoch 2/10
662/662 [==============================] - 0s 394us/step - loss: 0.1945 - val_loss: 0.1587
Epoch 3/10
662/662 [==============================] - 0s 397us/step - loss: 0.1453 - val_loss: 0.1444
Epoch 4/10
662/662 [==============================] - 0s 394us/step - loss: 0.1362 - val_loss: 0.1505
Epoch 5/10
662/662 [==============================] - 0s 406us/step - loss: 0.1309 - val_loss: 0.1412
Epoch 6/10
662/662 [==============================] - 0s 390us/step - loss: 0.1243 - val_loss: 0.1392
Epoch 7/10
662/662 [==============================] - 0s 395us/step - loss: 0.1166 - val_loss: 0.1333
Epoch 8/10
662/662 [==============================] - 0s 397us/step - loss: 0.1154 - val_loss: 0.1269
Epoch 9/10
662/662 [==============================] - 0s 396us/step - loss: 0.1091 - val_loss: 0.1233
Epoch 10/10
662/662 [==============================] - 0s 400us/step - loss: 0.1172 - val_loss: 0.1248
```

Fig. 25.11 EPOCH with price drop

images or videos, and the results could be compared to the results of a human observer.

State prediction: This experiment could test the accuracy of a deep learning model for predicting the future state of a car. The model could be trained on a dataset of historical data,and results could be compared to the actual state of the car.

Path planning: This experiment could test the ability of a deep learning model to plan a safe and efficient path for a car to follow. The model could be trained on a dataset of maps and traffic data, and the results could be compared the paths generated by a human driver.

Control: This experiment could test the ability of a deep learning model to control the speed, steering, and braking of a car. The model could be trained on a dataset of driving data, and the results could be compared to the control inputs generated by a human driver.

In addition to these experiments, it would also be important to evaluate the performance of the deep learning model in terms of safety, efficiency, and robustness. The model should be able to detect objects and predict the future state of the car accurately, and it should be able to plan safe and efficient paths. The model should also be robust to changes in the environment, such as different weather conditions or traffic patterns.

The results of these experiments could be used to improve the design of deep learning models for automated cars. The experiments could also be used to identify the strengths and weaknesses of different deep learning algorithms.

4. Results

Conduct cloning takes region in a simulated riding state of affairs conduct cloning simulates a riding scenario the use of a CNN in which we use the Elu function. The elu characteristic makes use of the rectangular of the mistake to validate the records. As we predicted, the training records performed better, however the two values of the schooling and test statistics are very near, which leads us to finish that the version explains a lot of correct matters.

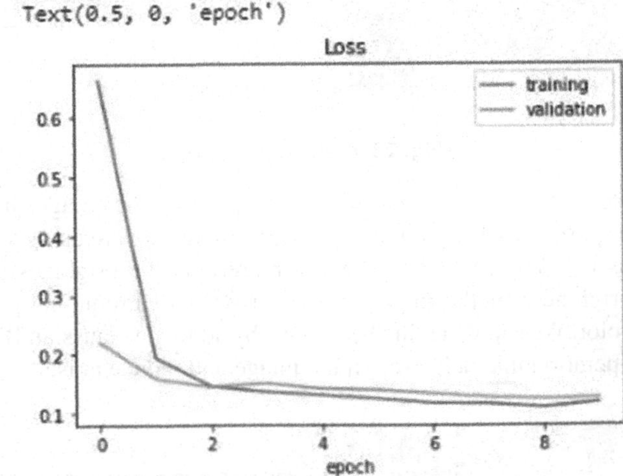

Fig. 25.12 Training and validation

After using the above approach, right here is the end result, the car running on the road, the result can be visible that the proper perspective is a speedometer. The training version can effectively control the device on unknown variables. The model can closing numerous laps without mistakes. With a bigger training dataset containing extra activities, the model's potential to govern the man or woman version will boom. take a look at runs can be found at: https://youtu.be/H50cCrUiOqc.

Fig. 25.13 Training version control the device

5. Conclusion

This article affords a method for independent riding the usage of deep gaining knowledge of techniques and cease-to-give up learning in a simulated surroundings. At its middle, the driver cloning algorithm is primarily based on Nvidia's neural network structure. The community includes five convolutional layers, a normalization layer, and 4 fully related layers that generate angles according to its output. Achieving autonomous driving is done in autonomous mode, following a predefined path in the simulation. The model trains using limited data generated independently in book form and thus generates specific training data. However, it is worth noting that there is room for improvement by using a more comprehensive approach to support. The current general limitations are due to the small amount of data that affects the application of the model to real-world situations. Currently, self-driving cars perform well in simulation along the proposed route.

6. Future Scope

The future scope of automated cars using deep learning is very promising. Deep learning has already been shown to be a powerful tool for a variety of tasks related to autonomous driving, such as object detection, state prediction, path planning, and control. As technology continues to evolve, driverless cars will become safer, more efficient and cheaper.

Here are some specific areas where deep learning is likely to have a significant impact on the future of automated cars:

- *Object detection:* deep learning is used to detect objects in the environment such as other cars, pedestrians and traffic signs. As technology continues to evolve, deep learning will be able to identify small, hard-to-see objects. This will make self-driving cars safer and more reliable.
- *State prediction:* Deep learning is also being used to predict the future state of a car, such as its position, heading, and velocity. This information can be used to plan safe and efficient paths for the car to follow. As the technology continues to improve, deep learning will be able to predict the future state of the car more accurately, which will make it easier for the car to avoid accidents.
- *Path planning:* Deep learning is also being used to plan safe and efficient paths for cars to follow. This information can be used to avoid obstacles and traffic congestion. As the technology continues to improve, deep learning will be able to plan paths that are even more efficient and safe.
- *Control:* Deep learning is also being used to control the speed, steering, and braking of cars. This information can be used to keep the car in its lane and to avoid collisions. As the technology continues to improve, deep learning will be able to control cars more precisely and safely.

In addition to these specific areas, deep learning is also likely to have a broader impact on the future of automated cars. For example, deep learning could be used to develop new features for automated cars, such as the ability to recognize and respond to emotions or the ability to learn from its own experiences. Deep learning could also be used to improve the safety and reliability of automated cars by detecting and preventing errors.

Overall, the future scope of automated cars using deep learning is very promising. Deep learning is a powerful tool that has the potential to make automated cars safer, more efficient, and more affordable. As technology continues to evolve, self-driving cars will appear on the roads in the next few years.

REFERENCES

1. Nicolas Gallardo.2017.Autonomous Decision Making for a Driver- less Car
2. S. Liu et al.2019.Creating Autonomous Vehicle Systems, Morgan Claypool Publishers
3. D. Bemstcin, and A. Kamhauser.2012.An Introduction to MapMatching far Personal Navigation Assistants.Princeton University, Princeton, New Jersey, August 2012
4. Joshi and M. R. James.2014.Generation of accurate lane-level maps from coarse prior maps and lidar
5. Qudsia-Memon, Shahzeb Ali, Wajiha Shah.2016. Self-Driving and DriverRelaxing Vehicle
6. Naveen S Yeshodara, Nikhitha Kishore.2014Cloud Based-Self-Driving-Cars.https://medium.com/swlh/behavioural-cloning-end-to-end- learning-forself-driving-cars-50b959708e5

Note: All the figures in this chapter were made by the author.

Advancement of Intelligent Computational Methods and Technologies (AICMT2023) – Dr. O. P. Verma et al. (eds)

26

Credit Card Fraud Detection using Supervised Machine Learning Algorithm

Abhay Kumar Verma, Ankesh Kumar, Anjani Kumar, Itesh Bansal
Delhi Technical Campus, Greater Noida, U.P

ABSTRACT: Detecting credit card theft is a crucial process to safeguard customers from unauthorized charges. By utilizing data science and machine learning, a model is developed using past fraudulent transactions as examples. This model is then employed to analyze fresh credit card transactions in real-time. Its goal is to reliably detect fraudulent activities while reducing the amount of legal transactions incorrectly marked as fraudulent. Through continuous refinement and updates, credit card companies can stay ahead of fraudsters and ensure a secure experience for their customers. By striking the right balance between precision and sensitivity, the system can effectively identify fraudulent transactions without causing unnecessary inconvenience to users. This way, credit card firms can protect their customers' financial interests and maintain trust in their services.

KEYWORDS: Fraud, Supervised machine learning, Training data, Testing data, Classification, Regression

1. Introduction

Credit card fraud has become a prevalent issue in today's digital age, posing significant challenges to financial institutions and cardholders alike. With the increasing reliance on online transactions and the rapid growth of e-commerce, fraudulent activities have also evolved, necessitating the development of sophisticated techniques to combat them.

Credit card fraud is a form of financial crime that involves the unauthorized or fraudulent use of credit card information for personal gain. It encompasses various fraudulent activities, including stolen card details, counterfeit cards, identity theft, and unauthorized transactions. Fraudsters continually adapt their tactics to exploit vulnerabilities in payment systems, making it crucial for financial institutions to deploy advanced methods for timely detection and prevention.

Traditional rule-based systems have been employed to detect fraud, relying on predefined rules and thresholds. However, these approaches often fail to keep pace with the evolving nature of fraud, as fraudsters find ways to circumvent these rules. As a result, financial institutions are increasingly turning to supervised machine learning algorithms to strengthen their fraud detection capabilities.

Supervised machine learning algorithms offer a data-driven approach to fraud detection, where models are trained on historical transaction data with known fraudulent and legitimate instances. By learning from these patterns and characteristics and using the algorithms new transactions should be classified as either genuine or bogus, thereby assisting in identifying potential fraud in real time.

The potential benefits of using supervised machine learning algorithms for detection of fraud are significant. They can improve the accuracy of fraud detection by uncovering complex patterns and anomalies that may not be apparent through rule-based systems (R. Brause et al. 1999). Additionally, machine learning models can adapt and evolve over time, continuously learning from new data and updating their detection capabilities.

[1]sharmauttam1610@gmail.com, [2]Rohanpal3232@gmail.com, [3]gouravsaroha@gmail.com, [4]Pulkitmathur4u@gmail.com, [5]yashu.shanker@gmail.com, [6]mdshamsuzzama19@gmail.com

DOI: 10.1201/9781003487906-26

What other Data Scientists got

Method Used	Frauds	Genuines	MCC
Naïve Bayes	83.130	97.730	0.219
Decision Tree	81.098	99.951	0.775
Random Forest	42.683	99.988	0.604
Gradient Boosted Tree	81.098	99.936	0.746
Decision Stump	66.870	99.963	0.711
Random Tree	32.520	99.982	0.497
Deep Learning	81.504	99.956	0.787
Neural Network	82.317	99.966	0.812
Multi Layer Perceptron	80.894	99.966	0.806
Linear Regression	54.065	99.985	0.683
Logistic Regression	79.065	99.962	0.786
Support Vector Machine	79.878	99.972	0.813

Fig. 26.1 Example of method used for detecting credit card malpractice

2. Literature Survey

The review encompasses a wide range of studies, articles, and research papers published up until the knowledge cutoff date of September 2021.

The review begins by emphasizing the significance of credit card fraud detection and its impact on financial institutions and consumers (Fabiana Fournier et al. 2015). It highlights the importance of employing effective and accurate fraud detection methods to mitigate financial losses and maintain customer trust.

Supervised machine learning algorithms have emerged as powerful tools for fraud detection. Logistic regression, decision trees, support vector machines (SVM), random forests, and artificial neural networks (ANN) are commonly utilized algorithms in this domain. These algorithms leverage labeled transaction data to learn patterns and classify transactions as fraudulent or genuine (Samaneh Sorournejad et al). The review examines the strengths and limitations of each algorithm, including their ability to handle imbalanced datasets, computational efficiency, and interpretability.

Feature engineering and selection play a crucial role in enhancing the performance of supervised machine learning models (David J.Wetson et al). The review discusses various techniques such as feature scaling, dimensionality reduction using Principal Component Analysis (PCA), and feature selection algorithms like Recursive Feature Elimination (RFE). These techniques aim to improve the models' ability to capture relevant features and reduce the dimensionality of the dataset.

Evaluation metrics are essential for assessing the performance of these fraud detection models. The evaluation focuses on measurements that are routinely utilised, including as accuracy, precision, recall, F1-score, and Area Under the Receiver Operating Characteristic Curve (ROC). These metrics provide insights into the models' effectiveness in correctly identifying fraudulent transactions while minimizing false positives and false negatives (Ribeiro, A et al. 2020).

The review also explores the challenges faced in credit card fraud detection, including evolving fraud patterns, class imbalance in the dataset, and the need for real-time detection systems (Arifin et al. 2019). It examines recent advancements and emerging trends, such as the integration of ensemble methods, deep learning techniques, and anomaly detection algorithms for improved fraud detection performance (Mehta et al. 2019).

Real-world datasets and benchmark datasets are essential for training and evaluating credit card fraud detection models. The review discusses the availability of such datasets, their characteristics, and the importance of dataset quality, size, and diversity in achieving reliable and robust models (Dey et al. 2019).

3. Problem Statement

Credit card fraud poses a significant threat to the financial industry, necessitating the development of robust detection systems. In recent years, supervised machine learning algorithms have gained attention as effective tools for detecting fraudulent credit card transactions. In this literature review, we explore the problem definitions associated with credit card fraud detection and the role of supervised machine learning algorithms in addressing these challenges.

3.1 Imbalanced Data

One of the key challenges in credit card fraud detection is the inherent class imbalance in the dataset. Legitimate transactions significantly outnumber fraudulent transactions, resulting in a skewed distribution. This imbalance poses difficulties for traditional machine learning algorithms, as they tend to prioritize the majority class, leading to poor detection of fraud instances (Sezer, F et al. 2019). Addressing this problem is crucial to ensure accurate and reliable fraud detection.

3.2 Evolving Fraud Techniques

Credit card fraudsters are continually adapting their techniques to evade detection systems. They employ sophisticated methods such as identity theft, account takeover, and transaction laundering, making it challenging to detect fraudulent activities solely based on predefined rules or patterns. Supervised machine learning algorithms offer the ability to learn and adapt to new fraud patterns by analyzing historical transactional data(Yu et al. 2019). However, staying ahead of the evolving fraud techniques remains a critical problem in credit card fraud detection.

3.3 Real-time Detection

Detecting credit card fraud in real-time is essential to prevent financial losses. Traditional methods that rely on batch processing or manual reviews are time-consuming and may delay the detection and response to fraudulent transactions. Supervised machine learning algorithms offer the potential for real-time detection by analyzing transactions as they occur, enabling immediate alerts and preventive measures. However, achieving real-time detection accuracy while maintaining low false positive rates is a significant challenge in this field.

3.4 Feature Engineering and Selection

The success of supervised machine learning algorithms depends heavily on the quality and relevance of the features used for training. Extracting meaningful features from credit card transactional data can be complex, as fraud patterns may be subtle and require careful analysis. Moreover, selecting the most relevant features from a large pool of variables is crucial to avoid over-fitting or including noisy data that may hinder the performance of the algorithm. Efficient feature engineering and selection techniques are vital to improving the accuracy and efficiency of credit card fraud detection systems.

3.5 Model Interpretability

The interpretability of machine learning models plays a critical role in credit card fraud detection. Financial institutions and regulatory bodies often require explanations for the decisions made by the models. However, some supervised machine learning algorithms, such as deep neural networks, are known for their "black box" nature, making it challenging to understand the underlying reasons for their predictions. Ensuring transparency and interpretability of the models without sacrificing detection performance is an ongoing research problem in this field.

4. Implementation

Recently, there has been an increase in credit card users, making the widely used Card Verification Value(CVV) the standard mode of remittance. These credit card services offer far more effectiveness and cost savings. However, given the quick spread of credit cards, it is now simpler for attackers to take advantage of victims by sending misleading messages or asking for OTPs. Logistics Regression is the classification algorithm employed in this case. Even though there are numerous of these algorithms, LR always provides greater accuracy.

4.1 Logistics Regression

It is a classification method based on machine learning algorithms. It is a technique for predicting a categorized outcome variable from a set of individual factors. Logistic regression uses a threshold to quantify the probability of 0 or 1. In most cases, values above the threshold are 1, but rounded data that meet the threshold are usually 0.

4.2 Dataset

Gathering datasets is the major problem for training algorithms. This data pertains to credit card transactions that cardholders submitted in September 2020. Out of his 284,807 transactions over the past four years, this dataset contains 492 fraudulent items. With fraud accounting for just 0.172% of all transactions, the data is extremely biased.

The numeric input variables are the result of a PCA transformation. The original data and any supporting information were not made public due to confidentiality concerns. 'Time' and 'Value' are the only variables that have not been transformed using the PCA. The variable 'Time' stores the number of seconds that have passed between each transaction and the first transaction in the data collection. The 'Amount' variable refers to the transaction's value. The

	Time	V1	V2	V3	V4	V5	V6	V7	V8	V9	...	V21	V22	V23	V24	V2
0	0.0	-1.359807	-0.072781	2.536347	1.378155	-0.338321	0.462388	0.239599	0.098698	0.363787	...	-0.018307	0.277838	-0.110474	0.066928	0.1285
1	0.0	1.191857	0.266151	0.166480	0.448154	0.060018	-0.082361	-0.078803	0.085102	-0.255425	...	-0.225775	-0.638672	0.101288	-0.339846	0.16717
2	1.0	-1.358354	-1.340163	1.773209	0.379780	-0.503198	1.800499	0.791461	0.247676	-1.514654	...	0.247998	0.771679	0.909412	-0.689281	-0.3276
3	1.0	-0.966272	-0.185226	1.792993	-0.863291	-0.010309	1.247203	0.237609	0.377436	-1.387024	...	-0.108300	0.005274	-0.190321	-1.175575	0.64737
4	2.0	-1.158233	0.877737	1.548718	0.403034	-0.407193	0.095921	0.592941	-0.270533	0.817739	...	-0.009431	0.798278	-0.137458	0.141267	-0.20601
5	2.0	-0.425966	0.960523	1.141109	-0.168252	0.420987	-0.029728	0.476201	0.260314	-0.568671	...	-0.208254	-0.559825	-0.026398	-0.371427	-0.2327
6	4.0	1.229658	0.141004	0.045371	1.202613	0.191881	0.272708	-0.005159	0.081213	0.464960	...	-0.167716	-0.270710	-0.154104	-0.780055	0.7501
7	7.0	-0.644269	1.417964	1.074380	-0.492199	0.948934	0.428118	1.120631	-3.807864	0.615375	...	1.943465	-1.015455	0.057504	-0.649709	-0.4152
8	7.0	-0.894286	0.286157	-0.113192	-0.271526	2.669599	3.721818	0.370145	0.851084	-0.392048	...	-0.073425	-0.268092	-0.204233	1.011592	0.3732
9	9.0	-0.338262	1.119593	1.044367	-0.222187	0.499361	-0.246761	0.651583	0.069539	-0.736727	...	-0.246914	-0.633753	-0.120794	-0.385050	-0.0697

10 rows × 31 columns

Fig. 26.2 Example of dataset

'Class' variable is the response variable (Target) and has a value of "1" in case of fraud and "0" otherwise.

After establishing the dataset and separating the input variables from the target variable, we imported the train_test_split function to divide the data into training and test sets. The train_test_split function divides data into training and test sets using a randomizer. In this instance, 30% of the data for testing and 70% of the data for training were defined. To guarantee that the same data is utilised for each run, the random seed (np.random.seed) is employed.

5. Experiments

The following actions are carried out throughout the construction of the fraud detection model in order to complete the model evaluation.

5.1 Data Pre-Processing

Data preprocessing is the stage of machine learning that prepares raw data for the training and development of machine learning methods. In fact, this is the first and most important phase in building a machine-learning model. When conducting machine learning projects, it's not common to come across meaningful raw data to complete this critical step. H. Perform pretreatment. To maximize the accuracy of the machine learning classifier, we ensured that all NaN values present in the dataset were replaced with a specific range of values.

5.2 Data Analysis

Analyze the data present in the dataset regardless of whether all integers are present in the dataset. If not, use the missing value technique and immediately fill in the spaces using Python pandas. Machine learning models can only understand numeric data, so vectorization techniques are used to convert all kinds of categorical data into numbers.

5.3 Training and Testing

Test data and training data are the two main parts of the data set. Data preparation creates an AI model and tests it against test data to ensure its accuracy. First, the dataset splits into two parts, 80% is used for training data, and the remaining 20% for testing data.

In this case, we should choose a large training set. Simulations with fewer model parameters are easier to validate and tune and can reduce test dataset length. If your system has many model parameters, you will need a large test set (although cross-validation should also be considered). If your model has no model parameters or is difficult to change, you also don't need a test set.

The training dataset is a subset of the dataset used to prepare the AI model, at which point the outcome was known. A test dataset is a subset of the dataset used to evaluate AI computations, and the model uses the test set to predict outcomes. To provide training only, or to adapt the system to a training dataset, use the Logistic Regression class from the sklearn package. After importing the classes, create a classification object and use it to validate the data for logistic regression. The logistic data model plots data on a graph based on probability values, resulting in a sigmoidal curve. Then evaluate the class labels of the given tuple.

Finally, generate a confusion matrix imported from the sklearn library and evaluate the model. From this method, we calculate all parameters such as accuracy, sensitivity, precision and recall.

6. Results

Classification matrices are used to score classifiers based on parameter accuracy, recall, accuracy, etc. The higher the accuracy, the more effective the trained model. Since the accuracy of the model is high, we can say that the accuracy of the model is also high. By training the data using a logistic regression model, we achieved an accuracy of 97.2%

7. Conclusion

This study looked at enhanced logistic regression and found it helped detect fraudulent transactions while reducing the number of false alerts. Regarding the domain of the system, supervised learning algorithms are the first in the literature. When these algorithms are linked to the bank's fraud detection system, they can predict fraudulent transactions as soon as they occur. A number of fraud prevention strategies can be employed to protect banks from large losses and minimize risk. The purpose of this study was approached differently than previous classification tasks, as there was a variable penalty for misclassification. Recommended system performance is evaluated using Precision, Recall, f1-score, Support, and Accuracy. Our classifier achieves 97.3% accuracy, which gives the best results.

8. Future Scope

While we haven't reached our goal of 100% fraud detection accuracy, we have developed a program that works given enough time and information. There is always space for improvement in a project like this. Because of the project's confidentially, we can use many methodologies as components and mix their results to improve the final product's quality. Additional algorithms can be used to improve this model.

The output of these algorithms, however, should have the same structure as the output of most other algorithms. As the script shows, modules can be easily added once the criteria are met. Beneficial. As a result, as the project continues to grow, different methods can be adopted to address this issue.

REFERENCES

1. R. Brause, T. Langsdorf, M. Hepp.1999. Neural Data Mining for Credit Card Fraud Detection.ICTAI '99: Proceedings of the 11th IEEE International Conference on Tools with Artificial Intelligence. (November 1999)
2. Fabiana Fournier, Ivo carriea, Inna skarbovsky.2015. "The Uncertain Case of Credit Card Fraud Detection", the 9th ACMInternational Conference on Distributed EventBased Systems (DEBS 15). (2015)
3. Samaneh Sorournejad, Zahra Zojaji, Reza Ebrahimi Atani, Amir Hassan Monadjemi, "A Survey of credit card fraud detection techniques: Data and techniques-oriented perspective".
4. David J.Wetson, David J.Hand, M.Adams, Whitrow and Piotr Jusczak "Plastic Card Fraud Detection using Peer Group Analysis" Springer, Issue 200
5. Ribeiro, A., Santos, V., & Soares, C. 2020.Credit Card Fraud Detection: A Realistic Modeling and a Novel Learning Strategy". IEEE Transactions on Neural Networks and Learning Systems, 31(9), 3311-3324. (2020)
6. Arifin, A. Z., Kim, K. S., & Kim, H. J.2019.Credit card fraud detection using semi-supervised deep learning with generative adversarial networks. Future Generation Computer Systems", 99, 366-376. (2019).
7. Singh, D., & Mehta, A.2019.Credit card fraud detection using deep learning with semi-supervised auto encoders. In 2019 9th International Conference on Cloud Computing, Data Science & Engineering (Confluence) (pp. 402-406). IEEE. (2019)
8. Dey, D., & Pal, S.2019.Semi-supervised learning for credit card fraud detection using self-organizing maps and random forest. Computers & Security, 82, 164-178. (2019).
9. Sezer, F., & Uyar, M. U. 2019.Credit card fraud detection using semi-supervised machine learning algorithms. In 2019 27th Signal Processing and Communications Applications Conference (SIU) (pp. 1-4). IEEE. (2019)
10. Yu, Z., Zhu, J., Chen, X., Li, Y., & Hu, Z. 2019.A novel semi-supervised deep autoencoder for credit card fraud detection". IEEE Access, 7, 5434-5443. (2019)

Note: All the figures in this chapter were made by the author.

Advancement of Intelligent Computational Methods and Technologies (AICMT2023) – Dr. O. P. Verma et al. (eds)
© 2024 Taylor & Francis Group, London, ISBN 978-1-032-78445-8

27

A Social Media Authentication Tool with Real-Time User Verification and Fraud Detection Capabilities

Tripti[1], Yashashvi Gupta[2], Monika Kumari Baghel[3], Geetika Thakran[4]
Delhi Technical Campus, Greater Noida, UP
Ankit Gambhir[5]
Assistant Professor, Delhi Technical Campus, Greater Noida, UP

ABSTRACT: Nowadays social media has become the most popular among the youngsters. Due to pandemic not only youngster but people from all age group has become addicted social media, it's quite good how people are getting in touch with their old friends as well as make new friends in social media from all over the world, but apart from this many illicit make fake account and do cybercrime. So in this paper authors are going to propose a discovery model, which predicts the authenticity of accounts on Instagram based on visual features such as profile picture, followers count and more using various machine learning methods.

KEYWORDS: Instagram, Authenticity prediction, Fake, Pandemic, Kaggle

1. Introduction

A recent study done to measure the impact points out that the social media consumption of an average user increased by around 72% in the recent times of COVID and the majority (44%) of the respondents used Instagram the most. This acted as an amazing opportunity for businesses to reach out to a wider range of audiences online. Therefore, the demand for Instagram Influencers increased a lot. But it is sad to note that a lot of people tried to game this system for their own good by gaining some fake Instagram followers and engagements to attract more companies. In this paper, we propose building a classification-based model to authenticate the followers and engagement of an Instagram account.

Authors have used Anaconda Kaggle. An open source available online for this research work using various machine learning algorithms have been used. In this paper, authenticity on the profile by listed 11 features have been checked.

- Profile picture
- Username length
- Full-name word
- Full-name length
- Name equals user name
- External url
- Private
- Post
- Followers
- Following

2. Methodology

While working on this research project various algorithms like KNN, logistic regression, decision tree, random forest in which Random forest gave us the best solution were considered. Authors have implemented one by one each algorithm mentioned then came out with this result.

[1]triptipushpa7674@gmail.com, [2]yashshvigupta01@gmail.com, [3]monikakumarib007@gmail.com, [4]geetikathakran748@gmail.com, [5]a.gambhir@delhitechnicalcampus.ac.in

DOI: 10.1201/9781003487906-27

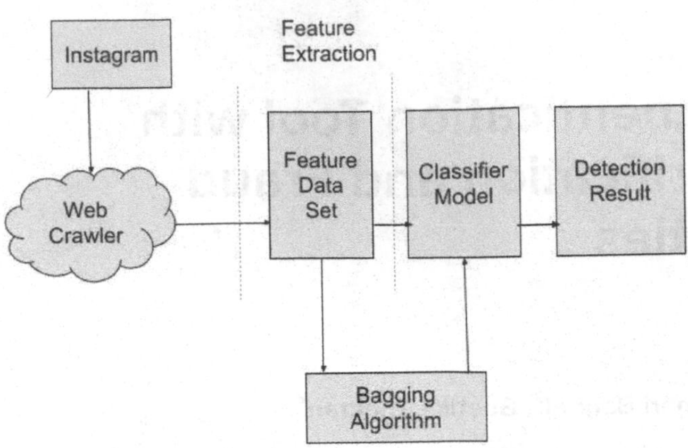

Fig. 27.1 Flow of feature extraction and result

2. Literature Review

"Large-Scale Fake Account Detection in Instagram" (Yang Yang, Guodong Long, Jing Jiang, Sheng-Uei Guan, 2018): This paper proposes a large-scale approach for detecting fake accounts on Instagram. The authors employ machine learning techniques and analyze various user-related features to identify fake accounts, achieving promising results.

"Deep Learning for Detecting Fake Instagram Accounts" (Charalampos Chelmis, Xiaojin Zhu, Polina Rozenshtein, 2019):

The authors present a deep learning-based approach to detect fake Instagram accounts. They leverage convolutional neural networks (CNNs) to analyze profile images and textual content, achieving improved accuracy in identifying fake accounts.

"Fake Instagram Profile Detection Using Machine Learning Techniques" (Ghida Ibrahim, Maria De Marsico, Michele Nappi, Fabio Narducci, 2018):

This paper focuses on detecting fake profiles on Instagram using machine learning techniques. The authors explore features such as the number of followers, followings, and engagement patterns, utilizing classification algorithms to distinguish between genuine and fake accounts.

"Detecting Fake Profiles on Instagram: A Deep Learning Approach" (Kun Liu, Hai Zhao, Ying Shen, Junwei Han, 2020):

This research paper proposes a deep learning approach for detecting fake Instagram profiles. The authors employ a combination of CNN and long short- term memory (LSTM) networks to analyze profile images, captions, and comments, achieving effective identification of fake accounts.

"Detecting Fake Instagram Accounts Using Convolutional Neural Networks" (Fatma Elsheikh, Hazem M. El-Bakry, Shafik M. El-Mekkawy, Sara S. El- Wahsh, 2020):

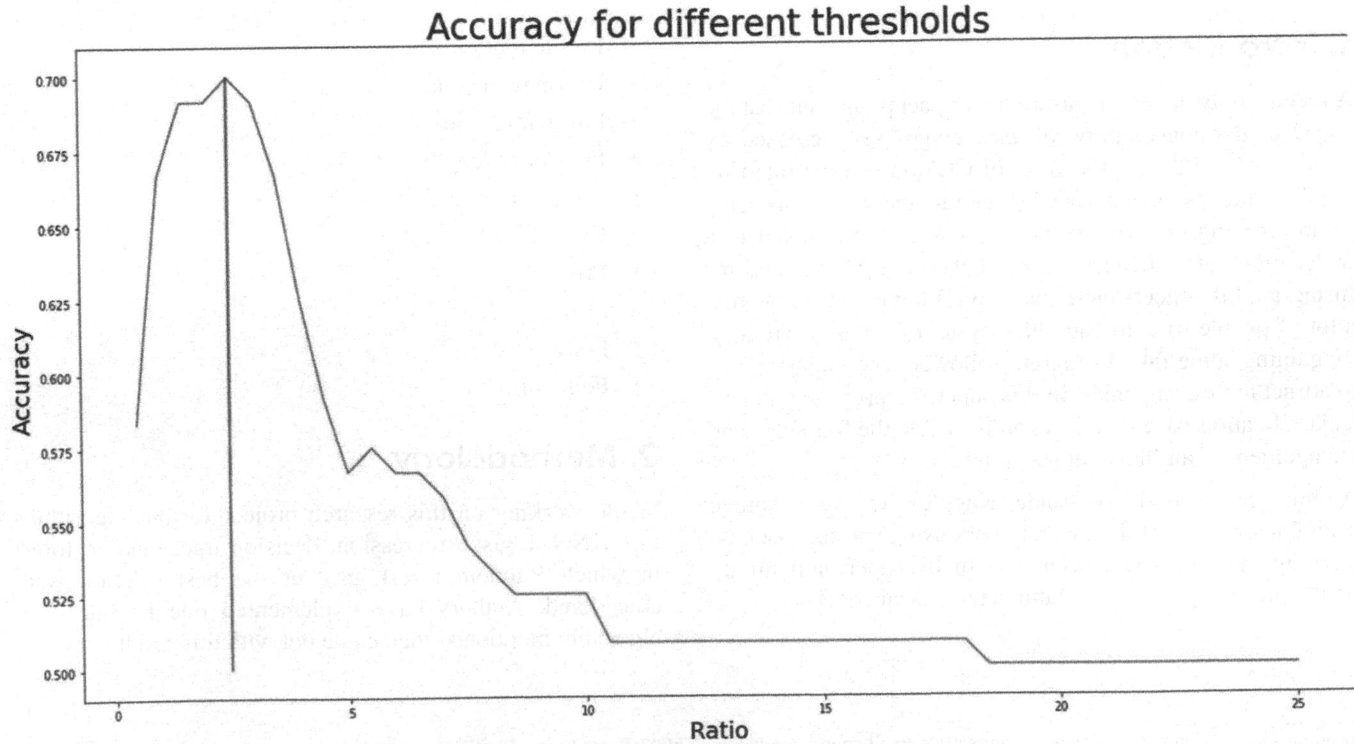

Fig. 27.2 Accuracy for different thresholds

The authors present a method to detect fake Instagram accounts utilizing CNNs. They extract image features and train the network to distinguish between genuine and fake accounts, achieving accurate classification results.

"Fake Instagram Account Detection Using User Behavioral Analysis" (Ruohan Zhang, Yong Zhang, Yulei Zhang, 2019):

This research focuses on detecting fake Instagram accounts through user behavioral analysis. The authors analyze various behavioral factors such as posting frequency, interaction patterns, and user engagement to identify suspicious accounts.

"Detecting Fake Profiles on Instagram: An Ensemble Learning Approach" (Navid Rekabsaz, Ali A. Ghorbani, 2019):

This paper proposes an ensemble learning approach to detect fake Instagram profiles. The authors combine multiple classification algorithms and employ a feature- based analysis, achieving effective detection of fake accounts.

"Detecting Fake Instagram Accounts Using Machine Learning Techniques" (Huda Nassar, Mohamed F. Tolba, Tamer Elnourani, 2020):

The authors propose a machine learning-based approach to identify fake Instagram accounts. They analyze user-related features and employ classification algorithms to distinguish between genuine and fake profiles.

"Fake Instagram Account Detection Using Machine Learning and Image Processing Techniques" (M. S. A. Ashraff, K. A. S. I. Lakshika, H. A. C. P. Herath, S. D. Wickramanayake, 2021):

This research paper presents a method to detect fake Instagram accounts using machine learning and image processing techniques. The authors analyze image- based features and employ classification algorithms to identify fake accounts.

"Fake Instagram Account Detection Using Ensemble Learning" (Jemima C. P, M. Durga Devi, 2021):

The authors propose an ensemble learning approach for detecting fake Instagram accounts.

3. Implementation

Authors have used python and various machine learning algorithms like logistic regression, KNN, decision tree, random forest.

Among all these classifiers the random forest is the only classifier that gave us the maximum testing accuracy.

Apart from this Authors have also used few extensions to improve efficiency of app., extensions like fake like detection, engagement rate. At last Authors have asserted our claims using social blade, which is an online tool that helps in checking various trends in the count of comments added or subtracted, count of likes, count of following and count of followers over a certain period of time.

4. Conclusion

After closely analyzing the account authenticity and media like authenticity of account X, authors found that the trends were almost similar to what we got through the SocialBlade Analysis. There were no suspicious hikes or draughts in the account following and media likes observed on accountX and therefore, both account authenticity, as well as the media like authenticity, came out pretty well.

On the other hand, for account Y, authors observed a few hikes and draughts on SocialBlade and therefore, this made us suspicious about the authenticity of Account Y. Interestingly, the Account Authenticity was very poor for Y but despite that, the Media Like Authenticity came out pretty well.

On the other hand, for Account Y, we observed a few hikes and draughts on SocialBlade and therefore, this made us suspicious about the authenticity of Account Y. Interestingly, the Account Authenticity was very poor for Y but despite that, the Media Like Authenticity came out pretty well. This can be explained by the Engagement Rate Analysis of Account Y. The engagement rate came out to be 0.42% which points out that only 0.42% of Y's followers actually engage with the things posted by it. Therefore, for Account X, it is concluded that both Account Authenticity and Media Like Authenticity came out pretty well and this was supported by the Social Blade analysis as well. This Points out that almost all of the followers of X are authentic and they also engage quite well with the things posted by X. For Account Y, it is concluded that the Account Authenticity was very poor but Media Like Authenticity was pretty good. This nature was further explained using the Engagement Rate analysis on Account Y which is indeed very poor. This points out that most of Y's followers are non-authentic and almost none of those non-authentic followers engage with the things posted by account Y. This was further supported by the SocialBlade analysis which pointed out a couple of suspicious hikes and draughts both in the following gains and the posts liked/commented.

5. Future Work

Detection of fake accounts is somehow important for us as deleting fake accounts can prevent many cyber-attacks, it can also help us to identify many fake business accounts which ask for money from the clients before starting business. Not only this, these people often share fake posts to flex their expenditures and fool anyone for.

REFERENCES

1. Yang, Yang, Guodong Long, Jing Jiang, and Sheng-Uei Guan. 2018. Large-Scale Fake Account Detection in Instagram.
2. Deep Learning for Detecting Fake Instagram Accounts." 2019. In Charalampos Chelmis, Xiaojin Zhu.
3. Ibrahim, Ghida, Maria De Marsico, Michele Nappi, and Fabio Narducci. 2018. Fake Instagram Profile Detection Using Machine Learning Techniques.
4. Liu, Kun, Hai Zhao, Ying Shen, and Junwei Han. 2020. Detecting Fake Profiles on Instagram: A Deep Learning Approach.
5. Elsheikh, Fatma, Hazem M. El-Bakry, Shafik M. El-Mekkawy, and Sara S. El-Wahsh, eds. 2020. Detecting Fake Instagram Accounts Using Convolutional Neural Networks.
6. Zhang, Ruohan, Yong Zhang, and Yulei Zhang. 2019. Fake Instagram Account Detection Using User Behavioral Analysis.
7. Rekabsaz, Navid, and Ali A. Ghorbani. 2019. Detecting Fake Profiles on Instagram: An Ensemble Learning Approach.
8. Detecting Fake Instagram Accounts Using Machine Learning Techniques." 2020. Huda Nassar, Mohamed F. Tolba, Tamer Elnourani.
9. Ashraff, M. S. A., K. A. S. I. Lakshika, H. A. C. P. Herath, and S. D. Wickramanayake, eds. 2021. Fake Instagram Account Detection Using Machine Learning and Image Processing Techniques.
10. Devi, M. 2021. Fake Instagram Account Detection Using Ensemble Learning.
11. Theobald, Oliver, and Author: Oliver Theobald, eds. n.d. "Machine Learning For Absolute Beginners: A Plain English Introduction (SecondEdition)." In Machine Learning For Absolute Beginners: A Plain English Introduction.
12. Kelleher, John D., Brian Mac Namee, -. John Author, D. Kelleher, Brian Mac Namee, and Aoife D' Arcy, eds. n.d. "Fundamentals of Machine Learning for Predictive Data Analytics: Algorithms, Worked Examples, and Case Studies."

Note: All the figures in this chapter were made by the author.

Advancement of Intelligent Computational Methods and Technologies (AICMT2023) – Dr. O. P. Verma et al. (eds)
© 2024 Taylor & Francis Group, London, ISBN 978-1-032-78445-8

28

Sign Language Detection App Using Random Forest

Chaitanya Chawla[1] , Archisman Tripathy[2], Neel Gupta[3], Kunal[4], Umnah[5]
Department of Computer Science Engineering, Delhi Technical Campus, UP, India

ABSTRACT: In the disciplines of computer vision & mortal-computer commerce (HCI), gesture recognition presents considerable obstacles. With the minimum information handed by a single RGB camera a decade ago, this bid appeared to be virtually insolvable. Hand gesture identification is now more practical thanks to recent developments in seeing technologies like time of flight and structured light camera, which have created new data source. In this study, exercising depth information obtained from one of the forenamed detectors, we offer a veritably accurate approach for relating static movements.

KEYWORDS: Computer vision, Gesture recognition

1. Introduction

Sign language and hand recognition are significant research areas within computer vision and machine learning. Recent advancements in sensing technologies have greatly improved the robustness and quality of solutions in these fields. Various approaches have been developed for recognizing static and dynamic gestures and poses. In general, sign language recognition methods can be categorized into two main groups:

Pose estimation: This approach involves estimating gesture parameters by analyzing hand poses.

Gesture recognition: This approach directly applies recognition techniques to raw image data or extracted image features.

Due to the complexity of hand pose estimation, more emphasis has been placed on the latter category. Section 2 of the research paper provides an overview of the current state-of-the-art methods in this domain. Recognition of static and dynamic motions can be used to better categorize sign language and gestures. Both of these motions are included in American Sign Language (ASL).

Recognizing static gestures presents several challenges, including:

The large number of signs (e.g., ASL consists of 24 static signs, or 26 in Russian sign language). Similarities observed among certain signs. Variations in appearance due to differences in viewpoint, referred to as intra-subject variation.

Differences in performance across individuals, known as inter-subject variation.

To address these challenges in sign recognition, research that specifically focuses on static sign recognition and proposes solutions for the aforementioned challenges. The study clearly distinguishes between static signs, dynamic signs, and accidental hand postures. Its primary emphasis lies in recognizing the full range of signs performed by an individual.

Earlier studies encountered difficulties in gesture recognition using a single camera. Initial attempts involved applying various image convolution techniques to extract feature vectors from RGB images of hands. For example, in (Bergh et al 2011), sea families based on edge images were employed as features to train a neural network for classifying 24 signs. In (Keskin et al 2012), Haarlet-like features were employed to classify 10 hand shapes using grayscale images and silhouettes. Some studies directly applied Principle Component Analysis (PCA) to images for hand pose

[1]00818002719@delhitechnicalcampus.ac.in, [2]05518002719@delhitechnicalcampus.ac.in, [3]35318002719@delhitechnicalcampus.ac.in,
[4]04818002719@delhitechnicalcampus.ac.in, [5]umnah@delhitechnicalcampus.ac.in

DOI: 10.1201/9781003487906-28

classification (Keskin et al. 2011). In a modified interpretation of Histogram of acquainted slants(overeater) descriptors was used to fete stationary signs in British subscribe Language. In, SIFT-feature based descriptions were employed for recognizing signs in American Sign

Language (ASL). These techniques, meanwhile, were very reliant on the background, subject, and lighting. Additionally, because these features were not rotation, position, and scale invariant, pose normalization was required prior to feature calculation.

Recent advancements in recognition using a single camera have been facilitated by the introduction of range sensors. The Microsoft Kinect sensors, in particular, has made significant contributions to human pose recognition. Human body parts have been classified using specific features calculated directly from depth pictures, and these features have been extended to hand position estimation and form classification. There are now techniques that entirely rely on segmentation obtained from deep learning data, as detailed in (Oikonomidis etb al 2011), because depth data makes hand detection and segmentation easier. Also, deep learning data is resistant to changes in illumination and subject appearance, allowing for the computation of image features directly from depth images still, these ways don't completely regard different viewpoints.

Another conventional method to hand sign recognition involves maintaining a 3D model and fitting it to a picture. This approach compares the rendered model in various configurations with the original image, proving successful in both sign recognition and hand estimation (Shotton et al 2011). However, the increased variation in rotation expands the parameter space, making the complement techniques unstable and time-taking.

Several existing studies focus on recognizing a small subset of signs. As mentioned earlier, significant challenges arise due to differences in viewpoint, environmental factors, and subject appearance.

In our work, we address these challenges by abstracting rotational, positional, and by scaling the invariant features. Moreover, similar to, we utilized the multilayered random forest (MLRF) algorithms for classification. The approach significantly reduces training time and memory consumption, enabling the chances of automatically re-training the forest within a short period of time using a PC.

We test our approach using simulated data to show how resistant the features are to pose fluctuations. Additionally, we contrast the two-level forest with our MLRF framework. A vector's cluster is identified by the forest at the first level, and the final class label is determined at the second level using the clustered label from the first level.

2. Contributions

Our approach focuses on improving sign language detection by incorporating two key ideas.

Firstly, we tackle the challenge of variations in appearance caused by different perspectives of hand signs. To address intra-class variation, we propose using rotational-, translational-, and by scaling the invariant image features extracted from 3D point clouds obtained from a depth sensor. These features can be classified into local & global types. After reviewing state of the art features for object recognition, we selected the ensemble of shape function (ESF) descriptor. This descriptor exhibits real-time computation and invariance to translation, rotation, and scale.

Secondly, we introduce the multi-layered random forest (MLRF) for classification. The main principle of this approach is to identify groups of same or similar feature descriptors and train separate classifiers for each group. This enables better differentiation of classes within each group. Ideally, each group should contain a smaller number of classes compared to the original set.

Using MLRF provides several advantages:

Potential for greater accuracy: At the first level, trees are averaged out, which lessens the chance that some trees' errors would spread to the second level. Because the second level random forests are trained on cluster with substantially less variation, they might potentially classify objects more accurately and with more robustness.

Reduced training time & memory requirements: Random forests consist of binary trees, and memory size increases exponentially with the forest's depth to store training parameters for each node. MLRF, with fewer nodes, significantly reduces memory consumption. For example, storing a forest with a depth (D) of 20 and 10 trees (T), with 5 parameters per node, requires a minimum of 560 Mb. In contrast, an MLRF with ten forests at the second level and a depth of 10 for both levels requires only around 6 Mb of memory. Similarly, an MLRF with depth of D1 = 13 and D2 = 12 requires only 26.5 Mb.

Since the suggested method does not depend on special features of a particular depth sensor, it is device independent. Hence, it can be applied with various devices such as the Kinect sensor or time-of-flight cameras, including the Intel Creative Gesture Camera used in our experimentations.

The factor of such techniques is to enhance the nearness of a photo by utilizing outfitting a predominant detectable quality with an unrivaled multifaceted nature or concealing unwaveringness. The major aim of this project is:

Enhance image detail: Another objective of image enhancement may be to enhance the level of detail in an image, making it easier to see small features or patterns.

Remove noise and artifacts: Many images suffer from noise or other artifacts that can obscure the underlying details. Image enhancement projects may aim to remove these unwanted elements to reveal clearer images.

Restore damaged or degraded images: Image enhancement may also involve restoring old or damaged images that have lost quality over time. This may involve removing scratches, tears, or other forms of damage.

Apply artistic effects: Image enhancement projects can also involve applying artistic effects to images, such as adjusting the color balance, adding filters, or creating stylized versions of the image.

Improve image analysis: In some cases, image enhancement may be necessary to improve the accuracy of image analysis techniques, such as object recognition or computer vision.

3. Feature Extraction

In the context of depth image preprocessing, the primary goal is to detect and segment the hand by thresholding deep learning data values, resulting in a point cloud that can be further processed. To achieve this, a series of steps are taken, including normalizing the deep learning image and transforming it into a real 3D point cloud using an inverse perspective transformation. This transformation involves equations that utilize intrinsic parameters from the OpenNI library for the Kinect sensor, such as focal length and camera center coordinates.

Using the random forest (RF) technique, subsequent analysis and classification are made possible. In the random forest machine learning technique, predictions are made using a collection of decision trees. The predictor in this case indicates the probability distributions of the class or cluster labels that reached each leaf node of the tree during training. The predictor contained in the leaf node determines the tree's forecast for a data vector when it reaches a specific node. Averaging the predictions of the different trees yields the overall prediction of the random forest for a given vector.

During the training phase of the random forest, several suggestions for splitting parameters are randomly sampled at each node. The best parameters are selected based on a chosen criterion, such as information gain. A specific type of separation plane function is employed, where two equals are aimlessly tried from the point vector. These parameters, along with others, characterize each node of the decision tree. Prior to training, feature vectors are normalized to ensure the distribution contains the mean value is equal to 0 and the variance is equal to 1, enhancing the effectiveness of the random forest.

In addition to classification, clustering is another important aspect of the data analysis pipeline. Random forest-based clustering is utilized in this scenario to improve classification accuracy by reducing the number of classes within clusters. An artificial training dataset is used to form clusters, and it consists of data that is intended to be clustered as one class and data that was generated randomly as another class. By selecting values from the marginal vector coordinate distributions in our TD (training data), we created the random data.A proximity matrix is then computed, measuring the similarity between samples. This matrix serves as an input of our clustering algorithm.

Hierarchical clustering is employed using complete linkage to identify meaningful structures and group similar signs together. The clustering algorithm aims to distinguish between the given data and randomly generated data that share the same range of values. The proximity matrix is transformed into a distance measure, which facilitates clustering. The clustering results show that similar signs are effectively grouped together, while noise and variations within the data result in clusters containing small portion of different classes.

In the training phase, the MLRF is constructed, consisting of 2 layers. Initially, the data is clustered to create clusters containing a reduced no. of classes. This pruning process involves merging small clusters into larger ones and removing classes with insufficient representation within a cluster. The first layer of the MLRF is trained using aggregated feature vectors, assigning a cluster label to each vector. Subsequently, separate random forests are trained for each cluster on the full feature vectors, enabling the discrimination of similar signs within each cluster.

The training method must include the normalisation of feature vectors in order to take into consideration the decreased variance found within each cluster. The performance of classification is improved by re-normalization, which makes sure that the variance is generated from the classes contained within the cluster. The depth data from the random forests in both layers are added to define the cumulative depth of the MLRF, which gives an idea of the robustness and complexity of the MLRF.

During testing, the first level forest was used to identify the cluster label for each sample in our dataset. The sample is then taken to the relevant forest in the second layer to find out what class it belongs to. This two-layer method enhances the MLRF's overall functionality and allows for precise categorization.

In summary, the depth image preprocessing involves transforming the image into a 3D point cloud using an inverse perspective transformation. A random forest algorithm is then employed for classification and clustering purposes. The random forest comprises decision trees, and during training, splitting parameters are selected based on information gain. Clustering is performed using hierarchical clustering with complete linkage, and the resulting clusters are utilized to train a multi-layered random forest. The MLRF consists of two layers, with the first layer assigning cluster labels and the second layer discerning class labels within each cluster. Normalization and re-normalization steps are applied to ensure optimal performance. The MLRF approach enhances accuracy and robustness, providing effective classification and clustering results for depth images.

4. Result Analysis

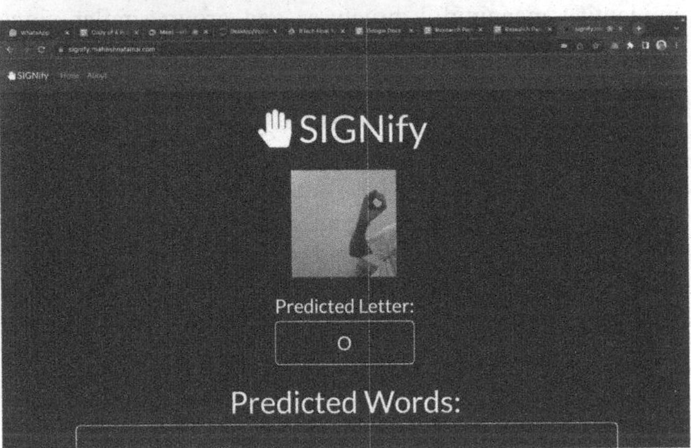

Fig. 28.1 Home page

Fig. 28.2 Alphabet detection

Fig. 28.3 Alphabet detection

Fig. 28.4 Alphabet detection

The web application has resulted in a user-friendly and accessible platform that allows individuals to communicate with sign language users in real-time. By simply capturing sign language gestures through a camera, the application can accurately interpret and translate those gestures into meaningful text.

5. Evaluation

We evaluated the effectiveness of our algorithm in a variety of contexts, including artificial data, databases of American Sign Language (ASL) signals that are readily accessible to the public (Wohlkinger et al 2011), deep learning data gathered from the Intel Creative Depth Camera, & synthetic data. We compared our method with the state of the art (Wohlkinger et al 2011)[using classification error, training time and memory consumption. The evaluation was performed with a MATLAB random forest implementation (Shotton et al 2011) on a single-core computer CPU.

6. Conclusion

In conclusion, the successful development of a web application using machine learning for sign language processing represents a significant accomplishment with immense potential for enhancing communication and promoting inclusivity within the deaf and hard-of-hearing community. The primary goal of this research was to close the communication gap between sign language users and others who do not comprehend sign language and spoken language.

REFERENCES

1. Amit, Yali and Donald Geman, 1997. "Shape Quantization and Recognition with Randomized Trees." *Neural Computation* 9 (1997): 1545-1588.
2. Ballan, Luca, Aparna Taneja, Jürgen Gall, Luc Van Gool, and Marc Pollefeys, 2012. "Motion Capture of Hands in Action Using Discriminative Salient Points." *Computer Vision – ECCV 2012*, 2012, 640–53. https://doi.org/10.1007/978-3-642-33783-3_46.
3. Billiet, Lieven, José Oramas, McElory Hoffmann, Wannes Meert and Laura Antanas.2013. "Rule-based Hand Posture Recognition using Qualitative Finger Configurations Acquired with the Kinect." *International Conference on Pattern Recognition Applications and Methods.*
4. L. Breiman, 2011. Random forests. Mach. Learn. 45(1):5–32, Measurement Systems and Applications(CIMSA), 2011 IEEE International conference on, pages 1–6, 2011.2
5. Van den Bergh, M., E. Koller-Meier, F. Bosche, and L. Van Gool.2009. "Haarlet-Based Hand Gesture Recognition for 3D Interaction." *2009 Workshop on Applications of Computer Vision (WACV)*, 2009. https://doi.org/10.1109/wacv.2009.5403103.
6. Hastie, Trevor, Jerome Friedman, and Robert Tibshirani.2001. "The Elements of Statistical Learning." *Springer Series in Statistics*. https://doi.org/10.1007/978-0-387-21606-5.
7. Oikonomidis, Iason, Nikolaos Kyriazis, and Antonis Argyros. 2011 "Efficient Model-Based 3D Tracking of Hand Articulations Using Kinect." *Procedings of the British Machine Vision Conference 2011*,. https://doi.org/10.5244/c.25.101.
8. Isaacs, J., and S. Foo. "Hand Pose Estimation for American Sign Language Recognition.2004." *Thirty-Sixth Southeastern Symposium on System Theory, 2004. Proceedings of the*, n.d. https://doi.org/10.1109/ssst.2004.1295634.
9. Keskin, Cem, Furkan Kirac, Yunus Emre Kara, and Lale Akarun.2011. "Real Time Hand Pose Estimation Using Depth Sensors." *2011 IEEE International Conference on Computer Vision Workshops (ICCV Workshops)*, 2011. https://doi.org/10.1109/iccvw.2011.6130391.
10. Keskin, Cem, Furkan Kıraç, Yunus Emre Kara, and Lale Akarun.2012."Hand Pose Estimation and Hand Shape Classification Using Multi-Layered Randomized Decision Forests." *Computer Vision – ECCV 2012*, 2012, 852–63. https://doi.org/10.1007/978-3-642-33783-3_61.
11. Oikonomidis, Iason, Nikolaos Kyriazis, and Antonis Argyros.2011. "Efficient Model-Based 3D Tracking of Hand Articulations Using Kinect." *Procedings of the British Machine Vision Conference 2011*, 2011. https://doi.org/10.5244/c.25.101.
12. Shotton, Jamie, Andrew Fitzgibbon, Mat Cook, Toby Sharp, Mark Finocchio, Richard Moore, Alex Kipman, and Andrew Blake.2011."Real-Time Human Pose Recognition in Parts from Single Depth Images." *CVPR 2011*, 2011. https://doi.org/10.1109/cvpr.2011.5995316.
13. Van den Bergh, Michael, and Luc Van Gool.2011. "Combining RGB and TOF Cameras for Real-Time 3D Hand Gesture Interaction." *2011 IEEE Workshop on Applications of Computer Vision (WACV)*, 2011. https://doi.org/10.1109/wacv.2011.5711485.
14. Wohlkinger, Walter, and Markus Vincze.2011. "Ensemble of Shape Functions for 3D Object Classification." *2011 IEEE International Conference on Robotics and Biomimetics*, 2011. https://doi.org/10.1109/robio.2011.6181760.

Note: All the figures in this chapter were made by the author.

Advancement of Intelligent Computational Methods and Technologies (AICMT2023) – Dr. O. P. Verma et al. (eds)

29 An Automated and Robust Image Watermarking System Using Artificial Intelligence/Machine Learning Including Neural Networks

Gunjan Ahuja[1], Onkar Mehra[2], Muskan Aggarwal[3], Jashn Tyagi[4]
Delhi Technical Campus, Greater Noida, U.P

Abstract: In this study, we describe a CNN-based method for watermarking images. Embedding and watermark extraction are his two phases of the process. A CNN model is trained in the embedding phase to embed the watermark in the image. This ensures that the watermark is imperceptible to humans while also being resistant to image processing manipulations and attacks. The extraction phase uses another CNN model trained to accurately identify and remove watermarks from updated images. Experimental results show that the proposed method is successful, with good embedding capacity and robustness. CNN-based solutions provide automatic and efficient watermarking for large-scale applications to help protect digital images and enforce copyright.

Keywords: Robust, CNN, Effectiveness, Watermark embedding, Watermark extraction, Imperceptibility

1. Introduction

The Watermark Generator creates the watermarks required for a specific application. A watermark may or may not be based on a specific key. The Embedder uses the embed key to insert the watermark into the cover object. The detector detects the presence of preset watermarks inside the cover object. Sometimes it is useful to extract the message from the watermarked cover object. Encoders and decoders are her two main components of a watermarking system. Add watermarks to digital documents.

Image watermarking using Convolutional Neural Networks (CNN) is a technology that protects the copyright and integrity of digital images. CNNs are known for their performance in computer vision applications and provide powerful methods for watermark embedding and removal. The technique consists of training a CNN model to embed watermarks in images while remaining invisible to human observers and resilient to common image processing operations and attacks. Another CNN model is trained to find and extract watermarks from the modified images. This CNN-based watermarking technique is automated and efficient, making it suitable for large scale applications in digital image protection and copyright enforcement.

2. Problem Definition

One of the drawbacks of watermarking strategies in secure image exchange is that the technology has not yet been widely deployed and the protocol has not yet been fully standardized. Another significant drawback is that the watermark method does not adequately thwart various forms of attack. In practice, a hybrid mix of encryption and watermarking is said to be used to increase the security of images on the untrusted Internet.

3. Need and Significance

Intellectual property protection: With the increasing use of digital photography on the Internet photographs can be easily reproduced, distributed and used without the owner's permission.

The artist's intellectual property rights are protected by a watermark to prevent unauthorized use of their work.

[1]gunjanahuja942@gmail.com, [2]onkar.mehra7@gmail.com, [3]muskan.aggarwal1401@gmail.com, [4]tyagijashn@gmail.com

DOI: 10.1201/9781003487906-29

Trademark protection: Adding your company emblem or brand name to your photos helps protect your brand identity and prevents unauthorized use.

Automated Efficiency: Watermarking your photos with our automatic watermarking system can save you time and effort, especially when dealing with a large number of images.

4. Existing System

His Lightweight Convolution Neural Organize (LW-CNN) approach to watermarking frameworks was proposed by (Teacher R. Dhaya 2021). The LW-CNN architecture has proven to be more resilient than other standard techniques. Feature selection in the LW-CNN framework has resulted in reduced computation time. The study also demonstrated his resilience to two separate attacks: a collusion attack and a geometric attack. This research project effectively increased the system's resilience against modern threats while reducing computing time.

(Mohiul Islam et al 2020) proposes a robust image watermarking method in the field of lifting wavelet transforms. To increase resilience to multiple attack situations, the system used multiple subbands and her SVM classifier during watermark extraction. In this study, we comprehensively examined the imperceptibility and robustness performance of the system across multiple subbands. (Kim et. Al. 2020) The goal was to maximize resistance to various attacks while maintaining a reasonable level of stealth.

The system's resilience was tested against various forms of attacks, including noise, denoising, image processing, lossy compression, and geometric attacks(Fierro-Radilla et. al. 2019). Higher frequency sub-bands have been found to provide better invisibility, but resilience varies with attack type. There is a performance consideration that not all attacks have the same effect on repeated parts of an image. For example, a compression attack affects all repeat components of an image more or less similarly, but including it in a large repeat run makes the system more vulnerable to lossy compression attacks(Zhong, X et. al. 2020).

5. Proposed Methodology

5.1 Functional Requirements

The figure shows the usual design of image watermarking technique, a methodology proposed for image encoders. Take a cover image called 'c' and put a watermark on it called 'w' to create a marked image called 'm'. The marked images are sent through the communication channel (Tao, H et al. 2014).

The watermarked information 'w' is extracted at this point from the watermarked image 'm' received by the recipient, possibly in a form in which 'm' has been modified by transmission attacks or distortions (Haribabu, K et al. 2015).

5.2 Algorithm used Convolutional Neural Network

Convolutional Neural Systems (ConvNet/CNN) is a deep learning strategy that can create mutually recognizable input images by assigning meanings (learnable weights and predispositions) to specific aspects/objects. ConvNet's plans are inspired by the nervous system region of the human brain(Amrit, P., & Singh, A. K. 2022). In the visual cortex, human neurons respond, so to speak, to impulses in a small area of the visual field called the response area.

5.3 CNN Used in Image Watermarking

Watermarked images are processed for watermark extraction via the same or equivalent CNN architecture. CNN analyzes the image and accurately detects relevant features to recover the encoded watermark. The learned features help the CNN distinguish between the original image content and the inserted watermark.

The advantage of using CNNs for image watermarking is that they can automatically learn and extract complex features, thus processing a wide range of images and watermarks. Additionally, CNNs can provide resistance to common attacks such as noise addition, compression, and geometric transformation by learning how to insert watermarks in a way that is resistant to these distortions.

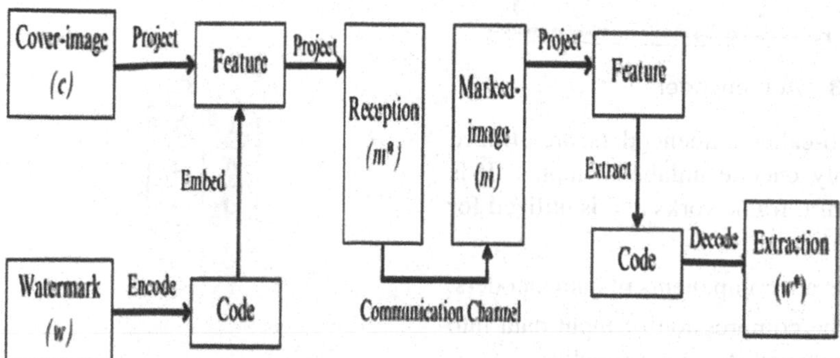

Fig. 29.1 Image watermarking process

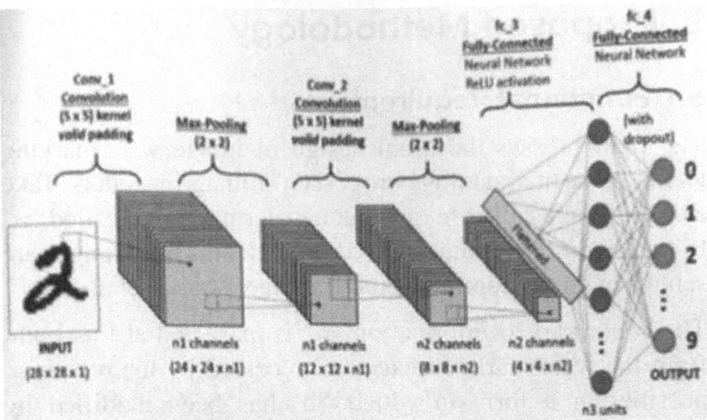

Fig. 29.2 A CNN sequence to classify handwritten digits

Source: https://saturncloud.io/blog/a-comprehensive-guide-to-convolutional-neural-networks-the-eli5-way/

Image watermarking uses robust methodologies including CNN algorithms, feature extractors, and learning-based methods to guide, detect, and remove watermarks in a safe and accurate manner.

6. Proposed System

This work centered on building an autoencoder that can work as both an encoder and a decoder. It was made utilizing fake bits of knowledge to make, recognize and remove watermarks from pictures. The foremost objective is to replicate input from learned coding. Autoencoders, a sort of fake neural organize, are utilized to memorize beneficial coding of unlabeled information through unsupervised learning.

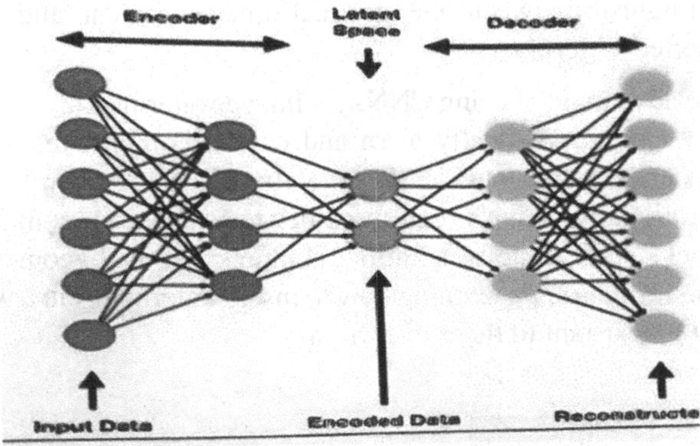

Fig. 29.3 Autoencoder

Fake neural frameworks, so-called autoencoders, are utilized to memorize how to viably encode unlabeled inputs. It is based on convolutional neural frameworks and is utilized for embeddings and extraction.

- Encoders and decoders are components of autoencoders.
- Encoder focused on the compression of input data into an encoded form by reducing its dimensionality.
- Decoder focuses on obtaining data from that is already encoded. It tries to obtain data as close to the original input.

7. System Design

An autoencoder consists of two parts encoder and decoder. The input is compressed into a latent space (usually smaller) by the encoder.

The encoding process can be represented by h = f(x). The input is reconstructed from latent dreams using a decoder. The goal is to make the reconstructed output, denoted by r, as close as possible to the original input x. This process can be represented as r = g(f(x)).

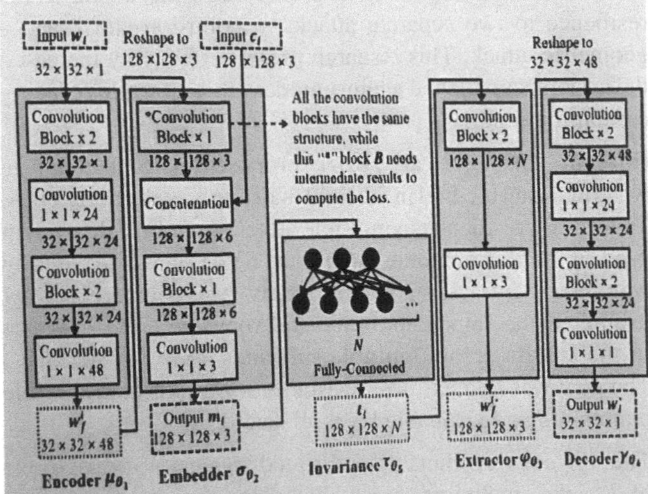

Fig. 29.4 Architecture of Autoencoder using CNN

7.1 Functioning Of CNN In Image Watermarking System

Input images are captured by a CNN model and assigned importance (learnable weights and biases) to distinguish different aspects or objects in the image.

The 3x3 image is converted by CNN into his 9x1 vector image and fed to a multi-layer perceptron for classification.

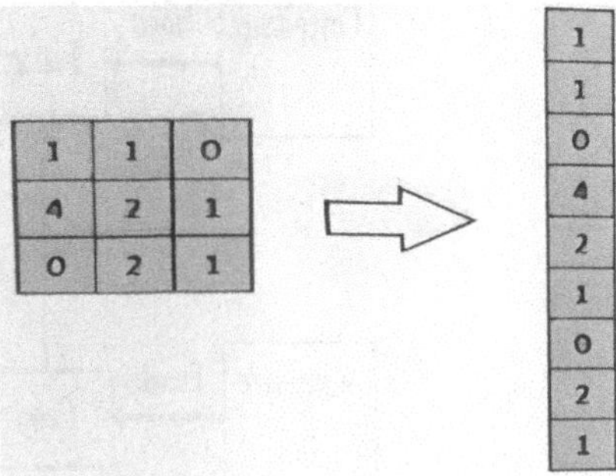

Fig. 29.5 Flattening of a 3x3 image matrix into 9x1 vector

ConvNets utilize channels to capture the spatial and temporal network of pictures to superior fit datasets with less parameters and reusable weights. This permits the arrange to way better see visual complexity and detail.

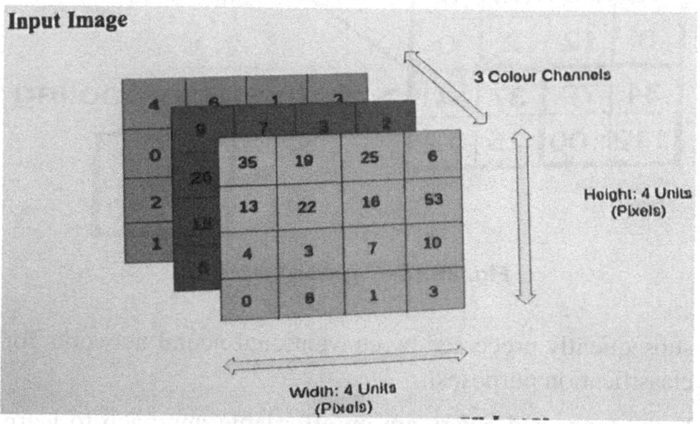

Fig. 29.6 4x4x3 RGB image

In this illustration, an RGB image is divided into red, green, and blue color planes. There are other color spaces such as grayscale, RGB, HSV, and CMYK. ConvNets can compress large images to a manageable size and process them effectively without losing important information, making them useful for scalable architectures with large amounts of data.

Convolution Layer — The Kernel: -

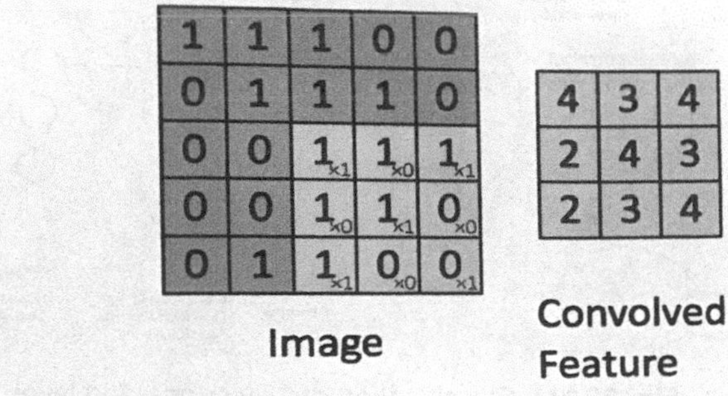

Fig. 29.7 The Kernel in Convolution Layer

A 3x3x1 convolution function is created using a 5x5 image and a 3x3x1 kernel. Image dimensions are 5 (height), 5 (width), 1 (number of channels, e.g. RGB). The green part of the demo resembles the input image with dimensions 5x5x1-. The kernel/filter labeled K represents the 3x3x1 matrix used to perform the convolution process in the first half of the convolutional layer.

Kernel/Filter,

	1	0	1
K =	0	1	0
	1	0	1

If the stride length is set to 1 and there are no objections, the kernel is moved nine times, and each time it performs a matrix multiplication operation 1 0 1 0 1 0 1 0 1 between K and the region P of the image where the kernel is positioned.

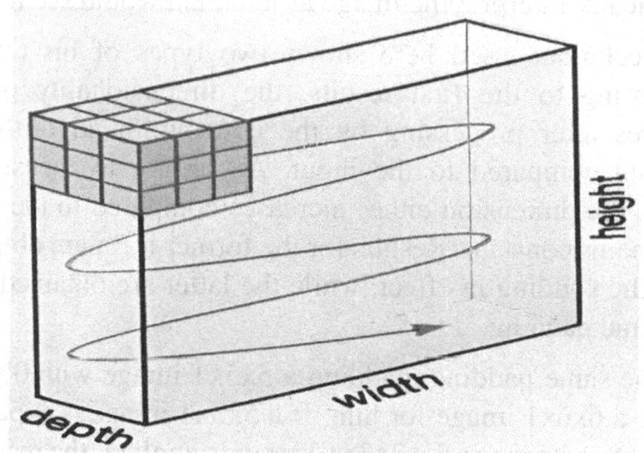

Fig. 29.8 Movement of the Kernel

The filter goes through the full width while sweeping at the specified step value. After the first step, we move to the top of the left side of the image and continue in the same manner until we have traversed the entire image.

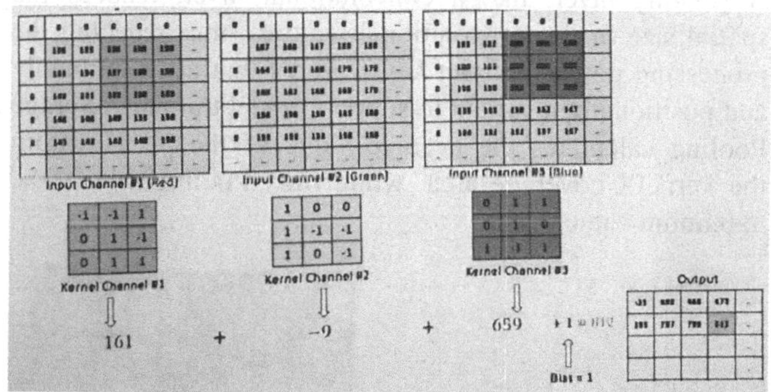

Fig. 29.9 Convolutional operation on a MxNx3 image matrix with a 3x3x3 Kernel

The kernel adjusts the input depth for multi-channel images such as RGB. Kn and In Stack is mutliplied ([K1, I1]:[K2,I2]:[K3,I3]) and sum the result with the bias to produce a compressed tortuous channel feature with depth.

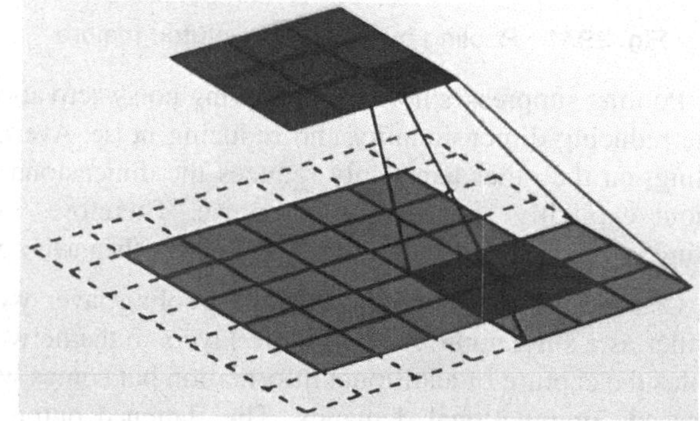

Fig. 29.10 Convolutional operation with stride length = 2

Convolution operations derive high-level properties such as edges from images. A ConvNet can have multiple layers. The first ConvLayer records low-level features, and subsequent layers adapt to high-level features, allowing the network to holistically interpret the image as a human would see it gain.

The technique used here shows two types of his results: According to the first results, the dimensionality of the features after processing by the convolution algorithm is reduced compared to the input. According to the second result, the dimension either increases compared to the input or remains constant. Results for the former form are obtained with the padding in effect, while the latter are obtained with the same padding.

For the same padding, padding a 5x5x1 image with 0's will create a 6x6x1 image for him. If a 5x5x1 image is expanded to a 6x6x1 image and a 3x3x1 kernel is applied, the resulting folded matrix is 5x5x1. This dimension retention is also known as "identical padding". If we repeat the same process without padding, the resulting matrix will have the same dimensions as the kernel itself (3x3x1).

This type of upholstery is called "effective upholstery". A pooling layer, like a convolutional layer, reduces the spatial size of the convolutional features, thus reducing the processing power. Extract key features that are rotationally and positionally invariant to support model training. Average Pooling calculates the average value of the pixels within the kernel's coverage area, while Max Pooling selects the maximum value.

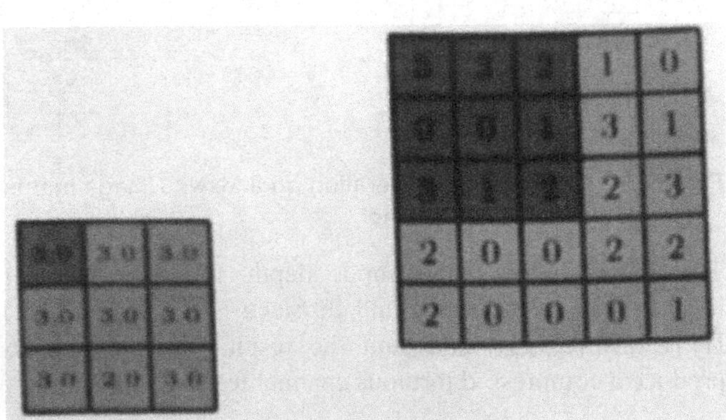

Fig. 29.11 Pooling over 5x5 convoluted feature

Max Pooling suppresses noise by removing noisy activations while reducing dimensionality and reducing noise. Average pooling, on the other hand only reduces the dimensionality without explicitly suppressing the noise. Therefore, max pooling is generally considered more effective than average.

In a CNN, the convolutional layer and pooling layer work together as a single unit. Adding more layers to the network enables the capture of additional information but comes with increased computational demands. The flattened output is

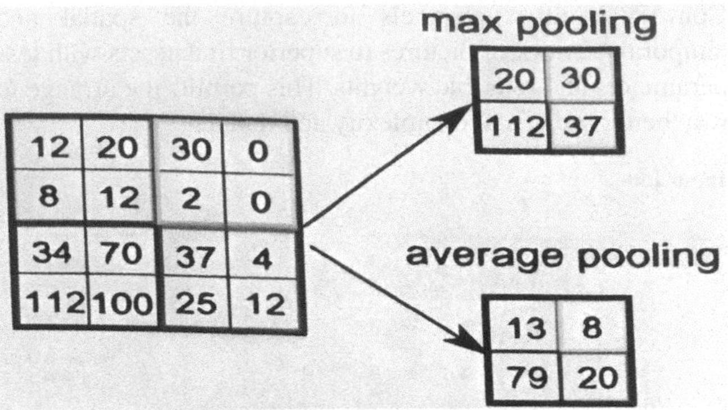

Fig. 29.12 Types of pooling

subsequently processed by conventional neural networks for classification purposes.

Fully connected layers are an affordable approach to learn complex and non-linear combinations of information derived from convolutional layers. They effectively operate within the feature space and enable the learning of non-linear functions. The flattened images are fed into a feedforward neural network trained with backpropagation. This network can effectively differentiate between dominant and low-level features and classify them using the softmax function over multiple training iterations.

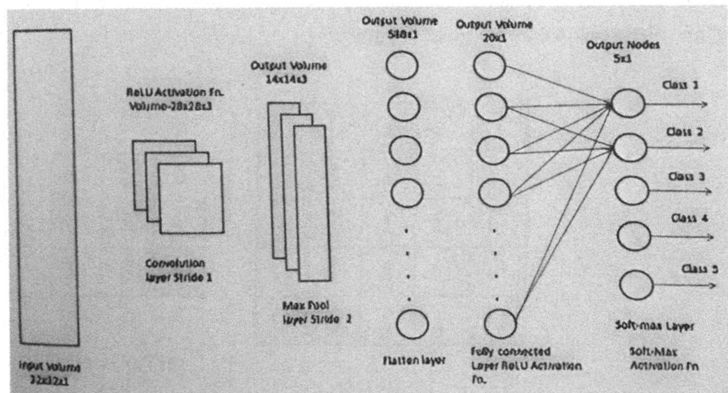

Fig. 29.13 Classification of fully connected layer

Based on the level, the following steps are taken:

- *Convolutional Neural Network (CNN):* Compute the dot product of the filter and the image field to compute the output volume.
- *Activation layer:* Applies an activation function to every layer of the element in order to produce output for a convolutional layer.
- *Flatten:* Convert the output of the convolutional layer to a one-dimensional array and generate a long feature vector. This vector is linked to the fully connected plane.
- *Fully connected:* In traditional neural network, there are several layers. One layer passes the value to the next

layer as an input, the next layer computes class values, and produces as many one-dimensional arrays as there are classes.

8. Conclusion

The proposed image watermarking system uses the adaptive features of deep learning to generalize image watermarking algorithms. It provides an architecture that can be trained unattended for watermarking applications, achieving resilience without requiring prior knowledge of potential biases. Deep neural networks are used to correct for geometric and perspective distortions, and approaches such as ablation studies are used to optimize scheme architectures, objectives, and loss functions. Although more research is needed, this study provides insight into interesting future avenues for image watermarking using deep learning.

REFERENCES

1. Dhaya, R. 2021. Lightweight CNN based robust image watermarking scheme for security. J. Inf. Technol. Digit World, 3(2), 118–132.
2. Islam, M., Roy, A., & Laskar, R. H. (2020). SVM-based robust image watermarking technique in LWT domain using different sub-bands. Neural Computing and Applications, 32(5), 1379–1403.
3. Kim, W. H., Kang, J., Mun, S. M., & Hou, J. U. (2020). Convolutional neural network architecture for recovering watermark synchronisation. Sensors, 20(18), 5427.
4. Fierro-Radilla, A., Nakano-Miyatake, M., Cedillo-Hernandez, M., Cleofas-Sanchez, L., & Perez-Meana, H. (2019, May). A robust image zero-watermarking using convolutional neural networks. In 2019 7th International Workshop on Biometrics and Forensics (IWBF) (pp. 1–5). IEEE.
5. Vukotic. V., Chappelier, V., & Furon, T. (2018, December). Are deep neural networks good for blind image watermarking?. In 2018 IEEE International Workshop on Information Forensics and Security (WIFS) (pp. 1–7). IEEE.
6. Kandi, H., Mishra, D., & Gorthi, S. R. S. (2017). Exploring the learning capabilities of convolutional neural networks for robust image watermarking. Computers and Security, 65, 247–268.
7. Zhong, X., Huang, P. C., Mastorakis, S., & Shih, F. Y. (2020). An automated and robust image watermarking scheme based on deep neural networks. IEEE Transactions on Multimedia, 23, 1951–1961.
8. Tao, H., Chongmin, L., Zain, J. M., & Abdalla, A. N. (2014). Robust image watermarking theories and techniques: A review. Journal of applied research and technology, 12(1), 122–138.
9. Haribabu, K., Subrahmanyam, G. R. K. S., & Mishra, D. (2015, December). A robust digital image watermarking technique using auto encoder based convolutional neural networks. In 2015 IEEE Workshop on Computational Intelligence: Theories, Applications and Future Directions (WCI) (pp. 1–6). IEEE.
10. Amrit, P., & Singh, A. K. (2022). Survey on watermarking methods in the artificial intelligence domain and beyond. Computer Communications, 188, 52–65.

Note: All the figures except Fig. 29.2 in this chapter were made by the author.

Advancement of Intelligent Computational Methods and Technologies (AICMT2023) – Dr. O. P. Verma et al. (eds)

30

Web Data Extraction Using DOM Parsing for Data Collection and Ontologies

Yuganshika Narang[1], Shamsher Singh Rawat[2], Devansh Sati[3], Ananya Singh[4], Ayasha Malik[5], Seema Verma[6]

Delhi Technical Campus, Greater Noida

ABSTRACT: In the digital era, the internet provides a wealth of valuable information. However, manually collecting and organizing this data can be inefficient and time-consuming. To tackle this challenge, web scraping and crawling techniques have emerged. Web scraping entails extracting data from websites, while web crawling involves automating the process of navigating through multiple web pages to gather information. These techniques enable the retrieval of structured data, including text, images, prices, reviews, and other relevant information. The main goal of this work is to leverage these techniques to automate the collection and analysis of data from various sources on the internet.

KEYWORDS: Web scraping, Web crawling, Business intelligence, Internet, Web pages

1. Introduction

This work is focused on extracting data from various types of websites, including industry-specific portals, e-commerce platforms, social media networks, news sites, and other online sources. Each website presents unique challenges such as dynamic content, authentication requirements, and anti-scraping measures. We will address these challenges during the development process by utilizing efficient web scraping and crawling algorithms, along with suitable tools and technologies. The objective of this work is to navigate through the target websites, extract the relevant data, and store it in a structured format that can be effectively analyzed. Throughout the work, we will strictly adhere to legal and ethical guidelines to ensure responsible web scraping practices, respecting the terms of service and privacy policies of the websites. Additionally, we will consider the impact of our scraping activities on the target websites and implement measures such as rate limiting and compliance with the crawling policies specified by each website. Our ultimate goal is to empower organizations by leveraging the vast amount of available data on the internet. We are committed to carrying out our project with integrity, respecting ethical standards, and honoring the rights and policies of the websites we scrape.

2. Related Background

Web scraping has been extensively researched, with a particular emphasis on its applications in various domains. Numerous studies have dedicated their attention to the legal and ethical concerns associated with web scraping. Additionally, researchers have developed techniques and tools such as XPath, regular expressions, and HTML DOM to facilitate the scraping process. In the realm of e-commerce, scholars have explored the utilization of web scraping for price monitoring and competitive analysis. For example, one study put forth a web scraping system designed to monitor competitors' prices in real-time. Another research endeavor delved into the examination of how web scraping influences price dynamics within the e-commerce market. Web data extraction technology is a highly beneficial tool for extracting content from various websites. It offers the advantage of scraping only the required content. With the rapidly evolving technological landscape, web data extraction has emerged as a new paradigm in recent years. Table 30.1 shows various

[1]yuganshikanarang1005@gmail.com, [2]35418002719@gmail.com, [3]35718002719@gmail.com, [4]03718002719@gmail.com, [5]ayasha07.am@gmail.com, [6]seemaknl@gmail.com

DOI: 10.1201/9781003487906-30

Table 30.1 Related work

Name(S)	Contribution
Irfan Darmawan et al.	Evaluating Web Parsing Performance with Multiprocessing Technical Applications Using XPath, Regular Expression, and HTML DOM (Darmawanet al., 2020)
B. Sathya and R. Anitha	An overview of web scraping and text mining techniques for social media analysis (Sathya, B and Anitha, R. 2018)
Y. Zhao and X. Liu	A novel web scraping approach for automatic generation of topic-specific dataset (Zhao, Y. and Liu, X. 2016)
T. Höllerer and M. Langer	The impact of web scraping on the quality of the web (Höllerer, T. and Langer, L. 2020)
B. Çakır and Ö. Özçalıkoğlu	Web data mining: a systematic review (Çakır, B. and Özçalıkoğlu, O. 2017)
Maldeniya, D., et al.	Herding a Deluge of Good Samaritans: GitHub Projects Respond to Increased Attention by Herding a Flood of Good Samaritans (Maldeniya, D., et al., 2020)
Singh, R. and Gupta, V.	A survey of web scraping techniques for extracting structured data from the web. (Singh, R. and Gupta, V., 2018)
Bernal, P. et al.	An investigation of web scraping tools for extracting and storing data from the web. (Bernal, P. et al. 2019)
Saurkar, A. and Gode, S.	A Guide to Web Scraping Techniques and Tools. (Saurkar, A. and Gode, S. 2018)

research work done in the context of web scraping and web crawling.

3. Proposed Methodology

3.1 Proposed Framework

Here, our proposed framework for web scraping consists of three key components: data collection, data cleaning, and data analysis.

The first component, data collection, entails utilizing web scraping tools to extract product data from e-commerce websites. To extract relevant information from the website, various scraping techniques such as XPath and regular expressions can be employed. Automation of the scraping process can be achieved through the utilization of tools like Beautiful Soup and Scrapy.

The second component, data cleaning, involves refining and formatting the collected data to ensure its suitability for analysis. This step is crucial in order to maintain the accuracy and reliability of the subsequent analysis. Tools like OpenRefine and Trifacta can be employed to clean the data by eliminating duplicates, handling missing values, and addressing any inconsistencies that may be present.

The final component, data analysis, encompasses the examination of the cleaned data to derive meaningful insights and facilitate informed decision-making. Several data analysis tools, such as Excel, R, and Python, can be employed to conduct a variety of analyses, including pricing analysis, trend analysis, and customer behavior analysis. HTML content to the DOM parsing library to create a structure.

By following this framework, we can effectively collect, clean, and analyze data obtained through web scraping, enabling us to gain valuable insights and make well-informed decisions.

3.2 Methodology

When it comes to web data extraction using DOM parsing, there are several methodologies you can follow. Here are some common approaches:

1. *Identify Target Websites:* Determine the websites from which you want to extract data. Consider factors such as the website's structure, accessibility, and the availability of the desired data within the DOM.
2. *Understand DOM Structure:* Analyze the structure of the target website's DOM (Document Object Model). Inspect the HTML source code and identify the specific elements and attributes that contain the data you want to extract.
3. *Choose a Programming Language:* Select a programming language that supports DOM parsing, such as Python, JavaScript, or Ruby. Different languages have various libraries and frameworks that facilitate DOM manipulation and parsing.
4. *Select DOM Manipulation Library:* Choose a library or framework that simplifies DOM manipulation and parsing. For example, BeautifulSoup for Python or jQuery for JavaScript provide convenient methods to navigate and manipulate the DOM tree.
5. *Establish HTTP Requests:* Use appropriate HTTP libraries (e.g., Requests in Python) to send HTTP requests to the target website's server. Make sure to handle any necessary headers, cookies, or authentication mechanisms required to access the data.
6. *Fetch and Parse HTML:* Retrieve the HTML content of the web page using the HTTP library. Then, pass the representation of the web page's DOM. By following these methodologies, you can effectively extract data using DOM parsing and collect the desired information from websites in a structured and automated manner.

4. Implementation and Result

After conducting web scraping, the obtained results typically consist of structured data that can be further processed or analyzed. The specific outcomes of web scraping depend on the targeted website and the desired data extraction.

1. *Structured Data:* The scraped data is often structured in formats such as JSON (JavaScript Object Notation), CSV (Comma-Separated Values), or XML (eXtensible Markup Language).
2. *Textual Data:* Scraped text data can be saved as plain text files or subjected to further processing for tasks like natural language processing.
3. *Image Files:* Image files can be stored locally or utilized for purposes such as image recognition, computer vision, or generating visualizations.
4. *URLs and Links:* Web scraping may involve extracting URLs and links from web pages. They can help in discovering related pages or navigating through the website's structure.
5. *Tabular Data:* Web scraping can capture tabular data, such as tables or lists present on web pages.

```
[ ] import requests
    from bs4 import BeautifulSoup
    url = "https://www.enjoyalgorithms.com/blog/decision-tree-algorithm-in-ml"
```

```
[ ] pip install html-table-parser-python3

    Looking in indexes: https://pypi.org/simple, https://us-python.pkg.dev/colab-wheels/public/simple/
    Collecting html-table-parser-python3
      Downloading html_table_parser_python3-0.3.1-py3-none-any.whl (15 kB)
    Installing collected packages: html-table-parser-python3
    Successfully installed html-table-parser-python3-0.3.1
```

Fig. 30.1 Importing libraries

```
[ ] # Get the title of the HTML page
    title = soup.title
    print(title)

    <title data-react-helmet="true">Decision Tree Algorithm in Machine Learning</title>
```

Fig. 30.2 Get titles of HTML page

```
[ ] # Get all the paragraphs from the page
    paras = soup.find_all('p')
    all_paras = set()
    for para in paras:
        if(para.get('p') != '#'):
            paraText = "Paragraphs = "+ para.text
            print(paraText)
    print(paras)
    print(soup.find('p')['class'])
    print(soup.find('div'))

    Paragraphs = EnjoyMathematics
    Paragraphs = Trees have a very close connection with almost every Computer Science domain, and Machine Learning is not an exception here. We might be aw
    Paragraphs = A Decision Tree is a hierarchical breakdown of a dataset from the root node to the leaf node based on the governing attributes to solve a c
    Paragraphs = But before moving any further, let's first learn some basic terminologies of tree-based algorithms.
    Paragraphs = 
    Paragraphs = Now, as we know the terminologies, it will be easier to follow the theory. To get better hands-on, let's take a very popular dataset of Pla
    Paragraphs = 
    Paragraphs = A decision tree is a visualization of attributes governing the decision hierarchically. Consider the dataset above. Fig.1 shows one of the 
    Paragraphs = If we closely examine another possible tree for the same example above, shown in Fig.2, the output of this tree will be the same as the pre
    Paragraphs = 
    Paragraphs = 
    Paragraphs = There is still a big puzzle for us: How do we decide which attribute/feature will give us the smaller tree? To decide the best attribute, w
    Paragraphs = In our loss function's blog, we learned about this term. Let's quickly revise it here. The Entropy of a dataset is the average amount of in
    Paragraphs = 
    Paragraphs = For an equally balanced categorical value, the Entropy is equal to 1. A real-world dataset may not necessarily be balanced. In the given ex
    Paragraphs = Any attribute chosen to partition a tree will result in a loss of Entropy. This means that on choosing any attribute to form a tree, the ba
```

Fig. 30.3 Content scraping

```
[ ] # get all images
    images = soup.find_all('img')
    all_images = set()
    for image in images:
        if(image.get('src') != '#'):
            imagesrc = "Image = " +image.get('src')
            all_images.add(image)
            print(imagesrc)

    Image = https://d33wubrfki0168.cloudfront.net/9f714f1c45bd93e3eb3d0a020d5a6c209b615687
    Image = https://cdn-images-1.medium.com/max/1760/1*S6IMQT4QkL8IOyhu9JOcPg.png
    Image = https://cdn-images-1.medium.com/max/1600/1*L3wbmF9htj1PFSCrm-Nr1Q.jpeg
    Image = https://cdn-images-1.medium.com/max/1600/1*YqOoY0vh0-oAKUdiR7b1FQ.png
    Image = https://cdn-images-1.medium.com/max/1600/1*oSdt_5xNMP6_Uw3YyCuJUw.jpeg
    Image = https://cdn-images-1.medium.com/max/1600/1*v7RY6N7vlsLxd7sHpAarzg.png
    Image = https://cdn-images-1.medium.com/max/1600/1*JUQLfZ7ttROa5ylhDEkQqw.png
    Image = https://cdn-images-1.medium.com/max/1600/1*sIDSaqGBJaYC2H14GZ6wJA.png
    Image = https://cdn-images-1.medium.com/max/1600/1*ibs4OfzYIEctFKTMVMEvSA.png
    Image = https://cdn-images-1.medium.com/max/1600/1*sIDSaqGBJaYC2H14GZ6wJA.png
    Image = https://cdn-images-1.medium.com/max/1600/1*o4ZWhY71I22xRsR5Nk_3WQ.png
```

Fig. 30.4 Image links scraping

```
[ ] # Get all the anchor tags from the page
    anchors = soup.find_all('a')
    all_links = set()
    #Get all the links on the page:
    for link in anchors:
        if(link.get('href') != '#'):
            linkText = "HREF Links :- " +link.get('href')
            all_links.add(link)
            print(linkText)

    HREF Links :- /
    HREF Links :- /courses/
    HREF Links :- /coding-interview/
    HREF Links :- /popular-tags/
    HREF Links :- /stories/
    HREF Links :- /contact/
    HREF Links :- https://www.enjoymathematics.com/
    HREF Links :- https://www.enjoyalgorithms.com/blog/classification-of-machine-learning-models/
    HREF Links :- https://www.enjoyalgorithms.com/blog/loss-and-cost-functions-in-machine-learnin
    HREF Links :- http://jmlr.csail.mit.edu/papers/v12/pedregosa11a.html
```

Fig. 30.5 Anchor link scraping

```
[ ]
    # converting the parsed data t/o dataframe
    print("\n\nPANDAS DATAFRAME\n")
    print(pd.DataFrame(p.tables[1]))

    [['Tag', 'Description'],
     ['table', 'Defines a table'],
     ['th', 'Defines a header cell in a table'],
     ['tr', 'Defines a row in a table'],
     ['td', 'Defines a cell in a table'],
     ['caption', 'Defines a table caption'],
     ['colgroup',
      'Specifies a group of one or more columns in a table for formatting'],
     ['col',
      'Specifies column properties for each column within a colgroup element'],
     ['thead', 'Groups the header content in a table'],
     ['tbody', 'Groups the body content in a table'],
     ['tfoot', 'Groups the footer content in a table']]


    PANDAS DATAFRAME

             0                                   1
    0      Tag                         Description
    1    table                     Defines a table
    2       th    Defines a header cell in a table
    3       tr            Defines a row in a table
```

Fig. 30.6 Table scraping

6. *HTML Markup:* In certain cases, web scraping may involve extracting the HTML markup of web pages.

In summary, the output of web scraping provides you with structured data suitable for further processing, analysis, or integration into your applications or databases. Figures 30.1, 30.2, 30.3, 30.4, 30.5, 30.6 are showing the various snippets of the code implemented for the method.

5. Conclusion

Web data extraction using DOM parsing is a highly effective and versatile method for collecting data from websites. DOM parsing involves programmatically accessing and extracting specific elements and data from the HTML structure of a webpage. Web data extraction using DOM parsing is a powerful technique that enables precise and flexible data collection from websites. It eliminates the dependency on APIs or pre-defined data feeds, making it applicable to a wide range of websites. By leveraging suitable libraries and frameworks, developers can streamline the extraction process and effectively overcome challenges associated with web scraping. Adhering to legal and ethical guidelines ensures responsible and respectful data extraction practices.

The future of web scraping and web crawling holds immense potential for advancements in data extraction, analysis, and automation. Integrating AI, ML, NLP, and other emerging technologies will enable more sophisticated and accurate data extraction and analysis. As businesses increasingly recognize the value of web data, the demand for advanced web scraping and web crawling solutions is set to grow, driving further innovation in this field.

REFERENCES

1. Darmawan, I. Maulana, M. Gunawan, R. Sono, N. 2020. Evaluating Web Parsing Performance with Multiprocessing Technical Applications Using XPath, Regular Expression, and HTML DOM
2. Sathya, B and Anitha, R. 2018. An overview of web scraping and text mining techniques for social media analysis. International Journal of Pure and Applied Mathematics, 119(12), 1881–1889.
3. Zhao, Y. and Liu, X. 2016. A novel web scraping approach for automatic generation of topic-specific dataset.
4. Höllerer, T. and Langer, L. 2020. The impact of web scraping on the quality of the web. Proceedings of the 2020 CHI Conference on Human Factors in Computing Systems, ACM, 1–12.
5. Çakır, B. and Özçalıkoğlu, O. 2017. Web data mining: a systematic review.
6. Maldeniya, D. Budak, C. Robert, L. and Romero, D. 2020. Herding a Deluge of Good Samaritans: GitHub Projects Respond to Increased Attention by Herding a Flood of Good Samaritans , ACM, 1–13.
7. Singh, R. and Gupta, V. 2018. A survey of web scraping techniques for extracting structured data from the web. International Journal of Computer Applications, 180(4), 21–27.
8. Bernal, P. et al. 2019. An investigation of web scraping tools for extracting and storing data from the web. Journal of Information Science, 45(2), 219–238.
9. Saurkar, A. and Gode, S. 2018. A Guide to Web Scraping Techniques and Tools. International Journal of Innovative Research in Technology, 4(4), 6–10.

Note: All the figures and table in this chapter were made by thc author.

Advancement of Intelligent Computational Methods and Technologies (AICMT2023) – Dr. O. P. Verma et al. (eds)

31

A Videoconferencing Framework for Real Time Applications Based on MERN Architecture

Qasim Malik, Rudra, Rajeev Kumar, Upasna Joshi*, Shivam Kumar

Department of Computer Science & Engineering, Delhi Technical Campus, Greater Noida, India

ABSTRACT: The MERN stack, consisting of MongoDB, Express.js, React.js, and Node.js, is a comprehensive technology stack widely recognized for its ability to develop scalable and robust web applications. MongoDB, a flexible NoSQL database, enables efficient handling of large data volumes with its schema-less structure. Express.js, a minimalist web application framework built on Node.js, simplifies server-side logic development and offers a robust middleware system. React.js, a powerful JavaScript library, facilitates the creation of dynamic and interactive user interfaces through its component-based architecture. Node.js, a server-side JavaScript runtime environment, enables fast and event-driven I/O operations, ensuring high application efficiency. The MERN stack's modular and component-based design promotes code reusability, enhancing development productivity. The stack's unified JavaScript-based workflow ensures consistency and simplifies the development process. Researchers benefit from the MERN stack's versatility, scalability, and real-time capabilities in building high-performance web applications. Its combination of MongoDB's scalability, Express.js streamlined backend development, React.js interactive UIs, and Node.js efficient runtime environment presents a comprehensive solution for research-oriented web applications. The MERN stack's wide adoption and successful implementation make it an attractive choice for researchers seeking to develop scalable and efficient web applications in their research endeavors.

KEYWORDS: Development, Web Application, Servlet, Efficient, Consistent

1. Introduction

The project at hand is a comprehensive web application built on the MERN stack, designed to revolutionize the way IT professionals and learners connect, collaborate, and share knowledge. With a focus on providing a feature-rich platform, this project aims to address the evolving needs of the IT industry. The development stack for this project comprises MongoDB, a flexible and scalable NoSQL database, Express.js, a robust web application framework for Node.js, React.js, a powerful JavaScript library for building user interfaces, and Node.js, a server-side JavaScript runtime environment. This combination of technologies offers a versatile and efficient foundation for creating a high-performance web application (Aggarwal et al. 2018).

The key objective of this project is to foster a vibrant community of IT enthusiasts by facilitating seamless knowledge sharing. The application provides dedicated discussion forums where users can engage in technical discussions, ask questions, and share their expertise. Real-time communication features such as video conferencing and chat capabilities enable users to connect with industry experts and participate in virtual meetups, enhancing collaboration and expanding their professional network.

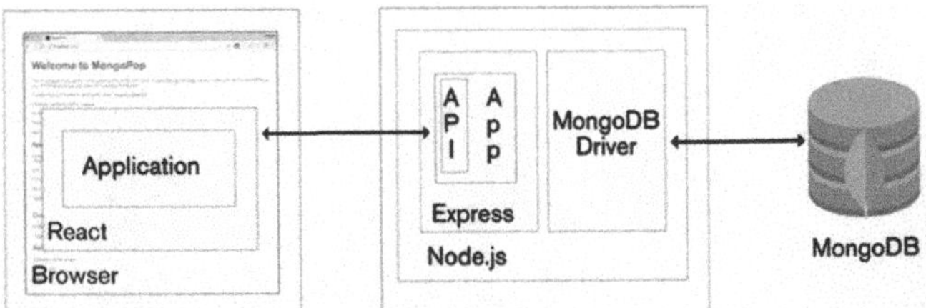

Fig. 31.1 MERN architecture

*Corresponding author: u.joshi@delhitechnicalcampus.in

DOI: 10.1201/9781003487906-31

Collaboration is paramount in the IT industry, and this project aims to streamline the process by providing powerful collaboration tools. Users can form teams, share project details, assign tasks, and track progress, ensuring efficient project management and enabling effective teamwork. By integrating task management features, the application empowers users to work together seamlessly, leading to improved productivity and innovative problem-solving.

Additionally, the project emphasizes networking and mentorship opportunities. Skill-based search functionality allows users to connect with individuals possessing specific technical skills or expertise, fostering networking and mentorship within the IT community. By facilitating these connections, users can seek guidance, explore career opportunities, and broaden their professional horizons.

The project prioritizes user experience by offering a responsive and intuitive interface. Leveraging modern web development technologies such as responsive design, data caching, and API integration, the application ensures a seamless and enjoyable user journey. The use of reactive components and client-side rendering with React.js enables dynamic and interactive user interfaces, enhancing usability and engagement.

Furthermore, the project harnesses the capabilities of the MERN stack to deliver a scalable and efficient application. MongoDB's document-oriented database model allows for flexibility and scalability, accommodating the storage and retrieval of large amounts of data. Express.js provides a robust and extensible middleware system, simplifying the development of server-side logic. React.js enables the creation of reusable components, enhancing code modularity and maintainability. Node.js facilitates fast and event-driven I/O operations, ensuring optimal performance and responsiveness

2. Literature Review

In the book "Web Development with Node and Express" by Ethan Brown, the author delves into the concepts and techniques surrounding web development using Node.js and Express.js. Brown highlights the advantages of using these technologies for building scalable and efficient web applications. The book emphasizes the importance of server-side JavaScript and showcases the capabilities of Node.js in handling concurrent requests and managing I/O operations effectively.

In (Bawane et al. 2022), the author explores the fundamentals of React.js and its role in creating interactive user interfaces. The article emphasizes the component-based architecture of React.js and how it promotes code reusability and modularity. The book also covers topics such as state management, routing, and handling user input, providing valuable insights into building robust and dynamic UIs.

In addition to the aforementioned literature sources, several other notable references contribute to the understanding and implementation of the MERN stack in web development.. Furthermore, (Maratkar et al. 2021), focuses on mastering the intricacies of React.js, including advanced topics such as Redux state management, server-side rendering, and performance optimization.

These literature sources collectively emphasize the benefits and capabilities of the MERN stack for modern web development.

3. Problem Statement

The IT industry is evolving at a rapid pace, demanding continuous learning, collaboration, and networking for professionals and learners. However, existing platforms for IT-related interactions often fall short in addressing these needs effectively, creating several disadvantages that need to be addressed.

One major problem is the lack of a centralized platform that caters specifically to the IT community. Many existing platforms offer generic discussion forums, but they fail to provide a focused environment where IT professionals and learners can engage in meaningful discussions and share their expertise. This fragmentation hinders effective knowledge sharing and collaboration, making it challenging to find relevant and reliable information.

Another problem is the limited availability of real-time communication features on existing platforms. Traditional text-based discussions often lack the immediacy and interactivity required for effective collaboration. The absence of video conferencing and chat capabilities restricts the ability to connect with industry experts, hindering opportunities for mentorship and networking.

Furthermore, the absence of dedicated collaboration tools hampers effective project management within the IT community. Existing platforms often lack features that enable users to form teams, share project details, assign tasks, and track progress. This results in inefficiencies, miscommunication, and hindered teamwork, ultimately impacting project success and productivity.

Additionally, existing platforms often lack robust search functionality based on specific technical skills and areas of expertise. This limits the ability to find and connect with individuals possessing the required skills, hindering networking opportunities and mentorship within the IT community. Without a comprehensive and efficient search mechanism, individuals struggle to seek guidance, explore career opportunities, and expand their professional networks.

The disadvantages created by these problems include a fragmented and inefficient knowledge-sharing landscape. IT professionals and learners spend valuable time sifting through multiple platforms and sources to find relevant information, leading to information overload and reduced productivity. The lack of real-time communication features limits opportunities for instant guidance, collaboration, and networking, impeding professional growth and innovation.

Moreover, the absence of dedicated collaboration tools hampers effective teamwork and project management, resulting in missed deadlines, miscommunication, and decreased productivity. The limited search functionality restricts the ability to connect with individuals possessing specific technical skills, hindering the growth of professional networks and access to mentorship opportunities.

To address these challenges, a comprehensive platform is needed that provides a centralized environment specifically designed for IT professionals and learners. This platform should offer real-time communication capabilities, robust collaboration tools, and efficient search functionality. By addressing these problems, the platform aims to enhance knowledge sharing, collaboration, and networking within the IT community, fostering a culture of continuous learning, innovation, and professional growth.

4. Implementation

To tackle the aforementioned problems in the IT industry, several implementation techniques, methods, and algorithms can be employed within the proposed platform. This section will outline the key approaches for addressing the challenges related to knowledge sharing, real-time communication, collaboration, and efficient search functionality.

4.1 Front end Development

The frontend development leverages Next.js and Tailwind CSS. Next.js provides server-side rendering and static site generation for improved performance and SEO. Tailwind CSS offers a utility-first approach to styling, enabling rapid UI development. React components are used for modular and reusable UI elements (Tilkov et al. 2010). The platform follows a mobile-first approach with responsive design and optimization. State management and data fetching are handled using React's capabilities and Next.js. The UI/UX is enhanced with intuitive navigation, interactive forms, smooth transitions, and visually appealing elements.

4.2 Backend Development

Backend development utilizes Node.js, Express.js, and JSON Web Tokens (JWT) to create a robust and secure server-side infrastructure. Node.js provides a scalable runtime environment, while Express.js simplifies API development. JSON Web Tokens enable secure user authentication and authorization. The backend handles routing, API development, database integration, and middleware functions for request handling and authentication. This combination of technologies ensures a reliable and efficient backend for the project, enabling seamless communication between the frontend and backend components.

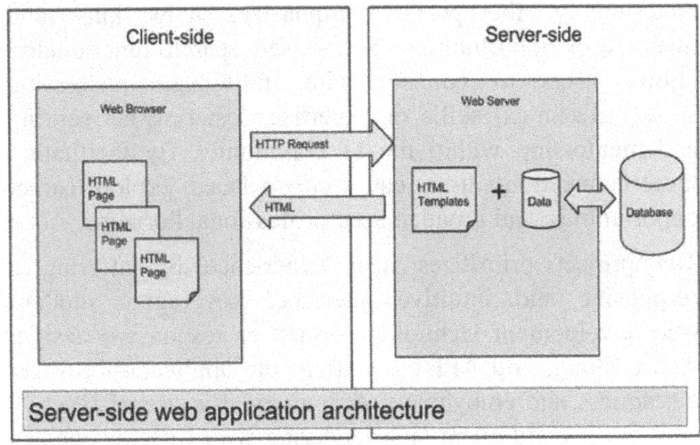

Fig. 31.2 NextJs architecture

Node.js Architecture

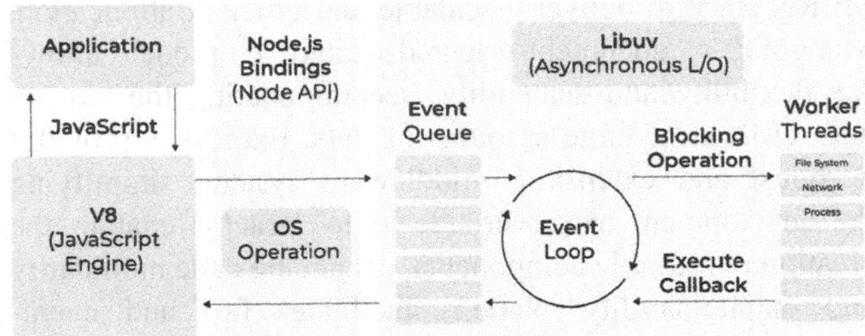

Fig. 31.3 NodeJs architecture

4.3 Data Management

MongoDB and Mongoose are used for data design and management. MongoDB is a flexible and scalable NoSQL document database, while Mongoose is a Node.js library that simplifies interaction with MongoDB through schema-based modeling (Banker et al. 2016). Schemas define the structure and properties of data entities, and Mongoose provides CRUD operations, relationships, referential integrity, data validation, and middleware capabilities. This combination ensures efficient data storage, retrieval, and manipulation while maintaining data integrity and consistency in the project.

4.4 Real-Time Communication

To enable effective real-time communication, the platform can incorporate WebRTC (Web Real-Time Communication) technology. WebRTC allows for peer-to-peer audio and video communication directly within the browser, eliminating the need for additional plugins or software. This technology can facilitate seamless video conferencing and chat capabilities, enabling users to connect with industry experts, participate in virtual meetups, and engage in interactive discussions (Nayyef et al.2018). The user interface (UI) design of the project focuses on providing an intuitive and seamless experience for users, enabling them to access the platform's features effectively. The design incorporates elements that facilitate smooth navigation, clear communication, and interactive engagement.

The UI design includes a visually appealing and responsive layout that adapts to different screen sizes and devices. It employs modern design principles, utilizing a clean and uncluttered interface that enhances readability and ease of use. The color scheme and typography are carefully selected to create a visually cohesive and aesthetically pleasing experience.

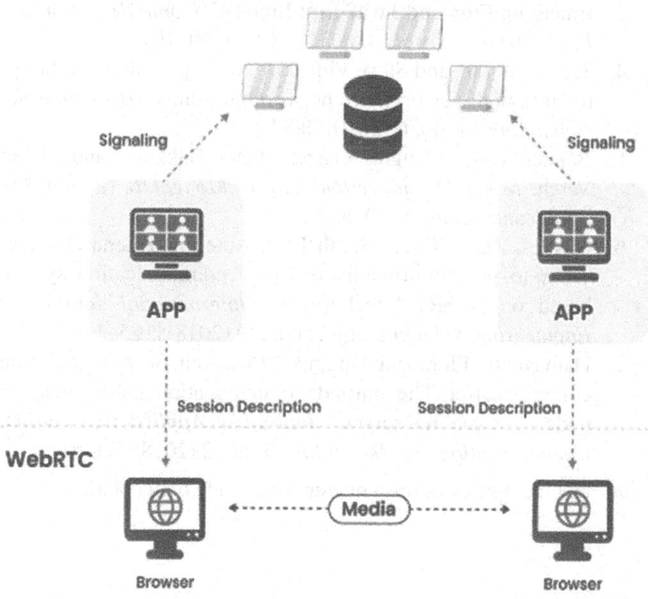

Fig. 31.4 WebRTC diagram

The prominent features of the UI design include the video chat and forum functionalities. The video chat interface is designed to provide a seamless and immersive experience for users engaging in real-time video communication. It includes controls for video and audio settings, screen sharing options, and a chat sidebar for text-based communication alongside the video stream.

The forum section of the UI design focuses on facilitating discussions and knowledge sharing among users. It incorporates a clear and organized layout that presents discussion threads, comments, and user profiles in a user-friendly manner (Damayanti et al.2018). The design allows users to create new threads, post replies, and engage in threaded conversations with ease. Additionally, features like notifications and search functionality enhance the user experience by enabling users to stay updated on relevant discussions and easily find topics of interest.

5. Results

The successful implementation of the project yielded significant positive outcomes and results, contributing to the advancement of IT-related interactions and knowledge sharing within the community. The results can be summarized as follows.

5.1 Enhanced Collaboration and Networking

The platform facilitated seamless video chat and forum functionalities, enabling users to engage in real-time communication, discussions, and knowledge sharing. This led to improved collaboration, fostering a sense of community and providing opportunities for users to network, seek mentorship, and connect with industry experts.

5.2 Improved Access to Information

The project's implementation resulted in an efficient search functionality, allowing users to easily discover relevant content, discussions, and resources based on their specific technical needs. This improved access to information empowered users to find accurate solutions, stay updated with industry trends, and expand their knowledge base.

5.3 Positive User Experience

The user interface design, incorporating a visually appealing and intuitive layout, contributed to a positive user experience. The seamless integration of video chat and forum functionalities, coupled with responsive design principles, enhanced user engagement, ease of use, and overall satisfaction.

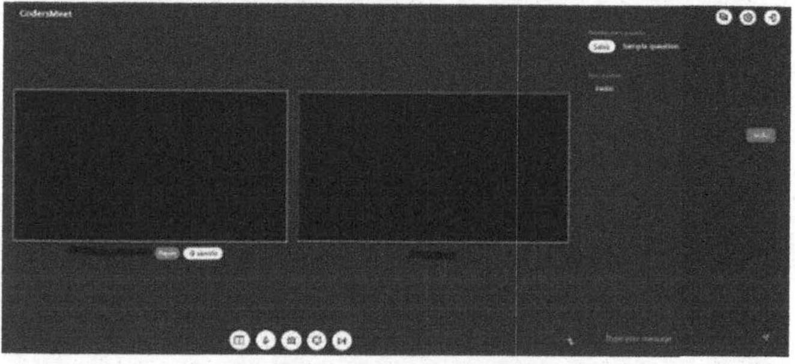

Fig. 31.5 Interaction page

6. Conclusion

In conclusion, the MERN project represents a significant advancement in the field of IT platforms, leveraging the power of the MERN (MongoDB, Express.js, React, Node.js) stack to create a highly sophisticated and technically advanced solution. Through its robust architecture, seamless integration of key technologies, and innovative features, the project offers a comprehensive ecosystem that addresses the challenges faced by IT professionals and enthusiasts. The project's successful implementation showcases the effectiveness of the MERN stack in building scalable and efficient web applications. The utilization of MongoDB as a NoSQL database ensures flexibility and scalability in handling vast amounts of data. Express.js provides a solid foundation for developing RESTful APIs, enabling seamless communication between the front-end and back-end. React's component-based architecture enables the creation of dynamic and interactive user interfaces, while Node.js empowers the server-side functionality with its event-driven and non-blocking nature. The research conducted during the project highlighted the importance of user-centered design and the integration of advanced technologies. The incorporation of real-time video chat and forum functionalities fosters collaboration and knowledge sharing, enabling users to connect, learn, and grow within the IT community. The work serves as a foundation for ongoing research and development, offering a solid framework for incorporating emerging technologies such as artificial intelligence, machine learning, and blockchain.

A pivotal direction for future enhancement lies in the integration of advanced collaboration tools, such as immersive virtual whiteboards and collaborative code editors. These tools would facilitate real-time collaboration, empowering users to engage in interactive code reviews, seamless brainstorming sessions, and collective problem-solving endeavors. By providing a highly immersive and interactive environment, these integrated tools would greatly enhance teamwork and promote efficient project collaboration among users.

Furthermore, the work can broaden its scope by enhancing networking opportunities within the platform. This can be achieved through the implementation of a comprehensive mentorship program, wherein seasoned professionals can extend their expertise and guidance to aspiring learners.

REFERENCES

1. Aggarwal, Sanchit, and Jyoti Verma. "Comparativeanalysis of MEAN stack and MERN stack." *International Journal of Recent Research Aspects* 5, no. 1 (2018).
2. Bawane, Mohanish, Ishali Gawande, Vaishnavi Joshi, Rujuta Nikam, and Sudesh A. Bachwani. "A Review on Technologies used in MERN stack." *Int J Res Appl Sci Eng Technol* 10, no. 1 (2022): 479–488.
3. Maratkar, Pratik Sharad, and Pratibha Adkar. "React JS-An Emerging Frontend JavaScript Library." *Iconic Research And Engineering Journals* 4, no. 12 (2021): 99–102.
4. Tilkov, Stefan, and Steve Vinoski. "Node. js: Using JavaScript to build high-performance network programs." *IEEE Internet Computing* 14, no. 6 (2010): 80–83.
5. Banker, Kyle, Douglas Garrett, Peter Bakkum, and Shaun Verch. *MongoDB in action: covers MongoDB version 3.0.* Simon and Schuster, 2016.
6. Nayyef, Zinah Tareq, Sarah Faris Amer, and Zena Hussain. "Peer to peer multimedia real-time communication system based on WebRTC technology." *International Journal of Engineering & Technology* 7, no. 2.9 (2018): 125–130.
7. Damayanti, Florensia Unggul. "Research of web real-time communication-The unified communication platform using node. js signaling server." *Journal of Applied Information, Communication and Technology* 5, no. 2 (2018): 53–61.

Note: All the figures in this chapter were made by the author.

Advancement of Intelligent Computational Methods and Technologies (AICMT2023) – Dr. O. P. Verma et al. (eds)
© 2024 Taylor & Francis Group, London, ISBN 978-1-032-78445-8

32

Automatic Exam Paper Generator Using Dynamic Structured and Intelligent Database

Avinash Singh, Lakshay Sharma, Akash Chauhan, Upasna Joshi*
Department of Computer Science & Engineering, Delhi Technical Campus, Greater Noida, India

ABSTRACT: Exams are necessary to assess a candidate's knowledge at each level for quality. It is beneficial to put pupils' knowledge and abilities in any discipline to the test. Therefore, holding exams at each level may result in various challenges or complications, such as a lack of time and other resources when manually producing the test papers. Therefore, a system that automatically creates test questions would simplify the work. Such challenges are taken into consideration when implementing the advance question paper generating system, which can produce paper with ease. In every organization, including universities, the question of an examination paper's accuracy is crucial. Exam paper writing is traditionally done by hand using the writers' expertise, experience, and writing style. Despite the questions' high rating, there are still some issues. The fundamental issue is poor paper quality, which is a result of human variables like instability and a relatively small number of themes. Exam paper writing requires a lot of time and effort from teachers. This has no impact on the distinction between instruction and assessment. In order to achieve the separation of teaching, automatic test paper generation using computers is a crucial step

KEYWORDS: Database, Java, Servlet, Exam generator, HTTP, JSP, JDBC.

1. Introduction

One of the most crucial aspects of our lives is education. There are many ways to learn things, but a teacher plays a crucial role in the early years of life. It is always necessary to have some background knowledge in order to comprehend or acquire knowledge from other sources, including books, research articles, and online videos (Naik et. al., 2014). After learning something, it's important to test your ability to put that knowledge to use by solving some related challenges. There are many different types of questions in the test or exam. While some of them are unfamiliar but pertinent to the topics the students have studied, others are known to the pupils. Almost all schools and universities base their paper levels on how well their students performed in prior years. Thus, we can have different difficulty levels for our question papers, such as easy, medium, and hard (Aaghade et. al., 2021).The Teachers at most reputable colleges are frequently preoccupied with research projects in addition to their academic responsibilities. Consequently, they typically do not want to linger for a long time arranging and producing the questions. Consequently, they require an automatic question paper generator that will pull the questions from the database (Singh et. al., 2021). The lecturers can freely select the topics while coming up with questions under this approach. Creating test questions has a different level of difficulty to assess a certain question's degree of difficulty. As characteristics of the questions tables in the database, these inquiries are kept.

2. Methodology

A separate GUI will be made available for question insertion. Questions will be shown, and a separate GUI will be available for question insertion. After successfully logging in, the user will be given the option to select the subject for which he wants to retrieve questions or prepare the paper. He is only allowed to focus on one issue at a time. He can, however, return and work on the other tasks that were given to him. User must choose the type of paper and the degree of difficulty. After selecting "Generate paper," a document will be produced and saved in your profile.

*Corresponding author: u.joshi@delhitechnicalcampus.in

DOI: 10.1201/9781003487906-32

Table 32.1 Tools

Front-end Tools : Servlet and JSP
Back-end Tools : Core Java and JDBC
Middle-end : Tomcat Apache Server

Table 32.2 Hardware requirements

Components	Minimum	Recommended
Processor	Intel Core i3-2100 2nd generation	Intel Core i7 generation 5th
RAM	2GB	8GB
Disk	128Gb	512Gb

2. Literature Review

It is the system that automatically generate exam papers are designed to cut down on the time and labor that teachers must expend when writing questions manually. These systems employ computer algorithms to produce test questions depending on established standards, including learning objectives, degree of difficulty, and distribution of topics. Due to their reliability, adaptability, and broad use, Java, JSP, JDBC, and Tomcat are often utilized technologies for constructing such systems. Several Common Errors.

In a study by (Kirby and Stephen, 2002), Java, JSP, JDBC, and Tomcat were used to construct an automatic exam paper generator. A database of questions organized by topic, degree of difficulty, and learning objective was used by the system. Based on user-defined criteria, the generator algorithm developed unique question papers by choosing the right questions. The system's ability to drastically cut paper creation time without sacrificing exam quality was demonstrated by the evaluation results.

A system for automatically generating exam papers was created by (Huang and Ning, 2017), using Java, JSP, JDBC, and Tomcat. The system had an adaptive algorithm that produced customized test questions by taking into account information about student performance. In order to design tests that were both difficult and appropriate for each student, the algorithm changed the difficulty levels of questions based on the ability of each individual student. The study showed that the customized strategy increased student engagement and better learning results.

Another work by (Kirkegaard et al. 2006), concentrated on the incorporation of machine learning methods into a Java, JSP, JDBC, and Tomcat-based automatic exam paper generator. To create questions that were appropriate for each student's level of cognitive development, the system used natural language processing algorithms to analyses student performance data. The study's conclusions demonstrated how well the machine learning method works for designing customized tests and improving the precision of question difficulty prediction.

There are various benefits to employing automatic exam paper generators that use Java, JSP, JDBC, and Tomcat. First and foremost, these technologies offer a dependable and expandable basis for creating solid systems. Second, the automation process frees up time and effort for teachers, allowing them to concentrate more on teaching activities. Additionally, the personalized strategy enhances learning outcomes and student engagement.

However, there are issues to take into account while putting autonomous exam paper generators into use. To prevent biased or repeated question selection, one difficulty is to ensure the question bank is high-quality and diverse. In order to effectively determine question difficulty levels and match them with students' abilities, efficient algorithms must also be devised. Additionally, the system should take into account elements like topic coverage, relevancy of the questions, and suitable formatting to produce well-organized and thorough question papers.

The literature review highlights the growing demand for Java, JSP, JDBC, and Tomcat-based automatic exam paper generators. These technologies give instructors useful resources to speed up the generation of exam papers, saving time and enhancing the learning process as a whole. In order to improve the capabilities of these systems, future research should concentrate on addressing the issues outlined and investigating cutting-edge methods like data mining and artificial intelligence.

3. Working Environment

Java is a computer language that makes it easier to create applications for various platforms. Learning Java will be useful whether you are creating server-side software, GUI programmed with desktop interfaces, or Android mobile applications.

A function of Java is core Java. Java applications are created using the core language of Java. It is a core Java concept, including swings, JDBC, and java beans. Without the technology at the core of Java, no one can advance the language. Any java technology will leverage the fundamentals of core Java. If you deal with advanced Java, you are familiar with core Java. Java is always used to launch the core Java package. To create standalone applications or system software that only runs on the system, core Java is utilized.

A Java application programming interface (API) called Servlet runs on the server computer and intercepts client requests before producing and sending a response. The

HTTP servlet, which offers ways to hook on HTTP requests utilizing well-liked HTTP methods like GET and POST, is a well- known example.

Although servlets can reply to any kind of request, they are most often used to construct Web server-based applications. The equivalent in Java of additional tools for dynamic web content like PHP and ASP.NET are such Web servlets.

To manage data coming from a form or particular URL. People typically layer a framework like Struts/Spring on top of servlets to make programming easier. The servlet should only analyse the received data before sending it on. A backend business layer implementation (against which test cases can be programmed).

Execution of Servlets involves the six basic steps:

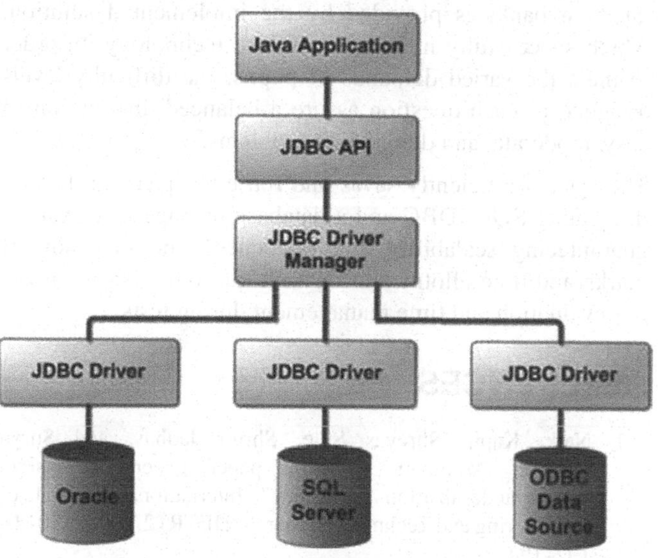

Fig. 32.1 JDBC architecture

It should then call a JSP to display the results by putting the values on the request or session.

JSP stands for Java Server Pages and is essentially HTML with Java code incorporated. Dynamic responses are to be produced via Java code. It is a server-side programming tool that makes it possible to construct Web-based applications in a dynamic, platform-agnostic way. If you wish to create code for your project's front-end view, you can utilize JSP. You can use HTML for the project's structure and JSP's scripting to automatically compile Java code without the requirement for compilation

The HTTP protocol is required for the application to be accessed from anywhere in the world, hence Tomcat Server has all of these HTTP protocols supported. As a result, it handles "Request" and "Response" automatically.

4. About The Technology

Programmers can connect to and communicate with databases using application programming interface (API) for Java Database Connectivity (JDBC). It offers means to access and modify database data with update commands like SQL's CREATE, UPDATE, DELETE, and INSERT as well as query expressions like SELECT. JDBC may carry out stored techniques as well. JDBC, like Java, works with a variety of operating systems, including MAC OS and Unix.

The JDBC API connects to databases making use of Java's standard classes and interfaces. There is a JDBC driver for that database server that supports the JDBC API necessary in order to link Java applications to that database server using JDBC.

The steps that JDBC takes to connect the Java programme to the database are as follows:

The driver can be loaded and offers an interface with the database. Making the relationship: After the driver has been loaded, a connection must be made. The database name, port number, and name of the computer are all included in the URL that the connection object uses. With the database object, it has communication carrying out SQL statements builds the SQL statement with the aid of an object. Delivering the outcome. Database queries are manipulated and retrieved using set. Records are fetched from the database's order from first to last row. The package then allocates or launches create a thread for the request, invokes serving as a servlet function, and gives the request and argument responses as objects. Based on the HTTP Request Method (Get, Post, etc.) given using the service () method, by the client determines which

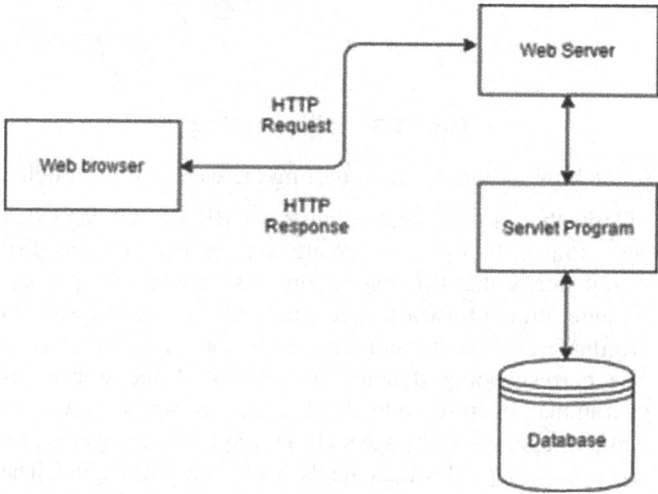

Fig. 32.2 Servlet architecture

servlet method, do Get () or do Post (), to call. For example, if the client sends a GET request over HTTP, the service () will run the do Get () method on the Servlet. The response is then written back to the client by the Servlet using the response object.

Java Server Pages (JSP) is a method for building Web pages with the ability to use dynamic content. Utilising certain JSP tags—the majority of which begin with "%" and "" %>—programmers may now insert Java code into HTML pages.

The web application's user interface in Java is supposed to be provided by a Java servlet called a Java Server Pages component. Web developers employ text files with embedded JSP actions and instructions, XML components, and HTML or XHTML code to generate JSPs.

JSP allows you to dynamically construct Web pages, utilise forms on Web sites to show data from a database or other source and collect user input.

Tags in JSP can be used for a wide range of functions, including transmitting control between pages, accessing JavaBeans components, registering user preferences, and getting data from databases, exchanging information sent between requests and pages, etc.

The processes that the web server takes to produce a webpage using JSP are listed below:

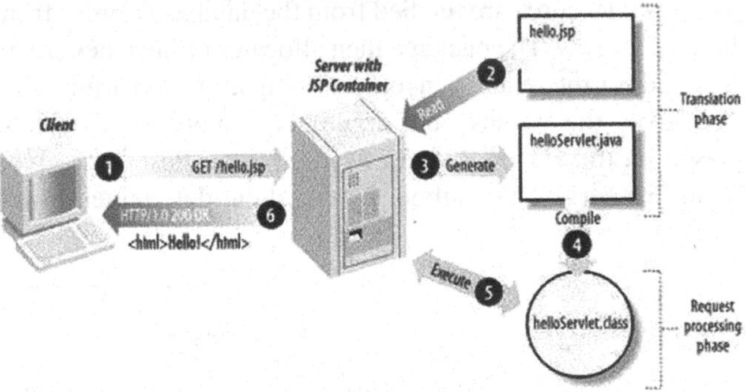

Fig. 32.3 JSP processing

In the browser makes an requesting the web server through

To do this, instead of.html, use a URL or JSP page that ends in.jsp. In order to create servlet content, the JSP engine loads the JSP page from disc conversion process is quite straightforward, converting text in all template to println () commands and Java code for all JSP elements. The corresponding dynamic behaviour of the website is operational by this code. HTTP, just as when viewing a regular page, the JSP page's HTTP request is recognised by the web server, who then sends it on to a JSP engine. The initial request is sent to a servlet engine by the JSP engine, which then compiles the servlet into an executable class. The servlet engine loads and uses the servlet.class, a component of the web server. The servlet generates an output in HTML format During operation. The servlet engine then sends the output as part of an HTTP response to the web server The output is then sent by the servlet engine to the web server as part of an HTTP response. Your browser receives the HTTP response from the web server as content in static HTML. Finally, the web browser treats the a dynamically created HTML page that functions just like a static page and is included in the HTTP response.

5. Conclusion

The approach intends to lighten the load on teachers and streamline the process of creating customized assessments for educational institutions.

A user-friendly interface for developing and managing exam question banks is provided by the implemented solution, which successfully makes use of Java technology. In order to meet the varied demands of pupils, the difficulty levels assigned to each question assure a balanced distribution of easy, moderate, and demanding problems.

The system efficiently saves and retrieves question data by integrating SQL JDBC and a database management system, guaranteeing scalability and resilience. The inclusion of marks and time allotments for each question also promotes fair evaluation and time management during tests.

REFERENCES

1. Naik, Kapil, Shreyas Sule, Shruti Jadhav, and Surya Pandey. "Automatic question paper generation system using randomization algorithm." International Journal of Engineering and Technical Research (IJETR) 2, no. 12 (2014): 192–194.
2. Aaghade, Shubham, Manan Parikh, Adwait Gudekar, and Shweta Sharma. "REVIEW ON AUTOMATIC QUESTION PAPER GENERATOR." (2021).
3. Singh, Prabhdeep, Rajesh Upadhyay, and Rupa Khanna Malhotra. "Automatic Questionnaire Generator System." Webology 18, no. 5 (2021): 3150–3156.Al-Ali, A. R., & Al-Rousan, M. (2004). Java-based home automation system. IEEE Transactions on Consumer Electronics, 50(2), 498–504.
4. Kirby, Stephen F. "Web-Based Mesoscale Model Execution aed Evataatloii Too!: A Prototype." (2002). Dietrich, Suzanne W., Susan D. Urban, and Ion Kyriakides. "JDBC demonstration courseware using Servlets and Java Server Pages." ACM SIGCSE Bulletin 34, no. 1 (2002): 266-270.
5. Huang, Ning. "Analysis and design of university teaching evaluation system based on JSP platform." International Journal of Education & Management Engineering 7, no. 3 (2017): 43–50.
6. Kirkegaard, Christian, and Anders Møller. "Static analysis for Java Servlets and JSP." In International Static Analysis Symposium, pp. 336–352. Berlin, Heidelberg: Springer Berlin Heidelberg, 2006.

Note: All the figures and tables in this chapter were made by the author.

Advancement of Intelligent Computational Methods and Technologies (AICMT2023) – Dr. O. P. Verma et al. (eds)
© 2024 Taylor & Francis Group, London, ISBN 978-1-032-78445-8

33

IoT Based Peltier Module Smart Refrigerator

Sarthak Aggarwal[1], Robin[2]
Mechanical and Automation Engineering, Delhi Technical Campus (Affiliated to GGSIPU), Greater Noida, Utter Pradesh

Mohd Atif Wahid[3]
Assoc Prof. Mechanical and Automation Engineering, Delhi Technical Campus (Affiliated to GGSIPU), Greater Noida, Utter Pradesh

Prabhat R. Prasad[4], Nidhi Sharma[5], Neha Jain[6]
Mechanical and Automation Engineering, Delhi Technical Campus (Affiliated to GGSIPU), Greater Noida, Utter Pradesh

ABSTRACT: With the rapid advancement of Internet of Things (IoT) technology, various aspects of our daily lives are being transformed, including the way we interact with household appliances. This research paper explores the integration of IoT capabilities into mini refrigerators, focusing on enhancing efficiency and the user experience. This research paper proposes a novel approach to utilize IoT in a mini refrigerator by leveraging data analysis techniques to generate recipes based on the available items inside the refrigerator. By employing sensors, connectivity, and data processing algorithms, the system can identify the items stored in the refrigerator, analyse their characteristics, and generate recipe suggestions using the available ingredients.

KEYWORDS: Internet of Things, IoT, mini refrigerator, data analysis techniques, sensors, data processing algorithms, recipe suggestions.

1. Introduction

1.1 Refrigeration Background

Refrigerators have become an essential appliance in households, commercial establishments, and various industries. They are designed to store and preserve perishable food items, beverages, medicines, and other temperature-sensitive products. The development of refrigeration technology has significantly transformed the way we store and consume food, ensuring its safety and extending its shelf life.

1.2 Types of Refrigerators

There are various types of refrigerators available today, catering to different needs and preferences. However, the characteristics of few which are introduced in this project have been listed:

- Compact/Mini Fridges: These smaller refrigerators are commonly used in dorm rooms, offices, or as secondary storage units. They are designed to fit in tight spaces.
- Smart Fridges: Smart refrigerators are equipped with features such as Wi-Fi connectivity, touchscreens, and advanced monitoring systems. They can interact with

[1]sarthakagg17@gmail.com, [2]robinsarraf420@gmail.com, [3]Wahidatif89@gmail.com, [4]Kishuraj421@gmail.com, [5]nidhi@delhitechnicalcampus.ac.in, [6]nehajain312@gmail.com

DOI: 10.1201/9781003487906-33

users, track inventory, and provide access to various apps and services.

1.3 Internet of Things

The integration of Internet of Things (IoT) technology has opened up exciting possibilities for enhanced functionality and convenience for users in practical life. This paper explores the potential benefits and challenges of its application in mini refrigerators, highlighting the impact on user convenience, reducing food waste, and encouraging creative cooking. The proposed system holds promise in revolutionizing the way users interact with their mini refrigerators, facilitating efficient meal according to a particular diet plan and fostering culinary exploration.

The motivation behind undertaking this project stemmed from several factors, including technological advancements, environmental concerns, and practical applications. The following are the key motivations

- *Energy Efficiency:* Peltier module refrigerators offer the potential for increased energy efficiency compared to conventional compressor-based refrigeration systems. This is because they operate using solid-state thermoelectric technology, which eliminates the need for refrigerants and mechanical compressors. By exploring and optimizing the energy efficiency of Peltier module refrigerators, the project can contribute to sustainable and environmentally friendly cooling solutions.
- *Compact and Portable Refrigeration:* Peltier module refrigerators are known for their compactness and portability. They are lightweight, require minimal installation space, and can be easily integrated into various applications, such as camping, portable medical cooling, and mobile refrigeration. The project can focus on designing and developing efficient and practical portable refrigeration solutions using Peltier modules.
- *Noiseless Operation:* Unlike traditional refrigeration systems that rely on compressors and fans, Peltier module refrigerators operate silently. This characteristic makes them suitable for noise-sensitive environments, such as bedrooms, offices, or laboratories. The project can explore the advantages of noiseless operation and design Peltier module refrigerators for specific applications where noise reduction is critical.
- *Educational and Research Significance:* Undertaking a Peltier module refrigerator project provides an excellent opportunity for learning and research. It allows for a deeper understanding of thermoelectric principles, heat transfer, control systems, and optimization techniques. The project can contribute to the existing body of knowledge by conducting experiments, analysing data, and proposing improvements in Peltier module refrigeration technology.

2. Literature Review

The authors (Kakade and Lokhande, 2016), projected a system, "IoT based Intelligent home using Smart Devices" These sensors can monitor the quantity and presence of specific items, providing real-time data about their availability.

The authors (Singh and Jain, 2016), have put forth the "Smart Refrigerator" system, which uses an application to send notifications to the user's mobile device when the weight of the food item drops below a predetermined level.

A project named "The Design and Implementation of Wifi Based User-Machine Interactive Refrigerator" (Mubeena and Swati, 2017) employs Wi-Fi for wireless communication. It shows how to monitor a refrigerator and alert the user via email.

A system called the "Automated Demand Response Refrigerator Project" was studied. They provided a medium to see the sensor data and operate the refrigerator remotely (Tran et al. 2015).

In their work, "Raspberry Pi Based Interactive Home Automation System through Internet of Things," (Ganesh et al., 2015) employed the Raspberry-Pi to connect embedded equipment to the internet.

The sensors were utilised in "Smart Refrigerator having IOT" to sense and monitor the contents (Prapulla et al., 2015). This smart refrigerator sends an email or SMS alert to the remote user.

To enhance the system's performance, authors presented linear regression in their article "Product recommendations using linear predictive modelling" (Xiao et al., 2014).

The demand prediction for inventory optimisation has been proposed by Guo, C Liu, W. Xu, Yuan, and M. Wang in "A Prediction Based Inventory Optimization Using Data Mining Models" (Xiao et al., 2014). They got sample data by using classification and prediction based on back propagation, and then they applied the formulations based on the results.

In order to identify or affect the organisational processes across a large number of people, the author reviewed extensive literature entitled "A Review on Predictive Analytics in Data Mining" (Kavya, 2016). This proposal provides a predicted score for each individual product.

A system using the wireless sensor and actuator network (WSAN) has been presented by M. Wang et al. as "An IoT based appliance control system for smart homes" (Wang et al., 2013).

A system called the "Smart Refrigerator using IoT" has been presented by Mahajan et al (Mahajan et al., 2017). where they offered the opportunity for dialogue with outsiders.

A system called "Low-Cost Smart Refrigerator" has been proposed by Hasin-Han Wu. It explains the general concept of a cost-effective Smart Refrigerator constructed with a Raspberry-Pi (Wu et al., 2017). It also features 2 sensors that are connected to the Raspberry Pi board and are in charge of each camera.

With the extensive literature review, various research gaps were identified. The study on the implementation of RFID technology and integration of IoT into the refrigerator has been scarcely conducted. Therefore, the objective of this research is to design and build an efficient thermo-electric refrigerator that uses the Peltier effect to cool while also utilising IoT technology to provide recipe suggestions based on the items that are kept in the fridge. In addition to this, the implementation of RFID technology and IoT was also done for the fabrication of a smart refrigerator.

3. Methodology

This section describes the materials and methods adopted to fabricate the smart refrigerator.

3.1 Developed System

We have created a portable refrigerator that utilizes peltier effect for cooling along with the potential for IoT integration in future. Fig. 33.1(a), (b) shows the physical representation of the model developed.

(a)

(a)

Fig. 33.1 (a) Isometric view of the model, (b) Back view of the model

Source: Author

The Peltier effect enables solid-state cooling, eliminating the need for compressors, traditional refrigerants, and moving parts, resulting in a refrigerator that is compact, lightweight, and ecologically friendly.

This refrigerator presents interesting potential for expanded functionality, user experience, and the ability to add the necessary sensing devices indicated in this paper.

3.2 RFID Readers

(Radio Frequency Identification) readers, as shown in Fig. 33.2, are devices that are used to read and collect data from RFID tags. RFID technology uses radio waves to communicate between the reader and the tag, allowing for wireless identification and tracking of objects or individuals.

These sensors identify the items stored inside the refrigerator and gather data about their characteristics, such as expiration dates, nutritional information, or ingredient types. This data is then sent to the microcontroller connected to them.

Fig. 33.2 RFID reader card

Source: Author

3.3 Raspberry Pi

The sensors provide the Raspberry Pi with data, which it then stores locally or in a database. The Raspberry-Pi is a series of small, single-board computers used in programming, coding, electronics, and other computing concepts, Raspberry Pi and its components are shown in Fig. 33.3.

This information includes the item identification, quantity, available ingredients, and their expiration dates.

It then compares this data with the recipe database to find recipes that can be made using the items available, chooses a set of recipe suggestions that best fit the ingredients available, and then sends notifications to a mobile device or displays them on a connected display.

Fig. 33.3 Raspberry Pi

Source: https://nemcd.com/wp-content/uploads/2017/01/raspberry-pi-3.png.

3.4 Database Development

A pre-existing recipe database is created, containing a wide range of recipes along with their ingredient requirements and preparation instructions. This database can be created by manually inputting recipes or by sourcing them from various online platforms.

3.5 User Interaction

The user can interact with the mobile application system to view the suggested recipes, select a recipe of their choice, or search for specific recipes based on preferences, dietary restrictions, or other criteria.

Fig. 33.4 User interface

Source: Author

3.6 Continuous Updates and Feedback

The system can continuously update the inventory data as items are consumed or added to the refrigerator. User feedback on the recipes can also be collected to improve the accuracy and relevance of future recipe suggestions.

3.7 Peltier Module

A Peltier module, as shown in Fig. 33.5, also known as a thermoelectric module, is a solid-state heat pump device which employs the Peltier effect to transport heat between two opposing sides of the module. The Peltier effect is the phenomena of heat absorption or release at the junction of two different materials when an electric current flows through them.

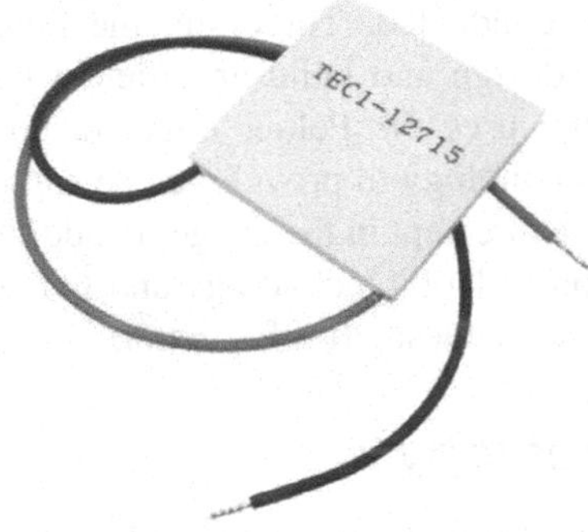

Fig. 33.5 User interface

Source: Author

A typical Peltier module is made up of numerous pairs of P-type and N-type semiconductor components placed between two ceramic plates. When a direct current is given to the module, an electrical current travel through the semiconductor pairs, causing heat to be transported from the cold side of the module to the opposite side, making it hot. The direction of heat transfer can be reversed by altering the polarity of the applied current.

4. Conclusion

In conclusion, this work focused on the development of an IoT-based Peltier module smart refrigerator with the objective of providing efficient cooling while leveraging IoT technology to create recipe ideas depending on the goods stored inside. Several main objectives were addressed during the research and development process, emphasising the need of precisely monitoring the products and providing personalised recipe recommendations based on user preferences, dietary constraints, and prior consumption patterns.

Furthermore, the study highlighted the intuitive and user-friendly interface accessible via the refrigerator's display or connected devices for seamless interaction with current smart home ecosystems, energy efficiency optimisation, and real-time inventory and recipe database updates. Overall, the IoT-based Peltier module smart refrigerator presented in this research paper provides a convenient and innovative solution for efficient cooling, inventory management, and recipe suggestions, with the potential to simplify meal planning and preparation while improving the overall kitchen user experience.

5. Future Scope

With the integration of Internet of Things (IoT) technology with Peltier module refrigeration systems, the project can offer:

- *Inventory Management:* IoT connectivity can enable smart inventory management within the refrigerator. Through sensors and embedded cameras, the system can detect and track items stored in the refrigerator, providing real-time updates on their quantity, expiration dates, and consumption patterns. Users can receive alerts when items are running low, create shopping lists, or even automate reordering through integration with online grocery services.
- *Adaptive Temperature Control:* IoT connectivity can enable adaptive temperature control based on user preferences and specific storage requirements. The smart refrigerator can recommend and automatically set ideal temperature levels for different types of food items, beverages, or medications. It can dynamically adjust cooling settings to accommodate varying storage needs, ensuring optimal freshness and minimizing energy waste.
- *Voice and Gesture Control:* Integrating voice recognition or gesture control capabilities into the IoT-based Peltier module smart refrigerator allows users to interact with the appliance more intuitively. Users can issue voice commands or perform gestures to adjust settings, check inventory, or retrieve information. This hands-free interaction enhances convenience and accessibility, especially in scenarios where manual control is impractical or inconvenient.
- *Enhanced Security and Safety:* IoT connectivity can enhance security and safety features in the smart refrigerator. It can incorporate features such as authentication, user access control, and tamper detection to prevent unauthorized access or tampering. Additionally, the system can monitor critical parameters like temperature deviations or equipment malfunctions and promptly alert users to prevent food spoilage or potential hazards.
- *Data Analytics and Insights:* The IoT-enabled smart refrigerator can collect and analyse data regarding temperature, usage patterns, energy consumption, and inventory. By leveraging advanced analytics techniques, the system can generate valuable insights for users, such as personalized food management recommendations, energy-saving suggestions, or predictive maintenance alerts. These insights can help users make informed decisions, improve efficiency, and reduce waste.

REFERENCES

1. Kakade N., S. D. Lokhande (June 2016). "IoT based Intelligent home using Smart Devices". International Journal of Innovative Research in Computer and Communication Engineering, 4(6), 2320–9798.
2. Singh D., Jain p. (July 2016). "IoT Based Smart Refrigerator System". International Journal of Advanced Research in Electronics and Communication Engineering (IJARECE), 5(7)
3. Mubeena, S, Swati, N. (April 2017). "The Design and Implementation of a Wi-Fi Based User Machine -Interacted Refrigerator", 6(14), 2319-8885.
4. Tran, J., Gilles, J., Mann, R, and Murthy, V. (October 2015) "Automated Demand Response Refrigerator Project", CE 186.
5. Ganesh, S., Venkatash S., Vidhyasagar P., Maragatharaj S., (March 2015). "Raspberry Pi Based Interactive Home Automation System through the Internet of Things". International Journal for Research in Applied Science & Engineering Technology (IJRASET), 3(3).
6. Prapulla B., Dr. Shobha and Dr. Thanuja (July 2015) "Smart refrigerator using internet of things" Journal of Multidisciplinary Engineering-Science and Tech. (JMEST), 2(7), 3159-0040.
7. Xiao, G., Chang L., Xu, w., Yuan, h. and Wang, M. (July 2014) "A Prediction Based Inventory Optimization Using Data Mining Models", Computational Sciences and Optimization (CSO), 2014 Seventh International Joint Conference on 4–6.
8. Kavya, Arumugam S (September 2016) "A Review on Predictive Analytics in Data Mining", International Journal of Chaos, Control, Modelling and Simulation (IJCCMS) Vol. 5, No. 1/2/3.
9. Kishore, R., Jain, V., Bose, S., Boppana, L., (2016) "Iot based smart security and home automation system", Computing, Communication and Automation (ICCCA), International Conference on.
10. Wang, M., Zhang, G., Zhang, J., Li, C. (June 2013) "An IoT based appliance control system for smart homes". Intelligent Control and Information Processing (ICICIP),2013 Fourth International Conference 9–11.
11. Mahajan, M. P., Nikam, R. P., Patil, V. P., Dond, R, D. (March-2017). "Smart Refrigerator using IoT". International Journal of Latest Engineering Research and Application (IJLERA) 2(3) ISSN:2455-7137, PP-86-91.
12. Wu, Hsin-Han, Chuang, Yung-Ting, (2017) "Low-Cost Refrigerator", Edge Computing (EDGE), EEE International Conference.

Advancement of Intelligent Computational Methods and Technologies (AICMT2023) – Dr. O. P. Verma et al. (eds)
© 2024 Taylor & Francis Group, London, ISBN 978-1-032-78445-8

34

Implementation of Machine Learning In IOT

Rohit[1], Nidhi[2], Alam Shadab[3], Nitish Sharma[4], Mohd. Atif Wahid[5]
Mechanical and Automation Engineering Department, Delhi Technical Campus, UP, India

ABSTRACT: The quick progression in equipment, programming, and correspondence advancements have worked with the development of gadgets associated with the Web that offer observational and information estimating capacities. By 2020, it's estimated that the all-out number of such Web-associated gadgets will run between 25 to 50 billion. With the expansion in gadgets and the development of advancements, the information created will correspondingly increment. The Web of Things (IoT), a new generation of Web-connected devices, expands the capabilities of the current Web by enabling communication and collaboration across the physical and technologically advanced realms. IoT produces Huge Information that is closely related to the growth in information volume and is characterized by speed and location reliance, a variety of modalities, and variable information quality. The development of sophisticated Internet of Things applications depends on how well this enormous amount of information is handled and examined. This essay evaluates various machine learning approaches to IoT information challenges with a crucial focus on vibrant urban areas. The main commitment of this study is the improvement of a scientific categorization of AI calculations, explaining how various methods can be applied to information to separate more elevated-level data.

KEYWORDS: Internet of things, Machine learning, Deep learning, Scheduling, Real-time systems, Graph representation

1. Introduction

1.1 Background

The advancement of innovation lately and critical enhancements to Web conventions and processing frameworks have smoothed out the correspondence between different gadgets. Conjectures propose that around 25-50 billion gadgets will be Web-associated by 2020. This has prompted the plan of the idea known as the Web of Things (IoT). As per the examination paper "Machine Learning for IoT information investigation", IoT amalgamates implanted advances concerning wired and remote correspondences, sensors, actuators, and Web-associated actual items. IoT requires information for further developing administrations to clients or improving IoT framework execution. Subsequently, the frameworks needed to obtain acrude information from different sources over the organization, break down this information and concentrate significant information. As One of the significant wellsprings of new information, IoT is set to extraordinarily profit from information science to make its applications smarter.

The objective of IoT is to establish a more brilliant climate, improve on way of life by saving time, energy, and cash, and lessen costs across various ventures. The significant speculations and progressing concentrates in IoT have made it a moving point as of late. IoT comprises of interconnected gadgets that trade information to improve execution without human mediation. IoT incorporates four fundamental parts: (1) sensors, (2) handling organizations, (3) information examination, and (4) framework checking.

The new advancement in IoT can be ascribed to the expanded utilization of radio recurrence distinguishing

[1]rohitranjan2400@gmail.com, [2]nidhi@delhitechnicalcampus.ac.in, [3]shadabkhan09@icloud.com, [4]nitishsharma9990542178@gmail.com, [5]wahidatif89@gmail.com

DOI: 10.1201/9781003487906-34

proof (RFID) labels, accessibility of minimal expense sensors, improvement of web innovation, and changes in correspondence conventions. Fundamental for IoT is availability, making correspondence conventions essential parts that need improvement.

In IoT, correspondence conventions can be arranged into three significant parts: 1. Gadget to Gadget (D2D): Works with correspondence between adjacent cell phones. 2. Gadget to Server (D2S): Gadgets send information to servers, which could be close or a long way from the gadgets. For the most part utilized in cloud handling. 3. Server to Server (S2S): Servers trade information with one another.

The information handling for these interchanges is an essential test. Different sorts of information handling techniques, For instance, data set-level edge inquiry, stream investigation, and IoT examination should be carried out. Two scientific techniques used in preparing information for transfer are handling clouds and haze. Information is gathered by sensors and IoT devices, extracted from raw data, and moved to other objects, devices, or servers via the Web as part of the IoT's overall project.

A critical test in executing machine learning with IoT is the information move cycle to the hubs for preparation. To handle this issue, we have taken on the MQTT (Message Line Telemetry Transport) convention. It's a client-server-based informing transport convention intended for machine-to-machine and IoT applications for obliged networks. To decide the most reasonable calculation for handling and dynamic savvy information produced from IoT gadgets, grasping these three ideas: the IoT application, the attributes of IoT information, and the information-driven approach of AI algorithms are fundamental.

1.2 Understanding Machine Learning

Artificial intelligence (AI)'s machine learning subfield gives computers the capacity to learn for themselves and get better based on prior knowledge, all without explicit programming. The core of machine learning is the "IMPLEMENTATION OF MACHINE LEARNING IN IOT" construction of computer programs that can learn on their own by accessing and utilizing data. Data inputs, such as observations, examples, firsthand experiences, or instructions, are often where the learning process begins. Finding trends in the data and improving decision making going forward are the objectives.

1.3 Different Methods of Machine Learning

Supervised Machine Learning

These algorithms use previously learned lessons applied to fresh data to forecast future events. It starts by looking at a training dataset that has been previously studied, from which the algorithm constructs a function to forecast output values. After adequate training, the system can predict targets for any new input.

Additionally, the formula can compare its results to the accurate results, spot mistakes, and adjust the model as necessary.

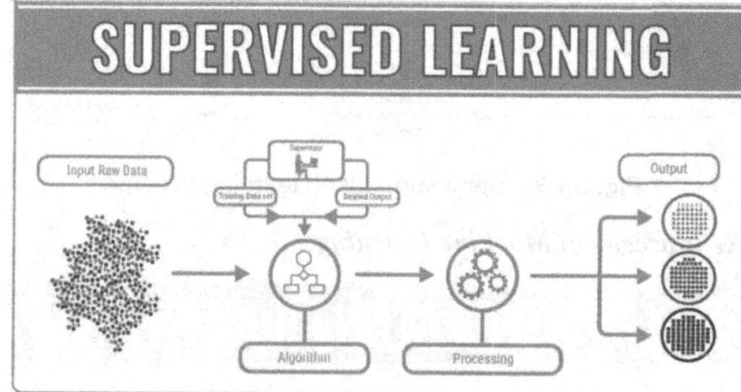

Fig. 34.1 Supervised learning process

The ultimate goal is to make it possible for computers to learn on their own, without the aid of humans, so that they can modify their behavior as necessary.

Unsupervised Machine Learning

When training data is neither categorized nor labeled, these algorithms are used. Unsupervised learning seeks to infer a function from unlabeled data that can describe a hidden structure. The system doesn't have a specific output in mind; instead, it wants to examine the data and deduce conclusions to explain any underlying structures.

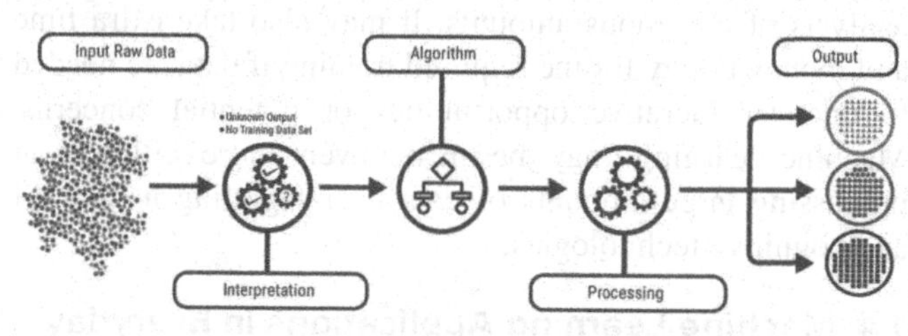

Fig. 34.2 Unsupervised learning process

Semi-supervised Machine Learning

These algorithms employ training data that are both labeled and unlabeled, frequently a small quantity of the former and a big amount of the latter, making them a mix of supervised and unsupervised learning. These tools can significantly increase learning accuracy supervised learning is frequently used when the labelled data available for training needs substantial resources to use or learn from, whereas unlabeled data is simpler to obtain.

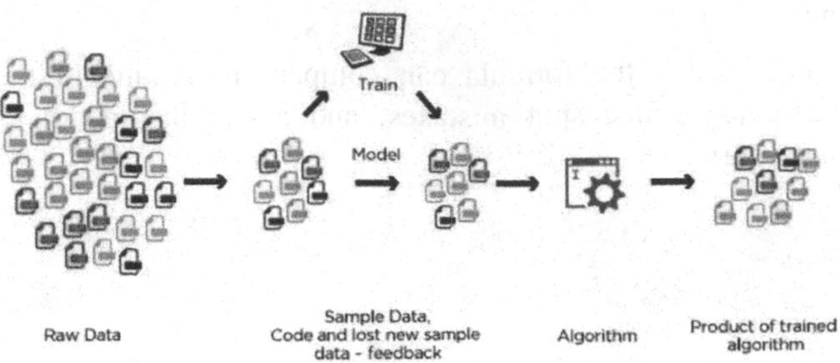

Fig. 34.3 Semi-supervised learning process

Reinforcement Machine Learning

Fig. 34.4 Reinforcement learning process

Algorithms that interact with their environment, carry out tasks, and identify errors or rewards. With the help of this technique, software agents and machines may decide what actions to take in a given situation to maximize performance.

The reinforcement signal, straightforward reward feedback, directs the agent to choose the optimum course of action. Although machine learning can speed up and improve the analysis of enormous amounts, It may also take extra time and money to pay for the required training if data are needed to uncover lucrative opportunities or potential concerns. Machine learning may be made even more efficient at processing large amounts of data by integrating it with AI and cognitive technologies.

1.4 Machine Learning Applications in Everyday Life

Digital Personal Assistants

Machine learning is used by digital personal assistants like Siri, Alexa, and Google Now to improve their responses based on prior experiences. These technologies are essential to products like Amazon Echo, Google Home, and Samsung Bixby on the Samsung S8, as they can respond to queries, carry out tasks, and deliver personalized information.

Commuting Predictions

Utilizing data gathered from drivers, machine learning helps GPS navigation services estimate traffic. Machine learning is used by ridesharing businesses like Uber to set prices and optimize routes.

Video Surveillance

AI-powered surveillance systems Eliminate the need for ongoing human monitoring by using machine learning to recognize suspicious activities and get better over time.

Social Media Services

By personalizing content, enhancing ad targeting, proposing possible friends, and enabling features like facial recognition, machine learning improves the user experience on social media sites.

Email Spam and Malware Filtering

To improve spam filters and identify malicious activity, machine learning techniques are deployed. This system can recognize coding patterns and quickly find new virus variants.

Online Customer Support

Machine learning is used by chatbots to deliver efficient customer service. They gradually gain a better understanding of customer inquiries and give better answers.

Search Engine Result Refining

Machine learning is used by search engines like Google to improve search results depending on user involvement and behaviour.

Online Fraud Detection

Machine learning assists in securing the internet by identifying fraudulent activity. For example, PayPal employs machine learning to prevent money laundering.

2. Internet of Things (IoT)

Interconnected physical devices that can gather and transport data over the Internet without human intervention are included in the Internet of Things (IoT).These devices, which have been given an IP address, can interact with their internal states orthe outside environment, which can have an impact on how decisions are made.

2.1 Significance of IoT

Devices can send and/or receive information when they are connected to the internet, giving the impression that they are "smart." IoT devices fall into three categories: those that receive and act on information, those that gather and transmit information, and those that do both.

2.2 Devices Collecting and Sending Information

Devices with sensors may automatically gather data from their environment and make an intelligent decisions. Examples of these sensors are temperature, motion, moisture, air quality, and light sensors.

2.3 Devices Receiving and Acting on Information

Many machines take information in and do something with it. For instance, a printer might receive a document file and print it, or a car might unlock its doors after receiving a signal from a set of car keys.

2.4 Devices Doing Both

When devices can both gather/send and receive/act on information, the whole potential of the Internet of Thing is realized. For instance, in farming, sensors can gather data on soil moisture, and the irrigation system can then use this data to autonomously water crops.

3. Literature Survey

3.1 Machine Learning in the Era of IoT

Industries have seen a radical change as a result of the convergence of low-cost sensors, widespread connection, and distributed intelligence, producing vast amounts of data that are beyond the capacity of human processing.

This prompts important queries: Will firms change rapidly enough to maintain their advantage over the competition? How can we use our environment's richness of knowledge and intelligence as humans? To properly use these new sources and data streams, organizations must streamline their internal data management. The era of intelligent, interconnected devices also portends an increase in decision-making autonomy, as devices will be able to adjust, correct, and repair themselves without human assistance.

Device networks occasionally can operate as integrated systems that can be modified in creative ways.

Larger systems made up of numerous device networks will share data and work together as a symbiotic ecosystem of data and devices. In this context, machine learning, a catch-all term for several methods of extracting insights from data, will be crucial. In addition, as businesses prepare for the Internet of Things (IoT), traditional business and data analysis methods will still be essential.

3.2 Neural Network

Artificial Neural Networks (ANN) find applications in diverse fields due to their interdisciplinary nature:

Speech Recognition: ANN facilitates easy interaction with computers via spoken language, although issues like limited vocabulary, retraining for different speakers, and varying conditions persist.

Character Recognition: ANN enables automatic recognition of handwritten characters and digits, a facet of pattern recognition.

Signature Verification: ANN helps authenticate individuals in legal transactions by classifying signatures as genuine or forged based on a trained neural network algorithm.

Human Face Recognition: ANN assists in identifying faces, a complex biometric task due to the characterization of non-face images. This involves image preprocessing, dimensionality reduction, and subsequent classification using neural network training algorithms.

3.3 Deep Neural Networks

An artificial neural network (ANN) with multiple layers between the input and output layers is referred to as a deep neural network (DNN). Whether there is a linear or nonlinear relationship between the input and the output, the DNN selects the right mathematical modifications to turn the input into the output.

3.4 Deep Learning

Artificial intelligence known as "deep learning" imitates the human brain's ability to recognize patterns and process data. It is a subset of machine learning in the field of artificial intelligence (AI) and uses networks that can learn unsupervised from unstructured or unlabeled input. It goes by the terms deep neural networks and deep neural learning (Agarwal et al., 2018).

3.5 Machine Learning vs Deep Learning

Compares machine learning to deep learning Machine learning is one of the most widely used AI techniques for large-scale data analysis. It is a self-adaptive algorithm that improves over time or in reaction to fresh data in terms of its ability to analyze and identify patterns. For instance, a business that manages digital payments might utilize machine learning methods to identify and prevent fraud in its network. All transactions on the digital platform are processed by the computational algorithm built into a computer model, which also analyses the information for trends and abnormalities.

As a subclass of machine learning, deep learning uses artificial neural networks with hierarchical layers to carry out machine learning tasks. Similar to how the real brain is built, these artificial neural networks have interconnected neuron nodes that form a network structure. Deep learning systems' hierarchical structure allows machines to interpret data in a non-linear manner, unlike conventional programs that analyze data in a linear form. Additional factors like time, location, IP address, store type, and other pertinent characteristics that could point to fraudulent activity are included in a deep learning approach. Deep learning takes into account more factors than a conventional system, which might merely take the transaction amount into account to find fraud or money laundering. Before being exported to the second layer of the neural network, raw input data from the first layer, such as the transaction amount, is processed there. The subsequent levels process the data from the preceding layer and add additional data, such as the user's IP address.

To increase the neural network's ability for pattern recognition, this process keeps moving up its tiers. Each layer takes in new raw information, like location.

3.6 The Role of Deep Learning in IoT

It becomes apparent that deep learning might be used to get precise insights from the unprocessed sensor data gathered by IoT devices placed in challenging locations. Despite having strict performance and power requirements, it enables IoT devices to comprehend unstructured multimedia input and react intelligently to the user and environmental events. Machine learning (ML) is generally applicable to a variety of IoT product use cases.

The number of products that collect environmental data and use conventional machine learning techniques to interpret it has lately increased in the IoT industry. For instance, Google's Nest Learning Thermostat logs temperature data and employs algorithms to comprehend human schedules and temperature preferences. However; it suffers from multimedia data that is not organized, such as audio signals and graphics. Modern deep learning technologies, which use neural networks to analyze their environment, are being used by emerging IoT gadgets.

For instance, Amazon Echo understands voice requests from people. It transforms auditory impulses into a word list, then searches for pertinent information using this word list.

Deep learning applications for IoT hardware usually have stringent real-time requirements. To respond rapidly to target events, security camera-based object-recognition activities typically require a detection latency of less than 500 ms. Intelligent IoT business equipment routinely offloads knowledge to the cloud

Due to expensive and constrained network connections, it may be challenging to meet real-time needs. Because deep learning on the device is unaffected by connection quality, it is a better option.

3.7 MQTT

The straightforward messaging protocol known as MQTT, or Message Queuing Telemetry Transport, was created especially for devices with little bandwidth. MQTT makes it possible to read and publish data from sensor nodes, control outputs with commands, and do much more.As a result, it makes the process of setting up communication between various devices simpler.

MQTT's main features include:

- Publish/Subscribe Mechanism for MQTT in this system, a device can subscribe to a topic to receive messages or publish a message under a certain subject.
- MQTT messages MQTT messages are used to communicate information between devices. Data or commands may be included in this information.
- MQTT topic areas To indicate interest in incoming messages or choose where to post a message, topics are used.
- Broker for MQTT the broker's main duty is to receive all communications, screen them to see who could be interested, ascertain who is interested, and then send the message to everyone who has subscribed. There are numerous brokers from which to pick. On desktop PCs or small-form-factor microcontrollers like the Raspberry Pi, Mosquittoan open-source broker, can be installed locally. Another choice is Cloud MQTT, a cloud-based broker.

3.8 Cloud MQTT Overview

The MQTT protocol, which offers simple methods for facilitating messaging via a publish/subscribe queueing approach, is implemented by Mosquito. You can focus on application development using Cloud MQTT rather than becoming distracted by worries about platform upkeep or broker scalability.

3.9 MQTT: A Publish/Subscribe Protocol for Wireless Sensor Network

Due to its potential in several fields, including industrial automation, asset management, environmental monitoring, and the transportation industry, wireless sensor networks (WSNs) have recently attracted more attention. Many of these applications involve sending data gathered by sensors to software running on conventional network infrastructure. WSNs must therefore integrate with these established networks.

Environmental data is gathered by a large number of battery powered Sensor/Actuator (SA) devices operating within

WSNs and sent to gateways for further transmission to the applications (Hunkler et al., 2008). For sensor administration, configuration, and software upgrades, information also flows the other way.

The publish/subscribe (pub/sub) communication paradigm is based on subscribers who want to consume specific information and publishers who produce it. By managing subscriptions, the broker organization makes sure data is delivered from publishers to subscribers.

The three main types of pub/sub systems are topic-based, type-based, and content-based. The topic-based pub/sub protocol MQTT allows character-string-based hierarchical topics, enabling the subscription to several topics (Li et al., 2018).

MQTT supports fundamental end-to-end Quality of Service (QoS). Depending on the required level of delivery dependability, MQTT offers three QoS levels (Dawei et al., 2017). A relationship between the client and the broker must be established before publications and subscriptions can be transferred. The broker keeps track of the health of the client or connection using a "keep-alive" timer. A crucial component of MQTT is support for the "Will" idea, which enables applications to identify device and link failures (Laxmi and Mishra, 2018).

4. Methodology

4.1 Overview

This research aimed to develop a flexible architecture for Internet of Things (IoT) devices that can analyze real-time data.

Think about a scenario where a swarm of IoT devices is installed in an industrial setting with a range of sensors to track the environment (such as brightness, humidity, temperature, wind, radiation level, etc.).

4.2 Approach

The steps in our strategy for this project are as follows:

1. Assembling an Internet of Things (IoT) gadget with sensors to gather data.
2. Real-time data delivery via the Internet using the MQTT protocol.
3. Obtaining the most recent data from our training nodes.
4. Delaying until our Mini-Batch Gradient Descent method has sent the training nodes the smallest number of records necessary.
5. Performing accuracy validation on the incoming data and training it.
6. The IoT devices share the weight matrix from the model that fits the data the best, giving them the freedom to choose their behavior.

4.3 Challenges

The following difficulties were experienced throughout the project:

- Limited availability of IoT devices to work with;
- Lack of access to a controlled and isolated environment to build a dataset free of noise.

To overcome these challenges, we addressed the first issue by simulating the data transmission of IoT devices using a static dataset. We were able to mimic the effects of real-time data transmission by sending data from other databases one record at a time. This allowed us to mimic IoT device behavior even when there wasn't a controlled and silent setting.

5. Results and Observations

When developing the neural network architecture, the appropriate number of neurons in the hidden layers must be taken into account. Despite not directly interacting with the outside environment, these layers have a substantial influence on the outcome (Mahdavinejad et al., 2018). It is important to carefully evaluate the number of hidden layers and the number of neurons in each hidden layer. Underfitting results from using too few neurons in the buried layers.

When there aren't enough neurons in the hidden layers to fully capture the signals in a difficult dataset, underfitting takes place (Yasumoto et al., 2016) Nevertheless, overusing neurons in the buried layers might result in a number of negative consequences. First, it could result in overfitting, which happens when a neural network has too much processing power and struggles to deal with the sparse data in the training set. Second, having a lot of neurons can make training the network difficult due to the training period being too long. There needs to be a balance between having too few and too many neurons in the buried layers (Earley, 2015).

The following suggestions are only a few of the general methods for determining the appropriate number of neurons in the hidden layers:

- Both the input layer and the output layer ought to have an equal number of buried neurons.
- The number of hidden neurons should not be greater than the sum of the sizes of the input and output layers and should be less than twice the size of the input layer.

These laws serve as a framework for thought. However, selecting the ideal neural network design typically necessitates trial and error. We constructed several nodes and trained them individually using varied real-time data from datasets to address this issue.

We developed a variety of models, varying the number of hidden layers and neurons in each layer, and we assessed the accuracy of each model separately.

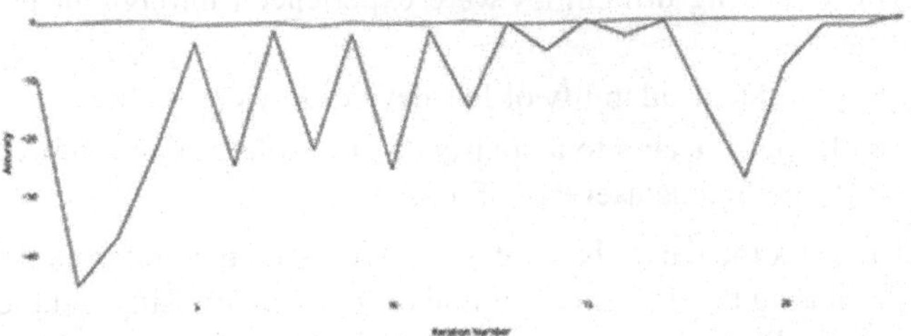

Fig. 34.5 Case 1-Accuracy model

The best-fit models consistently had accuracy, while under fitted models had low accuracy. Overfitted models initially had great accuracy but gradually lost it. For instance, when three hidden layers with 25, 20, and 15 neurons each were taken into account, the accuracy reached a high and then rapidly declined on the plotted graph.

In a second study, we contrasted two scenarios: the first used 10, 7, and 5 hidden neurons, while the second used 15, and 10 hidden neurons.

Since it oscillated less and maintained constant accuracy, the pink line on the graph, which represents the first scenario, was more effective than the red line, which represents the second scenario.

To determine the appropriate number of hidden layers and neurons, we tested with several combinations and created a graph based on the accuracy attained by each combination. The generated graph displayed the ideal outcomes as well as the positioning of the hidden layers and neurons in our neural network architecture (Maini, 2023).

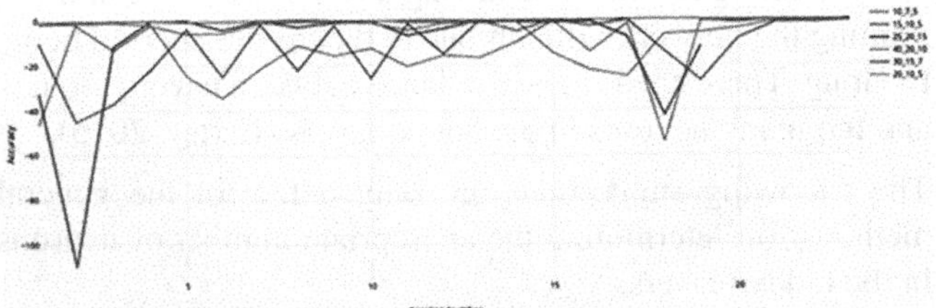

Fig. 34.6 Case 2- Accuracy model

6. Conclusion

Machine learning techniques are now frequently utilized to handle and analyze data from different sources to solve actual problems. Instead of retaining the sensor data, we used it directly to train our models. This approach was particularly helpful because it did not require a specialized server or specific database to store the data.

The key concepts and theories that are important to our endeavor are discussed in depth. We have discussed the methodology, jargon, and our reasoning for selecting a certain topic for the project. The multiple methodologies and technologies are explored in detail, including references to numerous scholarly research articles. Diagrams and charts are used to describe the implementation of the various algorithms employed at different project stages contains our implementation-phase data, a discussion of the impact of selecting different hidden layers, and graphs for visual assistance. Finally, the project's likely future directions and objectives are explained.

7. Future Scope

We have mentioned various enhancements that could be done because this project is currently in its early stages:

1. A Recurrent Neural Network (RNN) implementation is something we intend to do because data is time-sensitive.
2. We want to replace current data sets used for data transmission with IoT devices.
3. To enable autonomous operation and prediction-making, we want to send the best model to every IoT device.
4. Regularization in combination with gradient descent optimization approaches like Momentum and Adagrad may improve our operational effectiveness.
5. To assess the precision of prediction, we intend to develop a mathematical function for the generation of fictitious data that is augmented with Gaussian error.
6. With the help of the document "Enabling Embedded Inference Engine with the ARM Compute Library: A Case Study," we hope to accelerate the design.

REFERENCES

1. Mahdavinejad, Mohammad Saeid, Mohammadreza Rezvan, Mohammadamin Barekatain, Peyman Adibi, Payam Barnaghi, and Amit P. Sheth. 2018. "Machine Learning for Internet of Things Data Analysis: A Survey." *Digital Communications and Networks* 4 (3): 16175.https://doi.org/10.1016/j.dcan.2017.10.002
2. Yasumoto, Keiichi, Hirozumi Yamaguchi, and Hiroshi Shigeno. 2016. "Survey of Real-Time Processing Technologies of IoT Data Streams." *Journal of Information Processing* 24 (2): 195–202. https://doi.org/10.2197/ipsjjip.24.195
3. Earley, Seth. 2015. "Analytics, Machine Learning, and the Internet of Things." *IT Professional* 17 (1): 10–13. https://doi.org/10.1109/mitp.2015.3

4. H. Li, K. Ota and M. Dong. 2018. "Learning IoT in Edge: Deep Learning for the Internet of Things with Edge Computing". *IEEE Network* 32(1): 96–101. https://doi: 10.1109/MNET.2018.1700202.
5. U. Hunkeler, H Truong and Stanford-Clark, A. 2008 "MQTT-S A publish/subscribe protocol for Wireless Sensor Networks". *3rd International Conference on Communication Systems Software and Middleware and Workshops*, pg n. 791–798
6. Sun Dawei, Liu Shaoshan and Jean-Luc, Gaudiot.2017 "Enabling Embedded Inference Engine with the ARM Compute Library: A Case Study". arXiv:1704.03751 https://arxiv.org/pdf/1704.03751.pdf
7. Aggarwal, Charu C. 2018. *Neural Networks and Deep Learning*.Springer EBooks. https://doi.org/10.1007/978-3-319-94463-0.
8. Laxmi, A.R., and Mishra, A. 2018 "RFID based Logistic Management System using Internet of Things (IoT)". *Second International Conference on Electronics, Communication and Aerospace Technology (ICECA), Coimbatore, India* pp. 556–559, doi: 10.1109/ICECA.2018.8474721.
9. Maini, Vishal, and Samer Ssabri. 2023. Machine Learning For Humans: *Introduction to Machine Learning with Python.*

Note: All the figures in this chapter were made by the author.

Advancement of Intelligent Computational Methods and Technologies (AICMT2023) – Dr. O. P. Verma et al. (eds)
© 2024 Taylor & Francis Group, London, ISBN 978-1-032-78445-8

35

Review on Online Cloth Shopping

Udit Sharma[1], Ajay Krishnan[2] , Kashish Malhan[3], Shivam Saurabh[4]
Computer Science & Engineering, Delhi Technical Campus, Greater Noida, India

ABSTRACT: To give the popularity of Internet shopping is on the rise in the modern digital age, completely changing how people buy clothing. This abstract introduces "Seamless Styles," a cutting-edge online clothing store that provides fashion fans with a distinctive and immersive shopping experience. The most recent technological developments are embraced by Seamless Styles, which also offers a user-friendly interface and a large selection of high-quality clothing. Our website offers personalized recommendations based on users' tastes, body types, and style choices by utilizing cutting-edge algorithms, ensuring an improved and tailored purchasing experience. The website's user-friendly layout makes it simple for visitors to browse a wide range of clothing options, filter them based on their requirements, and examine in-depth product descriptions and high-resolution pictures. By enabling clients to virtually try on clothing and evaluate how well it fits and looks before making a purchase, the revolutionary virtual fitting room function reduces the likelihood of size-related disappointments. Seamless Styles offers secure payment methods, easy checkout procedures, and a hassle-free return policy to increase customer happiness.

KEYWORDS: Virtual fitting room, Augmented reality, Secure payment, Social media integration, Fashion, Sustainability, User-centric design, and Online clothing purchasing.

1. Introduction

With the flexibility and convenience of online shopping, we hope to give you a simple and delightful experience while you look for the ideal clothing to suit your preferences and style. We have a large selection to satisfy your needs, whether you're looking for activewear, special occasion outfits, formal wear, or casual clothing. We regularly refresh our collection with the newest styles and cutting-edge designs to keep you on top of your style game. You can quickly browse through our product categories and filter by size, color, price range, and more with our user-friendly navigation and search capabilities to discover exactly what you're searching for. Before making a purchase, you can use the thorough descriptions, high-quality pictures, and customer reviews that come with each item. Your personal and financial data is safeguarded on our website by a secure payment gateway. Additionally, we provide a variety of payment methods, such as credit cards, debit cards, and electronic wallets, to ensure flexibility and ease while carrying out your transactions. Along with our extensive range of clothes, we also offer outstanding customer service to address any questions or issues you might have. Our helpful and accommodating customer service team is on hand by live chat, email, or phone and ready to help you at any stage of your buying experience (Kawaf and Tagg 2012).

2. Problem Definition

The issue at hand has to do with an online clothes store. The website has seen a noticeable fall in client satisfaction and sales despite its popularity and wide selection of products. Numerous customers have expressed annoyance and a variety of problems while using the platform and making purchases. The website's user interface and general user experience are among the primary issues. Customers have complained

[1]uditsharmabca@delhitechnicalcampus.ac.in, [2]ajaykrishnanabca@delhitechnicalcampus.ac.in, [3]kashishmalhanbca@delhitechnicalcampus.ac.in, [4]shivamsaurabhbca@delhitechnicalcampus.ac.in,

DOI: 10.1201/9781003487906-35

that the poorly organized categories and subcategories make finding the clothing they want difficult. It might be frustrating and time-consuming to use the search feature because it frequently produces incorrect or irrelevant results (Molinillo et al. 2017). Additionally, customers are left in the dark about the material, sizing, and other crucial aspects because the website lacks clear and comprehensive product descriptions.

2.1 Objectives

Providing our consumers with a convenient and delightful purchasing experience is the main goal of our online clothing store. We strive to provide a broad selection of high-quality apparel options that accommodate different styles, sizes, and tastes. Our user-friendly website makes it simple for clients to browse through our huge selection, conduct precise product searches, and make purchases with confidence. We work hard to design an intuitive online shopping experience where shoppers can read thorough product descriptions, see crisp pictures of the clothing from all perspectives, and obtain precise sizing information. In order to improve the entire purchasing experience, we also provide personalized recommendations based on customer preferences and previous purchases (Ladhari, Gonthier, and Lajante 2019). The data flow diagram is shown in Fig. 35.1.

3. Technology Used

3.1 JavaScript

High-level programming languages like JavaScript are frequently used for creating websites. Although it may be used for server-side programming, mobile app development, and even desktop application development, its main function is to bring interactivity and dynamic elements to websites (Kim and Forsythe 2008).

3.2 .Net

Microsoft produced the well-known software development framework known as. NET. It offers developers a complete and adaptable framework for creating a variety of applications,

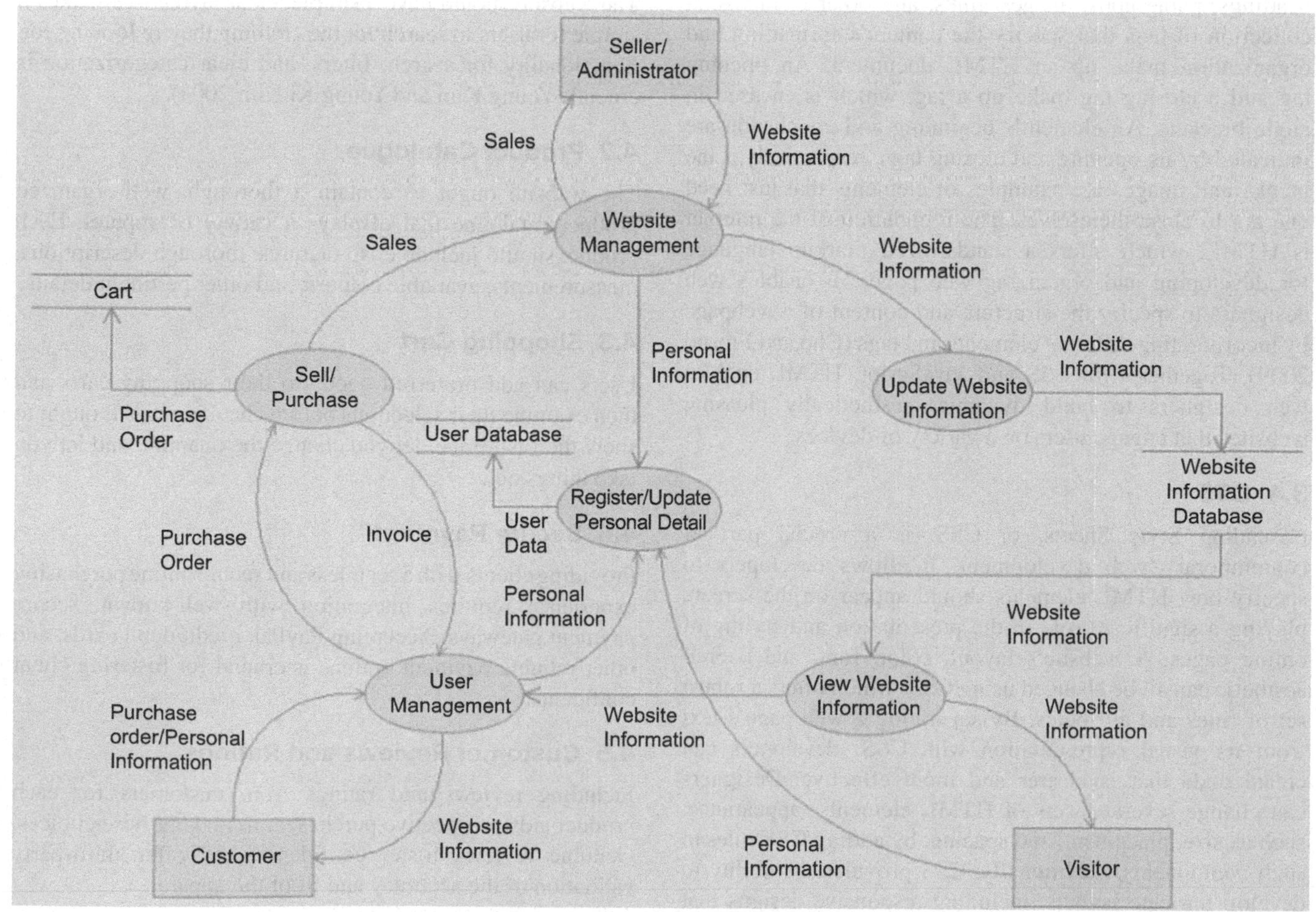

Fig. 35.1 Data flow diagram

Source: https://www.conceptdraw.com/How-To-Guide/online-store-dfd

from desktop and cloud-based programs to mobile and web-based ones. The support for several languages in.NET is one of its important features. Different programming languages, including C#, Visual Basic.NET, and F#, can be used by developers while still utilizing the underlying.NET infrastructure. Due to this flexibility, developers are free to select the language that best meets their needs or their level of comfort. The development process is streamlined by the extensive selection of libraries, frameworks, and tools provided by .NET (Hansen and Jensen 2009). It comprises the cross-platform.NET Core framework, which enables programmers to create apps that run on Windows, macOS, and Linux, as well as the.NET Framework, which is generally used for creating Windows applications.

3.3 HTML

The Hypertext Markup Language, also known as HTML, is a key component of the World Wide Web. It is used as the industry standard markup language to build web pages and organize their information. Web designers can use HTML to specify a webpage's structure and layout, including its headings, paragraphs, images, links, and other elements. A collection of tags that specify the content's formatting and organization make up an HTML document. An opening tag and a closing tag make up a tag, which is encased in angle brackets. An element's beginning and conclusion are indicated by its opening and closing tags, respectively. Line breaks and images are examples of elements that just need one tag to close themselves. The foundation of the internet is HTML, which offers a standardized markup language for developing and organizing web pages. It enables web designers to specify the structure and content of a webpage by incorporating different elements and tags (Cho and Fiorito 2009). Together with CSS and JavaScript, HTML enables web designers to build dynamic, aesthetically pleasing websites that engage users on a variety of devices.

3.4 CSS

Cascading Style Sheets, or CSS, is a crucial part of contemporary web development. It allows developers to specify how HTML elements should appear on the screen, playing a significant role in the presentation and styling of online pages. A website's layout, color, font, and overall aesthetic can all be changed using CSS, which offers a robust set of rules and attributes. By separating a web page's text from its visual representation with CSS, developers can create code that is clearer and more effective. Designers can change several facets of HTML elements' appearance, such as size, placement, and spacing, by adding CSS rules to such components. Additionally, CSS provides the ability to develop intricate layouts, including responsive designs that fluidly adjust to various screen sizes and devices.

3.5 MySQL

A substantial contribution to the field of data management has been made by MySQL, a strong and well-liked relational database management system. MySQL, created by Oracle Corporation, has become widely used because of its simplicity, scalability, and durability. For storing, retrieving, and modifying data across a range of applications and industries, it provides a trustworthy and effective solution. The capacity of MySQL to manage massive volumes of data while retaining great performance is one of its important advantages. It is appropriate for both small-scale applications and enterprise-level systems due to its design to optimize query execution and handle concurrent operations. MySQL provides versatility in data storage and management techniques by supporting a variety of storage engines, including InnoDB and MyISAM (Dennis et al. 2010).

4. Important Components

4.1 User Interface (UI)

The website should have a simple, clear layout that makes it simple for users to search for the clothing they're looking for. Functionality for search, filters, and clear categorization is crucial (Young Kim and Young Ki Kim 2004).

4.2 Product Catalogue

The website ought to contain a thorough, well-organized product catalogue that displays a variety of apparel. Each product should include crisp pictures, thorough descriptions, measurements, available colours, and other pertinent details.

4.3 Shopping Cart

Users can add preferred goods to their shopping carts and then examine their selections before checking out. It ought to show the final price, let you change the quantity, and let you take things out.

4.4 Secure Payment

Providing clients with a seamless and secure online purchasing experience requires integration with well-known, secure payment gateways. Accepting PayPal, credit/debit cards, and other reliable payment options is crucial for fostering client confidence.

4.5 Customer Reviews and Ratings

Including reviews and ratings from customers for each product aids prospective purchasers in making wise choices. Genuine reviews foster confidence and offer third-party validation of the accuracy and fit of the apparel.

4.6 Customer Service

It's critical to provide dependable customer service channels, such as live chat, email, or phone help. Customer loyalty and satisfaction can be increased by promptly responding to questions and concerns from clients and resolving any problems (Sekozawa, Mitsuhashi, and Ozawa 2011).

4.7 Personalized Shopping Experience

Online clothing retailers are now able to offer personalized shopping experiences because of developments in artificial intelligence and machine learning. These websites can provide customized recommendations, virtual changing rooms, and style guidance by analysing the data and tastes of their users, improving the overall buying experience.

4.8 Sustainable Fashion

Demand for ethically sourced and sustainable clothes is increasing as environmental issues and sustainability become more widely known. By offering a specialized platform for sustainable fashion businesses, online clothing retailers can capitalise on this trend and empower shoppers to make more thoughtful decisions.

4.9 Social Commerce Integration

Social networking platforms are increasingly crucial conduits for e-commerce. This is known as social commerce integration. Online apparel stores may communicate with customers, expand their following, and use user-generated material for promotion and social proof by integrating with social commerce.

4.10 International Expansion

Online apparel stores have the potential to transcend national boundaries and enter international marketplaces. They can serve clients from all over the world thanks to effective logistics and streamlined shipping procedures, increasing their clientele and earnings potential.

The online shopping flow has been shown below.

[Start]

[User Registration] → [User Login] Browse Products] →

[Select Product] → [Add to Cart] → [View Cart] → [Modify Cart]

[Checkout] → [Billing and Shipping]

[Payment] → [Order Confirmation]

[Order Processing] → [Shipping and Tracking] → [Delivery and Receipt]

[Feedback and Reviews] → [Returns and Support]

[Logout]

[End]

5. Conclusion

Development of online apparel purchasing websites has fundamentally changed how we buy clothing. Like never before, these platforms provide convenience, variety, and accessibility. Customers may browse through a wide variety of things from the comfort of their homes with only a few clicks, negating the need to go to physical stores. Consumers are now better equipped to make informed judgements thanks to the ability to compare pricing, read reviews, and access other information. Additionally, to ensure a smooth purchasing experience, online clothing shopping companies frequently offer thorough product descriptions, sizing charts, and simple return procedures. Deliveries to consumer doorsteps are convenient and save them time and effort, which increases their appeal. Additionally, these websites have provided tiny and independent designers with chances to demonstrate their abilities and connect with a global clientele. In general, online clothing purchasing websites have grown in popularity among fashion fans because they offer a convenient, interesting, and fun shopping experience.

REFERENCES

1. Kawaf, Fadia, and Stephen Tagg. "Online shopping environments in fashion shopping: An SOR based review." The Marketing Review 12, no. 2 (2012): 161–180.
2. Kim, Jinwoo, and Sandra Forsythe. "Adoption of virtual try-on technology for online apparel shopping." Journal of Interactive Marketing 22, no. 2 (2008): 45–59.
3. Molinillo, Sebastián, Begoña Gómez-Ortiz, José Pérez-Aranda, and Antonio Navarro-García. "Building customer loyalty: The effect of experiential state, the value of shopping, and trust and perceived value of service on online clothes shopping." Clothing and Textiles Research Journal35, no. 3 (2017): 156–171.
4. Ladhari, Riadh, Jérôme Gonthier, and Mathieu Lajante. "Generation Y and online fashion shopping: Orientations and profiles." Journal of Retailing and Consumer Services 48 (2019): 113–121.
5. Hansen, Torben, and Jan Moller Jensen. "Shopping orientation and online clothing purchases: the role of gender and purchase situation." European Journal of Marketing 43, no. 9/10 (2009): 1154–1170.
6. Cho, Hanna, and Susan S. Fiorito. "Acceptance of online customization for apparel shopping." International Journal of Retail & Distribution Management 37, no. 5 (2009): 389–407.
7. Dennis, Charles, Angela Morgan, Lisa T. Wright, and Charlene Jayawardhena. "The influences of social e-shopping in enhancing young women's online shopping behaviour." Journal of Customer Behaviour 9, no. 2 (2010): 151–174.
8. Young Kim, Eun, and Young Ki Kim. "Predicting online purchase intentions for clothing products." European Journal of Marketing 38, no. 7 (2004): 883–897.
9. Sekozawa, Takeshi, Hiroko Mitsuhashi, and Yoshinori Ozawa. "One-to-one recommendation system in apparel online shopping." Electronics and Communications in Japan 94, no. 1 (2011): 51–60.

Advancement of Intelligent Computational Methods and Technologies (AICMT2023) – Dr. O. P. Verma et al. (eds)

36

An Advanced Clone for Over the Top Platform

Shahbuddin[1], Siddharth Sharma[2], Raghav Sethi[3]
Department of Computer Applications, Delhi Technical Campus, affiliated by GGSIPU, Greater Noida, India
Tanupreet Sabharwal[4]
Department of Artificial Intelligence & Machine Learning, Delhi Technical Campus affiliated by GGSIPU, Greater Noida, India
Jatin Sharma[5]
Department of Computer Applications, Delhi Technical Campus, affiliated by GGSIPU, Greater Noida, India

ABSTRACT: In order to enable you develop your own on-demand OTT network similar to Netflix, where you can stream an unlimited number of films and TV series for a single cheap monthly fee, the project known as Netflix Clone was created. Netflix Clone streams films and TV episodes to new places with sizable viewership via the Internet. The ability of Netflix Clone Script to speak several languages also enables the streaming of films and programs in indigenous tongues. The largest online service sector in the market is the entertainment sector. The Netflix Clone has alluring qualities that are necessary for a profitable internet streaming service. Users may enjoy watching them in HD whenever and wherever they like. It allows users to watch TV series and films online, offering a variety of programs like drama, thriller, action, murder mystery, comedy, and documentaries. In this research paper, we tried to understand the working of Netflix, how it fetches the movies data and tried to build a Netflix clone using react. JS and TMDB API. We made the website using HTML and styled it through CSS. In this clone website, we have signup page, profile page. We can also fetch the details of any movie in the Netflix. It fetches the movies data from a third-party API. It also has the trailer pop-ups.

KEYWORDS: CSS, HTML, JS, Front-End, Back-End, Netflix, TMDB, API, OTT

1. Introduction

On a device with an internet connection, Netflix subscribers can stream films and TV series without being interrupted by ads. It makes use of the internet to stream films and TV episodes from our servers to your ISP's (Internet Service Provider) account on the internet. An exhaustive white label A "Netflix clone" is a website and mobile app that mimics Netflix but has more features and is extremely scalable (Khalifa et al., 2002). An on-demand video streaming service like Netflix is called a "Netflix clone." Before you can easily create a Netflix clone, it aids you in getting started with your own video streaming service. A Netflix original can get a full white label solution from a Netflix clone. In order to start your own on-demand OTT network similar to Netflix, where you can stream infinite films and TV series for one low monthly fee, you can use Netflix Clone expense on a monthly basis. Netflix Clone streams films and TV episodes to new places with sizable viewership via the Internet. Regional language broadcasting is also made possible by Netflix Clone Script's multilingual capabilities. This is a replica of the Netflix website made with Firebase as the backend and react. JS as the front end. It is not a copy, and it lacks some of the features found on the Netflix website. Thus, the whole idea is innovative and user friendly. With Netflix Clone, you can create your own on-demand OTT platform similar to Netflix,

[1]mshahbuddin216@gmail.com, [2]siddarthas378@gmail.com, [3]raghavsethi751@gmail.com, [4]t.sabharwal@delhitechnicalcampus.ac.in, [5]jatinsharmavip860@gmail.com

DOI: 10.1201/9781003487906-36

where you can stream an unlimited number of films and TV series for a single modest monthly fee. Netflix Clone streams films and TV episodes to new places with sizable viewership via the Internet. Regional language broadcasting is also made possible by multilingual capabilities.

2. Literature Review

The biggest provider of internet television in the world is Netflix, a very sizable entertainment firm. Nearly 38 million people worldwide subscribe to Netflix. Netflix's "original series"—original programming that is released by Netflix—featuring Shotgun Wedding, Hemlock Grove, The Ropes, House of Cards, Orange is the New Black, are watched for more than one billion hours per month. The cost of Netflix to the general public is $8.53 per month for either their on-demand internet streaming service or their DVD rental program. Members of Netflix are able to rank and comment on the content they have viewed on their TV or the Netflix website. With the help of billions of other ratings from other members, Netflix uses these ratings to precisely anticipate the kinds of episodes and films that will also be aired.

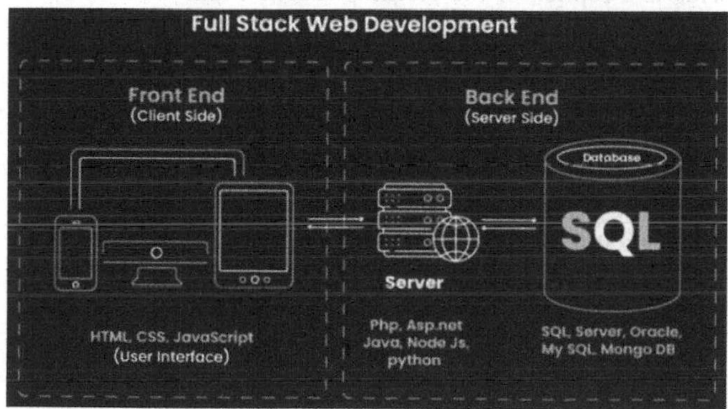

Fig. 36.1 Full stack web development (Malhotra et al., 2005)

Netflix based on your individual interests. Three distinct tiers make up the Netflix content catalogue. The lowest tier, which provides video and audio quality similar to that of a DVD, needs a constant downstream bandwidth of 1.5 Mbit per second. The intermediate tier offers quality that is better than a DVD while requiring twice as much bandwidth as the layer below it, at 3 Mbit per second. The fastest tier delivers 720p HD video with 5.1 and 7.1 surround sound for a limited number of shows and requires 5 Mbit per second.

3. Tools and Technologies

3.1 Front-End Technology

The upcoming section gives a detailed overview of HTML (Hyper Text Markup Language), CSS (Cascading Style Sheets), JavaScript and Node.JS. The capabilities are analyzed both practically and hypothetically.

HTML 5

HTML is an acronym of Hypertext Markup language. It is a markup language basically used to design web pages Hypertext create a linkage among different web pages. HTML5 allow us to build offline applications. The markup language is used to define the text document inside the tag that specifies the structure of web pages. HTML 5 refers to the fifth and most recent version of HTML. Application programming interfaces (API) and Document Object Models (DOM) have both been introduced, and document markup has been improved.

CSS

CSS (Cascading Style Sheets) enable user to styles web pages. Cascading Style Sheets in short, known as CSS. It provides user to make web pages attractive. The reason for using this is to entirely focus on overall appearance and minute specification and helps to create dynamic web pages. It contains variety of syntax t make web page presentable. More importantly, both HTML and CSS combines to form an entire web page.

3.2 Back-End Technology

JavaScript

JavaScript is globally used interpreted compiled programming language. Its prime working includes scripting a language for web pages. It is compatible for both client as well as server-side development. It is founded by Brendan Eich and developed in 10 days only. Its initial name was Live Script, later adopted by Microsoft and altered to Ecma Script or modern-day Java Script. Many great things can be achieved using JS features i.e., DOM which stands for Document Object Model and nowadays all websites are based on JS due to its functionality and popularity.

Node.JS

Node.JS, an open-source and cross-platform runtime environment based on Chrome's V8 JavaScript engine, can be used to execute JavaScript code outside of a browser. It provides a cross-platform runtime environment for event-driven, non-blocking (asynchronous), and I/O server-side applications written in JavaScript. Anckar et al., 2002 states that majority of people are unsure whether it is a framework or a programming language, which leads to misunderstanding. Node.js is heavily used in the development of back-end services such as APIs, online apps, and mobile applications (Hong et al., 2006). It is often used by large organizations such as PayPal, Uber, Netflix, and Walmart.

React.JS

React is an open-source, component-based front-end library.js is only concerned with the application's view layer. Facebook is in charge of it. It attempts to be both quick and versatile, and it employs a declarative paradigm that makes reasoning about your program easier. It generates simple views for each state in your application, and REACT will swiftly update and offer the best component anytime your data changes. When you use the declarative view, your code becomes more dependable and trouble shootable. Each component in a React project is responsible for rendering a distinct chunk of reusable HTML.

4. Proposed Framework

This work opens up and loads on a web page, so as soon as it does, the web page contains buttons for using Netflix clone features. The Netflix clone app shows the ability to upload large amounts of audio and video content simultaneously while automatically transcoding all of it! You can now easily track, sort, and organize the content in its entirety with just a few taps. With the ability to make customized thumbnails, present the philosophy of the complete video content in a single image. Create fantastically personalized theme images and thumbnails with this amazing tool rather than separate scripting languages for the server-side and client-side. Despite the fact that JavaScript code often has a.js filename extension, "Node.js" in this instance refers to the product rather than a specific file. Node.js' event-driven design allows for asynchronous I/O. These design choices are intended to maximize throughput and scalability for real-time web applications (such as browser games and real-time communication programs) as well as web applications with multiple input/output activities. With the help of a set of "modules" that handle different fundamental functionalities, JavaScript, and Node.js, it is possible to build Web servers and networking utilities. Networking modules (DNS, HTTP, TCP, TLS/SSL, or UDP), binary data (buffers), data streams, cryptographic operations, and other essential functions are available. The modules of Node.js make use of an API (Application Programming Interface) intended to Node. The API used by JS's modules is intended to make creating server applications less difficult.

5. Performance Analysis

This section describes the performance of Netflix clone in context to various features and activities. The performance is judged on the following parameters such as minimum, maximum, average values and standard deviation. The factors activities on which the performance in judged are as follows:

1. Catching up on or re-watching currently broadcasted TV shows
2. Discovering old or no longer broadcasted programs to watch
3. Viewing old or classic movies
4. Viewing new movies
5. Watching Netflix Originals

Table 36.1 Typical importance of Netflix clone features and activities

Factor	Min Value	Max Value	Average Value	Standard Deviation	Output
Re-watching TV shows	0	5	3.46	1.57	535
Old broadcasted programs	0	5	3.76	1.28	535
Viewing new movies	0	5	3.65	1.31	535
Viewing old movies	0	5	3.29	1.4	535
Watching Netflix Originals	0	5	3.66	1.42	535

Source: Author

6. Conclusion

This is a replica of the Netflix website made with Firebase as the backend and React.JS as the front end. It is not a copy, and it lacks some of the features found on the Netflix website. It's a clone of Netflix, demonstrating the proficiency with React.JS to create a sophisticated application like Netflix. The home page, sign-in and sign-up pages, browse page, and movie player are all included. With Netflix Clone, one can create their own on-demand OTT platform similar to Netflix, where one can stream an unlimited number of films and TV series for a single modest monthly fee. Netflix Clone streams films and TV episodes to new places with sizable viewership via the Internet. Regional language broadcasting is also made possible by Netflix Clone Script's multilingual capabilities.

REFERENCES

1. Tilson, D., K. Lyytinen, and R. Baxter. 2004. A Framework for Selecting a Location Based Service (LBS) Strategy and Service Portfolio. *37th Annual Hawaii International Conference on System Sciences, 2004. Proceedings of the, Big Island, HI, USA.*
2. Anckar, Bill and Davide D'Incau. 2002. Value-added services in mobile commerce: an analytical framework and empirical findings from a national consumer survey. *Proceedings of the 35th Annual Hawaii International Conference on System Sciences*: 1444–1453.
3. Khalifa, Mohamed & Cheng, S. 2002. Adoption of Mobile Commerce: Role of Exposure. *Hawaii International Conference on System Sciences.* 1. 46.
4. Hong, Se-Joon, Kar Yan Tam and Jinwoo Kim. 2006. "Mobile data service fuels the desire for uniqueness." *Commun. ACM* 49: 89–94.

5. Carlsson, Christer, Kaarina Hyvönen, Petteri Repo and Pirkko Walden. 2005. Asynchronous Adoption Patterns of Mobile Services. *Proceedings of the 38th Annual Hawaii International Conference on System Sciences*: 189a–189a.
6. Malhotra, A., and Segars, A. H. 2005. "Investigating wireless web adoption patterns" *in the U.S. Communications of the ACM*, Vol. 48, No. 10, 2005, pp. 105–110.
7. Knutsen, Lars Andreas, Ioanna D. Constantiou and Jan Damsgaard. 2005. Acceptance and perceptions of advanced mobile services: alterations during a field study. *International Conference on Mobile Business (ICMB'05)*: 326–332.
8. Flavián, Carlos and Raquel Gurrea. 2009 "Users' motivations and attitude towards the online press." *Journal of Consumer Marketing* 26: 164–174.
9. Luse, Andy Mennecke, Brian Triplett, Janea. 2013. "The changing nature of user attitudes toward virtual world technology: A longitudinal study", *Computers in Human Behavior,* Volume 29, Issue 3, 1122–1132.
10. Panda, K. C., & Swain, D. K. 2011. "E-newspapers and e-news services in the electronic age: an appraisal". *Annals of Library & Information Studies*, 58(1), 55–62.
11. Lavie, T., Sela, M., Oppenheim, I., Inbar, O., & Meyer, J. 2010. "User attitudes towards news content personalization". *International journal of human- computer studies*, 68(8), 483–495.
12. O'Brien, H. L. 2011. Exploring user engagement in online news interactions. *Proceedings of the American Society for Information Science and Technology*, 48(1), 1–1.

Printed in the United States
by Baker & Taylor Publisher Services